PERGAMON INTERNATIONAL LIBRARY
of Science, Technology, Engineering and Social Studies
The 1000-volume original paperback library in aid of education,
industrial training and the enjoyment of leisure
Publisher: Robert Maxwell, MC

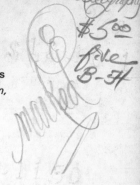

THE MORE
DEVELOPED REALM

A Geography of Its Population

D1307105

THE PERGAMON TEXTBOOK
INSPECTION COPY SERVICE

An inspection copy of any book published in the Pergamon International Library
will gladly be sent to academic staff without obligation for their consideration for
course adoption or recommendation. Copies may be retained for a period of 60 days
from receipt and returned if not suitable. When a particular title is adopted or
recommended for adoption for class use and the recommendation results in a sale
of 12 or more copies, the inspection copy may be retained with our compliments.
The Publishers will be pleased to receive suggestions for revised editions and new
titles to be published in this important International Library.

PERGAMON OXFORD GEOGRAPHY SERIES

Editor: W. B. FISHER

Other Titles in the Series

THE MORE DEVELOPED REALM

A Geography of Its Population

General Editor

GLENN T. TREWARTHA
UNIVERSITY OF WISCONSIN—MADISON (Emeritus)

PERGAMON PRESS

Oxford · New York Toronto · Sydney

Paris · Frankfurt

U.K.	Pergamon Press Ltd., Headington Hill Hall, Oxford OX3 0BW, England
U.S.A.	Pergamon Press Inc., Maxwell House, Fairview Park, Elmsford, New York 10523, U.S.A.
CANADA	Pergamon of Canada Ltd., 75 The East Mall, Toronto, Ontario, Canada
AUSTRALIA	Pergamon Press (Aust.) Pty. Ltd., 19a Boundary Street, Rushcutters Bay, N.S.W. 2011, Australia
FRANCE	Pergamon Press SARL, 24 rue des Ecoles, 75240 Paris, Cedex 05, France
FEDERAL REPUBLIC OF GERMANY	Pergamon Press GmbH, 6242 Kronberg/Taunus, Pferdstrasse 1, Federal Republic of Germany

First edition 1978

Library of Congress Cataloging in Publication Data

Main entry under title:

The More Developed Realm.

(Pergamon Oxford geographies)
1. Population—Addresses, essays, lectures.
I. Trewartha, Glenn Thomas, 1896–
HB871.M8   1977   301.32   76-39897
ISBN 0-08-020631-X (Hard cover)
ISBN 0-08-020630-1 (Flexi cover)

Typeset by Enset Ltd., Midsomer Norton, Bath
Printed in Great Britain by Page Bros (Norwich) Ltd.

CONTENTS

INTRODUCTION

A Geography of Population: World Patterns (Wiley, 1969) was the first of a conceived trilogy of books concerned with the earth's population geography. It is topical in its approach and emphasizes broad worldwide patterns of distribution. The second volume of the trilogy, *The Less Developed Realm: A Geography of Its Population* (Wiley, 1972) appeared a few years later. Unlike its predecessor, here the organization was regional, with the focus on the economically retarded continents, including Africa, much the greater share of Latin America, and East (excluding Japan) and South Asia. These represent the earth's traditional societies. This, the third and last unit of the trilogy, quite logically deals with the economically more developed realm and its modern societies. The first two books I had the daring to author myself; this third volume is multiauthored. The trilogy is intended mainly for a wide non-professional audience, including college undergraduates and the general reading public.

As a group, the economically advanced countries present to the writer concerned with the geography of population a quite different problem than that offered by the economically retarded populations. While in the latter instance it is usually the dearth, and many times the poor quality also, of the materials, statistical and otherwise, that confronts the would-be author of a population geography, it is, instead, the abundance of the published materials available for most of the economically advanced countries that poses a problem. Such abundance begs for a handling by specialists. For this prime reason, along with others less noteworthy, it was decided that the present endeavour should take the form of an edited volume, with regional specialists authoring individual chapters, and myself acting as general editor as well as author of one chapter. The result, of course, is a product with less coherence than likely would have been the case if it were the work of a single author. But at the same time it does have those other merits which derive from it being the product of individuals who are especially knowledgeable about particular countries and regions.

In the first general memorandum that I sent out to the prospective chapter authors, I disclaimed any intent as editor to impose a rigidity of content or structure upon them; indeed I positively encouraged variety. At the same time I pointed out the desirability of maintaining some degree of coherence as regards content and organization, both for the sake of the book in hand and to prevent too radical a departure in substance and flavor from those exhibited in the two preceding volumes of the trilogy. For one thing, I urged that in our writing a strong geographic flavor be maintained, so that the reader should be left in no doubt that it was our intent to write a *geography* of population. I also suggested that the dynamic element of population change, with its accompanying redistributions, be stressed, and that in the treatment of spatial distribution not only population numbers but also population characteristics or attributes should be involved. In addition it was pointed out that description of spatial distributions without some attempt at explanation provides an analysis that is less than complete.

That the several chapters in this book, prepared as they were by nine different authors, do indeed exhibit variety in approach and content no one can deny. What effects my other editorial admonitions may have had, I must leave to the reader's judgment.

GLENN T. TREWARTHA
General Editor

NOTE

The original manuscript of this book was composed of 14 chapters. Rising costs of publication eventually required a serious shrinking of its volume to about two-thirds the initial size. Such a drastic contraction led to the elimination of all footnotes and to a severe reduction in the reference lists as well. The materials on Argentina and Uruguay were sacrificed completely, mainly because these two more developed countries were dealt with in Professor John I. Clarke's book, *Population Geography and the Developing Countries*, Pergamon Press Inc., 1971. For a variety of reasons, three other chapters, in their original form, were selected for elimination—Northwest Europe, Historical Population Geography of the United States, and Canada and Alaska. In some measure their contents have been incorporated into other chapters, especially 2 and 7.

CHAPTER 1

THE MORE DEVELOPED REALM

JOHN I. CLARKE

University of Durham, England

Which Are the More Developed Countries?

This volume is concerned with the population geography of the more developed or economically advanced countries of the world, the "haves" rather than the "have-nots". Though the "haves" are economically and politically dominant in the world today, they have not always been so, and may not all remain in this privileged position. It is only during the last century or so that such nations have experienced the economic, social, and demographic transitions from traditional or pre-industrial societies to modern societies; in earlier periods other civilizations were more preponderant.

The greater *per capita* wealth of the more developed countries is reflected in a number of variables such as standards of living, medical and educational facilities, literacy, fertility and mortality, economic composition, consumption of inanimate power, urbanization, communication networks, and so on. Numerical indicators of these variables have fairly similar rankings, the more developed countries clustering at one end of the scale. As Brian Berry has said: "the highest ranking countries are, of course, those which trade extensively and have many international contacts and well developed internal systems of communications, including dense and intensively used transportation networks. They produce and consume much energy, have high national products, are highly urbanized and are well provided with such facilities as medical services." However, for some variables there is no marked dichotomy between the more and the less developed countries, but rather a changing gradation. The recent rise of many oil-producing states, for example, has tended to blur distinctions and confuse rankings of some variables; countries like Kuwait and Libya have very high *per capita* gross national products, but much lower levels of some other variables. The more developed countries are also difficult to isolate because of their profound interrelationships with the less developed countries. Little by little the latter are gaining greater political and economic independence, but they still owe much to the diffusion of innovations from a small number of technologically advanced countries. The significance to population dynamics of such innovations as vaccination, sterilization, and the motor-car is phenomenal, and as long as the present technological disparities persist the more developed countries will continue to exert an important demographic influence upon the rest of the world.

Whatever indicators or variables are used for purposes of definition, it is generally agreed that the more developed realm comprises Europe, the Soviet Union,

1

Anglo-American, Japan, Argentina and Uruguay in South America, and Australia and New Zealand. There are a few other borderline cases.

A Minority of Mankind

People living in the more developed countries often consider the less developed countries as unusual, but the reverse is the case. Far from being the norm, the more developed countries are those which have undergone a process of change, often called "modernization", though this is a word of broad connotation and dubious reliability. Moreover, they comprise only about 29% of the world's population and little more than 14% of its current annual population growth. Consequently, unless more countries join this select group they are likely to comprise a diminishing proportion of mankind. Yet this minority of the human race occupies 42% of the world's land (and higher proportions of its arable and forested land), and during the period 1960–70 produced over four-fifths of the world's goods and services. In addition, more rapid population growth in the less developed countries has meant that the gap in levels of living between these countries and the more developed countries has widened.

While the more developed countries are scattered in location, essentially they may be regarded as comprising three main concentrations: on either side of the North Atlantic Ocean and along the western Pacific. Certainly maritime trading has contributed greatly to their economic development, though it has not been a universal factor as we see in the case of the USSR. Another almost common factor is that nearly all of these more developed countries form part of the European cultural realm, largely peopled by Europeans disseminating the agricultural and industrial revolutions which originated in Europe and creating "New Europes" overseas. The process has mostly taken place during the nineteenth and twentieth centuries, but again there is a notable exception, this time Japan, a highly individual member of the more developed realm and the only wholly Asian one. It could well be a signal that domination of the world economy by European or Caucasian peoples will not go unchecked for long. It seems certain that the list of more developed countries is far from closed, though newcomers may not emulate the economic and demographic transitions of their predecessors. Unfortunately, the spread effects of economic development are not very efficient internationally, because international boundaries are barriers between peoples, their activities, and government policies. The progress of poor countries is insufficiently stimulated by the rich.

Fortunately, the spread effects of economic development are usually more rapid intranationally. Although the early phases of economic development within countries are characterized by marked localization at places where there are raw materials or markets or other industries, later phases usually involve the contrasting processes of greater spread of economic development across regions, and greater concentration in and around many large cities where there are the distinct advantages of abundant large labor supplies, markets, and centrality. Inevitably this means regional inequality within countries, but this is often less striking than in less developed countries because a number of factors have combined to reduce regional inequalities: more advanced and complex patterns of urban growth, diminution in the relative importance of agriculture, variety of industrial and service functions, spread of modern communications, expansion of middle classes, and ubiquity of low fertility, mortality, and growth rates.

Populations and Areas of the More Developed Countries

While it is a commonplace nowadays to consider the world population and the populations of the more developed and the less developed realms as collective units capable of
large scale solutions, still it is important to stress that national boundaries are demographic divides impeding the free movement of peoples, separating them to a greater or

TABLE 1.1. MAN–LAND RATIOS IN MORE DEVELOPED COUNTRIES

| | Population 1970 (millions) | Persons per km² | | | Agricultural workers per km² of agricultural land |
		(a) Total area	(b) Arable land	(c) Agricultural land	
Europe					
Albania	2.1	74	383	171	46
Austria	7.4	88	440	190	14
Belgium	9.7	311	1138	605	11
Bulgaria	8.5	77	188	141	32
Czechoslovakia	14.5	113	271	204	15
Denmark	4.9	114	184	184	10
Finland	4.7	14	172	167	20
France	50.8	93	264	153	9
Germany (Dem. Rep.)	16.1	150	337	258	16
Germany (Fed. Rep.)	59.6	240	733	439	19
Greece	8.9	67	245	100	21
Hungary	10.3	111	184	150	19
Iceland	0.2	2	20,500	9	0.7
Ireland	2.9	42	256	61	6
Italy	53.7	178	359	266	21
Luxembourg	0.3	131	515	252	10
Malta	0.3	1019	2038	2038	50
Norway	3.9	12	477	407	22
Poland	32.8	105	214	168	32
Portugal	9.6	108	220	197	25
Romania	20.3	85	193	136	39
Spain	33.3	66	162	91	11
Sweden	8.0	18	264	234	10
Switzerland	6.3	152	1555	288	10
The Netherlands	13.0	356	1502	594	14
United Kingdom	55.7	228	767	288	4
Yugoslavia	20.5	80	250	140	28
USSR	242.8	11	104	40	6
Japan	103.5	280	1879	1603	166
Oceania					
Australia	12.6	2	28	3	0.1
New Zealand	2.8	10	364	21	0.9
North America					
Canada	21.4	2	49	33	1
United States	20.5	22	116	47	0.7
South America					
Argentina	24.3	9	94	14	0.8
Uruguay	2.9	16	147	18	1

Source: *FAO Production Yearbook, 1971*. Arable land includes land under crops (double-cropped
areas are counted only once), temporary meadows for mowing or pasture, land under market and
kitchen gardens (including cultivation under glass), and land under fruit trees, vines, shrubs, and rubber
plantations. Agricultural land includes arable land plus permanent meadows and pastures. Agricultural
workers are those "economically active" in agriculture. Data are for about 1970.

POPULATION SIZE and GROWTH RATES of the MORE DEVELOPED REALM

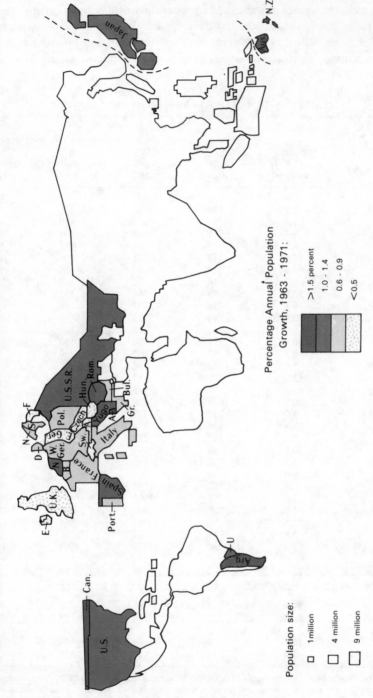

FIG. 1.1. Outline from Jan O. M. Broek and John W. Webb, *A Geography of Mankind*, McGraw-Hill, New York, 2nd edn., 1973, pp. 40–41.

lesser extent and thus impeding large scale solutions. Demographic diversity persists between and within nations, in particular the unevenness of population distribution; the momentum of the past is always present. Furthermore, the policies of governments, economic, social, and demographic, are having increasing influence upon the dynamics of population, numerically and spatially. One only has to think of Australia and New Zealand to realize how their policies restricting immigration have influenced population characteristics in those countries.

There are more than 35 more developed countries and they vary greatly in population (Fig. 1.1) and territorial size. At one end of the scale are the Soviet Union and United States with 248 and 209m. inhabitants respectively (1972 estimates), while at the other are micro-states with less than 1m. inhabitants: Andorra, Iceland, Liechtenstein, Luxembourg, Malta, and Monaco. Such disparities also exist in territorial size, a factor of considerable significance as it affects the relative importance of migration and natural change in population dynamics as well as many other aspects of population geography. On the whole, large countries like Soviet Russia, the United States, Australia, and Canada tend to contain most of their migrants within their own territories, while small countries experience a greater impact of external migration, so that large countries tend to have greater demographic stability than small ones. But the enormous areas of the macro-states also affect their patterns of population distribution and city location, their attractiveness to external migrants, the character of internal migration, their population structures, and their attitudes towards population size and growth.

Differences in population and territorial size inevitably mean differences in man–land ratios, which are once again extreme (Table 1.1). On the one hand, there are the high densities prevailing in Japan and many European countries (e.g. Belgium, West Germany, The Netherlands, and the United Kingdom) and low densities prevailing in the countries of the European cultural realm outside of Europe. The contrasts also exist with densities per square kilometer of arable land and agricultural land, and with the numbers of agricultural workers per square kilometer of agricultural land.

Two Main Cultural Realms—European and Japanese

Europe and Its Cultural Realm

Although there are massive differences in population distribution and density, the main features of population structure and dynamics within the more developed realm are less diverse than might be imagined, for all of its countries, with the exception of Japan, form part of the European cultural realm. Whatever its significance, if any, the more developed realm is located largely in the middle or "temperate" latitudes and is predominantly inhabited by Caucasoid peoples; the less developed realm, by contrast, is situated mainly in the tropics and subtropics and has a far larger proportion of Mongoloid and Negroid stock. Europe has long been one of the main cradles of mankind and of civilization, and in the middle of the eighteenth century, before the agricultural and industrial revolutions changed the face of the continent, it contained about 160m. inhabitants, probably just over one-fifth of mankind on one-twenty-eighth of the world land area. At that time Europe contained more people than the combined populations of the Americas, Africa, and Oceania (Table 1.2), and Europe and Asia together comprised well over four-fifths of mankind. It was Europe, especially western Europe,

TABLE 1.2. MEDIUM ESTIMATES OF POPULATION OF MORE DEVELOPED
AND LESS DEVELOPED REALMS, 1750–1970

	1750	1800	1850	1900	1950	1970
World	791	978	1262	1650	2515	3632
More developed realm						
Europe	125	152	208	296	392	462
USSR	42	56	76	134	180	243
North America	2	7	26	82	166	228
Oceania	2	2	2	6	13	19
Japan	30	30	31	44	83	130
Less developed realm						
Asia (excl. the USSR						
and Japan)	468	600	770	881	1298	1953
Africa	106	107	111	133	222	344
Latin America	16	24	38	74	162	283

Sources: J. D. Durand, The modern expansion of world population, *Proc. Am. Phil. Soc.*, vol. 111, no. 3, 1967, p. 137, and *UN Demographic Yearbook 1970*.
Note: Argentina and Uruguay are not considered as part of the more developed realm in this table.

which was to nurture the economic and social transformation that eventually brought about rapid economic and demographic growth and expansion to other parts of the world.

The process involved massive population redistribution, particularly through urbanization. Towns became the magnets for migrants from the marginal and mountainous lands and later from the areas transformed by modern mechanized agriculture. They became the main foci of population distributions. Today, the urban populations (variously defined) of the bulk of European countries constitute between one-half and four-fifths of the total populations. The proportion tends to vary according to the degree of industrialization, and is generally lower in the Communist countries of eastern Europe, partly because of high rural densities and partly because of the political system. The early phase of population redistribution and urbanization in Europe was associated especially with the new concentration of population in the coalfields and to a lesser extent in other mining areas, so that, as in pre-industrial societies, natural resources continued to exert a strong influence upon population distribution. Later, however, the emergence of other forms of power and the multiplication of means of communication helped to release people from the localizing constraints of natural resources. Gradually urban concentration has been succeeded by urban dispersal, involving as well large scale suburbanization and commuting which blur the distinctions between urban and rural.

In addition to widespread internal population redistribution, European countries have experienced considerable population growth. From 1750 to 1900 the population of Europe (excluding the USSR) rose from 125m. to 296m., and from 1900 to 1970 it rose by 166m. to reach 462m. Declining mortality has played the major role, though the reasons for this decline are a subject of much discussion. Many have attributed the drop in death rates to a great reduction in the decimating effects of epidemics (except during the world wars) along with improvements in medical facilities, sanitation, and hygiene. Others claim that early declines in mortality are more attributable to economic developments, particularly a substantial improvement in diets resulting from increases in food production. Whatever the reasons, the mortality declines of the nineteenth century were followed by fertility declines that acted to curb natural increase, especially in the older industrialized countries of northern and western Europe. Fertility declines were delayed among the more rural populations of eastern and southern Europe, where high natural rates were prolonged much longer into the twentieth century, though since World War II this differential has largely disappeared. The declines were associated with profound changes in Western Civilization: the wane of religious fervor, the rise of socialism, the spread of the rational mentality, the improved status of women, and the disintegration of the large family. In recent years both vital rates have fallen to or towards replacement levels, which may well result in the eventual stabilization of the sizes of populations in many of the more developed countries.

Until the last two to three decades, when fertility, mortality, and natural growth rates have declined to low levels over most of Europe (Table 1.3), there were strong spatial differences in these levels. Some of these differences accounted for the varied emigration streams which swelled during the nineteenth century to become a spate during the period 1891–1920, when some 27m. people left Europe. It replaced Asia as the main source of migrants of mankind, and Europeans proceeded to take possession of and occupy those regions of the world which seemed environmentally attractive, feebly populated, and inadequately exploited: the Americas, Oceania, Africa, and Siberia. Political control was more extensive than colonial settlement, but even this was extremely widespread. Pushed by poverty, population growth, political pressures, and economic crises, emigrants were drawn by the attractions of job opportunities and a new life in distant lands that were made much more accessible with improved maritime, rail, and road transport. The causes of such migrations were numerous and their consequences were correspondingly varied.

Most of the newly colonized lands which are developed countries today were only sparsely inhabited by indigenous peoples, and the early impact of Europeans upon groups like the Maoris, Aborigines, and American Indians was disastrous. Decimated, they are now found mainly in remote areas away from the major cities and population concentrations. The "New Europes" were mostly peopled by whites, whether "Anglo-Saxon", Latin, or Slav, though a substantial black minority evolved in the United States. Some, like Canada, South Africa, Australia, and New Zealand, were colonized mainly from the more industrialized countries of western Europe; others, like North Africa, Siberia, and most of South America, received immigrants mainly from the countries in eastern and southern Europe that were experiencing strong rural population pressure. Some, like New Zealand and Siberia, were peopled largely from one source country; others like Uruguay, Canada, and the United States received a mixture of immigrant nationalities.

Political independence and succeeding policies restricting flows of immigrants from Europe and other parts of the world meant that large scale immigration was staunched or greatly reduced (though not in the case of Siberia, forming part of the USSR), and these policies were dictated primarily by the concern to preserve some degree of ethnic uniformity as well as existing standards of living. The United States was the principal immigrant country; 34m. immigrants entered between 1800 and 1920, and their diverse origins led to an amazing ethnic mix. During the inter-war years the influx was greatly restricted through quotas, but in recent years the gates have opened wider again, so that immigration has renewed significance in annual population growth, though it accounts

TABLE 1.3. VITAL RATES OF MORE DEVELOPED COUNTRIES (EARLY 1970s)

	Birth rate (%)	Death rate (%)	Annual growth rate (%)	Projected population 1985 (millions)	Infant mortality rate (%)	Percentage Under 15	Percentage Over 65
Europe	16.0	10.0	0.7	515.0	—	25	12
Northern Europe	16.0	11.0	0.5	90.0	—	24	13
Denmark	14.4	9.8	0.5	5.5	14.8	24	12
Finland	13.7	9.5	0.4	5.0	12.5	26	8
Iceland	19.5	7.1	1.2	0.3	13.3	33	9
Ireland	21.8	11.5	0.7	3.5	19.2	31	11
Norway	16.6	9.8	0.7	4.5	13.8	25	13
Sweden	13.7	9.9	0.4	8.8	11.7	21	13
United Kingdom	16.2	11.7	0.5	61.8	18.4	24	13
Western Europe	15.0	11.0	0.5	163.0	—	24	13
Austria	15.2	13.4	0.2	8.0	25.9	24	14
Belgium	14.7	12.3	0.2	10.4	20.5	24	13
France	16.7	10.6	0.7	57.6	51.1	25	13
Germany (Fed. Rep.)	13.3	11.7	0.2	62.3	23.6	25	12
Berlin, West	9.5	19.0	−1.0	1.9	25.8	15	21
Luxembourg	13.2	12.3	0.1	0.4	24.6	22	12
Switzerland	15.8	9.1	1.0	7.4	15.1	23	11
The Netherlands	18.4	8.4	1.0	15.3	12.7	27	10
Eastern Europe	17.0	10.0	0.7	116.0	—	24	11
Bulgaria	16.3	9.1	0.7	9.4	27.3	23	9
Czechoslovakia	15.8	11.4	0.5	16.2	22.1	24	11
Germany (Dem. Rep.)	13.9	14.1	0.0	16.9	18.8	24	15
Berlin, East	14.5	16.4	−0.2	1.0	20.3	22	16
Hungary	14.7	11.7	0.3	11.0	359.0	21	11
Poland	16.8	8.2	0.9	38.2	33.2	28	8
Romania	21.1	9.5	1.2	23.3	49.4	26	8
Southern Europe	18.0	9.0	0.9	146.0	—	26	10
Albania	35.3	7.5	2.8	3.3	86.8	—	—
Greece	16.3	8.3	0.8	9.7	29.3	25	10
Italy	16.8	9.7	0.7	60.0	29.2	24	10
Malta	16.3	9.4	−0.7	0.3	27.9	28	9
Portugal	18.0	9.7	0.8	10.7	58.0	29	9
Spain	19.6	8.5	1.0	38.1	27.9	28	9
Yugoslavia	17.8	9.0	0.9	23.8	55.2	28	7
USSR	17.4	8.2	0.9	286.9	24.4	28	8
Oceania	25.0	10.0	2.0	27.0	—	32	7
Australia	20.5	9.0	1.9	17.0	17.9	29	8
New Zealand	22.1	8.8	1.7	3.8	16.7	32	8
North America	17.0	9.0	1.1	274.0	—	29	9
Canada	17.5	7.3	1.7	27.3	19.3	30	8
United States	17.3	9.3	1.0	246.3	19.2	29	10
South America							
Argentina	22.0	9.0	1.5	29.6	58.0	30	7
Uruguay	21.0	9.0	1.2	3.4	49.0	28	8
Japan	19.0	7.0	1.2	121.3	13.0	14	7

Source: 1972 World Population Data Sheet, Population Reference Bureau Inc.

for less than natural increase. Nevertheless, it has contributed massively to the growth in population of the United States from 5m. in 1800 to 211m. in 1974.

The character of colonization in the "New Europes" meant that they were demographically distinct from Europe itself, with unusual age and sex compositions marked by a surplus of young males. Moreover, population distributions were at first highly localized and peripheral, and these uneven patterns have persisted, particularly in those new countries which attracted smaller migrations streams. In general, although many of these countries have an agricultural image, they are highly urbanized and industrialized with higher proportions of their populations living in large cities than is the case in most European countries. Large coastal cities, functioning as ports, commercial centers and sometimes as capitals, are dominant in urban hierarchies, extreme examples being Buenos Aires and Montevideo with 36 and 45% respectively of the populations of Argentina and Uruguay. Cities along the Trans-Siberian railway may also be regarded as main links with Europe.

In contrast with urban localization and urban overpopulation, agricultural settlement of the New Europes was invariably at very low densities because of the small proportion of rural settlers and the availability of huge areas of land. Farming became extensive, with much machinery, few workers, and specialization in production of cash crops and livestock products for distant markets. The contrasts between the rural population patterns of Europe and the New Europes are therefore striking (Table 1.1).

By European and Asian standards, some of these "new" countries are still feebly populated both in absolute terms and in relation to their natural resources. New Zealand has about as many inhabitants as Rome or Washington, and Australia not many more than Tokyo or New York. Natural increase rates higher than those of most European countries have not been sufficient to raise densities to comparable levels, or to counter the view that they contain ethnically selected and privileged minorities of mankind. Some would hold that their gates should be opened wider to admit more peoples from the Third World and thereby reduce some of the manifest disparities in world population distribution and standards of living.

Japan and Its Cultural Realm

Japan is the single important country within the more developed realm that is racially non-Caucasoid, and non-European in its culture. But while this small insular country is only 37% larger than New Zealand (370,000 vs. 269,000 km²), and is beset with many similar natural handicaps, its population is vastly larger—106m. and 3m. respectively (1972 estimates). Japan is remarkable not only for its high population density, but as an Asian state which has modernized itself economically and demographically with great rapidity since its feudal isolation was broken in 1853 when Commodore Perry made his gunboat agreement to open up the country. At that time the population of Japan was roughly 30m., more than that of Anglo-America and almost as many as in Latin America. It has grown about $3\frac{1}{2}$ times since then, but these western regions have left it far behind, largely because Japan has experienced no major immigration and because natural increase has only briefly exceeded 1.5% during this century. Mortality and fertility remained fairly high until after World War II, when both plunged rapidly, so that the annual increase rate has generally remained above 1.0%. The rapidity of fertility decline is quite unparalleled in any modern nation, but this uniqueness is found in other aspects of Japan's society and economy. Its rate of industrialization has been especially impressive, and the growth of large cities is unlike that of the New Europes in that it perpetuates a pattern of city growth dating from the period of the Tokugawa seclusion (1537–1853); of the ten largest cities in Japan only Yokohama and Kobe date from the modern period. Such are the limitations of living space in Japan that many of these cities are only parts of extensive urbanized regions. A comprehensive discussion of Japan's population geography is the exclusive theme of Chapter 9.

Local Diversity

The above brief classification of large scale diversity in the more developed realm does little more than highlight salient differences of time and space relationships. At more local scales of analysis much more diversity appears: contrasts of population geography between The Netherlands and New Zealand, Kansas and Kyushu, and Queensland and Quebec extend far beyond considerations of density and distribution. The more developed realm includes Communist, Socialist, and Capitalist countries; Protestant, Catholic, atheist, and Shintoist countries; and countries of Asian as well as European culture. Studies at the micro-level reveal greater diversity of peoples and cultures, and demographic patterns which are very deviant from national norms. Internal patterns of age structure and sex ratios may be extremely complex, and the smaller the scale of analysis the greater the deviation from averages. Although this volume is a macro-population study in that it focuses on population aggregates and their average tendencies rather than on the behavior of small populations, all students of population should recall that the demographic characteristics of small populations may differ substantially from those of large populations, and that we should not expect the population of small Budleigh Salterton to exemplify that of Devon, Devon's that of the United Kingdom, or the United Kingdom's that of Europe. Moreover, the techniques and approach to the study of the population of Budleigh Salterton would be quite different from those used to study the population of Europe. A matter of scale is involved.

Although there are wide variations in the small scale population geography of the more developed realm, certain common threads are present such as high levels of living, literacy, mobility, fertility, growth, dependency, and juvenility—all of which encourage comparisons as well as contrasts.

Vital Rates and the Demographic Transition

The essential demographic difference between traditional and modern societies is that in the former fertility and mortality rates are usually high while in the latter they are universally low, and that between them there is temporal transition. The accelerated increase in humanity in the modern period resulted not from an increase in the reproduction rate, but rather from a reduction in mortality. The world's average birth rate is actually lower at present than it was two centuries ago, since birth rates in the more developed countries have declined markedly, although those in the traditional societies as a whole changed little, remaining almost universally high. Improvement in mortality, as measured by gains in life expectancy at birth, while certainly more impressive in the well developed realm, has been shared to some degree by the economically retarded countries as well. In possibly 20% of the latter current death rates are 15 per 1000 or below, and therefore classed as moderate to low. Observations of the relationships between these changes in fertility and mortality, on the one hand, and the social, economic, and cultural changes known as modernization, on the other, formed the basis of the oft-quoted *demographic transition theory*. It postulated that as death rates declined urbanization and industrialization increased along with literacy, living standards, and social and occupational mobility. Decline in fertility awaited the obsolescence of traditional social and economic institutions and the emergence of the new ideal of the small family. Children became more costly as their economic contributions to the family diminished, and women raised their status by reduced child bearing and new economic roles. Contraception, by traditional and modern methods, enabled birth restriction, but because of lowering infant mortality three pregnancies in a woman's reproductive life made possible as much population growth as six or more in pre-industrial days. Although it was realized by some that there were exceptions and variations to the theory, notably in the cases of France and the United States where early fertility declines appeared largely unrelated to either mortality decline or industrialization, transition theory offered a plausible explanation of general population trends in the more developed countries. The clearest evidence for the theory is found in nineteenth century Britain and western Europe, especially if industrialization is equated with modernization, and it also found support, for example, from the evidence of demographic changes in eastern and southern Europe.

Transition theory, however, has been subjected to a number of attacks, particularly from historical demographers, and on various grounds. But despite these criticisms, in general it remains true that modernized societies characteristically have lower fertility and mortality than pre-modern societies, though it should not be expected that there is one causal explanation for the complex and varying process of transition.

Transition took place earliest in Northwest Europe, and analysis of its space–time diffusion reveals that Anglo-America and Australia and New Zealand were next to change, then Uruguay and Argentina, followed by eastern Europe, southern Europe, the USSR, and Japan. This is the broad picture; the space–time details are much more complex. Several factors interfered with the smoothness of the transition, including the two world wars, their succeeding "baby booms" (particularly prolonged after World War II), the economic crises of the inter-war years, and the tendency towards earlier marriage. Moreover, within individual countries there have been substantial rural–urban and social–economic differentials, and these have changed with time. For example, although fertility decline was formerly greater among groups with high socio-economic status, in recent decades the middle classes have also generally experienced lower fertility.

Despite national variations in natural increase, all the more developed countries had by the 1960s achieved low fertility and mortality and a life expectancy of about 70 years. Resort to behavior that controls human fertility is a distinguishing quality of all modernized societies. Since then regional and national differences have been further flattened, so that there are now only weak differentials in vital rates (e.g. birth rates highest in the Southern Hemisphere and lowest in Northwest Europe), and perhaps, these should be stressed less than the basic similarities in population trends. In essence, the populations of the more developed countries are being controlled and, as Borrie puts it, "reproductive wastage has given way to reproductive efficiency". Certainly unwanted pregnancies occur, but the mean family size of two or three children is not too different from the desired size. Further improvements in mortality in the more developed countries can only have small effects upon growth rates, but if fertility should rise then very rapid growth rates would ensue.

At the moment a return to high fertility seems unlikely because of better contraceptive methods, the liberalization of laws against abortion, and growing concern about problems such as pollution, environmental conservation, and economic growth. But if affluence in the more developed countries continues to increase, then it is possible that fertility will rise again. In any case the proportions of young people are usually sufficient to ensure continued growth even with an average two-child family. Most developed countries will experience population growth until at least the end of the century, though it may be very slow in some countries such as Austria, Belgium, Hungary, Luxembourg, and East and West Germany.

Demographic Structures

Demographic transition involves radical changes in age composition, particularly in the proportions of young and old people. While mortality decline brings about broader based population pyramids, because initially it means a reduction in infant mortality, fertility decline has the reverse effect and reduces the proportion of young people, a process known as "aging at the base". Consequently, the demographic transition diminished the proportion of young people (aged less than 15) in more developed countries from 40–50% to 20–30%, though the sustained higher fertility after World War II had important effects upon percentages. Nevertheless, it may be noted in Table 1.3 that young people under 15 comprise only one-quarter of the population of Europe, while in Japan the proportion is slightly lower. In Anglo-America, the USSR, southern South America, and Australia and New Zealand, however, 28–32% are under 15—still a much lower proportion than in the less developed countries where the percentage is usually over 40.

As mortality has reached low levels among young and younger adult age groups, and fertility decline has reduced their proportions of the total populations, more developed countries have experienced "aging at the apex" of the population pyramid, or increasing proportions of old people. In Britain, for example, people aged 65 and over have risen from less than 5% of the total population during the whole of the nineteenth century to 13% today, slightly above the European average, like several other countries in northern and western Europe. In contrast, in the European extensions overseas and in Japan the average is 7–8%, except in the United States where it is 10%; but these levels are much higher than in the less developed countries. Increasing longevity and recent declines in fertility in many more developed countries ensure that the proportions of old people will continue to increase, as will the proportions of older adults.

Broad generalizations about percentages in the three age groups obscure detailed variations in age compositions which not only reflect demographic history but also have immense influence upon social, economic, and political activities and policies. In the French age–sex pyramid (Fig. 1.2), for example, one can detect the excessive mortality of males during the two world wars, the birth deficits of both wars, and post-war fertility rises.

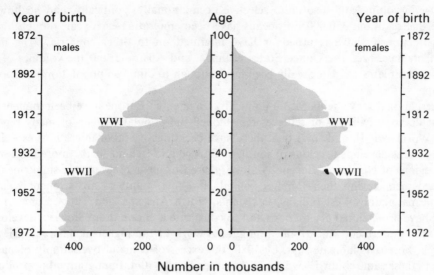

FIG. 1.2. Recent age–sex structure of France. Note the deficiencies caused by the two world wars.

More developed countries usually have a surplus of females, particularly in the case of countries greatly affected by war deaths, like the USSR, West Germany, Austria, and Poland. The general reason, however, is the greater longevity of females than of males in conjunction with the general trend towards aging of population. More old people mean more old women. In contrast, only a few countries have a surplus of males—Albania, Bulgaria, Iceland, and Australia—attributable to one or more causes such as high fertility with consequent young age composition, possible under-enumeration of females, or a selective immigration of males.

Population Mobility

As societies, economies, and transport systems evolve and modernize, and localities become more specialized in function, there is a tendency for more and longer movements of people and goods. The processes of interaction and diffusion augment so that mobility becomes a principal feature of modernized society. However, the diversity of human movement in terms of motivation, organization, distance, direction, duration, numbers, demographic composition, and consequences is so great that no simple classification is possible, though perhaps the most helpful typology is that based on the time factor, because the locational effects of human movement vary according to time.

Permanent migrations imply changes in location, and whether they are rural–urban, inter-urban, intra-urban, interregional or international they may be regarded as a response to opportunities and needs, and are one of the ways in which a society is able to achieve equilibrium, though all societies have a strong areal stability or inertia, so that present distributional patterns of population owe much to past social and economic conditions. The patterns of permanent migrations have changed a good deal in recent decades. Despite some easing of earlier restrictions, inter-continental migration streams to the New Europes no longer comprise the poor and unskilled masses; they are much smaller in volume and also more selective occupationally, politically, and healthwise. Nevertheless, about 350,000 Europeans have been emigrating each year, though a substantial minority have returned or have migrated on to other countries. The main recipients have been the United States, Canada, and Australia, but the volumes of the migration streams have not really been large enough to diminish population pressure in Europe.

International movements within politically fragmented Europe have been immense in recent decades. Millions of refugees refashioned the population map of many regions after World War II, and since then there have been massive labor migrations especially from the less developed regions of southern Europe and Ireland to the more industrialized regions of Northwest Europe. Many of these European migrants are single men, or married men leaving their families behind, and their numbers are swollen by non-Europeans, mainly West Indians, Pakistanis, North Africans, and Turks. Some of the latter have professional occupations and so constitute a "brain drain" for less developed countries. At present 3m. to 4m. immigrants work in the higher-income countries of Europe. Forecasts indicate that, by 1980, the excess of demand over supply of native labor in these same countries will be in the order of 8m.–10m. Immigrant labor produces many problems, such as wage levels, cultural and linguistic differences, residential segregation, and social assimilation, so that there are political pressures to control its volume, as in the United Kingdom; but controls on international movements are minimal in western Europe compared with those in the Communist Countries of eastern Europe.

While international migration generally accounts for only a minor part of national population growth of more developed countries, internal migration plays a major role in internal population change, both spatial and temporal. Continuous redistribution of population which is taking place involves a number of migratory movements which are not always easy to distinguish. Outward movements are from isolated, over-populated, or economically depressed rural areas, regions with declining coalfields, small towns, and the central zones of large cities. Inward movements are mostly into active industrial, commercial and retirement zones, large metropolitan areas, urbanized regions, and the suburban rings of large cities. Broadly speaking, population is concentrating in the more prosperous regions within countries, but within such regions there is much residential dispersal. However, the nature of intra-urban migration is very complex, involving many short moves which are influenced (a) by stages in the life-cycle of people, (b) by information fields (the geographical distribution within an individual group, of knowledge about other people or areas), and (c) by place utility (in which immigration is regarded as an adaptation to perceived changes in one's surroundings).

Regional concentration and residential dispersal along with growing affluence and improved transport facilities have contributed to a massive increase in temporary movements connected with journey to work, shopping and leisure, movements which vary greatly in volume diurnally and seasonally. Generally they reflect patterns of permanent location rather than alter them, but problems of traffic congestion have encouraged relocation or new locations of foci like supermarkets, airports, and seaside resorts.

Urbanization

"Urbanization" has been variously defined and is used to mean a variety of phenomena, but however defined there is no doubt that the more developed countries are the highly urbanized ones. Although urbanization is at present proceeding more rapidly in the less developed realm, the more developed realm still contains a majority of the world's urban dwellers. Presently about two-thirds of the total population of the more developed realm live in urban places (according to national definitions) and only one-quarter in the traditional societies. But by the end of this century the proportion will probably be four-fifths in the former, compared with two-fifths in the less developed realm (Table 1.4). By then, however, there may be twice as many urban dwellers in the less developed

TABLE 1.4. URBAN, RURAL, AND TOTAL POPULATION, BY WORLD AND MAJOR AREAS AND REGIONS AS PROJECTED FOR SPECIFIED YEARS, 1950–2000 (IN MILLIONS)

Region	Urban population	Rural population	Total population	Percent urban
World total				
1950	704	1782	2486	28.3
1970	1352	2283	3635	37.2
2000	3329	3186	6515	51.1
More developed regions				
1950	439	419	857	51.2
1970	717	374	1091	65.7
2000	1174	280	1454	80.7
Less developed regions				
1950	265	1363	1628	16.3
1970	635	1910	2545	25.0
2000	2155	2906	5061	42.6
Europe				
1950	207	185	392	52.9
1970	292	170	462	63.2
2000	438	131	569	77.0
North America				
1950	106	60	166	63.7
1970	169	59	228	74.2
2000	284	50	334	85.1
Soviet Union				
1950	71	109	180	39.5
1970	139	104	243	57.1
2000	252	77	329	76.5
Oceania				
1950	8	5	13	61.7
1970	13	6	19	67.9
2000	25	10	35	71.7
East Asia				
1950	105	552	657	15.9
1970	266	664	930	28.6
2000	722	703	1425	50.7
South Asia				
1950	111	587	698	15.9
1970	238	888	1126	21.2
2000	793	1561	2354	33.7
Latin America				
1950	66	97	163	40.5
1970	158	125	283	55.9
2000	495	157	652	75.9
Africa				
1950	30	187	217	14.0
1970	77	268	345	22.2
2000	320	498	818	39.2

Source: United Nations Population Division, *Urban and Rural Population: Individual Countries, 1950–1985, and Regions and Major Areas, 1950–2000*, ESA/P/WP.33/Rev. 1, 1970.

realm as in the more developed realm. Obviously, the proportions of urban dwellers throughout the more developed realm vary considerably, but are higher in North America and Oceania than in Europe and the Soviet Union, but the differentials are diminishing.

There has also been a great change in the world distribution of large cities with 1m. or more inhabitants (Fig. 1.3; Table 1.5). Formerly such giants were largely localized in the more developed realm, which contained two-thirds of the total number in 1950, especially in Europe and North America. Now there are nearly as many million-cities in the less developed realm, where their numbers are growing faster; but whereas they contain less than one-tenth of the total population of the less developed realm, the million-cities of the more developed realm comprise about one-fifth of its total population.

TABLE 1.5. MILLION-CITIES, 1950–85

Region	Number of cities			Million-city population as a percentage of total population		
	1950	1970	1985	1950	1970	1985
World total	75	162	273	7	12	16
More developed realm	51	83	126	15	20	27
Less developed realm	24	79	147	3	8	13
Europe	28	36	45	15	19	22
North America	14	27	39	23	32	38
Soviet Union	2	10	28	4	9	17
Oceania	2	2	4	24	27	37
East Asia	13	36	54	5	11	17
South Asia	8	27	53	2	6	10
Latin America	6	16	31	9	19	28
Africa	2	8	19	2	5	9

Source: United Nations Population Division, *The World's Million-Cities, 1950–1985*, ESA/P/WP. 45, 1972.

Urban population densities in more developed countries tend to decline exponentially outwards from a peak value near the center of the city, but the central business districts are invariably sparsely populated. Density gradients along the outer margins of cities are generally less steep than in less developed countries, particularly because of expansion outwards along main roads; compactness has been greatly reduced with the introduction of the tram, bus, and motor-car. There has also been growing dissociation of the residential and occupational zones of cities, with incumbent problems of journey to work and social area differentiation.

Urban populations differ from rural populations in their demographic characteristics, but such differences vary according to many factors such as the size, growth rate, age, and functions of cities, and these differences change considerably in time. Sex ratios and age structures, for example, are highly variable between cities, and also within them, so that average urban–rural differences may have little meaning. On the other hand, urban populations contain many of the immigrant minorities, such as Algerians in Paris, Jews in New York, and West Indians in London, as well as other minorities such as criminals, schizophrenics, and aliens. The urban concentration and social segregation of such groups are among the more difficult problems of urbanization.

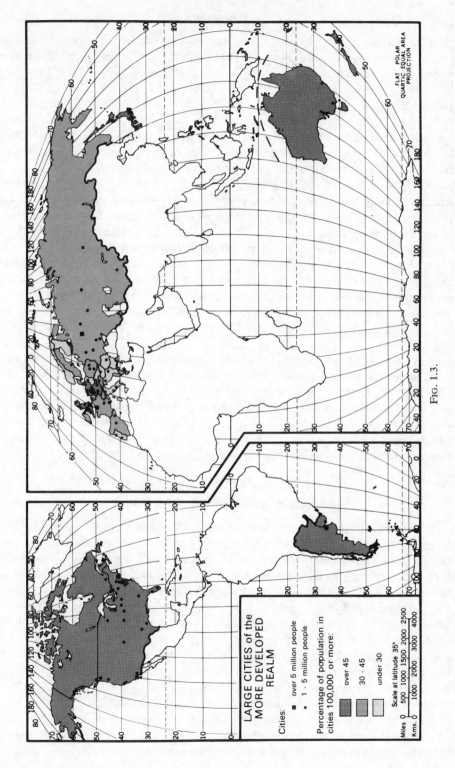

FIG. 1.3.

LARGE CITIES of the
MORE DEVELOPED
REALM

Cities: ■ over 5 million people
        • 1 - 5 million people

Percentage of population in
cities 100,000 or more:

over 45

30 - 45

under 30

Scale at latitude 35°

Miles 0 500 1000 1500 2000 2500
Kms. 0 1000 2000 3000 4000

FLAT POLAR
QUARTIC EQUAL AREA
PROJECTION

Rural Populations

While the number of rural dwellers in the less developed realm is growing enormously despite rapid urbanization, it is expected that the total rural population of the more developed realm will continue to decline, from an estimated 419m. in 1950 to about 280m. in 2000. The basic reason for this general decline in rural numbers is that out-migration exceeds natural increase, though of course the relationship of migration to natural change varies from region to region. In fact, many rural areas of more developed countries are suffering from both out-migration and natural decrease, the latter associated usually with aging populations and low proportions of women in the reproductive age groups. Isolated mountain areas often fall into this category.

Apart from declining rural totals, there is also a tendency for regrouping of rural populations in more favorable locations, where even semi-urban conditions may evolve. In Europe, at least, villages are becoming more urbanized because of the need for access to services, and they contain numerous commuter, service, and retired people. In North America also, though rural settlement is more dispersed, rural populations are increasingly non-farm, a composite category including a wide variety of socio-economic groups. On the whole, rural populations of more developed countries are much more hetero-geneous than those of less developed countries, and their links with the towns are much greater. There are massive daily movements connected with employment, goods, and services, so that the distinctions and limits between town and country are increasingly blurred.

Mention has already been made of the highly contrasted rural population densities of more developed countries, especially between Europe and Japan, on the one hand, and the New Europes, on the other. It should also be emphasized that low rural densities do not necessarily imply population decline, nor high rural densities rapid population growth. Much depends upon factors such as the nature of rural societies, the sizes of agricultural holdings, the number of agricultural workers, the degree of mechanization, the relationship to towns, and the numbers of rurally located industries.

Population, Resources, and the Environment

It is common to consider population numbers in relation to other phenomena such as food supply, natural resources and physical environment, economic or urban growth, military or economic manpower, and social interaction or organization. Almost in-evitably such relationships have been considered problematic, and often the blame for the existence of a problem has been laid on population numbers, although the problem may be ephemeral and more easily solved by necessary changes in the nature of the economy, society, or political organization. If population is inserted into an equation it should not be viewed as the only variable. There are so many variables—not merely population numbers but also the characteristics of population structure, mobility, and growth; not merely the quantity of natural resources but also their quality. In addition there are the human resources, the skills and technologies to utilize the natural resources, the standard of living of peoples, and their cultural attitudes and expectations, all of which influence human perception and utilization of the environment and its resources, and also change over time. These and other variables are interrelated in interacting systems which are not easily delimited territorially, especially in advanced countries. If we consider, for example, the use of resources and environment made by the inhabitants of one small European town we would find that it is worldwide. Indeed, the peoples of the more developed realm, particularly those of the non-Communist countries, are very much part of the world economy. Therefore operational indices of population–resource ratios and such terms as overpopulation, underpopulation, and optimum population are particularly elusive. So for our subjective assessments we tend to rely on inadequate indicators such as unemployment, unwanted children, *per capita* incomes, dependency ratios, and measures of population density. Small wonder that such assessments about the optimum population for Britain, for example, tend to be varied. We tend to generalize from our particular viewpoints, values, ideals, and experiences, so that what is intolerable overpopulation to some may be a desirable optimum, or even underpopulation, to others. For instance, many British and Japanese people consider the United States to be agreeably underpopulated, but that is not the prevailing view in America.

The more developed countries have ever-rising standards of living and ever-rising demands upon natural resources and these in turn result in an increasing pollution of the physical environment. It is said that every child born in the United States today will in his lifetime consume about 500 times the materials used by a child living in Central Africa, and as many of the materials are finite there is growing concern about overproduction in the more developed realm with its attendant use of the world's resources. There is much talk about the diseconomies of rising living standards and the need for limits to growth. Coupled with the aim of zero population growth, a goal frequently expressed in the West, there is also talk of a zero growth economy, though such an economy might cause more problems than it solves. Economic growth should not be arrested, for it is required to solve some of the difficulties associated with unequal distribution of income and wealth and to finance necessary technological developments, for example in the energy field. But it is also true that economic growth in some of the more developed countries has been excessively orientated towards luxury consumer goods at the expense of the environment, and that some reorientation is vital particularly in the direction of a better quality of life, though definitions of quality would be varied and difficult to formulate. Certainly many of the environmental and social problems of the more developed realm will become much more manageable if there are greater checks and controls upon economic and population growth.

Population Policies

The present reduction in population growth rates in most of the more developed countries is to be welcomed, for it has many more advantages than disadvantages. It can assist in dealing with problems of urban congestion, food supply, and environmental quality, but more particularly fertility decline fosters more social equality for women and for many disadvantaged minorities. Moreover, small controlled families generally mean healthier families.

The decline in population growth rates has taken place in countries with diverse prevailing religious and political beliefs. Today countries as dissimilar as the USSR, the United States, The Netherlands, Uruguay, and Japan all have annual growth rates around 1%. Despite the fact that some advanced countries have been pro-populationist and others anti-populationist, they have all arrived at a demographic situation of low or modest growth. In the past governments trying to influence population growth in more developed countries have mostly been pro-populationist, favoring fertility through family allowances, marriage loans, anti-abortion laws, and other legislation. France is an obvious example. It is only since World War II that we have seen anti-populationist policies emerge in Japan and eastern European countries, as well as strong calls for control of population growth in the United States, the United Kingdom, and elsewhere.

By population control many have meant fertility control, forgetting that it is only one of the variables of population change, and that direct control of numbers through mobility, mortality, and fertility is almost impossible. Populations are not easily managed. Most advanced countries have not a general population policy, but more often a policy with respect to one aspect such as immigration (e.g. Australia) or family planning (e.g. Japan). Government action is much more effective in controlling external migration than natural change, although the latter accounts for the greater part of population change. Moreover, generally governments have influenced natural change more by indirect measures such as health, welfare, and educational services than by direct measures, the latter being most successful when they have been similar to social norms. Indeed, most of the policies which affect population numbers have rarely been adopted for this specific purpose, most of them being social or economic in design, such as measures to assist the poor, the emancipation of women, or disadvantaged minorities. However difficult the task of controlling population, in many of the more developed countries there is growing recognition of the need for population policies, though some people fear that they could increasingly threaten individual rights to choose one's family size, rights which they are supposed to protect. Others maintain that society's needs and not the individual's desires are paramount.

There is also growing awareness that population policies which focus entirely on fertility and ignore other such fundamental issues as mobility and spatial distribution patterns will fail to come to grips with the fact that people live and work in specific environments, and that their relationships with those environments greatly affect the quality of their lives. It is gratifying that the Report of the Commission on Population Growth and the American Future clearly recognizes this fact, but regrettable that the Report of the Population Panel of the United Kingdom gives little consideration to internal redistribution of population. Fortunately more and more agencies and governments are realizing that demographic measures cannot be dissociated from multiple other aspects of society, economy, and environment. A holistic approach to population is necessary, and in such an approach spatial considerations are vital.

References

Barratt, John and Louw, Michael (1972), *International Aspects of Overpopulation*, Proceedings of a Conference held by the South African Institute of International Affairs at Johannesburg, Macmillan, London.
Beaujeu-Garnier, Jacqueline (1966), *Geography of Population*, Longmans, London.
Hauser, Philip M. and Schnore, Leo F. (1963), *The Study of Urbanization*, Wiley, New York.
National Bureau of Economic Development (1960), *Demographic and Economic Change in Developed Countries*, Princeton University Press, Princeton.
Population Crisis Committee in association with the Ditchley Foundation (1972), *Population Problems and Policies in Economically Advanced Countries*, Washington, D.C.
Report of the Commission on Population Growth and the American Future (1972), *Population and the American Future*, Washington, D.C.

Stockwell, Edward G. (1968), *Population and People*, Quadrangle, Chicago.

Thomlinson, Ralph (1965), *Population Dynamics: Causes and Consequences of World Demographic Change*, Random House, New York.

Thompson, Warren S. and Lewis, David T. (1965), *Population Problems*, McGraw-Hill, New York, 5th edn.

Wrigley, E. A. (1961), *Industrial Growth and Population Change*, Cambridge University Press, Cambridge.

Wrigley, E. A. (1969), *Population and History*, Weidenfeld & Nicolson, London.

CHAPTER 2

EUROPE: A GEOGRAPHY OF ITS POPULATION, PAST AND RECENT

DANIEL A. GÓMEZ-IBÁÑEZ

University of Wisconsin—Madison, USA

On a map of the world's population, Europe stands out as the home of a substantial fraction of mankind. From the deeply indented shores of the Atlantic and the Mediterranean to the Ural Mountains of Russia lives a sixth of the world's people. Even excluding the USSR, Europeans account for 12% of the world's population, but they occupy only 4% of the world's land surface. Indeed, the proportion of Europeans in the world was once even greater than it is today; at the time of Christ's birth it may have been as high as one-third or one-fourth. In the 2000 years since then, Europe's population has grown tenfold, though at rates which varied widely from place to place and at different times. The landscapes of Europe clearly show the effects of such a long occupance by so many people. Similarly, changes in the ways Europeans have interacted with their land illuminate much of the history of European population growth and the changes in its spatial distribution.

The present population map reveals a very uneven distribution of Europeans within the continent (Table 2.1; Fig. 2.7). A few areas appear relatively empty: central and northern Scandinavia, the Scottish and Welsh Highlands, and most of the mountainous districts of Europe. The Balkans and the interior of the Iberian peninsula (except Madrid) also are somewhat sparsely settled. On the other hand, the most notable concentrations of people occur in a belt which stretches from England to northern Italy (interrupted at the English Channel and the Alps). From this major north–south axis another belt of dense population stretches eastward, along the southern edge of the North European Plain, and then curves north to Moscow. There are a few other isolated patches of dense settlement, such as those occurring around the continent's capital cities. Most of the people in these regions, indeed most Europeans, live in towns and cities: in fact the most densely inhabited parts are conurbations or large clusters of cities. In the United Kingdom, Belgium, The Netherlands, West Germany, Switzerland, and Sweden, over 75% of the inhabitants are classed as urban dwellers.

But these aspects of Europe's population distribution are fairly recent. The present concentration of people in its northern and western parts represents a dramatic northward shift in the "center of gravity" of Europe's population since Roman times, when most Europeans lived around the Mediterranean Sea. While Rome flourished, what is now the Ruhr industrial district was mainly forest. The preponderance of urbanites is also

23

TABLE 2.1. 1975 POPULATION DATA FOR WESTERN EUROPE

Country	Population (millions)	Density (persons per km²)	Birth rate (births/1000 pop./yr.)	Death rate (deaths/1000 pop./yr.)
Austria	7.5	89	14.7	12.2
Belgium	9.8	321	14.8	11.2
Denmark	5.0	116	14.0	10.1
Finland	4.7	14	13.2	9.3
France	52.9	97	17.0	10.6
Germany (West)	61.9	249	12.0	12.1
Greece	8.9	67	15.4	9.4
Iceland	0.2	2	19.3	7.7
Ireland	3.1	44	22.1	10.4
Italy	55.0	183	16.0	9.8
Luxembourg	0.3	133	13.5	11.7
Norway	4.0	12	16.7	10.1
Portugal	8.8	96	18.4	10.1
Spain	35.4	70	19.5	8.3
Sweden	8.3	18	14.2	10.5
Switzerland	6.5	157	14.7	10.0
The Netherlands	13.6	333	16.8	8.7
United Kingdom	56.4	231	16.1	11.7

Source: Population Reference Bureau.

recent, a feature which is primarily a concomitant of the Industrial Revolution of the last 200 years. Of course, most of Europe's towns themselves are much older, but only rarely did the pre-industrial cities and towns of Europe include more than a few thousand persons. The "cities" of classical Greece, for example, today would appear to be little more than large agricultural villages.

Several attributes of Europe's population set it apart from that of other regions. Not least among these is the material well-being of Europeans themselves, and the great influence they thus wield upon the economic affairs of the world. Great population densities and relative affluence do not often coexist today. Yet Europe is not only one of the world's most crowded regions, it is also one of its most prosperous. Its affluence and its density make western Europe the world's greatest market after the United States—itself a child of Europe. The remarkable coexistence of prosperity and high population density in itself suggests that a historical examination of the relationships between population, culture, and environment in Europe might yield observations of general import. Europeans were the first to implement and experience the profound transformation of economy and society which we call the "Industrial Revolution". They thus became the first people to change radically their demographic patterns—especially those influenced by vital rates (births and deaths), urbanization, and internal and overseas migration. Since their beginnings in Europe, these developments have spread to most of the rest of the world, and so a study of the historical geography of Europe's population transcends merely parochial interests and may shed light on processes now affecting the lives of millions of non-Europeans. A further reason for presenting the historical geography of Europe's population here is that it is a field which has been well tilled by scholars, at least compared to other regions of the world, and so may serve as a conceptual starting point for similar studies of other societies.

How the number of Europeans grew, how their present distribution developed, and how the continent came to be dominated by its urban populations are some of the questions to which this chapter is addressed. Other questions concern cultural attributes of the population and the changing distributions of vital rates and their causes, occupational structures, standards of living, and migrations. In these respects, as well as population numbers and densities, the history of the European experience occupies a special place in the world.

Classical Populations

In the fifth century BC, when Europe's total inhabitants may have numbered 15m.–20m., the Mediterranean borderlands were the "center of gravity" of Europe's population map. There were not only the inhabitants of the city-states of fifth century Greece, but also their "offspring", in the colonies, and the inhabitants of other cities around the shores of the Mediterranean. The settlements of the toe of Italy and Sicily (Magna Graecia), like Syracuse and Catania, rivaled those in Greece itself in size and importance. In central Italy, Etruscan cities and their hinterlands represented fairly populous clusters, and the population of Etruria may have approached that at Attica, itself dominated by Athens, which was doubtless Europe's largest city. In the western Mediterranean the idea of the city was represented by the numerous but small Carthaginian and Greek colonies scattered along the shores of North Africa, Spain, and France, such as Carthage itself, or Gades (Cadiz, Spain), or the Greek settlement of Massilia (Marseilles).

Indeed, the notable feature of the population of the classical period is its concentration in "urban" places, and in a sense it is true that the predominantly urban character of modern Europe has its roots in the Mediterranean world, when the cities of the Aegean, Phoenicia, Sicily, southern and central Italy, and the shores of the western Mediterranean gave a distinctive stamp not only to society, economy, and politics, but also to the distribution of its population.

The Greek city-state, of course, is the archetypal classical city. But the city-states of the fifth century BC were more than urban places. They included an agricultural hinterland as well as the urban market, and in most of them the distinction between an agricultural village and a city might be difficult to discern, although all probably supported at least a few artisans, traders, and other non-farming specialists, and thus presented elements of an urban economy. The cities were also political entities, and the institution of democratic government is, of course, one of their most important contributions to western European culture.

The Aegean was the focus of much of this urban life, and in the fifth century BC no city-state in Greece exceeded Athens in population, although Sparta, spread over almost 8000 km^2, had an area three times as large. In Attica (Athens and the plain surrounding it) lived somewhere around a quarter of a million people (estimates range from 215,000 to 315,000; Beloch's is 285,000). If these estimates are correct, the population density of Attica would have been somewhere between 80 and 120 persons per km^2 and, as Beloch pointed out, the plain of Attica therefore must have been one of the most densely inhabited areas of the world in the fifth century BC. Its farmers not only grew enough grain to support themselves, but also produced a surplus which helped feed the city of Athens. Indeed, so large a market exceeded the ability of its hinterland to supply it with food, and we know that Athens relied also upon substantial imports of grain. Urban functions notwithstanding, farming sustained all the city-states and was the predominant economic activity. Athens was by far the largest of the city-states; the population of

B

other Greek cities probably averaged around 1000 inhabitants or less, though some, like Sparta, were larger.

Syracuse and Catania, on the eastern coast of Sicily, also were large cities, numbering with their neighbors perhaps a total of 350,000 persons. In addition there were perhaps another 150,000 living in the Greek cities of southern Italy. Of the Etruscan places we know somewhat less; their urban population may have attained 200,000. The Etruscan city of Caere has been estimated to have had 25,000 inhabitants. As for the Carthaginian cities and the Greek colonies of the western Mediterranean, Pounds estimates that their individual populations only rarely exceeded 10,000 inhabitants.

North of the Mediterranean, fifth-century (BC) Europe was overwhelmingly rural. Settlements which may have held 500–1000 inhabitants have been unearthed in central Poland, and these may indeed have had a few urban functions similar to those of the smaller Greek cities, but agricultural concerns predominated. During this period of Bronze and Iron Age technology, small farming villages of perhaps five to twenty houses, or dispersed farmsteads, were characteristic of the settlement pattern throughout most of non-Mediterranean Europe. In most places, the lighter and well drained forest soils (some of loessial origin) and sandy heaths were farmed in preference to the more refractory clay soils, although the tougher iron plowshare and coulter soon would begin to open up these soils to farming as well. Some areas such as the highland districts were probably only sparsely settled by hunters and gatherers and, perhaps, pastoralists. Where farms coalesced to form hamlets or villages, the settlement was sometimes fortified either by its position atop a hill or by earthen walls. Overall the pattern of population distribution was one of diffuse and scattered clusters. In between the farming communities of western Europe lay great expanses of uninhabited forested land. The forests of Gaul were less extensive than those east of the Rhine, but on a land-use map of western Europe, forested land doubtless would have predominated up to at least AD 1150. In general, the techniques of farming were not so advanced as they were farther south, and the very densely settled districts and the elegant urban architecture of the Mediterranean as yet had no northern counterparts.

Roman Europe

From the third century BC to the first century of the Christian era the hegemony of Rome grew, first in the Mediterranean Basin where it eclipsed that of the Greek city-states, and then northwards to include France and the lands west and south of the Rhine and the Danube, as well as Britain. By the second century AD, when Roman power was most widespread and the empire's achievements seemed greatest, the population of all Europe may have grown to about 50m. persons, perhaps three times what it had been during the fifth century BC. There is evidence for population decline during the next five centuries, with a recovery beginning after about AD 750, so that the figure of 50m. attained during the second century probably represents a density which was not equalled again until the twelfth century.

Although they amounted to less than a tenth of the modern total, the 50m. Europeans during the second century AD represented possibly one-fifth to one-fourth of the estimated population of the world at that time. Only the great concentrations of the North China Plain and northern India could rival the European cluster; and it is interesting that in these broad outlines the world's population map of almost 2000 years ago resembled that of today. The distribution *within* Europe, however, was quite different.

We know somewhat more about the numbers and distribution of peoples who were citizens of Rome than we do about the inhabitants of the rest of Europe because the Romans took censuses. The data are very difficult to interpret, however, because it is not known whether or not the census totals included women and children, or whether increases registered from one census to the next were the result of actual increases in the population or simply the extension of the privileges of citizenship. Slaves doubtless were not included and must be added to the census totals. The census of AD 48, for example, enumerated about 6m. *citizens* in the empire, but estimates of the total population of the Italian peninsula based on this count range widely from about 6m. to over 15m.

It seems likely that Italy was the most densely inhabited part of Europe in the second century AD. Certainly Rome was Europe's most populous city, and it may have had as many as 1m. inhabitants at its height. If so, Rome was then a city whose size would not be equalled again until 1801, when London became the modern world's first million-city. In the second century, the whole of the peninsula and Sicily may have had between 6m. and 10m. inhabitants, corresponding to a density of between 20 and 33 persons per km². Densities elsewhere in Europe were probably less than those in Italy, but the data are fragmentary and of uncertain quality. For example, Beloch's estimate of 6m. persons for Spain was based only on extrapolation from a single figure of 691,000 which Pliny gave as the population of Galicia, the Asturias, and northern Portugal. Others have argued higher estimates, but it seems likely that the truth lies somewhere within the range 6m. to 12m. Indeed, accuracy to within a factor of two is probably characteristic of estimates of Europe's population before the late medieval period. This is sufficient to yield at least an approximation of the population distribution, however. Figure 2.1 shows N. J. G. Pound's estimates for population densities in Europe during the second century AD. What stands out, besides the great density of Italy, is the importance of the Mediterranean littoral compared to the more sparsely inhabited northern and western parts of the continent. Densities of over 15 persons per km² were found only in Greece, southern France, eastern Spain, and especially in southern Spain, as well as Italy. These were also the areas where most of Europe's towns were to be found.

The growth in the number and size of Europe's towns was one result of Roman dominion. Under the relatively stable conditions imposed by the legions of Rome the urban idea spread northward from the Mediterranean Basin. The fortified hill villages or camps of Celtic tribes moved downhill to become the agricultural villages or provincial towns of the Roman Empire. There was some dispersal and extension of settlement as well, made possible by the peaceful conditions. Farmsteads and villas brought cultivation to what had formerly been heath or forest. The farmers' techniques had not changed very much, but relatively more people farmed, and fewer hunted and gathered, than had done before, and even beyond the borders of the empire the nomadic herders or hunters gradually yielded place to the sedentary husbandmen. The surplus from the farms supplied the towns with food, and in the empire commerce linked even distant regions. Thus, for example, the hams of southwestern France were consumed by Romans, to whom they were sent either by sea or overland along the system of roads which, like the language and laws of Rome, were to prove among the city's most durable legacies.

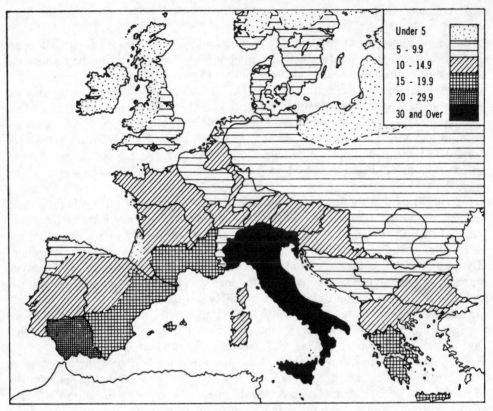

FIG. 2.1. Population density per square kilometer at the time of the Roman Empire. From N. J. G. Pounds, *An Historical Geography of Europe 450 BC–AD 1330*, Cambridge University Press, 1973, p. 111.

The Medieval Period

Along with the decline of Roman power after about the fifth century and its replacement by a mosaic of tribal kingdoms, the population of Europe also seems to have declined. The recession apparently lasted several centuries, so that not until the twelfth century did Europe again reach its second century densities, and the reduction in numbers was severe: Russell estimates there may have been but 18m. Europeans in about AD 650, and according to Pounds, the population about AD 800 may have numbered but 25m. persons, or about half the total in the second century. Why this decline should have happened is a matter of some conjecture, for we have even less information for this period than we do for the classical period which preceded it. The collapse of Roman authority and the decreasing security of the countryside meant that long distance trade was less practicable, or at least more costly, than during the Roman Empire, and so regions were thrown back upon their own agricultural resources without recourse to the variety and sureness of supply which commerce with other regions might have provided. Bad harvests in one locality could not be relieved by the surpluses of another, and so in the aggregate death rates may have risen. A series of epidemics of plague also swept

Europe during the sixth century, beginning in 542–544 and recurring in 556, 564, and continuing at intervals afterwards, although with diminished intensity. The sixth century also saw the northward extension of malaria into southern France. In addition, the Germanic invasions themselves and the turmoil, warfare, and violence which replaced the *Pax Romana* doubtless provoked population decline. Contemporary accounts speak of abandoned farmsteads and deserted villages, and pollen evidence shows forests or heaths retaking land which had been cultivated. The retreat of arable, the shrinking villages and towns, and the declining population seem to have been general throughout Europe, as was the resurgence after the eighth century. The evidence for regional differences in population growth rates is non-existent.

The documents which do remain, however, suggest a map having abrupt discontinuities in the pattern of settlement. Relatively densely inhabited farming areas on the easily worked soils alternated with wide, virtually uninhabited stretches of forests or heaths on heavy clays or poorly drained lands which were too difficult to exploit with the agricultural technology of the time. Thus, overall, Europe was sparsely settled, but in limited districts, as around Paris, populations nearly equalled those of the modern period. Population expansion and decline took place within the confines of these agricultural districts. Any increases in the birth rate seem to have been compensated for not by an expansion of the arable but by periodic waves of high mortality.

The significance of the early middle ages for the population map of modern Europe lies not so much in the regional redistribution of population numbers or of growth rates, but in the establishment of linguistic and cultural patterns. Europe's languages evolved considerably during the next ten centuries, but even by the eighth century the outlines of the modern divisions between the Slavic, Germanic, Romance, and Celtic languages could have been discerned on a language map. The expansion of Roman influence had brought Latin, or forms of speech derived from it, to most of the Italian peninsula, France, and Spain, overwhelming the Celtic tongues and pushing them to the continent's Atlantic shores, where Gaelic, Irish, Welsh, and Breton survive. Within the areas of Romance speech, local particularisms developed, fostered both by the decreasing influence of Rome and the varying effects of Gothic or Frankish invasions and settlements. Thus, for example, the speech of Italy came to differ from that of France, which in turn already showed a north-to-south gradient between the *langue d'oïl* and *langue d'oc*. A Romance language was not yet spoken in the southernmost parts of the Italian peninsula, where the use of Greek had persisted. Even in the twentieth century Greek dialects survived in some villages of Calabria. In Spain, Arab and Berber invaders from Africa reached the Pyrenees during the eighth century and some elements of their speech entered into the predominantly Romance dialects of the peninsula. Basque, unrelated to any other language, survived in the eastern Cantabrian Mountains of northwest Spain and the western Pyrenees. But the most striking boundary was, of course, that between Romance and Germanic languages; and it seems to have acquired its modern form by the ninth century and perhaps earlier. The same could be said of the distribution of Slavic tongues, though their eastern boundaries are less well known. The Magyars, too, settled in Hungary during the tenth century, bringing their Finno-Ugric speech to its westernmost outlier.

Other cultural patterns emerged during this period. For example, the melding of Arabic, Berber, and Roman institutions in the system of Hispanic law, and the distinction between Roman (written) law in the south and customary law in the north of France, have medieval roots. Also significant was the diffusion of Christianity during the early middle ages. By the beginning of the twelfth century it embraced all of Europe save a few areas around the Baltic Sea, and became one of the most important aspects of European culture. During the early medieval period, the church also played a role in assuring the continuity of urban settlements, for as commerce withered and the population of most towns declined, it was often only the church or cathedral which survived to be the nucleus of the reanimated towns of the twelfth century.

Late Medieval Population Growth

In the four centuries after about AD 950, Europe experienced a remarkable period of growth and development. The pace of change quickened during the period, and was especially notable during the twelfth and thirteenth centuries. What has been called the renaissance of the twelfth century saw a flourishing of literature, philosophy, technology, and the arts. The great universities of Europe trace their beginnings to this period. Commerce grew. The relatively closed and self-sufficient local markets of the preceding centuries slowly began to yield to the influence of larger, regional economies (for some but not all commodities), and trade over longer distances, such as had characterized certain aspects of the Roman Empire's economy, began anew. The supply of gold and silver increased and money circulated more freely, replacing barter as the medium of exchange. Towns and their industries prospered. The artistic achievements of the period—most notable are the many Romanesque and Gothic churches and cathedrals—made a legacy which is still admired.

What is perhaps more remarkable is that this relatively prosperous period was also a time of significant population growth. Since about the ninth century, Europe's population had been increasing, and the most rapid growth appears to have occurred from about 1150 to 1300. By 1340, only 8 years before it would be severely diminished by an epidemic of plague, the population of central and western Europe is estimated by Russell to have numbered approximately 62.5m. inhabitants, a figure which may have been about twice that of the preceding peak around the sixth century AD. Furthermore, the growing population of AD 1150 to 1300, instead of coming up against the limitations to subsistence imposed by the prevailing levels of technology and resources, seems instead to have met the challenges of growth by expanding or modifying both the resource base and the technology and social institutions capable of exploiting it. The result was a productive surplus of resources which the Europeans of the twelfth and thirteenth centuries could invest in trade, industry, urban life, and magnificent cathedrals.

New techniques and tools spread throughout the countryside and gradually effected changes in agriculture. The more productive three-course rotation replaced the two-course systems in many districts, augmenting yields by one-third. Three-course rotation also brought oats into wider cultivation, which in turn allowed horses to be substituted for oxen. Horses could do more work, especially since the advent of the wooden yoke around the tenth century, and thus heavier clay soils could be plowed and cultivated. Europeans, their numbers growing, put these new capabilities to productive use. The rise in population caused a rise in the prices of foodstuffs, which in turn increased the value of agricultural land. Farmers thus found it feasible to cultivate previously marginal lands. The abundance of people in the countryside also provided the manpower for the great clearing of waste and woodland which took place all over Europe at this time.

Indeed the outstanding process in the European landscape of the eleventh, twelfth, and thirteenth centuries was the tremendous expansion of the settled area which took place all over the continent, and which absorbed the increasing population of the older, thickly settled regions. As Europeans migrated to districts of pioneer settlement, the empty areas of the map of population distribution gradually filled up. Reclamation of land from the sea in the Low Countries (the word *polder* dates from the twelfth century), the draining of marshes, the eastward expansion of the Germans, and the movement of settlement up the valleys of the Alps, Pyrenees, and other mountain ranges, all proceeded apace. Where studies of population distribution have been made, it is apparent that the areas of greatest population growth from the twelfth to the fourteenth centuries were the areas which were least populous to begin with, something which had not characterized European growth patterns before. Everywhere axes and mattocks felled trees and put new fields into production. It was, as Bloch termed it, the great age of clearing.

In some districts clearing and settlement were fostered by monastic orders whose purpose was to bring cultivation and Christianity to what had been wild and uninhabited heaths or forests. Land was offered to whoever would clear and work it, and in this way large areas of new land were put to the plow. In many instances a monastery became the nucleus for a settlement. Elsewhere the clearing proceeded simply because it was profitable, and secular lords granted concessions to peasants who would thus increase the productivity of their domains. New villages and towns grew up to accommodate the growth.

A great eastward push by Germanic peoples into Slavic territory, the *Drang nach Osten*, thickened the density of settlement in the North German Plain, south of the Baltic Sea. Much of this Germanic colonization was organized and planned, either by local nobles or by the entrepreneurs acting for them. The clearing and cultivation of the eastern marshes of Germany was extensive enough to produce a surplus of grain for export from the region. By 1250 ships plied the Baltic laden with Polish grain, bound for places as far away as the northern coast of Spain.

Mountainous districts also absorbed an increase in settlement. In the Pyrenees, as in the Alps, many new villages were founded during these centuries, always upstream or upslope from the older villages which had literally fathered the new settlements. The increasing population was like a tide which carried people to higher elevations. Reclamation also took place in low-lying areas by dyking and draining. The fens of England and the coastal districts of the Low Countries were attacked by settlers during this period.

In a few regions, such as parts of the Pyrenees and the Alps, the practical limits of the settlement area were reached by about 1300: there has been only insignificant expansion since then. And in some districts, even population densities reached levels in 1340 which have not been exceeded since. In areas such as these, or where there might be relatively little uninhabited land available for new settlement, changes in agricultural techniques and institutions must attempt to cope with the increasing population. New methods of crop rotation or intercalation increased yields, as, for example, the increased use of legumes. The three-course system of crop rotation also was modified by communal regulations intended to maximize yields for the whole village. Thus villagers were required to follow identical schemes of rotation, often organized within large units of land containing fields belonging to several households. The rights of common were extended to include not only the common woodland and pasture beyond the arable, but also the private fields themselves, where villagers acquired the right to graze their live-stock on the stubble left after the harvest. Common rights also came to include the right of villagers to make temporary clearings in the common woods and pastures and cultivate these fields. As the press of people on the land grew greater, temporary clearings became permanent usurpations, and sometimes were the basis for the settlement of new villages.

A concomitant of the growth of population during the late medieval period was its

TABLE 2.2. POPULATION ESTIMATES (IN MILLIONS), AD 500–1450

	500	650	1000	1340	1450
Greece and Balkans	5	3	5	6	4.5
Italy	4	2.5	5	10	7.5
Iberian peninsula	4	3.5	7	9	7
Total—South	13	9	17	25	19
France and Low Countries	5	3	6	19	12
British Isles	0.5	0.5	2	5	3
Germany and Scandinavia	3.5	2	4	11.5	7.5
Total—West and Central	9	5.5	12	35.5	22.5
Slavia	5	3			
Russia			6	8	6
Poland and Lithuania			2	3	2
Hungary	0.5	0.5	1.5	2	1.5
Total—East	5.5	3.5	9.5	13	9.5
Total—All Europe	27.5	18	38.5	73.5	50

[Handwritten margin note: "Roman Italy 10 M"]

TABLE 2.3. POPULATION ESTIMATES (IN PERCENTAGE), AD 500–1450

	500	650	1000	1340	1450
Greece and Balkans	18.2	16.7	13	8.2	9
Italy	14.5	13.9	13	13.6	15
Iberian peninsula	14.5	19.4	18.2	12.2	14
Total—South	47.3	50.0	44.2	34.0	38.0
France and Low Countries	18.2	16.7	15.6	25.8	24
British Isles	1.8	2.8	5.2	6.8	6
Germany and Scandinavia	12.7	11.1	10.4	15.6	15
Total—West and Central	32.7	30.5	31.2	48.3	45.0
Slavia	18.2	16.7			
Russia			15.6	10.9	12
Poland and Lithuania			5.2	4.1	4
Hungary	1.8	2.8	3.9	2.7	3
Total—East	20.0	19.4	24.7	17.7	19.0
Total—All Europe	100	100	100	100	100

Source for Tables 2.2 and 2.3: J. C. Russell, Population in Europe 500–1500, in Carlo M. Cipolla (ed.), *The Fontana Economic History of Europe*, vol. 1, *The Middle Ages* (London: Collins, London, 1972), p. 36.

dramatic northward shift. The population of Northwest Europe grew almost three times faster than that of the Mediterranean countries between AD 1000 and 1340. At the beginning of the period there were more southerners than northerners, but at its end the proportions were reversed. And despite the northerners' relatively greater mortality during the period of epidemics and famines after 1340, there were still more people living in Northwest Europe in 1450 than lived in the Mediterranean countries (Tables 2.2 and 2.3). Such trends foreshadowed the modern distribution of population density.

Examined in greater detail, other modern patterns emerge on the map of medieval population. Northern Italy, for example, was characterized by its relatively denser, more urbanized populations when compared to southern Italy. The general urban renaissance of the twelfth century also initiated the dominance of the cities and towns of northern France, Flanders, and north Germany, as the map of urban places shows (Fig. 2.2).

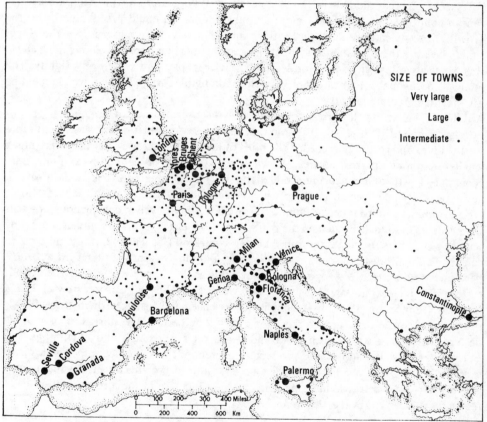

FIG. 2.2. European towns about 1330. From N. J. G. Pounds, *An Historical Geography of Europe 450 BC–AD 1330*, Cambridge University Press, 1973, p. 348.

Northern Europe developed a relatively sophisticated economy in which long distance trade, intensive livestock husbandry, and textile industries were especially important elements. Mining and metallurgical industries were still conducted on an almost craft scale and were scattered throughout Europe, especially in the mountainous districts, but the modern centers (which today support relatively dense populations) were among the most important even in the thirteenth century: the Rhine–Ruhr, Lorraine, southern Sweden, northwestern Italy, and northern Spain.

The growing commercial vitality of the North, and the cities it supported, were themselves important causes of and outlets for the region's upward surge in population densities. Only exceptionally, however, were the cities themselves nodes of natural population growth (that is, places where birth rates exceeded death rates). In fact, in most places only a heavy flow of rural-to-urban migration (most moves were over fairly short distances) offset the greater mortality of the cities compared to the countryside. The growth of the urban markets, as well as facilities for transport, also supported denser rural populations. Farmers near cities were able to intensify production and sell their surplus. The very high densities of the Paris Basin north of the city (from Pontoise to Meaux) lived by farming for the urban market.

It is also true that the North could support relatively greater growth than the Mediterranean countries because it had more surplus land which could profitably absorb the growth. Forest clearance and reclamation were relatively more important in the North simply because there was more to be reclaimed there. The Germans' *Drang nach Osten* was primarily a taming of the woods which Slavic peoples had settled only lightly. The land was both an absorber of people as well as a tangible form of capital which could be invested in economic growth.

It would be wrong, however, to exaggerate the overall rates of population growth during the period 1000–1340. It is true that the rates of population increase seem rapid for the times and certainly exceeded the rates of preceding centuries, yet they were much smaller than modern growth rates. We know that the pace of technological innovation, economic growth, and increasing productivity was slow compared to the modern period, yet it generally managed to keep up with the rising population during the late Middle Ages: accounts of hard times or famine before 1300 are relatively inconspicuous, whereas the products of affluence, such as the period's artistic legacy, are more numerous. Using Russell's estimates for population in AD 1000 and 1340 (see Table 2.2) it is possible to calculate annual rates of growth. Overall, the population of Europe increased at 0.19% per year. Mediterranean Europe's rate of growth was 0.11% per year during the period; eastern Europe grew at 0.09% per year, and western and central Europe grew at 0.32% per year. France and the Low Countries experienced the fastest growth rate—0.34% per year. Of course these are averages for a very long period. The normal demographic pattern was one in which both birth and death rates were high and fluctuating, and Europe's growth was simply the product of a preponderance of years in which births exceeded deaths. The overall trend was one of sustained growth, but it was maintained only by narrow and fragile margins. Only a slight increase in the already high rates of mortality sufficed to reverse the trend.

Population Decline After 1340

That is in fact what happened after about 1340. Again using Russell's estimates, the decline between 1340 and 1450 occurred at an overall rate of −0.34% per year. The decline was greatest in northwestern and central Europe (−0.41% per year), and least in the Mediterranean region (−0.25% per year). The period of decline began with a brief series of epidemics (e.g. amoebic dysentery in 1315–17), culminating in an epidemic of plague so severe that it came to be called the "Black Death." The Black Death, which spread northward from the Mediterranean through Europe in 1348–50, was only the first and worst of a series of visitations of plague which swept over Europe at intervals thereafter. Mortality was high: some districts lost half their inhabitants to the Black Death and overall perhaps 25% of Europeans succumbed, although births during the period may have limited the net loss to 20% or so. Adding to the deadliness of plague was a protracted period of late and insufficient harvests, cool, rainy summers, and harsh winters, beginning about 1300. Hunger and disease ravaged Europe until at least the middle of the fifteenth century, when the population decline halted and a period of slow recovery began. The patterns of decline were often quite localized, and varied through time as well as space. Between 1340 and 1360, J. D. Chambers has estimated that England's population was cut in half by disease: from about 4.1m. inhabitants to 2.1m.; the corresponding rate of decline is −3.3% per year. Most of the loss occurred in southern England. There were also other localized scourges, such as the campaigns of the Hundred Years War, which laid waste parts of Aquitaine during the period. Overall there were 32% fewer Europeans in 1450 than there had been in 1340 (see Table 2.2).

As a result of the decline, the area under cultivation receded, and both towns and villages grew smaller, the smallest often disappearing entirely. The abandonment of villages during this period was a general phenomenon: these were the "lost villages" of England, the *Wustungen* of Germany, the *despoblados* of Spanish chroniclers. In some areas the forest grew back over the clearings, and in the Alps and the Pyrenees, for example, the population receded downslope: the highest villages, settled but one or two centuries before, were the first to be abandoned.

Historians have advanced various explanations for the population decline. The frequent epidemics of the fourteenth and fifteenth centuries, of course, provide one of the simplest explanations, but alone they are probably insufficient to account for all the loss. Some historians have advanced the theory that by the first decades of the fourteenth century Europe's dense populations had reached a point of Malthusian crisis in which the number of people simply exceeded the capacity of the land to provide food. According to this theory, the rising population densities of the preceding period had obliged farmers to put ever more marginal land under cultivation, lands from which the fertility of the soil soon was exhausted, bringing harvest failures and famine upon the population, which, thus weakened, was susceptible to epidemic diseases.

The thesis of a Malthusian dilemma, however, is difficult to substantiate, for except in certain localities it appears most unlikely that the limits of the land's productivity had been reached by 1340—especially in Northwest Europe where depopulation was to be most severe. Neither would localized instances of depleted soil fertility have been able to produce such a widespread and long-lasting decline. The most plausible and best documented cause for the more frequent harvest failures (which need provoke but a slight increase in mortality to result in depopulation) is the general deterioration of Europe's climate which began sometime during the late thirteenth century. The previous two centuries had been characterized by an especially warm and clement climate which doubtless facilitated the expansion of the arable. After about 1300, as has been mentioned, winters tended to be more severe, and summers cooler and wetter, so the harvest failed or spoiled in storage more frequently. The growing season was on the average one or two weeks shorter than it had been. The climatic changes were gradual and certainly not drastic, but, as we have seen, the fact that both birth and death rates were high and somewhat unstable meant that it took no more than a slight increase in the number of bad years to change a growing population into a declining one. As for the epidemics, we now know that the incidence of plague depended far more on the fortunes (and the life cycles) of its vectors—the flea and the rat—than upon the vicissitudes of its victims. In fact the Black Death struck Europe just after several years of especially good harvest.

Modern Populations

The early modern period, from the Renaissance to the eighteenth century, saw the recovery and further growth of Europe's population. Recovery was rapid: from a low occurring about 1450, by about 1550 Europe again seems to have had as many inhabitants as in 1340. Growth slackened after around 1570, picking up again only in the late seventeenth or early eighteenth century. The most reasonable explanation for this growth lies in a lowering of the average death rate (over the long term)—primarily from an abatement of the acute and widespread crises of mortality with which Europeans literally had been plagued during the late fourteenth and fifteenth centuries. The growth was of course punctuated by a few local and relatively short lived crises which were the normal concomitants of a society living close to the means of subsistence and an economy in which most transactions were local. Under such conditions it is difficult to generalize about the regional distribution of growth.

Indeed, in Spain and Italy, population actually declined during the seventeenth century, probably from plague-borne waves of mortality. One scholar estimated the total population of Spain in 1594 at 8.5m. and 7.5m. in 1717; he was also careful to point out regional differences: most of the decline occurred in Castille and the southeast, whereas Catalonia and the North increased their populations. Pandemics of bubonic plague as late as 1630 and 1657 also reduced the Italian population in 1660 to the level of 1550. But the Italian plague of 1657 was the last to visit the peninsula; growth rates increased afterwards.

Italy is one of only a few countries for which reliable figures go back as far as the sixteenth century. In France the parish registers and other sources before about 1660 are fragmentary, and where they have been studied they reveal a complex—almost chaotic—mosaic of growth and decline so that it is impossible to draw conclusions about the demographic behavior of the whole country, except perhaps that growth was probably quite slow or sporadic and also marked by substantial fluctuations in the total during the sixteenth and seventeenth centuries. The slowness of the growth of France is better documented after 1660 followed by an increase in the growth rate after about 1760.

England's population seems to have followed more closely what is supposed to be the average for all Europe: a fairly rapid rise between 1480 and 1600, slower growth during the seventeenth century, and very rapid growth beginning around 1740. It is possible that England's population grew more than any other country's between 1500 and 1700 (it nearly doubled). Less is known about the situation in the German lands, although some have suggested that growth there, while following a similar rhythm, was slower than in England.

The quality and abundance of the data as well as the pace of population change increased after 1700. The keeping of parish records was better enforced, and the records themselves have been more completely preserved after the last decades of the seventeenth century. During the eighteenth century some European governments began tabulating these statistics on births, marriages, and deaths; and between 1749, when they began in Sweden and Norway, and 1861 (the year of the first Italian census), regular census enumerations became the norm in European countries. Despite this abundance of data, our understanding of the causes of what has been called the "demographic revolution" is still only tentative, because any study of the important period in which it began (before 1740) depends upon the careful analysis of parish registers—a branch of historical demography which is relatively recent.

Europe's population growth after 1740 was unprecedented. At the beginning of the period there were already more Europeans than ever before, and population densities were quite high even by world standards. The two centuries which followed were ones in which the average rates of increase were higher than the continent had experienced ever before, and the rates of growth themselves increased steadily until the first decades of the twentieth century (Table 2.4). The essence of this "demographic revolution" was

TABLE 2.4. GROWTH OF EUROPEAN POPULATION, 1650–1900

	Population (millions)		Mean growth rate (% per year)		
	Excluding Russia	Including European Russia	Excluding Russia	Including European Russia	
1650		100			
1700	110–115			0.337	1650–1750
1750	125	140	0.211		1700–1750
1800	152	187	0.392	0.581	1750–1800
1850	208	266	0.629	0.707	1800–1850
1900	296	401	0.708	0.824	1850–1900

Sources: J. D. Durand, The modern expansion of world population, *Proc. Am. Phil. Soc.*, vol. III, no. 3 (June, 1967); and A. M. Carr-Saunders, *World Population: Past Growth and Present Trends*, Clarendon Press, Oxford, 1936.

a great and sustained fall in mortality combined with a birth rate which was maintained at relatively high levels for several generations before it too declined to levels approaching that of the death rate. The consequent large excess of births over deaths during much of the period 1750–1900 produced very high rates of natural increase. In fact the figures presented in Table 2.4 obscure the *natural* growth of Europe's population during this period both because they are 50-year averages for the whole continent and because they present only net growth—that is, they omit the many persons who emigrated from Europe during this period (about 27.5m. left during the nineteenth century alone (Fig. 2.3). Thus the natural rate of increase (the difference between the birth and the death rates) in England and Wales in five decades from 1851 to 1900 was never less than 1.2% per year. Most western European countries experienced peak decades sometime during the late nineteenth century when their rate of natural increase was between 1.0% and

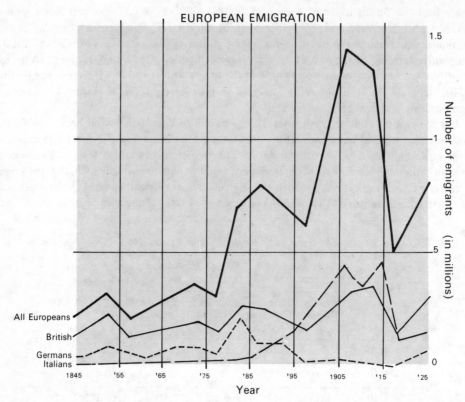

FIG. 2.3. Emigration from Europe, 1845–1925. Source: Marcel Reinhard, André Armengaud, and Jacques Dupaquier, *Histoire générale de la population mondiale*, Montchrestien, Paris, 1968, p. 397.

1.5% per year. Most of the emigration also occurred during the last half of the nineteenth century. The countries of Northwest Europe provided the first substantial flow of overseas migrants, especially Great Britain, Germany, and Scandinavia. After the 1880s they were joined by the eastern and the Mediterranean Europeans—from the Iberian peninsula, Italy, Austria-Hungary, and Russia. Emigration from the Balkans began late in the nineteenth century and gathered strength in the twentieth century. French emigration, also mainly during the last half of the nineteenth century, amounted to only a trickle compared to the flow from other countries.

The rapid and sustained population growth after 1740 was part of the great transformation of European society and economy during the Industrial Revolution. Innovations and achievements in agriculture, transport, commerce, technology, industry, urbanization, and social patterns wrought rapid and profound changes upon the landscape, and in general brought about substantial improvements in the "standard of living" of most Europeans. But it would be a mistake to argue, as some have done, that the material achievements of the Industrial Revolution produced the tremendous surge of population which accompanied it. Without the advances in productivity which the Industrial Revolution made possible, the continent could not have continued to support its ever-growing population, but what *initiated* the population growth is still unclear. It may have been simply a fortuitous drop in what J. D. Chambers has called the "autonomous death rate," which later was sustained and amplified by Europe's technological and social progress.

Thus in its first stages, the great population growth after 1740 was not unique and probably resembled that of the twelfth and thirteenth centuries and also the sixteenth century. The "crisis" death rate (which in years of famine and epidemic could soar as high as 200 per 1000) abated in Europe so that after 1740 mortality rarely exceeded a "normal" pre-industrial level of between 30 and 45 per 1000. Plague ceased to visit western Europe after 1720, and there were relatively few epidemics or famines involving large regions thereafter, except an influenza epidemic in 1761 and a variety of infectious fevers, such as cholera, which did reach epidemic proportions in its first visit to Europe in the 1830s. But mortality even from these did not approach the levels attained by the bubonic plagues of the fourteenth century. At the beginning of this new period of lower death rates, there also seems to have been a rise in birth rates in most countries.

What made the eighteenth and nineteenth century growth distinctive was the further drop in the "normal" death rate after 1740, to levels which by 1900 averaged between 15 and 20 per 1000, as the expectancy of life at birth increased for Europeans. Several factors in this decline may be mentioned. During the Industrial Revolution, advances in medicine and public health, and general improvements in living conditions, gradually lessened the effects of disease. Improvements in the infrastructure of transport meant also that areas were no longer entirely dependent upon their own resources, so that famines in one area now might be alleviated by bringing in surpluses from another area. The improvement in diet in turn made Europeans more resistant to some types of disease. All these factors doubtless contributed towards the definitive elimination of the high death rates associated with crises, and also helped lower the rate of "normal" mortality, especially as they influenced infant mortality, which had constituted a significant proportion of the whole death rate. But improvements in medicine, sanitation, transport, and diet alone cannot have *caused* the death rate to drop, because in most areas it began to decline before the effects of these improvements had been felt.

Thus in England and Wales, the death rate, which may have risen in 1700–40, began to decline after 1740, from about 36 per 1000 then to perhaps 26 per 1000 in 1800, 22 per 1000 in 1850, and 18 per 1000 in 1900. Yet there is no evidence that significant advances in medicine were widely available before the nineteenth century, or that an increase in agricultural output may have preceded and stimulated the fall in mortality. On the contrary, the rise in agricultural output in Great Britain during the eighteenth century did not quite keep pace with the increase of population (imports of foodstuffs also increased). From the timing of events both in Britain and elsewhere, it appears more likely that increasing agricultural production was the result rather than the cause of population growth. For example, most of the initial increase in output was achieved simply by increasing the arable acreage rather than by structural or technical innovations in agriculture (these came later).

In fact the very structural and social changes in agriculture which had been devised to cope with increases in population in the twelfth century, such as certain rights of common and the communally regulated systems of crop rotation, were considered in the eighteenth and nineteenth centuries to be impediments to the further improvement of agricultural productivity which the new population growth necessitated. Farmers who wished to adopt new crops, new methods of cultivation, new machinery, or new schemes of rotation, or who wished to enclose and cultivate common land (so as to intensify live-stock production, for example, by substituting forage crops for pasturage) often came up against the conservatism (and vested interests) of the whole village community, and found it an almost insuperable obstacle to innovation. Enclosure in England, for example, usually required an Act of Parliament. Such structural and technical changes in agriculture were difficult and expensive, and must be justified by the increased value of land and food which *prior* increases in population had brought about.

The elimination of the "crisis" death rate was general throughout Europe and many regions experienced population growth during the eighteenth century. But because of the fortuitous nature of the decline in mortality, growth rates were at first unevenly distributed and did not necessarily reflect the economic performance or potential of regions. E. A. Wrigley has tabulated rates for several European regions which show clearly the nearly random distribution of rapid population growth during the eighteenth century (Table 2.5).

TABLE 2.5. POPULATION GROWTH IN THE EIGHTEENTH CENTURY (% PER YEAR)

France, 1700–89	0.31	England and Wales, 1751–1801	0.80
France, 1740–89	0.45	East Prussia, 1700–1800	0.84
England and Wales, 1701–1801	0.45	Silesia, 1740–1804	0.94
Italy, 1700–1800	0.45	Austria, 1754–89	0.94
Württemburg, 1740–1800	0.56	Bohemia, 1754–89	1.18
Sweden, 1749–1800	0.59	Hungary, 1754–89	3.01
Pomerania, 1740–1800	0.80		

Source: E. A. Wrigley, *Population and History* (Weidenfeld and Nicolson, London, 1969), p. 153.

The *continued* population increase of regions during the nineteenth century, however, depended more on the further lowering of the "normal" death rate, and this could be sustained best by an economy and society in which changes in agriculture, commerce, and industry were taking place. The usual manifestation was a pronounced decline in infant and juvenile mortality, with a consequent improvement in the expectancy of life at birth. On the other hand, societies in which population increases exceeded the growth of the agricultural and commercial economy subsequently experienced increased mortality, as during the famines in Hungary in 1788–9 and 1816–17, or in Bohemia, where the death rate rose from 30 to 40 per 1000 between 1789 and 1809.

For these reasons the geographical pattern of changes in mortality during the late eighteenth and nineteenth centuries shows the countries of Northwest Europe as the first to drop below about 30–35 deaths per 1000, the tendency spreading only later to central, eastern, and southern Europe. Death rates in Sweden, England, and, more slowly, France (and probably also Denmark, Belgium, and Switzerland) moved steadily downward after about 1750. By the middle of the nineteenth century, these countries had death rates below 25 per 1000 and were in advance of others which had also joined the trend, such as Austria-Hungary, Finland, Germany, and The Netherlands (with death rates between 25 and 32 per 1000), and these in turn were followed by Russia and the Mediterranean countries, where death rates were still greater than 30–35 per 1000. In most cases changes in the infant mortality rate accounted for most of the drop in the overall death rate.

The geographical distribution of changes in birth rates was more complex than those for mortality, because more factors influenced it, including the average age at marriage, expectation of life after marriage, age and sex selective patterns of migration, economic conditions, and attitudes about child bearing or birth control. In general, couples tended to adhere to traditional values and so in most countries the decline of the birth rate (which was more sensitive to changes in the cultural or psychological than the physical or economic environment) lagged considerably behind the falling death rates. It was this lag, or period of substantial disparity between birth and death rates, which produced Europe's massive population growth during the nineteenth century.

France was the country which first experienced a substantial and prolonged fall in the birth rate. In fact, the case of France was remarkably unlike that of any other European nation in that the birth rate declined very early in conjunction with the death rate. The reasons for this anomalous performance are unclear, except that some means of voluntary birth control must have been used by French couples from about 1775 when the birth rate began to drop steadily. The result was that France did not participate in the population growth associated with the Industrial Revolution to the extent that other European countries did. The greatest rate of natural increase in France occurred in 1810–15, when it was about 0.6% per year. Indeed, in the nineteenth century the slow growth of the population *vis-à-vis* its rapid growth in other European nations was a cause of concern to Frenchmen, because it seemed to them to threaten the balance of power and France's status as one of Europe's most populous and influential states.

The birth rate in Sweden and England oscillated between 30 and 35 per 1000 during the first part of the nineteenth century. Sweden's began to drop after about 1850, whereas England's dropped only a generation afterwards, after peaking at 35.5 per 1000 in 1871–80. Germany's birth rate also began to decline in the same decade, though it started from a higher point (39 per 1000). Again, the countries of eastern and southern Europe lagged behind those of the northwest. On the eve of the First World War, most eastern European states still had birth rates greater than 38 per 1000, while Spain, Italy, and Portugal's rates were between 32 and 35 per 1000. The countries of Northwest Europe then varied from 29.5 (Germany) to 19.5 per 1000 (France).

The fall in birth rates, as well as massive emigration from Europe to colonies and to North America (which affected mainly younger males and was itself one of the causes of lowered natality), also changed the age structure of the population. (Decreasing death rates had not altered age structures appreciably because the decrease mainly involved infant and juvenile mortality, so that there was an increase in persons of all ages.) After the mid nineteenth century, the average age of the European population increased, as fewer children were born. Like the changes in birth rates, these changes in the age pyramid also spread from France and Northwest Europe eastward and southward during the nineteenth century.

The map of nineteenth century growth rates reflects the distribution of both vital rates and emigration (Fig. 2.4). The greatest increases occurred in the northwest. France, with its low rate of increase, is anomalous. The similarity of the French and Spanish rates of course masks their different causes: in France both vital rates descended together, whereas in Spain growth was relatively slow because the death rate remained high until late in the century—the demographic revolution came later to the Iberian peninsula. The case of Ireland is exceptional. There, famine, hardship, and limited economic opportunity in mid-century provoked rapid (and age-selective) emigration. The average

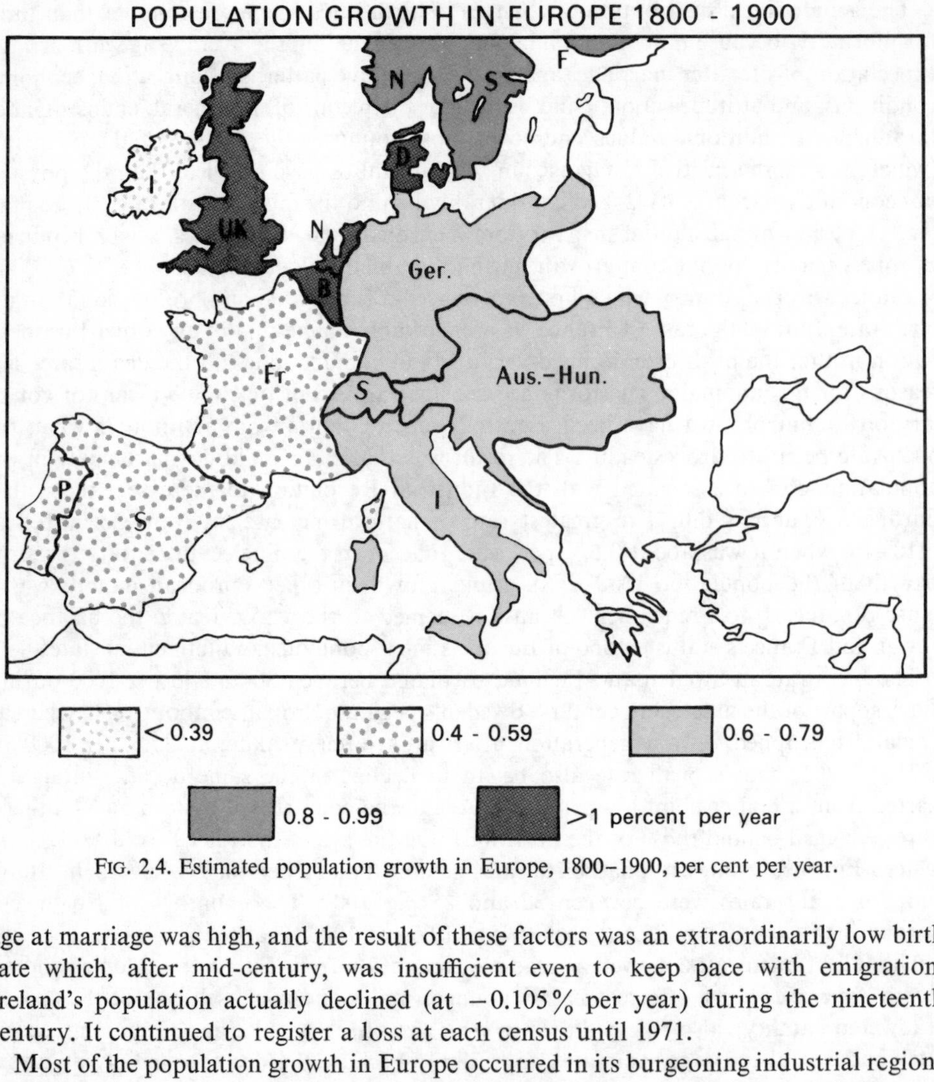

POPULATION GROWTH IN EUROPE 1800 - 1900

Fig. 2.4. Estimated population growth in Europe, 1800–1900, per cent per year.

age at marriage was high, and the result of these factors was an extraordinarily low birth rate which, after mid-century, was insufficient even to keep pace with emigration. Ireland's population actually declined (at −0.105% per year) during the nineteenth century. It continued to register a loss at each census until 1971.

Most of the population growth in Europe occurred in its burgeoning industrial regions largely as a result of the rapid urbanization and the shift in the occupational structure associated with the Industrial Revolution. The physical expansion of cities and their suburbs startled contemporaries with its speed. Thus, of Birmingham in the early nineteenth century, one regular visitor wrote: "The traveller who visits once in six months supposes himself well acquainted with her, but he may chance to find a street of houses in the autumn, where he saw his horse at grass in the spring." Such rapid growth often exceeded the ability of the cities to supply the necessary municipal services, and was in part responsible for the notorious slums of the Victorian period as well as the cities' higher death rates.

Nineteenth century cities tended to grow faster than the rural areas despite the fact that their birth rates were usually lower, and their death rates higher, than those of the country. Massive rural-to-urban migration increased the cities' populations. Nevertheless, Europe's rural areas also increased their population, at least in the first half of the nineteenth century, except in France (where overall growth was insufficient). Figure 2.5 shows the growth of both urban and rural counties in England, 1700–1815. In the last years of the nineteenth century, however, the number of rural dwellers either remained stable or declined in most Northwest European countries.

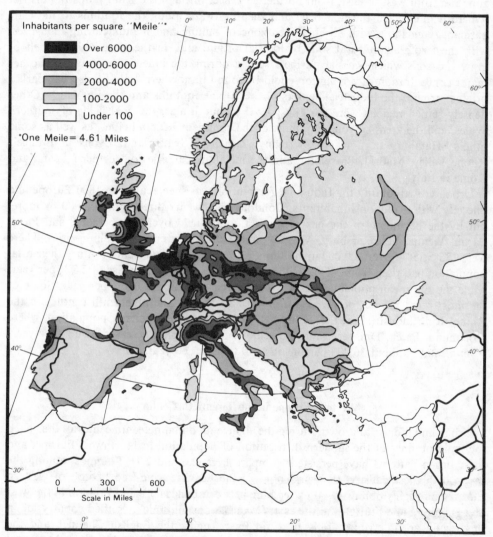

FIG. 2.5. Population density in Europe about 1870. (Modified from map by E. Behm and H. Wagner, in *Petermann's Geographischen Mitteilungen*, no. 35, 1874, pl. 2). From Glenn T. Trewartha, *A Geography of Population; World Patterns*, Wiley, New York, 1969, p. 65.

Two intersecting, industrialized, urban belts of high population densities became prominent in Europe during the nineteenth century, although since both had earlier origins, their nineteenth century growth did not create new patterns so much as it accentuated old ones. The greatest of these zones extended from the several urban and industrial concentrations of the English Midlands—around Leeds, Liverpool, Manchester, and Birmingham—south and eastward through London and the cities of the Low Countries to the conurbations of the Ruhr Valley and its tributaries. There the belt of dense populations turned south, to include the cities of the Rhine Valley (and its tributaries the Main and the Neckar) as far south as Strasbourg and Stuttgart. The other zone ran from west to east, from northern France, through the Ruhr industrial district (where it intersected the first belt) and then eastward along the foothills to the Carpathians, coinciding with an elongated zone of mining and manufacturing industries, with the fertile agricultural soils of loessial origin, and, in the east, with the belt of grassland soils which Russian farmers settled during the nineteenth century. Another major concentration of population could be found in northern Italy (it also had earlier origins) around the industrial centers of the Alpine foothills and the Po Valley. Other densely settled regions were the Glasgow–Edinburgh axis, the coal fields of southern Wales, and the areas surrounding most of the continent's capital cities, as well as some others: Hamburg in northern Germany, Zurich in Switzerland, Lyons in France's Rhone Valley, Madrid, Barcelona, and the metallurgical cities of northern Spain, and Rome in Italy.

Urban growth during the Industrial Revolution was spectacular. In 1800 Europe had one city with a million inhabitants (London) and twenty-three with 100,000 or more, but by the beginning of the next century London held over 4m. persons, and Paris, Berlin, Vienna, St. Petersburg, Moscow, and Hamburg were also million-cities. There were 135 cities of over 100,000 inhabitants, and during the nineteenth century their total population had risen from 5.5m. to 46m. This represented an increase of 2.2% per year, while the European population as a whole increased at about 0.7% per year. Some of the most rapid growth occurred during the last half of the nineteenth century in the Rhine–Ruhr industrial area, crossing point of the two great belts of population, where Dortmund, Essen, Duisberg, and Dusseldorf, for example, increased at 6% per year, from a total of about 36,000 persons in 1850 to 1.2m. 60 years later.

Western Europe in the Twentieth Century

Urban and industrial growth during the eighteenth and nineteenth centuries thus fixed the main outlines of the modern distribution of population in Northwest Europe, and these broad patterns have persisted (compare Figs. 2.6 and 2.7). Foremost among the zones of highest density, then and now, is the heavily urbanized "core" of western Europe: a roughly oblong region stretching between Lancashire and London in the west and Hamburg and Stuttgart in the east. Conurbations and thickly settled countryside in this region are interrupted only by rural East Anglia, the English Channel, and the uplands of the Ardennes and the Rhineland Palatinate. Everywhere else densities exceed 250 persons per km^2 (Fig. 2.7). This core and the major belts of population stretching out from it (Fig. 2.6) reflect the opportunities for industrialization which existed in areas having important mineral deposits (mainly coal and iron) or easy access to transportation (as port cities on the English coasts, the North Sea, and the Rhine River). While these broad patterns have persisted despite twentieth century improvements in communications and shifts in the sources of energy and minerals, the *details* of population distribution in western Europe are changing very noticeably. Thus, as will be shown in this section,

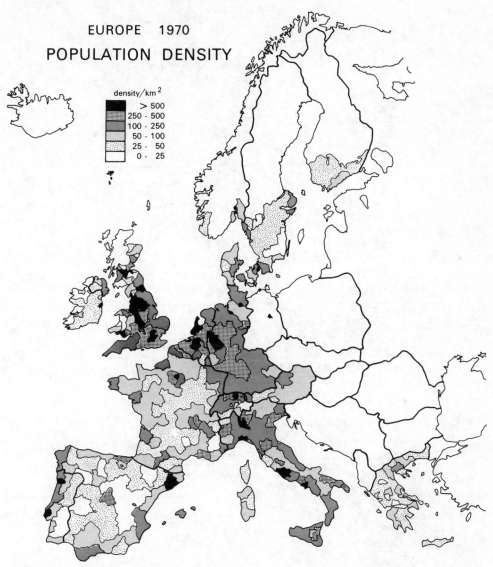

EUROPE 1970

POPULATION DENSITY

density/km^2

> 500
250 - 500
100 - 250
50 - 100
25 - 50
0 - 25

FIG. 2.6. Modified from a map in *Atlas of Europe*, F. Warne and Bartholomew, London and Edinburgh, 1974, p. 26.

affluence and the well-developed (and nearly ubiquitous) infrastructure of communications in western Europe today make residential choices appear more flexible and responsive to individual tastes.

By the first quarter of the twentieth century the decline of both birth rates and death rates in Europe began to slow down. The birth rate then converged with the death rate, completing the "demographic cycle" which had begun two centuries earlier. Vital rates stabilized first in western Europe, later in eastern and Mediterranean Europe. The

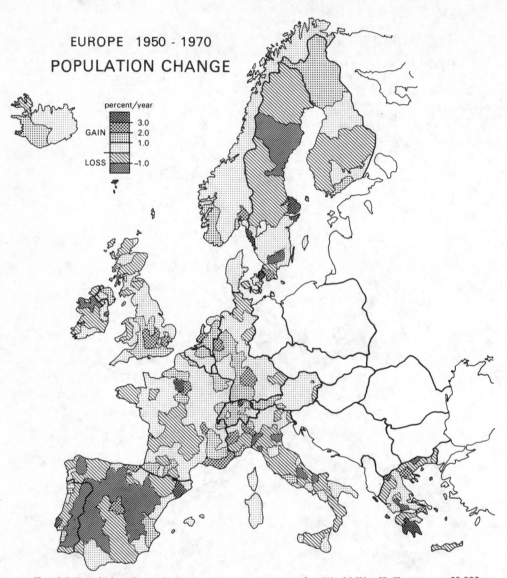

FIG. 2.7. Population change in Europe, per cent per year, after World War II. Towns over 50,000 are excluded. The data refer to slightly different time periods, but for most countries it is about 1950–70. Modified from a map in *Atlas of Europe*, F. Warne and Bartholomew, London and Edinburgh, 1974, p. 32.

average birth rate in all Europe in 1975 was 16 per 1000 and the average death rate was 10 per 1000. By 1975, country-to-country variations in these two figures were relatively small. Except for Ireland, there was a slight tendency towards lower birth rates and higher death rates (and thus lower growth rates) in the north and west, and slightly higher birth rates and lower death rates (thus higher growth rates) in eastern and Mediterranean Europe, than the European average. The birth rates ranged from 12 (West

Germany) to 19 per 1000 (Spain) and 22 per 1000 (Ireland); and the death rates from 12 per 1000 (East and West Germany and Austria) to 8 per 1000 (Spain). Correspondingly, growth rates ranged from 0.2% (Germany, Austria) to 1% (Spain, Ireland). The population of Europe in 1975 was also much older than it had ever been before. The median age was 32 years (the highest median age of any society in the world) and only 24% of Europeans were age 14 or under (again a world record). The average life expectancy at birth was everywhere over 70 years.

The progression towards these modern figures, however, was not always a smooth one. It was in particular punctuated by two world wars, both of which had important demographic impacts. Despite the severity of wartime experiences, however, the general population trends in Europe were not substantially altered by the wars. Even the population of France never stopped growing, albeit slowly, and the progress of birth and death rates depended upon the ever-changing attitudes of society and improvements in the standard of living rather than upon catastrophic occurrences as had beeu the case before the Industrial Revolution.

In many other respects the population patterns established after the beginnings of the Industrial Revolution in the eighteenth century persisted into the twentieth. The populations of European cities continued to grow rapidly, although the causes and results of this urban growth gradually changed. Indeed, the greatest change in the European landscape during the late nineteenth and twentieth centuries was the enormous growth in the size of cities, a product of the changing composition of the workforce (from an agricultural to an industrial and commercial basis), and of the technical development of the urban and transportation infrastructure.

The nineteenth century core of industrial centers, including parts of Great Britain, France, Germany, Belgium, and The Netherlands, continued to grow faster than the rural areas. Then, during the twentieth century, both industrial growth and urban population growth spread outwards from this core to include the Scandinavian, eastern European, and Mediterranean countries. The modern expansion of cities in eastern and southern Europe is described elsewhere in this book. North of the Mediterranean, the especially rapid growth of the Scandinavian capital cities after 1900, coupled with stagnation or decline in the southern and western French provinces, caused a northward shitt in the center of gravity of the population of Northwest Europe, although for the continent as a whole this was more than offset by the growth of Mediterranean cities. By 1970 no less than 14 western European cities had over a million inhabitants, whereas a century earlier only three (London, Paris, and Berlin) had been as large. Their ranking illustrates not only the persistence of the traditional industrial centers but also the rapid ɹise of cities at the periphery of western Europe (Table 2.6). Excluding the countries east of the Iron Curtain, almost 30% of Europeans (95,400,000) lived in the 292 cities of more than 100,000 inhabitants in 1970.

The components of urban growth in Europe changed during the late nineteenth and twentieth centuries. Old industrial centers and towns which had at first grown largely as a result of migration from rural districts eventually grew more from their own natural increase than from rural-to-urban migration. City-to-city and town-to-city population transfers overwhelmed the rural component in the internal migration patterns of Europe. In part this was due simply to the absolute dominance of urban populations: England had become a nation of town dwellers as early as 1821 (when for the first time half of its inhabitants lived in towns of 2000 or more). The nations of the continent lagged

TABLE 2.6. POPULATION OF EUROPEAN CITIES, 1970 (1000)

London	7418	Marseilles	889
Madrid	3146	Athens	867
Rome	2731	Cologne	866
Paris	2591	Genoa	842
Berlin	2134	Amsterdam	831
Hamburg	1817	Lisbon	782
Barcelona	1745	Stockholm	740
Milan	1702	Essen	705
Vienna	1603	Rotterdam	687
Munich	1326	Dusseldorf	681
Naples	1277	Frankfurt-am-Main	660
Turin	1177	Palermo	659
Brussels	1071	Valencia	654
Birmingham	1013	Dortmund	647
Glasgow	894	Copenhagen	630

Source: Bartholomew/Warne, *Atlas of Europe*, John Bartholomew, (Edinburgh, 1974). Figures are for 1970 except France, 1968; and Austria, Greece, and United Kingdom, 1971.

somewhat, but Germany achieved this status before 1900, and most other countries in Northwest Europe became predominantly urban during the first third of the twentieth century. As with so many other demographic trends which spread outward from an Anglo-Saxon hearth, the countries of the periphery—Portugal, Spain, Italy, Greece, and the eastern European nations—were the last to develop this urban dominance. By 1975 all the countries of western Europe except Portugal held more than half their population in towns of 2000 or more inhabitants.

The decreasing importance of rural-to-urban migration for the growth of towns was also a result of lessening differences between urban and rural vital rates. During the late eighteenth and early nineteenth centuries, urban death rates tended to be higher and birth rates lower than those of rural areas. The resulting differences in rural and urban growth potentials were then more than counterbalanced by a strong current of rural-to-urban migration. In the late nineteenth and twentieth centuries, however, the vital rates of town and country became similar as rural fertility and urban mortality both decreased.

Indeed, this decreasing surplus of rural dwellers became a deficit in many places as emigration from the countryside eventually exceeded the natural increase of the local population. Furthermore, the emigration was generally a youthful movement, so that the population remaining in rural places came to include more aged persons than the national average. This exacerbated population decline by increasing local crude death rates and decreasing the number of births.

Ireland and France experienced absolute population declines in some rural districts as early as the nineteenth century. The exceptional case of Ireland has already been mentioned. In France, where birth rates fell earlier than elsewhere in Europe, rural depopulation began as early as the 1830s or 1840s. Low natality has been especially pronounced in southern France. For this reason, and because of emigration, the western Massif Central and the Pyrenean region, for example, have been drained of population continuously since the mid nineteenth century. France thus produced some of the most disparate regional growth rates in Europe, as the Paris region and the industrialized northeast grew at the expense of the south and west.

Although rural emigration has been widespread during the last 150 years, *absolute* population decline in rural areas is a relatively recent phenomenon in most countries of Europe except Ireland and France. After World War II (earlier in some areas), falling rural natality and continued emigration to areas of greater economic opportunity produced absolute population declines in many other parts of Europe (Fig. 2.7). The Highlands and Islands of Scotland, Wales, rural Scandinavia, villages in the northeastern borderlands of the Federal Republic of Germany and portions of Bavaria, eastern Austria, almost all of Italy's rural districts, central, southern, and western France, and most of the rural interior of the Iberian peninsula—all were losing people by the 1950s. Because the emigration was often over short distances, from villages or farms to provincial towns or local market centers, the population decline may not show up on any but the most detailed maps. Figure 2.7, which excludes towns over 50,000 population, gives some idea of the post World War II rural exodus, but larger scales would reveal an even more pervasive decline. Rural emigration has also been most rapid in those regions which have been the latest to experience it.

Since the 1960s the growth of the largest western European cities and conurbations has slowed somewhat, whereas many medium-sized provincial towns and cities have enjoyed a reneissance of population growth and economic development. It may be that the inconveniences of daily life in very large cities are beginning to appear more important than the opportunities in the eyes of the relatively affluent Europeans. This diffusion of growth, so to speak, is facilitated by the very complete development of Europe's infrastructure of communication.

Similarly, there is a growing tendency in Northwest Europe for upper middle class and upper class families to leave the city to settle in its less congested suburbs. This local reversal of the traditional migration flow is again the product of affluence and mobility. Automobile ownership in Northwest Europe has become widespread since the 1950s and the recent evolution of city-scapes reflects this. Today the daily journey to work from suburb to city (often by private automobile) is the most important short distance migratory movement. (And it is possible that tourism may now be the most prevalent form of long distance movement.) As in the United States, the population densities of Europe's urban districts are decreasing because of the suburbanization of their formerly rural fringes, even though the cities continue to grow in population and size.

Another characteristic of twentieth century urban and industrial development in Northwest Europe is the selective decline of certain industrial areas. This is especially visible in regions where industrial prosperity during the nineteenth century was based on coal mining. Southern Wales, northeastern Britain, and the Borinage district of Belgium declined as coal was replaced by other forms of energy, especially imported petroleum after World War II. These declining industrial districts, as well as those rural districts which have lost population, have been the focus of much government concern aimed at slowing the processes of regional disequilibrium which seem to be part of Europe's twentieth century economic development. Britain, for example, attempts to discourage the steady drift of jobs and people to the southeast (London region) by offering a variety of financial concessions and incentives to industries establishing offices or plants in the northeast or other relatively disadvantaged regions. Likewise, Italy has attempted to encourage the economic development of its poor but still populous southern half, and most other western European countries have similar policies. Most of the policies, however, have been only occasionally successful.

The tendency towards population concentration is also an international phenomenon.

For example, international migration of labor has produced an important flow of population in modern Europe, where it is mainly a south-to-north movement. Germany and Switzerland especially are labor deficit areas which have "imported" thousands of foreigners into their workforces. In Switzerland, one worker in five is a foreigner; Germany has a smaller proportion, but the absolute number of foreign workers there is much larger (over 1m.). Sweden, Belgium, Luxembourg, and France also import substantial numbers of foreign laborers. Most of the workers come from the nations surrounding the Mediterranean Basin, plus Portugal—a labor surplus region. They usually stay several years in the host country. Some have made the move a permanent one, but in most countries this is discouraged. The European Economic Community (EEC) or Common Market (France, Germany, Italy, Belgium, The Netherlands, Luxembourg, United Kingdom, Ireland, and Denmark) is exploring ways to counteract the tendency towards concentration of economic opportunity and people in the international core area which stands out so clearly on the map of population density (Fig. 2.6). The very removal of international barriers to trade and commerce (and the free movement of workers across EEC boundaries) which the EEC has fostered probably are responsible for even greater concentration in the core area than might have been the case had the EEC never existed.

Conclusion

In the relationship between population, culture, and environment it is often tempting to assign a dominant role to one element or another and to assume that any changes in the others are merely the result of changes in the first. It should be clear from this brief review that the real world is more complex than this. Furthermore, each factor in the interaction is itself made up of complex relationships of elements. In the case of population these are fundamentally birth and death plus migration. An almost infinite variety of "feedbacks" exists. For example, in a particular environment and at a given level of technical achievement, changes in the density or size of a population will affect its economy and its environment, which in turn may influence mortality or perhaps the decision to have children or to migrate. Similarly, the evidence from the late Middle Ages and from the eighteenth century may indicate that where radical social or technological evolution occurs, population may function as a quasi-independent variable: that *prior* population growth may have been a necessary stimulus for technological and cultural change, especially in the agricultural sector, rather than the reverse, as many have implied.

If a generalization can be made, it is perhaps that of the three components of population change—mortality, birth, and migration—cultural factors, mainly economic circumstances, social values, and individuals' perception of their environment generally have wielded more influence upon the last two than upon the first. Mortality has often appeared to vary almost autonomously, responding to external factors beyond human control, as during the waves of plague which swept Europe in the fourteenth century, or during the eighteenth century when death rates fell, fortuitously as it were, all across Europe. To the extent that demographic change or population patterns have been influenced mainly by one or another of the three components mentioned above, it may be possible to identify cultural or environmental influences as being primarily responsible for particular changes.

The lowering of death rates during the last two centuries, however, was largely the result of deliberate human intervention to postpone the inevitable visit of death. This was an extraordinary achievement, one which gives the appearance at least of attenuating the former importance of environmental influences upon the death rate and thus perhaps upon the whole human condition. This single phenomenon has made a profound demographic and psychological impression upon the world. Whether or not the achievement can be sustained over the long term remains to be seen, but it is likely to be tested first by the more developed countries of the world, where the contamination of the ecosphere upon which we ultimately depend is proceeding fastest.

References

Armengaud, André (1973), Population in Europe, in Carlo M. Cipolla (ed.), *The Fontana Economic History of Europe*, vol. 3, *The Industrial Revolution*, Collins, London, pp. 22–76.

Chambers, Jonathan D. (1972), *Population, Economy, and Society in Pre-industrial England*, Oxford University Press, London.

Durand, John D. (1967), The modern expansion of world population, *Proc. Am. Phil. Soc.*, CXI, 136–59.

Glass, D. V. and Eversley, D. E. C. (1965), *Population in History; Essays in Historical Demography*, Aldine, Chicago.

Pounds, Norman J. G. (1973), *An Historical Geography of Europe 450 BC–AD 1330*, Cambridge University Press, Cambridge.

Reinhard, Marcel, Armengaud, André and Dupaquier, Jacques (1968), *Histoire générale de la population mondiale*, Montchrestien, Paris.

Russell, J. C. (1958), Late ancient and medieval populations, *Trans. Am. Phil. Soc.*, XLVIII, part 3.

Russell, J. C. (1972), Population in Europe, 500–1500, in Carlo M. Cipolla (ed.), *The Fontana Economic History of Europe;* vol. 1, *The Middle Ages*, Collins, London, pp. 25–70.

Smith, C. T. (1967), *An Historical Geography of Western Europe before 1800*, Longmans, London.

Toutain, J.-C. (1963), La population de la France de 1700 à 1959, *Cahiers de l'Institut de Science économique appliquée*, suppl. no. 133 ["Histoire quantitative de l'économie française" (3)].

Wrigley, Edward A. (ed.) (1966), *An Introduction to English Historical Demography from the Sixteenth to the Nineteenth Century*, Basic Books, New York.

Wrigley, Edward A. (1969), *Population and History*, Weidenfeld & Nicolson, London.

CHAPTER 3

EAST-CENTRAL EUROPE

L. A. KOSÍNSKI

University of Winnipeg, Canada

Introduction

East-Central Europe, located between the Soviet Union and western Europe, has been defined and termed differently in the past. Today it can best be defined in terms of the political system prevailing in the eight countries (East Germany, Poland, Czechoslovakia, Hungary, Romania, Yugoslavia, Bulgaria, and Albania) jointly comprising the region. At the close of World War II the area was under Soviet control and the Communist political systems evolving thereafter were very much dominated by the Soviet Union. The degree of this control has varied over the past 20 years, but all countries retained the social and political systems they adopted in the 1940s. Nationalization of economic life, collectivization of agriculture, centralized government control and planning are all very characteristic of the countries involved. These political characteristics have in turn influenced to a great degree the demographic patterns and processes in the region. For these reasons it seems reasonable to treat these countries jointly as a major subdivision of Europe, the assumption being that the differences within, great as they may be, are less than the differences without.

In many respects, this area represents a transition between western Europe and the Soviet Union. A line dividing Eastern and Western Christianity, and at the same time Eastern and Western cultural realms, cuts across East-Central Europe. This dichotomy is reflected not only by two different alphabets, Cyrillic and Latin, both used within the region, but also by differing attitudes spawned by the prevailing religious ideologies. East-Central Europe also includes the only part of the continent (Albania, Yugoslavia, and Bulgaria) still influenced by Islam. Until recently, peasant agricultural economies have dominated the economic life of most of the region. Processes of industrialization and urbanization, although operative since the nineteenth century, did not have a profound effect until the last few decades. In this sense the region is only now approaching the level of modernization characteristic of the more advanced western portions of the continent.

There is also a considerable variety within the region. Despite the existence of a supra-national economic organization (COMECON) and the powerful Soviet influence, the economic and social life of the individual countries remains isolated. International transfers of labor, mass movement of tourists, capital flows, etc., all taken for granted in western Europe, are hardly felt in the eastern part of the continent. Secondly, modern

53

development is still limited to selected areas despite the planning efforts to the contrary, and these variations in level of development are reflected in differing demographic trends. Thirdly, although the countries of East-Central Europe have drastically reduced the ethnic diversity of their populations, important ethnic minorities still exist in a number of them. Moreover, the populations of Czechoslovakia and Yugoslavia consist of several major nationalities.

The purpose of this chapter is to describe the population trends and patterns of the region after World War II, and also the differences between and within the countries which compose it.

Population Change

East-Central Europe with its 126m. people accounts for little more than one-fourth of the total European population (excluding the Soviet Union). The region's growth has approximated 1m. people per year during the two post-war decades. However, trends in individual countries depart substantially from the regional average. East Germany reached its maximum population in early post-war years (19m. in 1948) due to the influx of refugees, but has declined steadily since. Hungarian population has been remarkably stable. The largest absolute increase has occurred in Poland (7.5m.) while the largest relative growth took place in Albania where population almost doubled.

In order to understand the overall population trends one has to take a long time perspective. The total population of the seven countries (excluding East Germany) of East-Central Europe when they emerged from the ravages of World War I amounted to 81m. by 1920. By 1940, on the eve of World War II, this population had increased to nearly 102m., but that conflict caused a substantial drop to 88m. in 1950. If East Germany and the territories incorporated into Poland are included, the drop between 1940 and 1950 was even more impressive (from 128m. to 106m.). These changes were caused by three major factors—direct war losses, territorial exchanges, and population transfers.

War losses for the whole of East-Central Europe were estimated at 13.5m. people, or more than 10% of the pre-war population (Table 3.1). The largest losses occurred in Poland, Yugoslavia, and East Germany. War losses were highly selective in nature, affecting young males more than other groups. In Poland Jews were overrepresented among people killed and exterminated, and the Polish intellectual leadership was decimated by deliberate actions of the enemy.

Twenty-seven million people lived in areas affected by territorial changes. In addition, 16.8m. lived in what was later to become the German Democratic Republic. It should be emphasized that the number of people who were actually transferred between countries as a result of territorial changes differs from the above estimate since mass migrations that took place simultaneously substantially altered populations of the areas involved.

Major changes which altered boundaries of the region of East-Central Europe included annexations by the Soviet Union in 1939–40 (eastern Poland and Bessarabia and northern Bukovina from Romania) and 1945 (Sub-Carpathian Ruthenia from Czechoslovakia and the northern part of East Prussia from Germany), and by Yugoslavia (Istria, several Mediterranean islands, and the enclave of Zadar-Zara from Italy). In addition there were some changes within the region, with southern Dobrudja being transferred from Romania to Bulgaria in 1941; the Free City of Danzig and several

TABLE 3.1. POPULATION LOSSES CAUSED BY WORLD WAR II

County/Territory	Losses in thousands	Source
East Germany	1300	(5)
Former German provinces incorporated in Poland and USSR	2000	(1)
Danzig (former Free City)	100	(1)
Poland within pre-war boundaries (Poles, Jews, and Germans only)	6300	(1+4)
Czechoslovakia	670	(1+2)
Hungary	520	(1+2)
Romania	600	(1+2)
Bulgaria	20	(2)
Yugoslavia	2000	(1+3)
Total	13,510	

Sources: 1. *Die deutschen Vertreibungsverluste*, 1958, 38, 45, 46.
2. Frumkin, 1951, 169–70.
3. Vogelnik, D. (1952), Demografski gubici Jugoslavije u drugom svetskom ratu. *Statistički Revija* 2, 1.
4. *Sprawozdanie w przedmiocie strat i szkód wojennych Polski w latach 1939–1945* (1947), Warsaw.
5. Burgdörfer, F. (1951), *Bevölkerungsdynamik und Bevölkerungsbilanz*, Munich.

former East German provinces were incorporated into Poland in 1945. The above estimates do not include populations of the areas temporarily re-assigned from one country to another.

World War II caused also large scale migrations in which at least 25m. people were involved. Mass transfers of ethnic groups were undertaken in East-Central Europe prior to and following World War I. Hundreds of thousands of people left areas separated from defeated countries (Germany, Austria, and Hungary) to re-establish themselves in what remained of these nations. In addition, substantial transfers of Greeks, Bulgarians, and Turks were undertaken in the Balkans. It is very likely that these transfers and migrations included close to 4m. people not counting the 1.25m. who were repatriated from the Soviet Union to Poland in the early 1920s.

The transfers caused by World War II can be divided into three categories. Firstly, mass transfers were undertaken by Nazi Germany and her allies as part of the new order in Europe. Ethnic Germans left in the areas considered to be outside of the legitimate sphere of German influences were encouraged or forced to return to Germany. This affected so-called *Volksdeutsche* from the Baltic states, USSR, Romania, Bulgaria, Yugoslavia, and Hungary. Most of them were settled in the newly conquered Polish territories. In addition, German settlers and administrators were brought from the interior into the newly acquired lands. Similar transfers on a smaller scale were undertaken in Czechoslovakia in connection with partition of the country in 1939, and later in Yugoslavia and Transylvania. The second wave of migration took place in the later stages of the war when hostilities forced many people, especially Germans exposed to the onslaught of the Red Army, to flee for their lives. The third and final stage came as the result of transfers organized after cessation of hostilities. All in all, some 13m. Germans, 7.5m. Poles, 2m. Czechs and Slovaks, more than 0.5m. Yugoslavs, and 0.5m. Ukrainians and Belorussians were involved in these moves. The grand total, 25m., does not include deported prisoners of war, slave laborers, people transferred to annihilation camps (mostly Jews and gypsies) and military personnel.

Political transformations and slow economic recovery of the countries of East-Central Europe caused continuous out-migration from this region to the west. But detailed and reliable data are very difficult to come by. Increased outflow of Czechs followed the Communist coup in 1948 and later the Soviet invasion of 1968; Hungarian emigration culminated after their unsuccessful bloody revolt of 1956. In numerical terms flight from East Germany was by far the most impressive, involving over 2m. people between 1945 and 1961, when the Berlin Wall reduced the flow to a trickle.

Vital Rates, Natural Increases, Total Growth

The comparison of total growth with natural increase for the period 1950–70 indicates that most countries have a negative migration balance (Table 3.2). The estimate for Yugoslavia, contained in the table, is obviously faulty despite the fact that it is based on official government data. The main component of growth is the natural increase, estimated for the whole region at 21.8m. between 1950 and 1970.

TABLE 3.2. COMPONENTS OF POPULATION GROWTH, 1950–70
(IN THOUSANDS)

Country	Total population at the end of year		Total growth	Natural increase	Implied migration
	1950	1970			
East Germany	18,360	17,057	−1303	1114	−2417
Poland	25,035	32,605	7570	8140	− 570
Czechoslovakia	12,464	14,366	1902	2051	− 149
Hungary	9,383	10,347	964	1127	− 163
Romania	16,388	20,366	3978	4195	− 217
Bulgaria	7,273	8,515	1242	1393	− 151
Yugoslavia	16,487	21,452	4965	4834	+ 131
Albania	1,228	2,136 (69)	908 (51–69)	902 (51–69)	− 6

Source: Author's compilation.

Rates of population increase, rather high in early post-war years (especially in Albania, Poland, and Yugoslavia), later declined so that at the present time Albania remains as the only country of the region, and indeed of all Europe, with extremely high rates of increase (Fig. 3.1). At the other extreme, East Germany has an excess of deaths over births since 1969. This indicates that in addition to migration losses, reduced to a trickle after 1961, that country is now faced with a natural decrease in population. In all remaining countries natural increase diminished after the relatively short period of higher rates immediately following World War II. Decline in mortality can be explained by improved public hygiene, better medical care, and changes in nutrition. However, the long term trend has recently been reversed, with crude death rates increasing slightly in all countries (except Albania). This is caused mainly by an increased proportion of old people; age specific rates continue to decline.

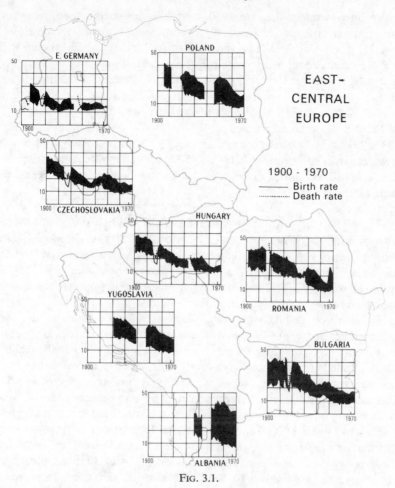

Fig. 3.1.

Fertility rates reached their maximum in the late 1940s and early 1950s after which they declined steadily until a few years ago, when a reversal took place in several countries. Factors accounting for fertility trends are more complex than those affecting mortality. Crude birth rates were adversely affected by changes in the proportions of women in the child-bearing ages, but other factors, including increased urbanization and changes in the occupational structure, are also involved. These resulted in a lower proportion of the population engaged in agriculture, improved educational attainment, increase in family incomes and living standards in general, increased employment of women, weakening of religious attachment, and an all-to-slow improvement in housing conditions. Population policies pursued in East-Central Europe, which recently aroused so much interest in the West, also had an important influence on fertility trends. Abortion laws were considerably liberalized in the mid 1950s. Although the main argument put forward at that time was of a social nature (women should have a right to make decisions affecting themselves and their families), the legislation had a very profound demographic impact. Since the decline in fertility which took place despite various other social measures such as family allowances, maternity leaves, etc., was considered excessive, new

C

policies were introduced in the late 1960s aimed at off-setting the downward trend. Czechoslovakia and Hungary emphasized economic inducements (increased bonuses); Romania relied mainly on "legislative–administrative" measures. Changes in Romanian abortion laws brought about a spectacular upsurge in the number of births in 1967 (Fig. 3.1), followed by a decline. Czechoslovakia, Hungary, Poland, and Bulgaria have succeeded in reversing the declining trends in fertility, even if sometimes only temporarily. In the early 1970s the numerous cohorts of the post-war "baby boom" will vastly increase the number of potential parents.

In 1970 the lowest birth rates occurred in East Germany and Hungary (13.9 and 14.7 per 1000 respectively), they ranged between 15.8 and 17.6 in Czechoslovakia, Bulgaria, Poland, and Yugoslavia, in this order, and reached the highest level in Romania (21.1) and Albania (35.3).

Birth rates by administrative subdivisions presently range between 10 and 36 per 1000 (Fig. 3.2). The highest rates occur in Albania and the neighboring Yugoslav region of Kosovo, which is inhabited predominantly by Albanians. Fertility rates in the northern more developed regions of Yugoslavia are much lower, Vojvodina being least fertile of all. A wide range of conditions are found in Romania with northern, rural Moldavia and more developed Banat (with high proportions of ethnic minorities) representing two extremes, high and low, respectively. In Bulgaria, fertility is lower in the central districts, including industrialized Pernik, whereas the highest rates are found in the peripheral and isolated counties of the south and east. The remaining four countries are characterized by smaller ranges and lower rates. Poland has relatively high fertility throughout, with the western and northern provinces having lost their earlier predominant positions. An unbalanced age structure in these areas is partly responsible, since young adults, the most fertile age groups, are underrepresented. The only exceptions are two newly settled northern provinces (Olsztyn and Koszalin) which continue to retain a high fertility. They are followed closely by two southern districts (Kraków and Rzeszów) known for their fragmentation of farms and high rural densities. Large Polish cities have the lowest fertility. In Czechoslovakia the spatial pattern of fertility rates is fairly uniform, but with the eastern provinces (especially east Slovakia) having the highest rates and central Bohemia by far the lowest. In East Germany, the more industrialized and urbanized south has crude birth rates that are somewhat lower than are those of the rural north (rates range between 12.4 and 15.2 per 1000).

The spatial distribution pattern of death rates is equally interesting (Fig. 3.2). In East Germany high mortality in most cases is coincidental with low fertility. The northernmost district, Rostock, with its youthful population, is at the opposite extreme, featuring low mortality accompanied by high fertility. In Poland the newly settled western and northern provinces stand out as an area of low mortality. In Czechoslovakia the two newly resettled western districts and the Slovak lands have lower rates, thereby contrasting with central Bohemia where an aged population suffers high mortality, comparable to those of some German regions. The southern portions of Hungary, long affected by depopulation, presently have a higher mortality rate than the more youthful northern industrial areas.

Budapest, with its high proportion of the elderly, also has a high mortality rate. The high mortality zone continues into Banat in Romania which is distinguished from the remainder of the country and especially the Moldavian districts and Dobrudja with its youthful population. Hilly, southern Bulgaria, the southern provinces of Yugoslavia,

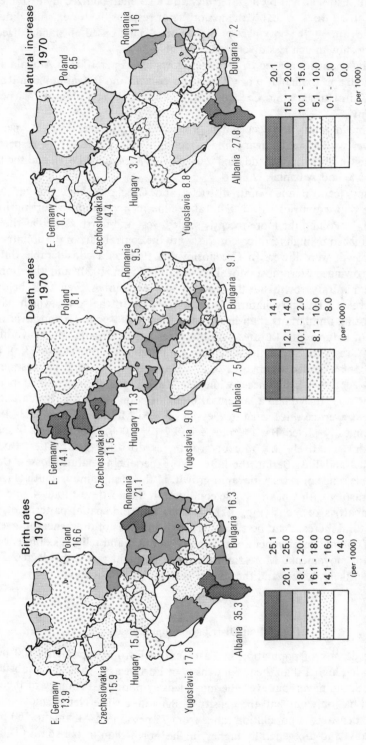

Fig. 3.2. East-Central Europe; regional variations in birth rates, death rates, and natural increase rates per 1000 inhabitants, 1970.

and Albania, all distinguished by high fertility, are also characterized by extremely low mortality. Age structure is probably the major factor responsible for existing differences in mortality rates among the provinces of the region. A map based on standardized rates would probably show much less diversification.

Death rates by countries ranged in 1970 from lows of 7.5 per 1000 in Albania and 8.2 in Poland through approximately 9 per 1000 in Yugoslavia and Bulgaria, 9.6 in Romania to 11.4 and 11.7 in Hungary and Czechoslovakia, and reaching a high of 14.1 per 1000 in East Germany.

Natural decline in population occurred in 1970 only in East Germany (−0.2 per 1000), increase was very slight in Hungary and Czechoslovakia (3.0 and 4.4 respectively), somewhat higher in Bulgaria, Poland, and Yugoslavia (7.2, 8.6, and 8.7), and the highest in Romania (11.5) and Albania (27.8).

East Germany (central and south districts) and Czechoslovakia (Prague and its region) are the only countries with a natural decline in population occurring in some areas (Fig. 3.2). In Poland the more recently settled west and north as well as the south-east, all distinguished by high fertility, contrast with the central part of the country where the rates of growth were lower. In Czechoslovakia there is a considerable difference between the growing easternmost Slovak district (11.7 per 1000) and the Bohemian districts where natural growth hardly exceeds, and sometimes even falls below, the replacement level. In Hungary natural increase is lower in the south which has been continuously losing immigrants than in the more developed north. Yugoslavia has the greatest range of natural growth rates with more developed Croatia and Vojvodina (3.7 and 2.5 per 1000 respectively) contrasting with mountainous Montenegro (13.3), Bosnia (13.9), and Albanian settled Kosovo (27.4). In Hungary, the natural increase gradient reflects mostly economic differences, while for Yugoslavia, social contrast plays the most important role. In Romania, a central block of counties (Transylvania and Wallachia) with near average rates separates less developed Moldavia (rates 15.3–19.7 per 1000) from ethnically mixed Banat (rates 2.7–3.7 per 1000). The capital, Bucharest, stands out with a relatively low rate of growth, as do other great cities, Budapest, Warsaw, Prague, and East Berlin, the latter two experiencing natural losses. Bulgaria has a remarkable range of rates with rapid growth in the mountainous south (11.7–17.6 per 1000) contrasting with a nearly stable condition in the northwest (0.6–4.3 per 1000).

Precursory analysis of maps (Fig. 3.2) indicates that the spatial patterns of births, deaths, and natural increase can best be interpreted in terms of differences in age structure, level of economic development, accessibility, cultural and religious differences, and recent settlement movements. More rigorous research might reveal the degree of interrelation between these factors and the spatial patterns of vital rates.

Population Distribution and Density

The average density of population in East-Central Europe approaches 100 per km² which is somewhat higher than the mean density of Europe as a whole. It is substantially higher than in Scandinavia, but even the most densely populated country of the region, East Germany, has only one-half the density of Belgium or The Netherlands.

By countries densities of population range from 75 per km² in Albania to 160 per km² in East Germany, and are generally higher in the north than in the south (Table 3.3;

TABLE 3.3. AREA AND POPULATION OF EAST-CENTRAL EUROPE IN 1970

Country	Area (km²)	Population in 000's (mid-year estimate)	Density per km²
East Germany[a]	108,174	17,257	160
Poland	312,677	32,805	105
Czechoslovakia	127,869	14,467	113
Hungary	93,030	10,331	111
Romania	237,500	20,253	85
Bulgaria	110,912	8,490	77
Yugoslavia	255,804	20,527	80
Albania	28,748	2,168	75
Total	1,274,714	126,298	99

Source: *UN Demographic Yearbook 1970*, table 2, pp. 110–11.
[a]Including East Berlin.

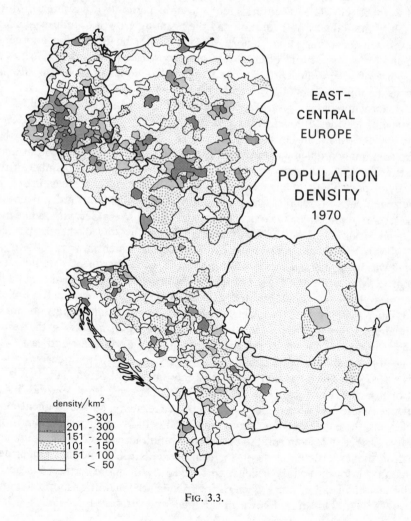

EAST-
CENTRAL
EUROPE

POPULATION
DENSITY
1970

density/km²
>301
201 - 300
151 - 200
101 - 150
51 - 100
< 50

FIG. 3.3.

Fig. 3.3). Density of population depends in part on fertility and growth rates, but also on the population retention capacity of a country or a region. This capacity can be high if an area is industrialized and can support a large population at a relatively high standard of living. However, a high density can also result from overpopulation of rural areas and the lack of attractive emigration opportunities. In this case one may say the retention rate is high, but only at the expense of the social and economic well being of the population involved. In other words, the retention results from the economic capacity of an area, including both conditions of natural environment and economic and social structure. On the other hand, the retention can be, as it were, artificially lowered or increased as a result of mobility of population or lack of it. All these factors are involved in explaining the intricate patterns of densities occurring in East-Central Europe.

A zone of high density extends across southern Germany and northern Bohemia eastwards to Poland, then bends southward across Moravia to northern Hungary, and eventually dissipates along the middle Danube and northeastern Yugoslavia. This zone is an eastward extension of a more extensive high density zone evident on any population map of Europe, and while of centuries long duration, certainly it has intensified recently as a result of the Industrial Revolution and the resulting growth of industrial and urban complexes. On the other hand, a northern belt along the Baltic and another in the eastern and southern portions of East-Central Europe have much lower densities despite the existence of several nuclei of extremely high urban concentration. Density patterns differ considerably among countries and within them (Fig. 3.3).

In East Germany striking contrasts exist between the more industrialized and developed south, where densities frequently exceed 300 per km^2 (especially around Zwickau, Leipzig, Halle, Erfurt, and Dresden) and the less populous and more rural north where densities commonly are below 40 per km^2. However, it should be pointed out that these contrasts are diminished relative to pre-war conditions. The post-war influx of refugees was partly responsible for the increased density of the agricultural areas. People usually were accommodated in regions where housing was most available and war devastation was less severe. In subsequent years, many refugees fled to West Germany, some migrated to more industrialized regions of East Germany, but many stayed, thereby permanently altering the pattern of densities in the country. Berlin, which grew rapidly in pre-war years, but was badly damaged during World War II, was subsequently stunted due to its partition. Leaving aside the legal position of both parts of Berlin, one can say that, in fact, East Berlin was incorporated with the German Democratic Republic, while West Berlin remains a foreign enclave tightly separated from its natural hinterland. This situation prevents further growth of the metropolitan area with the result that densities drop rapidly outside of the city, especially to the southeast and east.

A zone of low grade sandy, podzolic soils, not very conductive to intensive agriculture, extends across East Germany and farther east into northern Poland. This belt is characterized by very low densities, generally less than 50 per km^2. Low densities had earlier characterized these areas when they were a part of Germany, and subsequent repopulation following the exodus of the original inhabitants did not alter the pattern. In fact, there was a further shift from rural to urban areas, and especially to metropolitan regions centered on the large Baltic ports of Szczecin and Gdańsk. Somewhat higher densities occur along the lower Vistula which is privileged by its more fertile soils and easier accessibility both in earlier times when rivers provided the main transportation and later in the railway age. This area, known in the inter-war years as the "Polish Corridor", was also less affected by post-war population transfers. Low densities extend along the western and eastern boundaries of Poland, where inferior agricultural capacity, a high proportion of forested areas, and a relatively undeveloped agriculture coupled with a lack of industry are the main retarding factors. The zone of highest density extends along the southern frontier. Its core is the industrialized region of Upper Silesia from which it extends eastward along the Sub-Carpathian axis, known for its agricultural overpopulation and now the main region of commuting to newly established industries. This is an area of small private farms where people frequently combine industrial and agricultural occupations. To the west, the Lower Silesian plains and industrialized basins in the Sudety Mountains have been successfully repopulated after World War II. In fact, the density of post-war settlement frequently exceeds previous densities, especially in the more urbanized and industrialized counties. Generally speaking, the overall pattern of densities within the present territory of Poland has changed very little despite the mass transfers of population. The same zonal pattern that developed through the ages persists even today.

Czechoslovakia ranks second in overall density of population after East Germany. Densities vary, however, and are much the highest in Bohemia, especially its central part surrounding Prague and in the north along the Ore Mountains. The latter were known for their varied and plentiful natural resources, especially minerals, that gave rise to the development of numerous industries. Post-war expulsion of the German population drastically reduced densities in these previously highly developed regions, and despite post-war repopulation density still remains somewhat lower than before. However, even yet it continues very high in a national context. Northern Moravia with its industrial agglomeration centered on Morava represents the highest population concentration in the central part of the country. Brno and Bratislava are the two main high density clusters in this region. Density drops substantially in southern Bohemia and in most of Slovakia. In many rural and highly forested mountain areas densities reach only one-fourth of the national average.

Density patterns for Hungary and Romania as represented in Fig. 3.3 are more coarse due to the fact that the distribution is based upon larger administrative units. In Hungary the zone of highest density extends along its northern frontier and centers on the capital. This reflects to a great extent the history of the country and its present economic development. Southern and eastern Hungary was exposed for centuries to the devastations of wars that not only hampered further growth, but even reduced population below the levels of early medieval times. In the nineteenth century there was a substantial recovery, but the great plains never really caught up with the more fortunate western and northern regions which are favored with greater natural resources and industrial development. The patterns of internal migration themselves reflect differences in density and in turn contribute to these differences. In general people are moving from the south and east to the north and west, and especially to metropolitan Budapest.

In Romania densities are surprisingly uniform if the highest-order administrative units (Judet) are compared. The only area of distinctly higher density is located north of the capital city, whereas minima occur in some mountain regions and northern Dobruja, including the Danube Delta. However, more detailed maps of population densities indicate that the arch of the Carpathians and its Sub-Carpathian foreland, separating Transylvania located in the northwest from Wallachia in the south and Moldavia in the east, have very low densities. By comparison, the southern and eastern plains, as well as the central part of the Transylvanian Basin, support densities which are substantially higher due to greater agricultural and urban development. Urban centers in the low density zone include the industrial cores of Brasov, Sibiu, and Hunedoara. Frequent alterations of the political boundaries of Romania during the last half of the century did not greatly affect population numbers, even though international transfers did occur following both world wars. Rural population is remarkably stable; the small scale migration which results in urban growth does not alter the overall distribution pattern.

The average density of population in Bulgaria is lower than in Romania, and internal differences are not as pronounced as in the northern countries of East-Central Europe. Mountain regions in the west stand out as areas of low general density despite the fact that Sofia, situated in these highlands, represents the largest metropolitan unit in the country. However, more detailed maps reveal a low density zone coincident with the Balkan mountains that extend longitudinally across the country, with higher densities both on the plateau to the north and in the river basins to the south and east. These latter are known for their intensive, specialized agriculture that has made Bulgarian farming famous throughout East-Central Europe. New industrial development has also taken place in this general area, extending to various locations in the Rhodope Mountains which stretch along the southern frontier. In the eastern part of the country, continuous emigration of the Turks has lowered overall densities. But at the same time the growth of industry, centered mainly on the largest Black Sea port of Burgas, is clearly reflected on the density map.

Yugoslavia has only a slightly higher average density of population than Bulgaria, but the contrasts in densities within the country are striking. Among its republics and autonomous districts, Kosovo ranks first with a high and rapidly increasing density (114 per km^2) due mainly to a very high natural increase not alleviated by out-migration. The region remains predominantly agricultural, and population pressure is becoming a problem. The autonomous district of Vojvodina in the northern part of Serbia also has densities (94 per km^2) which exceed the national average. Here, however, well developed agriculture taking advantage of the fertile Pannonian Plain and fairly well developed industry create much better economic bases for the local population. Serbia proper (94 per km^2) is also fairly densely populated, especially around the capital city of Beograd along the Morava River which represents the central axis of accessibility and development for the republic. Another republic that exceeds the national average is Slovenia, located in the northwestern extremity of Yugoslavia (85 per km^2). Despite the fact that mountains occupy large portions of the area, the urban region of Lubljana and the eastern counties serve to lift the overall average. Intensive agriculture and well developed industry create a good economic base for Slovenia's population.

The republic of Croatia, where density is close to the national average (78 per km^2 in 1971) includes large portions of the coast, the desolate Dinaric ranges, and the fertile plains between the Sava and Drava rivers. Dalmatia, with its narrow but fertile coast and numerous hilly islands, has a highly uneven pattern of population distribution. Its inhabitants are concentrated along the coast which has recently developed into a recreational area of international renown. Whereas villages located in the mountains or on isolated islands are being abandoned, the Dalmatian coastal strip presently is experiencing a housing boom. Human carrying capacity of the Dinaric ranges has never been very high. There population is concentrated in the fertile "Polja", or inter-montane basins, separated from one another by dry and inaccessible mountain barriers. This is an area where growth potential is limited and large numbers of emigrants are recruited. The northern and eastern plains with long established agriculture and well developed cities (notably Zagreb, the capital) have higher population densities than the hilly regions of the republic. The centrally located region of Bosnia and Hercegovina, with its culturally and religiously diverse population, is relatively less developed and less densely populated (73 per km²). Resource based industries have recently evolved, especially around Zenica and the capital city of Sarajevo, resulting in higher densities in these localities than in the remaining parts of this mountain region. The average density of Macedonia in the southeast is only three-quarters of the national average (64 per km²). The extremes are represented here by the region of Skoplje, third largest metropolitan area of Yugoslavia, and the remaining parts of which are underdeveloped and less populated. Montenegro's density (38 per km²) is less than half of the national average. Settlement is concentrated along the coastal strip and also in mountain basins, especially around the capital Titograd.

Population density in Albania is the lowest of the entire region of East-Central Europe. However, due to its recent rapid growth and lack of emigration, the average density is rapidly approaching that of Bulgaria. Highest densities occur in the central coastal lowlands, and in the valleys leading inland, especially around the capital and largest city, Tirana. The latitudinally oriented mountain zone, with its traditional agriculture, is less thickly populated, with densities frequently falling below 40 compared to a maximum of 197 per km² in county Durrsit. Along the eastern frontier, somewhat higher densities occur in the upland basin of Korca with its intensive agriculture.

Internal Mobility

The period immediately following World War II was characterized by extreme internal mobility in East-Central Europe. Three types of movement may be distinguished. First, mass evictions and forced transfers during the war left many people stranded away from their previously permanent homes. Another factor responsible for dispersion of population was the guerrilla warfare and the fighting between regular Soviet and German troops in the last stages of the war. As soon as conditions permitted, people attempted to return to their homes, but often they found their farms or residences destroyed, prompting them to move on. These secondary movements were by far the largest in Poland, Czechoslovakia, and Yugoslavia, which nations were most affected by the war. In Poland, large scale evictions by the German authorities affected several hundreds of thousands, the largest single event being the eviction from the capital city of Warsaw in 1944. In Czechoslovakia, war transfers affected mostly Czechs living in areas incorporated into Germany in 1938. In Yugoslavia, movement was caused more by guerrilla warfare than by planned evictions. The second type of population migration consisted of people moving in order to fill vacancies created by deaths or departure of former residents. Such migrations had both nodal and regional effects. An example of the first was the movement of Polish peasants into towns and cities to replace the Jewish population exterminated during the war. Interregional flows were much more common, however. They included repopulation of the newly acquired northern and western parts of Poland (vacated by forcibly transferred Germans); Czech frontier lands restored to Czechoslovakia and vacated by its German inhabitants; and the northeastern Yugoslav district of Vojvodina vacated by former German settlers who either fled or were transferred to Germany and/or the Soviet Union. A third type of internal movement involved people who recently immigrated from abroad or from provinces lost as a result of the war. Such recently uprooted migrants were more mobile than the rest of the population and so were over-represented among internal movers. East Germany, Poland, Czechoslovakia, Romania, and Hungary were most affected by this latter type of movement.

This spatially and temporally specific mobility growing out of the war lasted through the late 1940s, and then gradually subsided in the early 1950s when it was replaced by a more "normal" or peace-time pattern of population movement, most important of which was the rural–urban migration prompted by rapid urbanization. Net migration gains of cities within East-Central Europe exceeded 1m. per year between 1950 and 1970; total flows between rural and urban sectors, on both local and interregional scales, were much higher. A large proportion of the interregional migrants moving from central Poland to the new northern and western territories settled in cities, thus increasing the urban proportion relative to the pre-war situation. Rural-to-rural migration was also considerable, part of it due to the rural colonization programs sponsored by various governments (most notably in Poland, Czechoslovakia, and Yugoslavia) to repopulate vacated lands, and part a result of attempts to change the structure of rural settlements by concentrating people in larger, better equipped villages (most notably in Bulgaria). Urban-to-urban flows were rather limited in the post-war years, although their proportion gradually increased. Finally, urban-to-rural flows, characteristic of large metropolitan areas in the Western world, were of little significance.

In all countries of the region except Yugoslavia, information on internal migration based on current registration of moves is available. The annual number of migrants within East-Central Europe declined from some 3.5m. in 1955 to 2.25m. in the late 1960s, the decrease being more noticeable in the northernmost countries of the region (East Germany, Poland, Czechoslovakia, and, after 1958, Hungary). It has been suggested that this downward trend reflects a change from the unusual fluid situation of early post-war years, accentuated by social upheavals, to a new equilibrium characteristic of more stable societies in recent years. There is no doubt that the highly mobile, uprooted populations of the early post-war years have in the meantime settled. The transformation of agriculture and the forcible collectivization of the rural sector which took place in the early 1950s undoubtedly affected the migration of population and particularly the rural–urban moves. The scarcity of labor in the industrial sector can influence mobility in two ways: on the one hand, employers attempt to retain labor by offering more attractive work conditions; on the other, labor is attracted by better wages or working conditions elsewhere. Recent housing policy tends to reduce mobility because more apartments are built or sold by cooperatives and condominiums. People who own their residences are less likely to move than are tenants.

It appears that an increasing proportion of total population movement takes place within regions (however defined) rather than among them. This could indicate that the average distance moved is declining and also that the pattern of moves has become more locally oriented, with nodes of attraction growing at the expense of their hinterlands.

The spatial pattern of migration corresponds to a great extent with the pattern of economic development, with more active regions attracting migrants from less developed rural areas. In East Germany, regions gaining by net in-migration include those located in the southeastern portion of the country (reflecting the concentration of new industries along the Neisse and Oder) and in the rapidly developing coastal region of Rostock. In Poland, the western and northern regions, incorporated into the country after World War II, have been consistently gaining through net in-migration, with the exception of the two less developed northern provinces of Koszalin and Olsztyn. The Warsaw region and Upper Silesia, the two largest industrial complexes in the country, have also gained through net in-migration. In Czechoslovakia, central Bohemia, including Prague and northern Moravia around the industrial node of Ostrava, gained through net in-migration in the early 1960s, while the rest of the country experienced net migrational losses. In Hungary, net migration gains have been concentrated in the northwestern provinces, especially in and west of Budapest, and in two regions in the extreme northeast (Miskolc) and south (Pécs). In Romania, during the intercensal period 1956–64, migrational gains were concentrated in the southeast including the capital region of Bucharest, as well as Dobruja, Banat, and southern Transylvania, all three regions offering settlement opportunities due to the departure of ethnic minorities. The central Moldavian region which has become intensively industrialized in recent decades has also gained. In Bulgaria, growth exceeding the average (thus implying migration gains) has occurred around the capital of Sofia, in the eastern region of the Burgas industrial node, and in the southern regions of recent resource development. In Yugoslavia, the more developed north and Macedonia have attracted migrants, whereas hilly southern Serbia and most of Bosnia and Hercegovina and Montenegro have experienced migrational losses. It bears repeating that internal migration had a profound impact upon density and structure of population in areas of both origin and destination.

Urban Population

Despite the existence of several large cities and the historical importance of a number of urban centers, the overall degree of urbanization, measured by the proportion of the population which lives in towns and cities, was until recently relatively small in East-Central Europe, the only exception being the eastern portion of Germany. In the early 1930s, Poland, Czechoslovakia, and Hungary had about one-third of their populations urbanized; Romania and Bulgaria only about one-fifth; and Yugoslavia and Albania hardly one-seventh. This modest level of urbanization was related to the small degree of industrialization and also the overpopulation of extensive rural areas dominated by a peasant economy. World War II devastated the cities in the northern part of the region, resulting in the reduction of the urban share in both Poland and what is now East Germany; Berlin, Warsaw, Danzig-Gdańsk, Breslau-Wrocław were almost totally destroyed. The high proportions of Jews in Polish cities who were exterminated by the Nazis accentuated this effect. Reduction in the number of urban dwellers also occurred in Hungary, Romania, and Czechoslovakia, but without a shrinking in the urban proportion. In East Germany, with its influx of refugees from the east, the urban population actually increased in numbers between 1939 and 1946, although the percentage that was urban declined somewhat. Total urban population in the whole region increased from some 36m. in the early thirties (35%) to more than 40m. a decade later (38%), only to drop to 37.5m. in the late 1940s (36%).

After World War II, urban population increased in all countries of East-Central Europe, and its overall proportion grew from 38% in 1950 to 48% in the 1960s. The progress of urbanization reflected the drive towards industrialization sponsored by the ruling Communist parties. At the present time, East Germany leads with about three-quarters of its population urbanized, followed by Czechoslovakia, Poland, Hungary, and Bulgaria, in which countries the urban population accounts for about one-half the total. The remaining three countries are less urbanized (Table 3.4). However, the reader

TABLE 3.4. URBAN AND RURAL POPULATION AFTER WORLD WAR II

	Year–Data[a]	Total		Urban		Rural	
		000's	%	000's	%	000's	%
East Germany	1950–C	18,388	100	13,040	71	5,348	29
	1970–E	17,057	100	12,570	74	4,487	26
Poland[b]	1950–C	25,008	100	9,605	39	15,009	61
	1970–C	32,589	100	17,007	52	15,582	48
Czechoslovakia[c]	1950–C	12,338	100	5,446	44	6,892	56
	1970–C	14,362[d]	100	7,878	55	6,479	45
Hungary	1949–C	9,205	100	3,531	38	5,673	62
	1969–E	10,316	100	4,648	45	5,667	55
Romania	1948–C	15,873	100	3,713	23	12,160	77
	1970–M	20,253	100	8,258	41	11,995	59
Bulgaria	1950–E	7,273	100	2,000	27	5,273	73
	1970–E	8,515	100	4,510	53	4,005	47
Yugoslavia	1953–C	16,991	100	3,145	19	13,846	81
	1961–C	18,549	100	5,265	28	13,284	72
Albania	1950–C	1,219	100	250	21	969	79
	1970–M	2,136	100	719	34	1,417	66
Total	1950	106,295	100	40,730	38	65,170	61
	1970	105,228	100	55,590	53	49,632	47
	(excluding Yugoslavia)						
	1970	123,777	100	60,855	49	62,916	51
	(including Yugoslavia in 1961)						

[a] C=census; E=end-of-year estimate; M=mid-year estimate.
[b] Including 394,000 in 1950 and 370,000 in 1970 who were not distributed between rural and urban population.
[c] Urban population includes all inhabitants of places with more than 5000 and one half of those living in places with 2000–5000 inhabitants. According to census definition (available for 1961 only) the proportion of urban population amounted to 47.6% (according to the present definition 49.3%). In some Czechoslovak sources all those living in communities over 2000 are classified as urban (1950, 51.3%; 1970, 62.4%).
[d] Including 4000 with no permanent address.

should be warned that the definition of urban varies somewhat between the different countries of East-Central Europe; hence precise comparisons are difficult. Detailed maps showing the proportion of the population which is urban at the level of minor administrative subdivisions would indicate a close correlation between the degree of urbanization and the degree of industrialization, especially in those countries where these two processes are most advanced (e.g. East Germany, particularly in the south; Poland, notably in the west and southwest; and Czechoslovakia, particularly in Bohemia).

In the late 1960s there were about 3600 towns and cities of all sizes in East-Central Europe. Most of the urban and semi-urban centers were relatively small; only about 500 exceeded 20,000 inhabitants. Towns developed mostly as local service centers and until recently this has been the chief function performed. However, the Industrial Revolution brought about changes in the urban pattern, especially in the northern part of the region where large urban–industrial complexes developed, most notably in Upper Silesia and the southern part of East Germany. Political independence favored the growth of capital cities. However, changes during the last several decades drastically altered territorial patterns, affecting the growth potential of various urban centers (Fig.

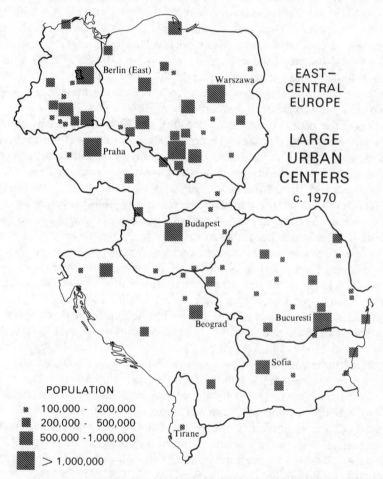

FIG. 3.4. Data are for cities in most countries; they are for metropolitan areas in Poland and Romania.

3.4). East Germany, for example, inherited part of Berlin, the former capital of a much larger country. With its 1m. inhabitants, East Berlin remains the largest city in the German Democratic Republic. Since 1961 it has been separated from the western part of the city, which remains as an enclave linked with West Germany. The remaining larger cities concentrate in the more urbanized southern portion of East Germany. If metropolitan criteria were to be employed, the largest urban concentration is the complex of

Halle–Leipzig–Karl-Marx-Stadt (2m.) followed by the agglomerations of Berlin (1.8m.), Zwickau (1.6m.) and Dresden (1.1m.).

In Poland, the largest urban concentration developed in Upper Silesia following intensive industrialization of that area during the Industrial Revolution. The area is still growing very rapidly, especially in the peripheral zone. Its population exceeds 3.25m. The Warsaw agglomeration ranks second with 1.8m. Lódź (900,000) which follows is also a product of industrialization in the nineteenth century. Three large regional centers, Kraków (760,000), Poznań (565,000), and Wrocław (540,000), developed as regional nodes isolated from one another, especially during the partitions of Poland. The rapidly growing tricity of Gdańsk–Gdynia–Sopot (720,000) continues the tradition of the ancient commercial center and free city-port of Danzig-Gdańsk.

In Czechoslovakia, Prague is the only major city (1.1m.), by far exceeding the next ranking Brno (340,000), the industrial center of Moravia, and Bratislava (300,000), capital of the Slovak republic. Despite its high degree of industrialization, Czechoslovakia has not developed a very concentrated urban network.

The primate position of Budapest, which accounts for 40% of the urban population and 20% of total population of Hungary, reflects the recent history of the country. The city's beginnings go back to Roman times, but it was only in the latter part of the nineteenth century that the enormous agglomeration, now approaching 2m., began to develop. As a capital of the autonomous Hungarian part of the Austro-Hungarian Empire, the city developed as the cultural, economic, and political center of a much larger country. The result of World War I was to drastically reduce the size of its national hinterland. Hungary has never been able to completely recover from the shock of the 1919 partition and Budapest remains as an overgrown metropolis of a small country. It is the largest single urban center of the whole of East-Central Europe.

While Romania belongs to the less urbanized countries of East-Central Europe, still she has 17 metropolitan areas each with more than 100,000 inhabitants. The largest of them is the capital city, Bucharest (1.6m.), followed by the much smaller urban centers of Constanta (240,000), port and center of a rapidly developing resort area; Ploiesti (220,000), center of the old established oil-producing area; and several regional centers.

In the remaining three countries of East-Central Europe, cities are generally smaller and the capitals do not exceed 1m. inhabitants. In Bulgaria, the capital, Sofia (860,000), ranks first followed by Plovidv (240,000), the old regional and industrial center, and Varna (220,000), a Black Sea port and center of resort development.

In Yugoslavia, differences in the size of capitals of constituent republics are relatively small. Belgrade, capital both of the federation and of the constituent republic of Serbia, ranks first (770,000), followed by the capitals of Croatia (Zagreb, 560,000), Macedonia (Skoplje, 290,000), and Bosnia-Hercegovina (Sarajevo, 223,000). Five other cities exceed 100,000.

The capital of Albania (Tirana, 170,000) is the only large city in a country which otherwise has numerous small towns, including some centers with Greek or Roman roots.

The urban population of East-Central Europe from 1950 to 1970 increased by about one-half, from 41m. to 61m. Increases occurred everywhere except in East Germany where persistent emigration led to the reduction of population in cities as well as in rural areas. The increase was naturally more rapid in countries which were initially less urbanized, that is, the southern portions of the region. During the same period, overall rural population declined somewhat from 65m. to 63m. people. However, in two countries, Poland and Albania, distinguished by consistently high fertility rates, rural population actually increased. In Romania and Hungary, rural population remained stable. By comparison with western Europe the rural sector still remains very prominent.

Age and Sex Structure

The effects of World War II were clearly reflected in the sex and age structure of the region as a whole in the late 1940s, when the proportions of males to females was generally low and large deficits occurred in various age and sex groups (Fig. 3.5). Later

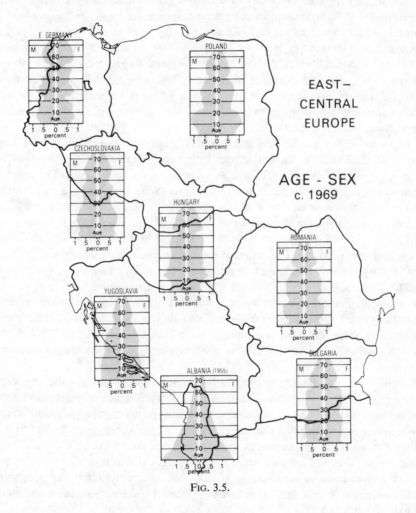

FIG. 3.5.

demographic development somewhat reduced the overall deficits of males, but they continued to be noticeable in particular age–sex groups.

The post-war masculinity ratio (males to females) was lowest in East Germany (80 males per 100 females in 1950) where even today it remains at 85. Thus the sex structure has been more unbalanced in East Germany than in any other country of the region during the whole post-war period. Its age pyramid also shows great scars left by the economic depression of the 1930s, the war losses, birth deficits suffered during both world wars, and the lack of a high compensatory fertility after the war. Flight from East Germany prior to 1961 deprived the country of large numbers of working age groups, and thereby contributed also to the process of aging which is considerably more advanced there than elsewhere in the region. The proportion of the young (below 14) remained stable around 23% during the post-war years, while that of older people (65 and over) increased from 11 to 16% between 1950 and 1969. However, changes within the working age group and high mortality among the elderly caused the median age to decline from 37 to 34, thus placing East Germany in a unique position in East-Central Europe, for in the remainder of the region median ages have increased.

Poland ranked second lowest in 1950 as far as the masculinity ratio was concerned with 88 males per 100 females. However, there was a substantial change during post-war years, for the ratio had increased to 95 by 1969. Poland's age pyramid has a large bulge in its young ages caused by the post-war "baby boom," and it is separated from the next bulge in the middle ages by smaller cohorts of those born during World War II. The proportion of young population (0–14) was third highest in the early post-war years, and despite a slight decline (30–28%) it ranked second highest in 1969. World War II took a heavy toll of old people and as a result the proportion of those over 65 was only 5.4% in 1950, the lowest in the entire region. It had increased to 7.8% by 1969, which was second lowest in East-Central Europe, exceeded only by Albania. The median age increased somewhat (from 26 years in 1950 to 28 in 1969), but it still remains the lowest in East-Central Europe (excluding Albania and Yugoslavia for which there are no data).

In Czechoslovakia the masculinity ratio increased insignificantly during the post-war years (from 94.6 to 95.4 between 1950 and 1969), while the median age also changed only slightly (from 31 to 32). The proportion of young people declined from 25.4 to 23.6 between 1950 and 1969 and is presently similar to that of East Germany. The proportion of the elderly increased from 7.8 to 10.8% over the same interval.

In Hungary the demographic structure is similar to that in Czechoslovakia except that the masculinity ratio remains lower (94% in 1969) despite a slight post-war improvement. The proportion of the young is now the lowest in East-Central Europe (21.7 in 1969 as compared to 24.9 in 1949), and the median age has increased to the level of East Germany (34 in 1969).

In Romania the masculinity ratio is rather high (97 in 1969) and the age structure shows fewer distortions than in the countries of the northern part of the region where war dislocations and devastation were more severe. The post-war "baby boom" created a bulge which has now moved to the upper teens, and the subsequent decline in fertility has caused a drop in the proportion of the youngest age group from 27.5 to 25.7 between 1956 and 1969. This decline occurred despite a recent upsurge of fertility which is reflected in a most unusual expansion at the base of the age pyramid. The proportion of old people increased from 6.4 to 8.6 between 1956 and 1969 and the median age increased accordingly (from 27 to 31).

In Bulgaria the masculinity ratio has remained remarkably stable around 100 and the differences in the size of age groups are not as pronounced as elsewhere in East-Central Europe. Nevertheless the proportion of the youngest group declined substantially from 28 to 23% between 1946 and 1969, while that of the oldest group almost doubled (9.3%

in 1969 as compared to 5.8% in 1946). Increase in the median age was the highest for the entire region (from 26 to 33 years during 23 years).

Yugoslavia had a relatively low masculinity ratio in 1948 (93) but it increased to 97 by 1971. The age pyramid shows the impact of both world wars and the compensation period of the 1940s. The proportion of young people declined from 30.5 to 26.7% between 1948 and 1971, while that of old people increased during the same period from 6 to 8%.

Albania has a population age and sex structure that is relatively unlike those of the seven other countries included within East-Central Europe. It is the only one with a substantial excess of males (103 in 1945; 106 in 1960), a feature that may reflect the country's backward condition with accompanying high mortality of females during childbirth, and also an underregistration of young females in this traditionally Moslem area. Despite a decline in the proportion of the young (0–14 years) within the total population (from 39 in 1945 to 33 in 1960), Albania still ranks first in East-Central Europe in the youthfulness of its inhabitants. At the same time, it has the smallest proportion of old people and the proportion has continued to decline, a trend which runs counter to that evident in the region as a whole, and results from high birth and natural increase rates.

Differences in age and sex structure are evident within national boundaries as well as across them, internal migrations being the most important cause. Newly settled Polish northern and western territories, Czech borderlands, and Yugoslav Vojvodina are prime examples of areas having numerous young settlers, and consequently are distinguished by their relatively higher fertility, a higher proportion of young population, and a low proportion of the elderly. Continuous out-migration from rural to urban areas, highly age and sex selective in character, affects age and sex structure as well as fertility and mortality in both regions of exit and entrance. The impact of external migration has been relatively slight and restricted to East Germany and more recently Yugoslavia. According to population forecasts, the process of aging will continue, with the proportion of old people approaching or exceeding 10% in all countries by the year 1990.

Ethnic Diversity

When the political map of East-Central Europe was being redrawn after World War I, attempts were made to create viable national states for which the political boundaries would follow as closely as possible the ethnic boundaries. Complete elimination of minorities was clearly impossible since the situation that had developed over a long period of time was altogether too complicated. This ethnic mixture came about as a result of several factors. First, frequent devastating wars fought in the frontier areas left them depopulated, and attempts at resettlement were often associated with importing settlers from various countries. Sometimes these groups were organized into semi-military settlements located along volatile frontiers; sometimes they simply replaced population losses resulting from wars. This factor explains the presence of Saxon settlers in southern Transylvania, and the mixed population in the southern part of the Pannonian Plain in Hungary. Second, foreign nationals often came as invited immigrants, who were sought in order to develop certain resources for which special skills were necessary. This explains the presence of Dutch settlers in the marshlands of Poland and German miners in southern Poland, Czechoslovakia, and Hungary. Immigration of farmers (often Germans) or foreign tradesmen (Jews, Armenians, and Greeks) are also included in this category. Third, some foreign powers actually encouraged settlement of their ethnic nationals within foreign areas, looking towards the subjugation of newly acquired territories. Isolated islands of German, Russian, or Turkish speaking people often developed as a result of these policies. Fourth, processes of assimilation, or lack of them, also were responsible for ethnic or cultural variety. Adoption of Islam by Albanians, and particularly true of large numbers of southern Slavs, led to their assimilation into the Turkish culture. Likewise northwestern Slavs were gradually assimilated into the German culture. In some areas ethnic mixtures reflected different stages of an incompleted process of assimilation.

However, even in those situations where it was possible to separate two ethnic groups by political boundaries, this has not always been done for various historical, political, or economic reasons. Insistence on re-creation of historical boundaries led to inclusion of foreign nationals into newly emerging countries (Germans in Czech Sudetenland; Lithuanians, Belorussians, and Ukrainians in Poland). Economic arguments, such as the necessity to secure enough fertile agricultural land for eastern Czechoslovakia and Yugoslavia, led to inclusion of an appreciable Hungarian population within these two countries. The desire to reduce the potential threat from former enemies would strengthen the claims of victorious countries (Romania, Czechoslovakia, and Yugoslavia) to absorb Hungarian populations living in their frontier zones. Consequently, newly formed countries were burdened with high proportions of ethnic minorities, especially Poland, Czechoslovakia, and Romania (Table 3.5).

It is extremely difficult to describe precisely the ethnic diversity existing in East-Central Europe. The available official data utilized in the present study have often been judged by representatives of minority groups or by the foreign press as inaccurate and unreliable. This criticism applies in a certain degree not only to current data, but even more so to data collected in the inter-war period or prior to World War I. Apart from deliberate distortions caused by attempts to statistically eliminate minorities, it was often impossible to obtain clear answers relative to the national feelings of the population. Regardless of the question asked (whether relating to language spoken or to national identity), large groups of the population living in isolated rural communities could not clearly identify their nationality. This led to such categories as "local population" (Polish census, 1931), and "Moslems in ethnic sense" (Yugoslavia, 1961). Jews, especially numerous in Poland, differed from the majority not only in their religion but also in their language (Yiddish), mode of dressing, and general way of life. Their nationalist leaders insisted that they should be treated not only as a religious but also as an ethnic minority. On the other hand, German and Hungarian Jews were culturally largely assimilated, and in fact often belonged to extreme nationalist factions within their respective countries. The number of gypsies often fluctuated as reported in successive censuses as they variously declared themselves Turks, Tartars, gypsies, or members of other dominant ethnic groups.

In the inter-war years the largest ethnic minorities in East-Central Europe were represented by (1) Ukrainians residing in east and southeast Poland, eastern Czechoslovakia, and northeastern Romania; (2) Germans dispersed all through the northern part of the region, especially Czechoslovakia, Romania, and Poland; and (3) Jews concentrated in urban communities of eastern Poland and northeastern Romania. Large numbers of Hungarians lived in contiguous portions of Czechoslovakia, Romania, and

TABLE 3.5. ETHNIC STRUCTURE IN EAST-CENTRAL EUROPE

Country	Year	Majority	Minorities % of minorities	Minorities Principal minorities
East Germany	1960	Germans	0.7	Sorbs (Lusatians)
Poland	1931	Poles	32.3	Ukrainians (13.9), Jews (9.8), Belorussians (5.3), Germans (2.3)
	1961	Poles	1.5	Ukrainians (0.6), Belorussians (0.5)
Czechoslovakia	1930	Czechoslovaks	33.7	Germans (22.5), Hungarians (4.9), Ukrainians (3.9)
	1971	Czechs and Slovaks	5.7	Hungarians (3)
Hungary	1930	Hungarians	7.9	Germans (5.5), Slovaks (1.2)
	1960	Hungarians	1.8	Germans (0.5), Slovaks (0.3)
Romania	1930	Romanians	28.1	Hungarians (7.8), Germans (4.1), Jews (4), Ukrainians (3.2)
	1956	Romanians	14.3	Hungarians (9.1), Germans (2.2), Jews (0.8)
Bulgaria	1926	Bulgarians	16.9	Turks, Tartars, Gagauz (10.7), Gypsies (2.5), Romanians (1.3)
	1956	Bulgarians	14.5	Turks, Tartars, Gagauz (8.7), Gypsies (2.6)
Yugoslavia	1931	Serbs, Croats, Slovenians	14.9	Albanians (3.6), Germans (3.5), Hungarians (3.3)
	1961	Serbs, Croats, Slovenians, Moslem Slavs, Montenegrins, Macedonians	10.8	Albanians (4.9), Hungarians (2.7), Turks (1.0)
Albania	1938	Albanians	7.5	Greeks (3.5), Gypsies (2.8), Romanians (1.2)
	1955	Albanians	5.0	Greeks (3.0), Macedonians (0.8)

Source: Kosiński, 1969.

Yugoslavia detached from Hungary as the result of the Treaty of Trianon. Many Turks were left behind in the eastern parts of Romania and Bulgaria, especially along the Black Sea, as well as in the interior of Yugoslavia (Macedonia). The great powers of Europe did not really trust the newly emerging countries to treat the minorities fairly, and hence guarded their rights through a series of special treaties co-signed by the League of Nations and the individual countries of East-Central Europe. Although the major powers such as Germany and the USSR were not required to sign the treaties, later experience showed that minorities in those two countries were not necessarily better off. Generally speaking, relations between ruling majorities and the minority groups were rarely harmonious. Governments were often distrustful of their minorities, especially if these were represented by members of formerly ruling nations (Hungarians, Germans, and Turks) who lived in contiguous areas where they were often disloyal and troublesome, especially if they were unjustly treated or had been included within another country against their will. The ethnic conflicts and minority problems were not solved by various international arrangements, and reciprocal accusations multiplied, particularly in the 1930s. Later in the decade, minority problems were used by Hitler as a pretext to invade neighboring countries, thus precipitating World War II, which was responsible for changing profoundly the ethnic mosaic of East-Central Europe.

World War II losses were selective in the minority groups they affected. Jewish minorities practically disappeared, destroyed by Nazi terror. The residuals of this group mostly emigrated after the war; only a small fraction thereof remained. Many of those staying were people committed to the Communist cause, which later led to conflicts with majority groups who suspected highly placed Jews of being the spokesmen of foreign interests. This argument was raised again some 20 years later in Poland, leading to renewed emigration of Jews in the late 1960s. The powerful German minorities dwindled as a result of mass transfers of population undertaken in the late 1940s. The only country which continues to have a substantial number of Germans is now Romania, where they are concentrated in southern Transylvania and to a lesser extent in Banat. The third formerly numerous minority, the Ukrainians, has disappeared as a result of boundary changes discussed earlier. At the present time there exist three leading minority groups: 2.6m. Hungarians whose numbers and distribution did not change much; 880,000 Turks whose numbers are steadily diminishing as a result of emigration; and 900,000 Albanians whose numbers are increasing as a result of an extremely high birth rate.

The proportions of ethnic minorities has declined in all countries of East-Central Europe, but especially in Poland and Czechoslovakia where they accounted for about one-third of their inter-war populations (Table 3.5). Three countries where minorities still represent a sizeable share of the population are Bulgaria, Romania, and Yugoslavia.

In Bulgaria the Moslem–Turkish minority, a leftover from earlier Turkish rule, is concentrated in the northwest and west. Agreements concluded between Bulgaria and Turkey provide for a continuing transfer of this ethnic group to the homeland.

In Romania the proportion of the total population made up of ethnic minorities was reduced by half between 1930 and 1956, but they still account for about one-seventh of the total population (Table 3.5). Jewish and German minorities declined, but Germans are still fairly numerous in southern Transylvania (descendants of medieval Saxon settlers) and southern Banat (eighteenth century Swabian settlers repopulating the then war ravaged parts of the Pannonian Plain). Hungarians remain the most numerous and influential minority, their proportion and absolute numbers having increased relative to what they were in pre-war years. They are concentrated in Transylvania, which until World War I was part of the Hungarian Empire, and during World War II was in part temporarily annexed by Hungary. Hungarians represent a strong majority in one region (Regiunea Autonomă Magiară) of eastern Transylvania which for some time enjoyed an autonomous status until retraction of its autonomy in the process of administrative reforms in 1968. The coastal zone of Dobruja and the marshy delta of the Danube remain ethnically the most diversified areas of the country, harboring Ukrainians, Russians, and some Turks and Tartars.

Yugoslavia is a multinational country with six nationalities officially recognized as ruling Slavic nations, and each of them forming a constituent republic of its own. The most developed republic, Slovenia, is inhabited almost exclusively by Slovenians. In Croatia, apart from Croats, there are lesser numbers of Serbs, Hungarians, and Italians. The coastal province of Dalmatia has been strongly influenced and at times in the past controlled politically by Italy, which had resulted in residual cultural influences particularly in language and architecture. In Serbia, the larger ethnic minorities were given special consideration by the creation of two autonomous districts, Vojvodina in the north with a large number of Hungarians, and Kosovo in the south, almost exclusively Albanian. In Serbia proper there are also some Romanians and Bulgarians along the eastern boundary. Montenegro is inhabited by Montenegrins who have been treated in the past as Serbs. Separate Macedonian identity was recognized by the Yugoslav central government only during and after World War II. Turks and Vlachs, along with some Albanians, represent minority groups in this republic. In Bosnia, apart from the majority population classified officially as "Moslems in ethnic sense," there are some Serbs and Croats. In the past, Yugoslavia has suffered from tensions between its two major groups, Croats and Serbians, and some of these tensions and conflicts persist even until today. In so far as minorities are concerned, Albanians (or Shiptars as they are called in Yugoslavia), whose number and proportion have increased drastically as a result of their extremely high birth rate, sometimes create difficulties for the central government, particularly in view of the fact that they inhabit a zone contiguous to the Albanian republic. Their changing attitudes very much depend on the political situation in Albania proper. The German minority, which was rather powerful in the northern parts of the country, has disappeared as a result of World War II and the position of the remaining Hungarians has been gradually weakened by the addition of Slavic settlers in the northern part of Vojvodina.

Proportions of ethnic minorities are much smaller in the remaining countries of East-Central Europe. In East Germany, the only minority is the Serbs (original Slavic population of that area) who inhabit the southeastern part of the country. Their present number is estimated at about 100,000, but the degree of assimilation is high. In Poland the unofficial estimate puts the proportion of ethnic minorities at 1.5%. Ukrainians, dispersed in the newly acquired northwestern provinces, and Belorussians concentrated in the northeastern part of the country, account for the bulk of this group.

In Czechoslovakia, 600,000 Hungarians represent the only numerous minority; they are concentrated in the southern part of Slovakia. The remaining Germans are dispersed along the western and northern frontiers in so-called Sudetenland, which was at one time almost exclusively German. A small Polish island remains in Moravia-Silesia. Czechoslovakia is the second country within East-Central Europe which has a federal structure based on the distinction between the two ruling nationalities, Czechs and Slovaks. As in Yugoslavia, disputes arise between the two groups, with the Slovaks complaining of unfair treatment and inferior status as compared to the Czechs. Slovaks are concentrated in Slovakia but some of them went to Bohemia, especially to the northern and western frontier zone repopulated after World War II. Out-migration of Czechs from more developed Bohemia was by comparison very limited.

In Hungary, small minorities include the considerably Magyarized Germans in the south and Slovaks dispersed throughout the north and on the plains. Finally, Albania has only a tiny Greek minority, and that is located in the extreme south.

Ethnic tensions and problems have waned considerably in the post-war period, partly because the size of minority groups declined, partly because the tensions surface only rarely. In contrast to the inter-war years, there are now no international treaties protecting minority groups. Civil and political rights are granted to individuals, but no political activity by ethnic groups is allowed. In autonomous districts selection of local authorities is based on ethnic considerations, but even here the heavy hand of the central government is felt. Officially, ethnic culture is encouraged, use of minority languages is permitted, and ethnic schools and newspapers exist. However, one may suspect that in long term perspective minorities are expected to either merge with the dominating culture or emigrate.

References

Berent, J. (1970), Causes of fertility decline in eastern Europe and the Soviet Union, *Population Studies* **34** (1) 35–58 and (2) 247–92.

Combs, J. W. (1963), Recent demographic changes in eastern Europe, in US House of Representatives, Committee on the Judiciary, Subcommittee no. 1, *Study on Population and Immigration Problems*, Washington DC, GPO, 47–71.

Frumkin, G. (1951), *Population Changes in Europe since 1939*, A. M. Kelley, New York.

Kosiński, L. A. (1969), Changes in the ethnic structure in East-Central Europe, 1930–1960, *Geographical Review* **59** (3) 388–402.

Kosiński, L. A. (1972), Internal migration in East-Central Europe, in Adams, W. P. and Helleiner, F. M. (eds.), *International Geography 1972*, vol. 2, University of Toronto Press, Toronto, 1142–3.

Kosiński, L. A. (1973), Urbanization in East-Central Europe after World War II, *East European Quarterly* (in press).

Kostanick, H. L. (1970), Significant demographic trends in Yugoslavia, Greece and Bulgaria, in G. W. Hoffman (ed.), *Eastern Europe: Essays in Geographical Problems*, Praeger, New York, 395–424.

Mauldin, W. P. (1954), *The Population of Poland*, Washington DC, US Bureau of the Census, International Population Statistics Report, Series P-90, no. 4.

Myers, P. F. (1970), Demographic trends in eastern Europe, in US Congress, Joint Economic Committee, Subcommittee on Foreign Economic Policy, *Economic Developments in Countries of Eastern Europe*, Washington DC, GPO, 68–148.

Myers, P. F. and Campbell, A. A. (1954), *The Population of Yugoslavia*, Washington DC, US Department of Commerce, Bureau of the Census, International Population Statistics Reports, Series P-90, no. 5.

Siegel, J. S. (1958), *The Population of Hungary*, Washington DC, US Department of Commerce, Bureau of the Census, International Population Statistics Reports, Series P-90, no. 9.

Wynne, W. (1953), *The Population of Czechoslovakia*, Washington DC, US Department of Commerce, Bureau of the Census, International Population Statistics Reports, Series P-90, no. 3.

CHAPTER 4

MEDITERRANEAN EUROPE

ALLAN L. RODGERS

Pennsylvania State University, USA

This chapter is concerned with the contemporary population geography of Mediterranean Europe, or the three great peninsulas of Iberia, Italy, and Greece (Yugoslavia excluded). To be sure, the modern features of population distribution in southern Europe have evolved from those of the ancient and medieval past, but these earlier distributions are dealt with in Chapter 2 and so are referred to only incidentally here.

The Mediterranean Basin was, of course, the home of Western Civilization. However, it was clearly only one of the regions of advanced early cultures and urbanization in the then developing world. Mesopotamia, the Indus Valley, and the Huang Basin also nurtured major early civilizations and their important concentrations of people. But the Mediterranean borderlands became the site of not one, but several successive flourishing cultures, among them Egyptian, Minoan-Cretan, Grecian, Phoenician, Roman, Byzantine, and Islamic.

Students of Grecian history believe that from the eighth to the sixth century BC there was a rapid increase in the number of inhabitants comprising the city-states of Greece proper. Population pressure therefore may well have been one factor leading to the systematic hiving of people from the mainland to form new coastal and insular colonies, particularly in the eastern Mediterranean. These included the Black Sea margins, parts of northeast Africa, Sicily, mainland Italy, and southern France. Thus the early Greek population, which may have reached about 3m. by the fourth and third centuries BC, consisted mainly of isolated and widely distributed clusters.

Unlike Grecian colonization which was largely confined to the eastern Mediterranean, some centuries later Rome spread its control and settlers into the western and north-central parts of the basin, along the littoral of northern Africa, and even into the western and central parts of Europe. Thus Roman settlements were more widespread and more continuous than those of Greece. And while Greek colonization was oriented toward the sea, that of Rome was to a greater degree land oriented. One estimate credits the Roman Empire with having a population of more than 50m. early in the first century AD.

The three great Mediterranean peninsulas probably experienced an overall decline in population during the late classical period, followed likely by a degree of recovery, erratic and fluctuating in character, during the middle and late medieval periods. In Italy there occurred a notable northward shift in the center of gravity of its population, accompanied by a commensurate growth of cities in the north. Some like Genoa and Venice were the durable seats of powerful trading empires, while others like Florence,

Bologna, and Milan were more localized in their reaches. Within Iberia a perceptible spatial arrangement had emerged in which the high densities, with rare exceptions, concentrated along the maritime periphery. The seaward attraction reflected both the Islamic penetration of Iberia via the sea from North Africa as well as the environmental advantages provided by the coastal lowlands. In the early Modern period (after about 1650) population growth in Mediterranean Europe lagged behind that in Northwest Europe where the industrial and demographic revolutions began earlier, leading first to a decline in death rates and somewhat later to a fall off in birth rates as well. In the three southern peninsulas both birth and death rates continued high until later.

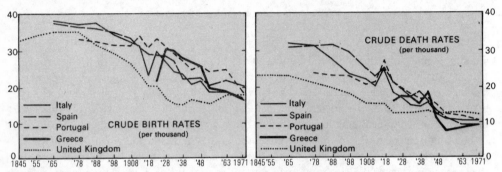

FIG. 4.1. Crude birth and death rates for countries in southern Europe, 1845–1971. United Kingdom included for comparison.

Figure 4.1 portrays the evolution of birth and death rate patterns for southern Europe since the nineteenth century. The United Kingdom was chosen as a reference level because it provides an excellent example of the trend in vital rates as a nation moves through the demographic transition. However, the graphs are incomplete, for the pattern of declining death rates began at an earlier stage in Britain than was true in southern Europe. Thus death rates in England and Wales, which were over 30 per 1000 in the mid seventeenth century, had declined to about 22 per 1000 a century later. Note how much later reductions in the level of death rates began in the northern Mediterranean. Similarly, there was a lag in the reduction of birth rates in southern Europe, as is evidenced by Fig. 4.1, but the period of retardation was considerably shorter.

TABLE 4.1. VITAL RATES FOR SOUTHERN EUROPE IN 1970
(UNITED KINGDOM INCLUDED FOR COMPARISON)

Country	Crude birth rate (per 1000 population)	Crude death rate (per 1000 population)	Crude natural increase (per 1000 population)	Infant mortality (per 1000 live births)
United Kingdom	16.2	11.7	4.5	18.3
Italy	16.8	9.7	7.1	29.2
Spain	19.6	8.5	11.1	27.9
Portugal	18.0	9.7	8.3	47.6
Greece	16.3	8.3	8.0	29.3

Source: *Statistical Yearbook 1971*, United Nations, New York, 1972, p. 79.

By 1970 a general pattern of low birth rates and low death rates prevailed in southern Europe. This is demonstrated by the national figures in Table 4.1. Cross-national and subnational variations in vital rates within the northern Mediterranean are primarily the result of spatial variations in degrees of urbanization in that region. These are in turn closely associated with regional contrasts in levels of industrialization, income, and education. Comparatively high birth rates in rural Iberia and southern Italy still reflect the influence of the Roman Catholic Church with its pro-natalist policy and its strictures on the adoption of artificial birth control measures.

The Present Settlement Pattern

The population of the Mediterranean's northern borderlands was approximately 98m. (excluding Yugoslavia) in 1970. Its distribution and density patterns are depicted on the national maps that follow. However, these generalized views of urban and rural settlement in Iberia, Italy, and Greece obscure an extraordinary diversity of patterns that can only be discerned on larger scale regional maps. These intricacies are the result of a vast array of complex forces: economic, social, political, and physical, both present and in the past. Our analysis of the population geography of the nations that comprise Mediterranean Europe assesses the relative weight of these forces in the shaping of the present population distribution patterns of that region.

Italy

The treatment of the population geography of Italy is more comprehensive than that of Iberia or the Greek peninsula. This emphasis is deliberate, and reflects the author's greater first hand knowledge of Italy, as well as the fact that Italy is a microcosm of patterns found throughout the whole northern Mediterranean. Those departures from regional "norms" which do exist are portents of impending demographic changes in other parts of southern Europe. The treatment will be confined to "modern Italy," or the period since unification, with special emphasis on regional developments during the past two decades.

Population Growth

The population of Italy, within its present territorial confines, almost doubled during the past century, reaching 54m. at the time of the 1971 enumeration. Table 4.2 records the average annual percentage growth rates for the various census intervals. These values are comparatively low when compared, for example, with those of the nations of western Europe during their period of economic "take-off." Thus the comparable value for Britain during the early nineteenth century was 1.4%. However, as will be demonstrated later, the Italian values are understated because of unusually high net out-migration which was concentrated mainly in the period from 1880 to World War I. The low growth from 1912 to 1921 appears to reflect the effect of that conflict. Conceivably, it resulted from a combination of military and civilian deaths and low birth rates associated with separation occasioned by the war.

TABLE 4.2. GROWTH OF THE ITALIAN POPULATION, 1861 TO 1971[a]

Census year	Population (within present boundaries) (millions)	Average annual percentage change[b] (census intervals)
1861	26.3	
		0.67
1871	28.2	
		0.57
1881	29.8	
		0.66
1901	34.0	
		0.86
1911	37.1	
		0.24
1921	37.9	
		0.86
1931	41.0	
		0.65
1936	42.4	
		0.74
1951	47.5	
		0.64
1961	50.6	
		0.65
1971	54.0	
		0.66 (estimate)[d]
1986 (estimate)	60.0[c]	

[a] *XI Censimento Generale della Popolazione, 1971*, vol. I, Rome, 1972, p. 3.
[b] Using compound interest formulation for census intervals.
[c] M. Livi Bacci and Pilloton, F., *Popolazione e Forze di Lavoro delle Regioni Italiane al 1968*, Svimez, Rome, 1970, p. 26.
[d] Percentage increase estimate for the period between 1966 and 1986.

Judging from the birth and death rate values presented in Fig. 4.1, Italy has clearly experienced the vital rate changes associated with demographic transition. The nation, viewed as a whole, is now in the low birth rate/low death rate phase hypothesized for highly developed nations (see the 1970 values in Table 4.1). Its position in that descriptive model is also illustrated in the evolution of the nation's age structure between 1861 and 1969. In the earlier period, Italy's age composition was one with a high proportion of children and a very small percentage in the oldest age groups. Thus 34% of the population were under 15 years of age and 4% over 65. In contrast, the current age structure is rapidly approaching that of western Europe. The values for 1969 (Table 4.3) were 24% of the population under 15 years of age and 9% over 65. These phenomena are typical of nations whose birth rates and death rates are both low.

As noted above, the intercensal increases in population numbers and the average annual rates of growth for Italy involve two factors—natural increase and net migration.

TABLE 4.3. ESTIMATED COMPARATIVE AGE STRUCTURE FOR THE UNITED KINGDOM AND SOUTHERN EUROPE (%)

Country	Age groups				
	0–14	15–44	45–64	65 and over	Total
Italy (1969)	24.4	44.5	21.1	9.1	100.0
Spain (1969)	28.1	41.9	20.4	9.6	100.0
Portugal (1969)	28.8	41.0	19.6	10.6	100.0
Greece (1969)	25.1	44.7	20.6	9.6	100.0
United Kingdom (1969)	23.5	39.1	25.4	12.9	100.0

Source: *Demographic Yearbooks, 1970* and *1971*, United Nations, New York, 1971–2, various pages.

Between 1861 and 1961 the natural increase of population (within present political boundaries) was roughly 31m. but there was a net out-migration during the same period of over 7m. inhabitants, so that the actual increase was only 24m. Thus, in the Italian case, emigration has been a major restraint upon overall growth.

Any analysis of emigration patterns starts out with a major handicap. While there are abundant data on out-migration, statistics on return flows are incomplete. Systematic collection of such data commenced only in 1904, several decades after the start of massive outflows abroad. Neglecting the feature of return migration, it can be stated that the volume of out-migration during the past century was truly enormous considering the size of the base population. However, much of the migration was ephemeral, with permanent expatriates accounting for only a fraction of the total. Thus between 1871 and 1930 the total number of emigrants was nearly 18m., while the net outward migration has been estimated at 5m., or less than one-third of that number. Nevertheless, it is clear that emigration played a major role in slowing population growth, and hence retarding the rise in population pressure. It is also true that the migrants' foreign remittances helped to support the nation's economic development during the past century. On the negative side, it has been argued that this age specific migration presumably drained away young adults who would have contributed to sustained national economic growth.

The major peak in Italian emigration came during the period from 1876 to World War I, after which time the enactment of bars to immigration abroad, followed by Fascist legislation against Italian emigration in the thirties, stemmed the outflow. This period logically falls into two time segments. From 1876 to 1900 the number of emigrants totaled over 5m., for an average of about 210,000 per year. The volume increased markedly from 1901 to 1913, when the total reached 8m., for an annual average of over 600,000 persons. If trans-Atlantic and European destinations are considered separately, the earlier period was one in which the flows were divided evenly between the two destinations. The second witnessed a modest shift in favor of overseas terminals.

Although population pressure prior to 1913 was intense throughout Italy, on a relative scale it was less so in the North because of that part's greater agricultural productivity and its comparatively higher levels of industrialization. Yet the numbers of emigrants from North and South were remarkably similar. The southerners came predominantly from Campania and Sicily, for these were the regions of greatest population pressure in the South. In the case of Campania, the exodus resulted from sheer population numbers relative to the available agricultural land; in the second instance, the out-migration resulted from Sicily's history of political instability, its land tenure system, and its environmental handicaps. The southern emigrants went mainly to the Western Hemisphere, particularly to the United States and Argentina. In contrast, the northern Italians migrated almost exclusively to countries in close proximity, especially France and Switzerland. The most important source region was Veneto in the eastern Po Plain, a badly drained region of comparatively low agricultural productivity. The available evidence indicates that the largest proportion of the northern emigrants were males, their movements were mainly temporary, and there were disproportionately heavy return flows. The converse was true of the southern emigration, for although, here too, there were large numbers of returnees, the migration was far more permanent. Entire family units commonly emigrated at the same time.

There has been a renewed emigration abroad since World War II. The data at hand, which cover the period from 1956 to 1970, show an outward flow for this 15 year period of 1,450,000 persons and a return movement of 904,000, for a net out-migration of 546,000. It must be emphasized, however, that these statistics are based on official change of residence records, but many more leave the country and return without such registration formalities. Three-fifths of these flows originated in southern Italy, and the movements were about evenly divided between overseas and European destinations.

Population Distribution

Figure 4.2 shows the distribution of population in Italy mapped on the basis of arithmetic densities for each of the nation's 8000 communes. It is a simplification of a far more detailed map produced by Pinna from the 1951 census. No such map exists for 1971, but given the modest population changes that have occurred in the past 20 years (an average annual increase of 0.65%), these patterns are still a valid base for the description and interpretations that follow. The present discussion of distribution, with considerable updating, is patterned after the Pinna analysis.

With a population of approximately 54m. (1971) and an area of over 300,000 km², the average density of population in Italy was 179 per km² (464 per square mile). Our analysis begins with those areas whose densities are lower than 50 per km² (130 per square mile). As a broad generalization it can be noted that all of these low density regions are characterized by physical handicaps which have restrained settlement. Typically, such disadvantages include high altitudes, often associated with rough terrain; thin and infertile soils; low and irregular precipitation; inadequate supplies of surface water; and poorly drained land, this last commonly correlated in the past with malaria. The most striking and certainly the most continuous of these sparsely populated regions is the Alpine zone along the northern fringes of the country. Note the relative continuity of the belt of low density stretching from the Cuneo and Valle d'Aosta areas on the west through Sondrio, Bolzano, Trento, and ultimately to Udine on the east. The only penetration of a zone of higher density through this belt is the one reaching from Milan northward to the Ticino region of Italian Switzerland. Within the Alps, as is true of the Apennines, there are, of course valleys of greater than average fertility which support relatively large rural populations, often reinforced by the presence of urban centers lying astride major transport arteries. In contrast, the slopes themselves are largely devoid of settlement other than those associated with pastoral activities and, increasingly today, tourism. A second but less continuous zone of low density follows the Apennine spine from the Ligurian highlands on the northwest to L'Aquila and Campobasso in east-central Italy. Note also the large zone of sparse population on the coast extending from south of Livorno to Latina, broken only by the Roman conurbation. The area south of the capital has a somewhat higher density today as a result of recent industrial and urban growth. However, the main zone of low density to the north, termed the Maremma, still persists. This can be explained mainly by physical handicaps such as the prevalence of low lying, formerly malarial marshes juxtaposed with rough terrain and thin sterile soils. The Maremma has had a long history of insecurity resulting from piratic incursions which though long past have also left their imprint. Further south there are the expected low densities of highland Basilicata and the mountain areas of central Calabria. The only other extensive region within this low density category, evident on the map, is the island of Sardinia. Note the striking contrast with Sicily, an island of roughly similar areal extent but one with three times the former's population

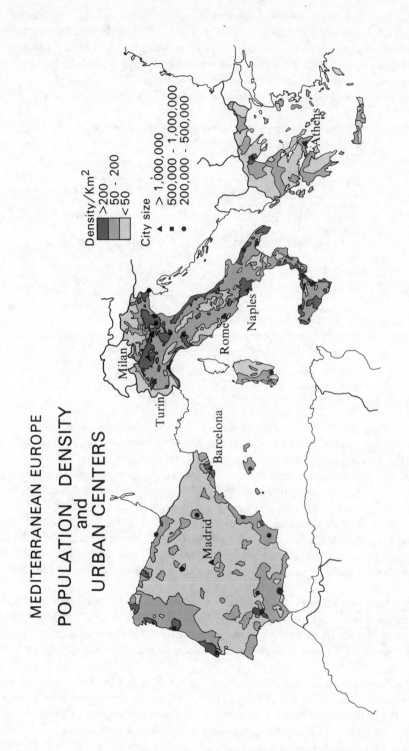

MEDITERRANEAN EUROPE
POPULATION DENSITY
and
URBAN CENTERS

Density/Km²
>200
50 - 200
<50

City size
> 1,000,000
500,000 - 1,000,000
200,000 - 500,000

Milan
Turin
Barcelona
Madrid
Rome
Naples
Athens

Sardinia exemplifies practically all of the physical problems noted in connection with other areas of low population density in Italy. These constraints were reinforced by the relative isolation of the island from the mainland; a long history of piracy which repelled the settlement along its coasts; relatively uncontrolled banditry; and the persistence of a semi-feudal way of life which retarded social and economic development.

Finally, a word with respect to the depopulation of the Italian highlands. Table 4.4

TABLE 4.4. THE SHARE OF THE ITALIAN POPULATION BY
LANDFORM CATEGORIES FOR 1871[a] AND 1971[b]

	Percentage of population			
	Mountains	Hills	Plains	Total
North Italy[c] 1871	23.1	42.5	34.4	100.0
North Italy 1971	12.5	32.4	55.1	100.0
South Italy[c] 1871	24.0	54.4	21.6	100.0
South Italy 1971	13.2	50.2	36.6	100.0
Italy 1871	23.5	47.5	29.0	100.0
Italy 1971	12.8	38.8	48.4	100.0
Italy: share of area	35.2	41.6	23.2	100.0

[a]*Popolazione Residenti e Presente dei Comuni ai Consimenti dal 1861 al 1961*, Istituto Centrale di Statistica, Rome, 1967, various pages.
[b]*Censimento Generale della Popolazione, 1971*, vol. I, Rome, 1972, various pages.
[c]Northern Italy includes both the *North* and the *Center*.

shows the share of the Italian population in 1871 and 1971 by three terrain groups: mountains, hills, and plains. These percentages demonstrate a striking decline in the share of the Italian population contained within the upland regions.

In the past, the hills and mountains served as refuge areas in times of political insecurity. During this century, however, there has been a significant depopulation of the Italian highlands, a feature which is amply documented in the literature. The decline is due, in part, to the low agricultural productivity of these regions, exacerbated by severe soil erosion resulting from deforestation and poor farming practices. It is also a function of economic opportunities afforded by tidewater towns and cities. The result of both forces has been a significant relative and absolute growth of population on the coastal plains of Italy.

We now turn our attention to the highest density category, delimited in Fig. 4.2, or those areas with over 200 persons per km² (518 per square mile). This group includes regions of moderate to excellent environmental quality where the population is dominantly agricultural, as well as urbanized areas whose economies are typically linked to industry.

The Po Plain is clearly the most extensive region of high population density in Italy. In its extreme northwestern part, or Piedmont, a region of nearly 3m. inhabitants, there is a series of discontinuous population clusters dominated by the city of Turin (1,178,000). There the remarkable population growth in recent decades is largely attributable to an influx of immigrants from the south, drawn to this area by expanding employment opportunities. In Turin and its industrial satellites, the key attraction has been the expansion of the Fiat Works and linked industrial plants.

Further east there is a far more continuous and extensive cluster of high density in Lombardy; the bulk of its 8.5m. inhabitants is concentrated in urban centers, particularly Milan (1,724,000). That sprawling urban and industrial conurbation, the nation's most important, has acted as a magnet for tens of thousands of migrants from southern Italy. However, unlike Piedmont, this region does have several rich agricultural districts which, though dwarfed by the industrial centers, together do support a sizeable rural population. Third and last of the major high density clusters of the northern Italian plain is that furthest east in Emilia and Veneto, representing a total of 8m. inhabitants. Unlike the regions to the west, this is a zone of mixed urban and rural settlement. Industry does play a role, and there are important manufacturing centers such as Bologna (490,000) and Padua (232,000). However, the area is also one of high fertility and supports a large agricultural population. In general densities decline east of Padua, the only major exceptions being the population clusters around the cities of Venice (364,000) and Trieste (270,000).

Southward from the Po Plain the regions of high population density become less extensive and more discontinuous, largely in response to topographic constraints. One narrow belt follows the Adriatic from Ravenna to Pescara and Chieti. Here the population of the coastal zone has expanded rapidly since the thirties as maritime activities have expanded and tourism has flourished. In addition there are also pockets of intensive agriculture along parts of the coast. However, this Adriatic zone still contains less than 1m. persons. In contrast, the northwestern littoral, Liguria, which is even more constrained by the Maritime Alps and the Apennines, is far more densely settled. Its population in 1971 was nearly 2m.; its largest city is Genoa (812,000), Italy's leading port and a major center of heavy industry. The narrow coastal plain is characterized by unusually dense rural settlement economically based on horticulture, which in turn is fostered by the mild climate. It is also a world-famous resort area which has traditionally been a magnet for domestic and foreign tourists. The intensive development of this Ligurian littoral has been enhanced by its relative ease of access to western Europe via France, and to the Po Plain via low passes in the Apennines.

Further south, in northern Tuscany, high population density is particularly typical of the Arno Valley which is dominated by the city of Florence (462,000). Here labor intensive, high value added manufacturing employs a large share of the urban work force, but the area is also one of the most agriculturally productive in all Italy. The only other notable center of population concentration in central Italy is the relatively isolated pocket of high density around Rome (2.8m.).

Southern Italy, also known as the Mezzogiorno, had about 20m. inhabitants in 1971 or 35–40% of the nation's total population. Since the early fifties this region has been the focus of a major government subsidized development designed to reduce the social and economic disparities existing between the South and the far more prosperous North and Center. By far the largest share of these moneys have been used to support new industrial development and the improvement of the road network. Although in cost–benefit terms the results of the program have been comparatively modest, it has had a significant impact on the growth of urban centers.

The high density regions of the South are typically well endowed lowland areas of comparatively high agricultural productivity. These in turn focus on market and administrative towns. Some of the urban nodes are, of course, far larger than others not only because of the size of population in their hinterlands, but also because of their roles as ports and/or industrial centers. Most important of mainland southern Italy's population concentrations are to be found on the plains of Campania, which is the hinterland of Naples (1,233,000), the Terra di Bari, and the Salentino Peninsula, both in Puglia (the southeastern coast). Bari, that region's chief city, had a population of 357,000 in 1971. The island of Sicily, with over 4.5m. inhabitants, has two main population clusters, one coincident with the Conca d'Oro or the hinterland of Palermo city (651,000), located on the northwest coast, and the Catania lowland on the east side.

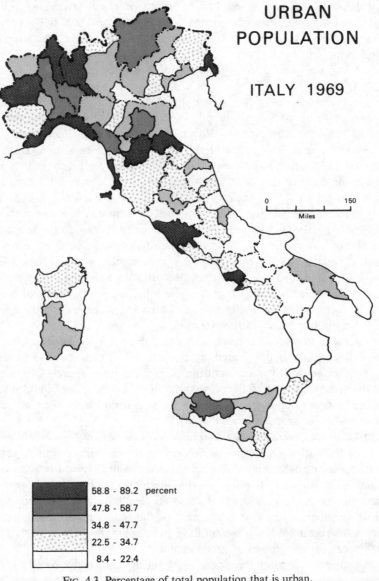

FIG. 4.3. Percentage of total population that is urban.

Urban–Rural Residence

Definitions of the terms urban and rural vary widely among nations. But accepting as an arbitrary definition for urban that proportion of a region's total population which lived in communities with over 20,000 inhabitants in 1961, the following values result: Italy, 37%; southern Europe as a whole, 27%; western Europe, 54%; and the United States, 46%. Thus Italy's level of urbanization was clearly higher than that of its neighbors in the northern Mediterranean, but below those of the more highly industrialized nations.

Since 1951 Italy has employed a multiple-criteria definition of urban. Thus communes are classified as urban or rural based on the share of their population that is concentrated in the "principal center," and this is supplemented by a series of socio-economic characteristics. In addition, communes are automatically classified as urban if they are the capitals of their provinces or if their population exceeds 70,000 inhabitants.

Distribution of the degree of urbanization within Italy is shown in Fig. 4.3. Clearly there is a far higher degree of urbanization in the North than in the South. Compared with a national average of 48%, the value in the North was 59%, that for the Center 52%, and for the South only 35%. The highest values were in industrialized provinces like Genoa (89%) and Milan (84%), and, as expected, for Rome (82%). Values in the depressed agricultural regions of the South were extremely low, dipping to levels of only 8–10% in the southern Apennines (Frosinone and Potenza), and 11% in parts of Sicily and Sardinia (Enna and Nuoro).

Italy is currently in the throes of a major urban crisis arising from the recent flood of migrants directed to its cities, many of whom have emigrated from the rural regions of the Mezzogiorno. This mushrooming urban growth has either been unplanned or at best poorly conceived. The Italian press speaks increasingly of the need to restrict urban development because of the diseconomies of metropolitan concentration. Air pollution, noise, traffic congestion, and crowded substandard housing are among the everyday ills of cities like Milan and Rome.

Cafiero and Busca, in a recent study of urbanization in Italy, have attempted to delimit the metropolitan areas and forecast their growth through 1981. In all, 32 areas were delimited, of which 10 are in the Mezzogiorno. Table 4.5 illustrates in a summary fashion the growth of those areas from 1951 through 1971. The tabulation illustrates the rather explosive growth described above. Compared with a national population growth of approximately 14%, the metropolitan areas grew by almost half, while there was a modest decrease in the population of the remainder of the nation. As will be seen shortly, these differences can be attributed to migration rather than to natural increase. The share of the Italian population contained in the metropolitan areas increased from 33% in 1951 to 43% in 1971. The urban increase was greatest in central Italy and least in the South where out-migration was strongest. The most notable increases came in the Milan and Turin areas of the Po Plain. Rome, too, was a major area of growth.

The Cafiero–Busca study also attempted to project the probable areal limits of the metropolitan areas by 1981. It must be emphasized that these were conservative estimates based on demographic and economic projections. Yet even on this basis, the metropolitan regions would have an estimated population of more than 35m. by 1981, or over three-fifths of the total Italian population. If their hypotheses are accepted, then there will be an almost continuous urban corridor along the Po Plain from Turin to Venice,

D

TABLE 4.5. CHANGES IN THE POPULATION OF ITALIAN METROPOLITAN AREAS FROM 1951 TO 1971

Region	1951 population (000's)	1971 population (000's)	Absolute change (000's)	Relative change (%)
Metropolitan regions of northern Italy[a]	7,221.4	11,034.0	+3,812.6	+52.8
Metropolitan regions of central Italy[b]	3,553.0	5,715.1	+2,162.1	+60.8
Metropolitan regions of southern Italy[c]	4,730.7	6,436.5	+1,705.8	+36.1
Total metropolitan areas	15,505.1	23,185.6	+7,680.5	+49.5
Non-metropolitan	32,010.5	30,839.6	−1,170.9	−3.7
Italy	47,515.6	54,025.2	+6,509.6	+13.7

[a]Milan, Turin, Genoa, Venice, Trieste, Padua, Brescia, Verona, La Spezia-Carrara, Biella, Udine, Vicenza, and Allessandria.
[b]Florence, Bologna, Livorno, Ferrara, Parma, Modena, Rimini, Ancona, Reggio-Emilia, and Rome.
[c]Pescara, Naples, Bari, Taranto, Reggio Calabria, Messina, Palermo, Catania, and Cagliari.

and also along the eastern edge of the Apennines from Milan to Ancona. Both axes follow major "autostrada" transport arteries. Some metropolitan growth will also take place in southern Italy, but such expansion will likely be comparatively modest in scale and highly fragmented.

Recent Internal Growth, Redistribution, and Migration

Italy's population grew by roughly 14% between 1951 and 1971, or 0.7% annually. Table 4.6 shows the regional variations in these growth patterns absolutely and relatively. It is evident that the South had a far lower rate of increase than the national average and a minimal absolute growth in its population. However, these values obscure a significant redistribution of the nation's population resulting from regional variation in vital rates, internal migration, and emigration.

It was noted earlier that Italy's vital rate patterns over time (see Fig. 4.1) replicated the declines postulated in the demographic transition model. Current birth and death rate values, viewed for the nation as a whole, are roughly comparable to those of the nations

TABLE 4.6. POPULATION GROWTH, BY MAJOR REGIONS, FOR ITALY FROM 1951 TO 1971[a]

Region	Population 1951 (000's)	Population 1971 (000's)	Relative increase (%)	Absolute increase (000's)	Natural growth (000's)	Net migration[b] (000's)
North	21,172	24,919	17.7	3,747	2,175	1,572
Center	8,670	10,305	18.9	1,635	1,305	330
South	17,698	18,801	6.2	1,103	5,181	−4,078
Italy	47,540	54,025	13.6	6,485	8,661	−2,176

[a]Calculated from M. Natali, "Stima Retrospettiva nella Popolazione Residente Provinciale nel Periodo 1951–1961," *Sviluppo della Popolazione*, pp. 138–53, and *Notiziario ISTAT*, Series 3—Population—Foglio 37, Istituto Centrale di Statistica, Rome, June 1972, p. 3.
[b]Net migration includes both internal and international migration estimates.

of western Europe. Yet national data obscure internal contrasts that are evident in Table 4.7, which demonstrates the evolution of birth and death rates over the past century for the three major subdivisions of the country. It is apparent that such differences were minimal in the late nineteenth century, for all three regions exhibited the high natality/high mortality patterns common today in the developing world. However, between 1910 and 1930 both the North and the Center experienced a sharp decline in birth and death rates associated with economic development and urbanization. The lag in such changes in southern Italy is clearly evident. Currently death rates are slightly lower in the Mezzogiorno than in the rest of the nation, reflecting the relatively youthful age structure of the South. More significantly, birth rates are considerably higher there than in the northern and central subdivisions of the country. This is a result of the persistently higher proportion of the South's population engaged in agriculture, and the effects of the Roman Catholic Church's pro-natalist policy. Traditionally, the Church has been more powerful and effective in the South than in northern Italy. Thus the natural increase of population in the Mezzogiorno is still quite high. The counter-balancing element, of course, has been the heavy net out-migration from that region, particularly to the North and, on a less permanent basis, abroad.

TABLE 4.7. CHANGES IN VITAL RATES FOR NORTHERN, CENTRAL AND SOUTHERN ITALY, FROM 1881 TO 1971[a]

Period	North		Center		South	
	BR[b]	DR[b]	BR	DR	BR	DR
1881–90	36.0	25.8	36.6	26.3	40.0	29.1
1891–1900	33.8	23.0	35.1	24.0	37.0	26.4
1901–10	32.4	20.6	30.2	20.0	33.6	23.2
1911–20	25.1	20.3	25.5	20.3	30.9	25.2
1921–30	25.0	15.4	26.4	15.2	33.5	18.1
1931–40	20.0	13.0	21.4	12.4	29.4	15.8
1941–50	17.0	12.4	18.2	11.9	26.2	13.6
	North and Center					
	BR	DR				
1951–60	14.4	9.9			23.3	9.0
1961–70	16.1	10.3			22.8	8.5

[a]Compiled from data provided by ISTAT (Istituto Centrale di Statistica).
[b]BR=crude birth rate per thousand, DR=crude death rate per thousand.

It should be re-emphasized at this point that the Mezzogiorno has a larger share of its population in the younger age groups than has its northern counterpart. Thus in 1961 47% of the population of southern Italy were less than 25 years of age, while the comparable value for the North and Center was only 36%. The youthful population coupled with continuing high birth rates portend a continuation of relatively rapid natural increase in the growth. However, such growth will continue to be tempered by net out-migration, whose volume will be dependent on changing levels of economic development within the South itself and conversely upon employment opportunities in northern Italy and abroad.

It was noted earlier that the growth of population (a resultant of natural increase plus net migration) of southern Italy was one-third that of the North and Center. However, these regional values mask the marked subregional variations that are to be observed in Fig. 4.4. There were provinces within all three regions that experienced losses in population, while others grew at rates that were appreciably above their regional averages. The explanations for the striking internal variations in population growth within each of the three major subdivisions of Italy are not primarily functions of differential vital

POPULATION CHANGE
ITALY 1951 - 1971

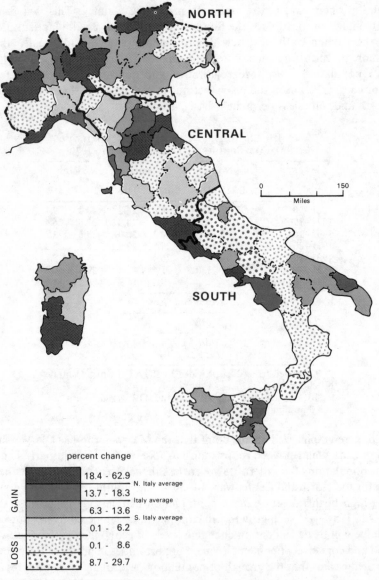

FIG. 4.4. Italy: percentage change in population by provinces, 1954–71.

rates, but rather reflections of internal migration in conjunction with spatial variations in economic opportunities and income levels in Italy.

Migration patterns during this two-decade interval, 1951–71, were extremely complex. The leading centers of in-migration in northern Italy were the key industrial centers of Milan and Turin. Another significant destination was the coast of Liguria, particularly Genoa. Migrants to all of these areas came predominantly from the South and from the eastern Po Valley.

Central Italy also had its growth poles, notably Bologna and Florence, which attracted in-migration, but the magnitude of these flows was less pronounced than in the North. Here the immigrants moved relatively short distances, for they came predominantly from the impoverished highland areas nearby. Rome, too, is here considered to be part of central Italy, but it actually straddles the border between North and South. The capital has traditionally been a magnet for southerners seeking to take advantage of employment opportunities in its huge administrative apparatus. During this era, Rome rivaled the giants of northern Italy as a destination for southern migrants.

Unlike the North and the Center with their variegated migration patterns, southern Italy was, in a sense, homogeneous in that every province lost population through net out-migration during the period between 1951 and 1971. Its outflows have been so heavy that the process has been termed "the hemorrhage" of the Mezzogiorno. There is some evidence of a modest waning of these flows resulting from government subsidized industrial development, but the results to date are still not encouraging. Out-migration patterns within the South clearly reflect spatial variations in population pressure and economic differentials within that region. The belt of heaviest out-migration follows the highland spine from the northern tier of provinces in the Abruzzi to Calabria in the South. Central and western Sicily have also been areas of major outflows.

In sum, our overview of the population geography of Italy has stressed the fact that the country is part of two worlds. Its northern areas are comparable in many respects to western Europe as far as their levels of economic development, urbanization problems, and projected dimensions of population growth are concerned. In contrast, the Mezzogiorno is a region in process of change. Despite massive government subsidies, it is still an underdeveloped region. As such, its level of urbanization is low, and its vital rates are transitional between those of the industrialized and urbanized nations of the West and those of the developing world. Population pressure, exacerbated by heavy natural increases in its population, has been and will continue to be a major element propelling out-migration. The coming decade may give some firm evidence as to the degree which government investment in the region will channel the migration to growth poles within the South itself.

Spain

The population of Spain as of the most recent census (December 1970) is approximately 34m. Despite the heavy loss of life resulting from the Civil War of the 1930s, the Spanish population has been growing at a faster pace than those of its neighbors in southern Europe, and far more rapidly than was true for the United Kingdom, representing conditions in western Europe (see Table 4.1). These variations in growth rates are reflections of regional differentials in vital rates shown in Fig. 4.1. Table 4.3 compares the age composition of the Spanish population with those of other nations in the northern

Mediterranean and with patterns for the United Kingdom. Spain's comparatively youthful population, coupled with its relatively high birth rates, all portend a more rapid rate of growth in the next decade than was projected for Italy. In fact, Spain's demographic traits resemble those of southern Italy.

Worthy of emphasis is the fact that the average density of population in Spain in 1970 was only 68 persons per km², one of the lowest in Europe, and less than half that of Italy. This low density is partly a result of physical constraints such as aridity, infertile soils, and rugged terrain, all of which, in combination, have retarded the development of agriculture, still the nation's most important economic activity. Equally significant, perhaps, has been the persistence of a semi-feudal socio-economic system, reinforced by the general isolation of Spain from the main currents of development in western Europe.

Contrary to the complex Italian pattern, the broad outlines of population distribution in Spain are relatively simple (Fig. 4.2). With the exception of the large and comparatively isolated node of higher density around Madrid, the capital and metropolis, there is a striking contrast between the sparse and predominantly rural population of the dry interior uplands, or the Meseta, and the far higher densities of the maritime periphery.

Several of the coastal regions, particularly those around Valencia, in the east, and the zone from Murcia to Algeciras, in the south, are areas of highly productive irrigated agriculture which support heavy rural population densities. More important, in a quantitative sense, is the heavy clustering of urban population on the north and east coasts, regions which have witnessed an extremely rapid growth of population in recent decades, attributable particularly to economic opportunities associated with developing industry. The north is Spain's only significant center of heavy manufacturing, fueled by coal from Asturias and iron ore from the Basque region. Here the chief cities are Santander, Bilbao, and San Sebastian. In contrast, the Catalonian area of the east coast, with its major metropolis of Barcelona, is a region with a wide range of labor intensive industries, particularly textiles. Both the northern and the eastern coastal areas have attracted numerous migrants from the interior. These flows originated mainly in the north-central regions of Leon, Old Castile, and Aragon, parts that were far more populous a century ago. In contrast, Galicia in the northwest and Andalusia in the south are zones of high rural population densities, low incomes, and considerable population pressure. Galicia, in particular, has been a major region of emigration to Argentina, Uruguay, and Venezuela.

Tables 4.8 and 4.9 summarize the internal variations that have occurred in the distribution of Spain's population since 1950. These shifts have taken two forms: first, a shift from the interior to the periphery, and, second, an explosive growth of the largest urban centers, especially Madrid and Barcelona. While one could hardly term modern Spain an industrialized nation today, still the share of its laboring population engaged in manufacturing had risen by 1970 to 27%, although much of its industrial employment is even yet in establishments of small scale with limited capital investments and low productivity. Paralleling this modest industrialization there has been a decline in agricultural employment together with a striking rural exodus.

Table 4.8 reveals the disproportionate population growth on the periphery, particularly the northern and eastern margins of the nation. With the exception of Madrid, the growth disparity between the center and the periphery has widened. Between 1960 and 1970, twenty-four of the fifty provinces (almost all in the interior) had an absolute decline in population.

TABLE 4.8. REGIONAL VARIATIONS IN THE GROWTH OF THE SPANISH POPULATION, 1950–70[a]

Regions[b]	Population 1970 (000's)	Absolute change 1950–60 (000's)	Relative change 1950–60 (%)	Absolute change 1960–70 (000's)	Relative change 1960–70 (%)
North	3,855	470	17.3	662	20.7
Eastern Mediterranean	8,186	851	15.4	1798	28.1
Madrid	3,761	687	37.7	1251	49.8
Northwest	2,676	29	1.1	− 55	− 2.0
Central North	4,207	21	0.5	− 288	− 5.2
Central South	5,490	137	2.3	− 538	− 8.9
Southern Mediterranean	4,088	219	5.9	139	3.5
Total[c]	32,387	2428	9.0	3016	10.1

[a]Organization for Economic Cooperation and Development (OECD), *Spain*, January 1973, p. 38.
[b]North = six provinces including such industrial areas as Asturias and Bilbao; Eastern Mediterranean = seven provinces of which Barcelona is the industrial area; Northwest = the Galician region; Central North = fourteen provinces including moderately industrialized areas like Valladolid and Zaragoza; Central South = nine provinces including Seville.
[c]Excluding the external possessions.

TABLE 4.9. GROWTH OF THE URBAN POPULATION OF SPAIN, BY SIZE OF CENTER, FROM 1950 TO 1970

Size class	1950[a] Inhabitants (000's)	1950[a] Share of total population (%)	1970[b] Inhabitants (000's)	1970[b] Share of total population (%)
500,000 plus	3,407	12.2	6,093	17.9
100,000–500,000	3,333	11.9	6,396	18.8
50,000–100,000	1,743	6.2	2,470	7.3
20,000–50,000	2,658	9.5	3,834	11.3
Subtotal	11,141	39.8	18,793	55.3
Total population	27,977	100.0	33,956	100.0

[a]*Anuario Estadistico España, 1969*, Madrid, 1969, p. 56. Data include external possessions.
[b]*Demographic Yearbook, 1971*, p. 389. Data include external possessions.

Along with the population shift to the northern and eastern margins of the country, and to the metropolis of Madrid, there has taken place an overall rapid urbanization, with the proportion of the total population living in communities of over 20,000 inhabitants growing from 39.8% in 1950 to 55.3% two decades later. The major growth has come in those urban centers with over 100,000 inhabitants, which cities now account for 36% of Spain's total population. Within this group, Madrid with over 3m. inhabitants and Barcelona with 1.75m. have been the outstanding growth poles. Madrid, alone, almost doubled its population in the two decades 1950–70, while the overall national growth was only 12%. Aside from its role as the chief administrative center in a highly centralized state, Madrid is the leading service center for interior Spain. In recent years the capital has also been a magnet for new industrial investment particularly in consumer oriented, non-durable goods. However, the bulk of the industrial employment is still concentrated in comparatively primitive workshops, unlike Barcelona whose long industrial tradition is reflected in more modern larger scale establishments.

It becomes evident that there are, in a sense, *two* Spains as there are two Italies. In the Spanish case, the contrast is between the Center (excluding Madrid) and the maritime periphery, as opposed to the North–South dichotomy in Italy. However, the difference is not merely locational, for despite the growth of the periphery and Spain's rather striking urbanization in recent decades, the country's economy is still backward. Average *per capita* income is considerably below that of Italy and far below those of the industrialized nations of western Europe.

Portugal

Portugal's inhabitants numbered 8,124,000 in 1970, resulting in an average density of 92 persons per km² (238 per square mile), a value which was only half that of Italy but considerably higher than the Spanish average. The distribution pattern is shown on the map of Iberia (Fig. 4.2). In broad terms there is a gradual decline from high densities north of the Tagus River to very low values in southern Portugal (Fig. 4.2). Densities also decline towards the interior. Portugal is still basically an agricultural society with comparatively high rural population densities. The north, a region of marine climate with mild temperatures and abundant effective precipitation, has particularly high densities, especially around Porto, a region of intensive horticulture. In contrast, southern Portugal, plagued by lower rainfall, summer drought, higher temperatures, excessive evaporation, and infertile soils, is a land of low agricultural productivity with densities that are one-third the national average.

The country's total population declined by approximately 2% between 1960 and 1970 despite moderately high birth rates (19–20 per 1000), for the increase was offset by emigration to the industrialized nations of western Europe. Within Portugal, declines were not uniform. Thus 12 out of 15 provinces experienced declining population during this period, with the sharpest decreases registered in the south. In contrast, as has been true elsewhere in Mediterranean Europe, there has been an internal drift to urban centers. This is reflected in the growth of three areas: Lisbon, Setubal, and Porto. The urban agglomerations of these provinces now account for almost half of Portugal's population. Lisbon, the capital, had 782,000 inhabitants in 1970, and its total urban agglomeration accounted for roughly one-fifth of the nation's population. Recent growth has come exclusively in its urbanized suburbs rather than in the city itself. Aside from its administrative function, Lisbon is a major commercial center, related in part to its role as the only major port in western Iberia. It is also a focus of road and rail routes linking the diverse regions of Portugal and tying them to the rest of the Peninsula. Porto, in the north, has a far smaller population (310,000), but it, too, experienced a sharp growth within its sprawling residential suburbs. In 1970 that urban agglomeration was credited with 1,315,000 inhabitants.

Greece

The distribution patterns of the nearly 9m. Greeks (1971) are exceedingly complex. If we exclude the Athens–Salonika urban area, densities vary from a low of 34 per km² in Epirus and Thessaly in the north to 80 in Ionia and 145 on Corfu, islands off the western coast (Fig. 4.2). To a large extent the variations in rural density result from contrasts in agricultural intensity, which in turn reflects differences in environmental quality (especially relief and precipitation), kinds of crops grown, and availability of water for irrigation. The highland regions which account for roughly two-thirds of the area of the mainland support less than two-fifths of its population. There has been a gradual depopulation of the mountain areas of Greece over the past half century, a clear replication of the recent history of settlement in Italy. In the lowlands densities are highest in areas of intensive horticulture, where crops like citrus, deciduous fruits, and tobacco are the staples. In contrast, regions of grain farming and pastoralism support far lower numbers.

Like most of southern Europe, Greece, too, has experienced a shift of its population to urban centers. Thus, in 1940 less than 33% of the nation's inhabitants lived in communities with over 10,000 population. By 1961 that share had risen to over 43%, and it was probably higher a decade later. Athens and Salonika are the two major agglomerations; together they accounted for 35% of the Grecian population in 1971. Over 2.5m. lived in Greater Athens, while more than 0.5m. resided in Salonika, the chief urban center of eastern Greece.

It was noted earlier that the Portuguese population had suffered a decline over the past decade despite relatively high birth rates. Greece, in contrast, with a significantly lower birth rate (16 per 1000) has shown a steady increase in the number of inhabitants, the growth during the period 1961–71 being almost 11%, or close to what it was in the previous decade. The difference between the two countries is apparently a result of differing levels of emigration. In the Portuguese case, the economy continues to be based almost exclusively on agriculture; in contrast, Greece appears to be on the road toward industrialization. The movement is admittedly slow, but domestic and foreign funds are being channeled into a variety of industrial ventures, resulting, in part, from a state-sponsored regional development program. No such movement appears on the immediate horizon for Portugal.

References

Cipolla, Carlo (1965), Four centuries of Italian demographic development, in D. Glass and D. Eversley (eds.), *Population in History*, Chicago, pp. 570–87.

Cole, John (1964), *Italy*, London.

Dickinson, Robert (1955), *The Population Problem of Southern Italy*, Syracuse.

Kish, George (1969), *Italy*, New York.

Kosínski, Leszek (1970), *The Population of Europe*, London.

Pounds, Norman (1969), The urbanization of the classical world, *Annals of the Association of American Geographers*, **59**, 135–7.

Rodgers, Allan (1976), Migration and industrial development: the southern Italian experience, *Economic Geography* **46**, (2), 111–36.

Toniolo, A. R. (1937), Studies of depopulation in the mountains of Italy, *Geographical Review* **27**, 473–7.

Way, Ruth (1962), *A Geography of Spain and Portugal*, London.

Walker, David (1958), *A Geography of Italy*, New York.

Wise, Michael (1954), Population pressure and national resources: some observations upon the Italian population problem, *Economic Geography*, **30**, 144–56.

CHAPTER 5

USSR: POPULATION IN THE PAST AND ITS PRESENT DISTRIBUTION

PAUL E. LYDOLPH

University of Wisconsin—Milwaukee, USA

Introduction

The Soviet Union is a relatively new country but it occupies the territory put together by the Russian Tsars over half a millennium by the accretion of peripheral territories that were occupied by diverse groups of people. Tsarist Russia in turn evolved from a complex background of population movement and settlement on the East European Plain that dates back to at least the third or fourth millennium BC. The present population of the Soviet Union, then, is a polyglot, rather than a meld, of widely varying groups of peoples whose long occupance of the same territories has developed and perpetuated traditions and attitudes which are now so deeply ingrained that even the monolithic Soviet system has not been able to alter them very rapidly. This diversity lends color to the Soviet population, but it also presents many internal problems to the Soviet regime.

Population Growth and Redistribution in the Past

What was to become the Russian Empire had its beginnings in the region around Moscow in the thirteenth to fifteenth centuries AD. During the sixteenth and seventeenth centuries the Russians pushed southward and eastward from this core region into the rich black soil grassland regions west of the Urals, and the wooded steppe in particular became a continuously settled land with agriculture occupying all of the usable acreage. At about the same time Russian adventurers and pioneers in small numbers swept completely across the vast area of Siberia to the Pacific Ocean and thus secured that domain. Agricultural development in Siberia at this time was minor; the prime interest was in the collection of pelts from the native peoples who did the actual hunting and trapping. The first official estimate of population within the Russian Empire was given as 17.9m. in 1724.

The 1897 Census

The first all-Russian census taken in 1897 counted approximately 125m. people in the empire; they were concentrated mainly in the European part of the country west of the

Volga River. Population was most dense in the highly urbanized area around Moscow where Moscow Province averaged between 60 and 80 persons per km². The density was equally great in parts of the western Ukraine. Much of the rest of the European part of the country averaged between 25 and 60 persons per km². Generally densities were greater in the transitional forest steppe than in either the forest belt to the north or the true steppe to the south. Belorussia, with its poor drainage conditions, stood out as an area of lesser density, while St. Petersburg Province, containing the capital city, had emerged as a region of higher density than its surroundings.

By 1897 the ecumene of the country had pretty well taken shape. An eastward tapering wedge of above average density of population extended from the western border of the country eastward across the Urals into southwestern Siberia where it butted up against the Altay Mountains, beyond which it continued eastward to the Pacific in the form of discontinuous clusters coincident with scattered intermountain basins. The middle and southern Urals averaged between 5 and 15 persons per km², and much of western Siberia and what is now Kazakhstan averaged between 1 and 5 persons per km². Much of the rest of Siberia and the Far East, as well as the northern part of European Russia, averaged less than 1 person per km². Two significant outliers of population were the Caucasus and Central Asia.

This distribution of population very closely correlated with the agricultural potentials of the land. The wedge across the central portion of the country occupied the natural zones of the mixed forest, wooded steppe, and steppe in the west, and the wooded steppe and steppe in the east. The wooded steppe and steppe zones contain the famous "black earths" of Russia whose color reflects their high humus content produced by their development under natural grass vegetation. Although drought is a hazard in these grassland zones, the soils are so fertile that such areas offer the greatest potentials for agriculture.

This general distribution of population at the close of the nineteenth century, which fits so closely the agricultural potentials of the land, has been maintained essentially the same down to the present time. The growth of population since 1897 and the urbanization and industrialization that have taken place primarily during the Soviet period have generally increased population densities throughout the settled portions of the country and have produced intensified nodes of urban population in regions that have spawned large cities for one reason or another, but the basic pattern of population distribution has not changed significantly during the last 75 years.

The census of 1897 also recorded the numbers of people who had moved into and out of individual areas. Those regions that were receiving the greatest influx of population immediately prior to 1897 were the Far East and most of Siberia, particularly Tomsk Province which contained the Kuznetsk Coal Basin. In many of these provinces more than 30% of the resident population had recently moved in from other regions of the Russian Empire. The only other area which had such high in-migration was the soil-rich Kuban territory of the northern Caucasus. Much of the European part of the country was experiencing heavy out-migration. This was particularly true of the central provinces as well as of some provinces in the west and northwest, where more than 12% of the population had moved to other parts of the empire.

A striking feature of the eastern or Pacific regions, already observable at that time, was the high degree of out-migration as well as in-migration, which signified the unrest of the peoples of those regions and their transitory nature. This was particularly true in

Sakhalin Province. The high mobility of the eastern populations is still one of the characteristic features of these regions, and it plagues the economic planners because of the very high labor turnover.

By 1897 the urbanization process was already under way. Urban in-migration was quite high throughout much of the country, and was particularly high in the Far East and certain provinces of Central Asia and Kazakhstan. The pattern of rural in-migration was significantly different. The Far East still appeared as an area of high in-migration for rural population as well as urban, but there was no rural in-migration to speak of in the southern regions other than in Kuban district in the North Caucasus. Rural in-migration was rather heavy in western Siberia, particularly in Tomsk Province, and a significant rural in-migration was going on throughout much of eastern Siberia. Most of the European part of the country was losing population through migration processes.

Summary of Migration, 1500–1900

Over this period of several centuries the mixed forest zone of the European part of the country served as a reservoir of natural population growth which supplied migrants to new outlying regions as the Russian Empire expanded. The wooded steppe zone to the southeast, as well as the coniferous forest zone to the northeast, first received an influx of population from the earlier settled mixed forest zone, and later joined the mixed forest zone to form a larger reservoir of population which sent people to other parts of the expanding empire.

Much of the steppe zone in southern European Russia, southern Siberia, and northern Kazakhstan received immigrants during this long period as Russian control continually extended the frontier southeastward into the drier steppes where the rich soils enticed agricultural settlers. This was particularly true in the eighteenth and nineteenth centuries when the more humid parts of the steppe regions experienced a rapid transition from an economy of nomadic and seminomadic herding to one that was predominantly based on sedentary agriculture.

The initial wave of Russians moving across Siberia left little imprint on the land, since there were too few Cossacks to do more than exercise nominal control over the region and exact tribute from the natives in the form of furs.

The first modern settlers penetrated into the Far East from the Transbaykal region in 1855. They were largely Cossacks who had been discharged from governmental services and were granted rather extensive tracts of land. They were joined by Cossacks and peasants from the Urals and as far west as the Ukraine, and by a much larger arrival of Ukrainians brought in by the long sea route through the Suez Canal and Singapore Straits. After the completion of the Trans-Siberian Railroad in the 1890s the sea traffic dwindled to nothing, and a new wave made up of individual peasant families who arrived by rail encroached upon the large communal landholdings of the original Cossack villages.

Intercensal period 1897–1926

Between the 1897 census and that of 1926 so much chaos occurred in the Russian area that it is impossible to follow the trends of population growth and distribution through the intervening period. As a result of World War I and the Revolution, the Soviets lost Finland, the Baltic republics, and Poland. The 1926 census counted little more than 147m. persons in the newly formed Soviet Union, up only 22m. from what it was 30 years earlier. The average birth rate was a little lower than it had been in 1897, and the death rate was considerably lower, so that the natural increase was significantly higher than in 1897. Life expectancy had been increased from 32 years in 1897 to 44 years in 1926 (Table 5.1). But the chaos of World War I and the ensuing revolutions and civil strife had taken their toll, and the 1926 population pyramid showed a constricted number of children in the 5–9 age group and significantly more women than men in ages above 15 (see Fig. 6.3).

The war, revolutions, and civil strife also acted to arrest the processes of urbanization and industrialization that were beginning to make headway before World War I. The percentage of the population classified as urban rose from 12.4 in 1897 to 18.0 in 1914, but at the time of the 1926 census it still was no higher than it had been in 1914 (Table 5.1). The portion of the labor force in agriculture actually rose from 57.6% of the total in 1897 to 65.1% in 1926. Industry had occupied 13.4% of the labor force in 1897, and in 1926 it occupied only 12.1%.

The population density map for 1926 reveals a general increase in densities throughout the occupied territory of the country. Rural population densities of more than 70 people per km^2 characterized the central Ukraine west of the Dnieper River, and rural densities between 50 and 70 persons per km^2 continued the high density zone eastward and north-eastward into the Central Black Earth Region of Russia. The population was predominantly rural throughout the country except in Moscow and Leningrad Oblasts.

Intercensal period 1926–39

During the 1926–39 intercensal period the birth and death rates continued to drop as urbanization increased rapidly, and the natural increase of the population remained fairly constant through the period at about 1.9% per year. The life expectancy continued to creep slowly upward. In 1939 the total population of the Soviet Union was estimated to be 170,467,000, of which almost one-third were urban dwellers. The age–sex structure of the population had not changed greatly since 1926.

The population distribution continued much as it had been, but with population densities increasing throughout the settled areas and with a rapid growth of clusters of cities in the Central Industrial Region around Moscow, in the Donets Coal Basin of the eastern Ukraine, and in many individual cities along the Trans-Siberian Railroad in southern Siberia and the Far East.

The industrialization drive got under way in the Soviet Union with the initiation of the five-year plans in 1928. This induced a rapid influx of people into the cities and brought about for the first time absolute decreases in rural population over large portions of the western half of the country. That process has continued down to the present time, and the rural population has continued to decrease in practically all regions except Central Asia and parts of the Caucasus.

Between the 1926 and 1939 censuses it appears that more than 4m. persons migrated to Siberia, the Far East, and Kazakhstan. This was approximately equivalent to one-fifth of the natural population increase in the country during the period. It seems that during

TABLE 5.1. POPULATION OF RUSSIA AND THE USSR

Year	Source	Population (000's)		Percent				Rates per 1000			Life expectancy (years)		
		Pre-1939 boundaries	Post-1939 boundaries	Urban	Rural	Male	Female	Births	Deaths	Natural increase	Male	Female	Total
1724	1	17,900						43.7	27.1	16.6			
1801	2	37,540						52.4	39.4	13.0			
1850	2	68,513		5.5	94.5			48.7	34.2	14.5			
1880	2	97,705		12.9	87.1								
1897	2 (3)	125,640	(124,600)	12.4	87.6	(49.0)	(51.0)	49.4	32.4	17.0	(31)	(33)	(32)
1913	2 (3)	161,723		14.6	85.4	(49.7)	(50.3)	(47.0)	(30.2)	(16.8)			33[4]
1920	2	137,093		16.7	83.3			29.1	38.1	–9.0			
1926	2 (3)	147,028		17.9	82.1	(48.3)	(51.7)	(44.0)	(20.3)	(23.7)	41.0	45.1	44[4]
1939	2 (3)	170,467		32.9	67.1	(47.9)	(52.1)	(36.5)	(17.3)	(19.2)			47[4]
1950	3		178,500	39	61	43.9	56.1	26.7	9.7	17.0			
1959	3		208,827	48	52	45.0	55.0	25.0	7.6	17.4			
1970	3		241,720	56	44	46.1	53.9	17.4	8.2	9.2	65	74	70
August 9 1973	5		250,000	59	41				8.5				70

Sources:
1. Lorimer, Frank, *The Population of the Soviet Union: History and Prospects*, League of Nations' Geneva, 1946.
2. Eason, Warren W., *Soviet Manpower: The Population and Labor Force of the USSR*, University Microfilms, Ann Arbor, 1959.
3. *Narodnoye khozyaystvo SSSR v 1970g.*, Statistika, Moscow, 1971.
4. Osipov, G. V. (ed.), *Town, Country, and People*, Studies in Soviet Society, vol. 2, Tavistock Publications, London, 1969.
5. *Soviet News*, August 14, 1973, p. 360.

Note: Census dates are in italics.

this time an equilibrium was reached between population and resources in the south, so that the movement southward essentially ceased.

Intercensal period 1939–59

The intercensal period 1939–59, of course, was a very abnormal period because of World War II. Shortly after the 1939 census was taken, about 20m. people were added to the Soviet Union by the annexation of the Baltic republics and parts of Finland, Poland, and Romania. Later, during the war, Tanu Tuva became a part of the Soviet Union, and at the end of the war the Soviet Union acquired the eastern end of Czecho-slovakia and the southern half of Sakhalin Island and the Kuril Island chain.

The war produced chaos in the most heavily populated parts of European USSR and caused great losses of life, particularly of young men of military age and of infants. In addition, there were great birth deficits as families were not being formed and children were not being born. It is unknown exactly what the war losses were, but it has been estimated that as many as 25m.–30m. excess deaths may have occurred because of war related causes and as many as 15m. births might not have been realized because of the war. The cities suffered most from the ravages of war and recuperated most slowly afterward. Although births increased significantly in the cities after the war, they were fewer than in the countryside. Thus in 1959 there were many more children in the rural population than in the urban.

Regardless of the war, birth and death rates declined continually throughout the 1939–59 period as industrialization and urbanization took place. The natural growth rate remained steady at around 17 per 1000 after a sharp drop during the war (Table 5.1). In 1959 the national birth rate was 25 per 1000, the death rate was 7.6 per 1000, and the natural increase was 17.4 per 1000.

At the end of the war mass exchanges of people took place in border areas where territories had been transferred. About 1.8m. Poles and Jews were expatriated to Poland and 500,000 Ukrainians, Belorussians, and Lithuanians were moved into the Soviet Union.

The net effect on population distribution during the 1939–59 period was to add about 18m. people to the regions east of the Urals. The other 20m. gained during the period were accounted for by the addition of new territories in the west. Thus, the 20 year period which included World War II resulted in only an 18m. increase in population if the 20m. new people in the west are discounted. And all of the 18m. population increase occurred in the eastern regions. While the entire Soviet population increased 7.7%, the population of the Urals increased 32%, western Siberia 24%, eastern Siberia 34%, the Far East 70%, Kazakhstan 53%, and Middle Asia 30% (Fig. 5.1). During the 20 year span, the share of the East in the total population of the country rose from 29% to 35%. During the 1939–59 period the population of "old Russia" remained almost exactly the same.

Intercensal Period 1959–70

During this last intercensal period the Soviet population increased by 16% or an average of about 1.5% per year, and reached a total of 242m. But the growth rate varied

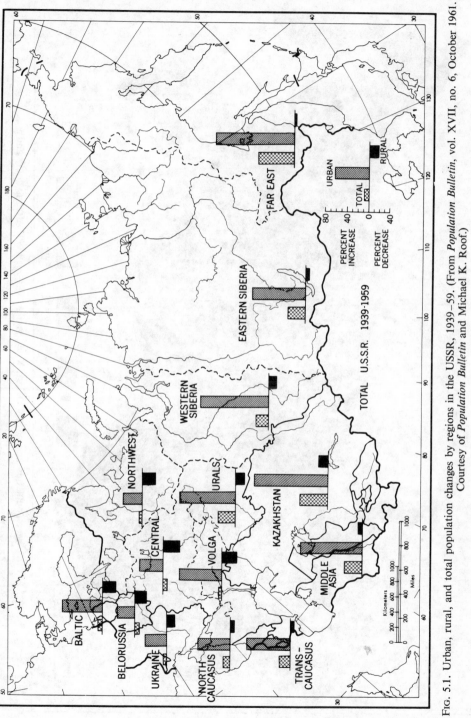

FIG. 5.1. Urban, rural, and total population changes by regions in the USSR, 1939–59. (From *Population Bulletin*, vol. XVII, no. 6, October 1961. Courtesy of *Population Bulletin* and Michael K. Roof.)

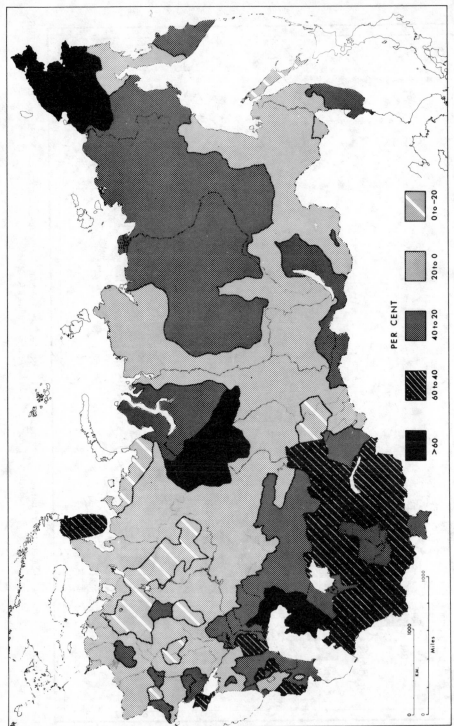

Fig. 5.2. Percentage population changes by Oblast, Kray, and ASSR, 1959–70. After Lydolph and Pease.

among regions (Fig. 5.2). Most striking is the fact that while in the two previous inter-censal periods it was the eastern regions (Urals, Siberia, the Far East, and Kazakhstan) that grew most rapidly percentagewise in number of inhabitants, due largely to a net in-migration, these same regions grew at a rate below the national average in the 1959–70 intercensal period—the Urals only 7%, western Siberia 8%, and eastern Siberia 15%. Evidently sometime in the 1950s the direction of net migration flow had reversed, and what had earlier been a west-to-east movement had changed to one in an opposite direction. The population growth that took place in the eastern regions during the latest intercensal period was in almost all cases due to natural increase; the net migration for most of the eastern regions was negative. In some parts of the eastern regions there was an actual loss in total numbers. To be sure, there were certain sections within the eastern regions that grew rapidly percentagewise, but these were generally sparsely settled areas where large numbers of inhabitants were not involved. The three regions which experi-enced the greatest percentage increases, all of this type, owed their rapid growth rates to newly initiated mining activities.

Any cartographic representation of percentage population changes by regions entails distortions in visual impressions because of the great differences in sizes of regions and differences in their population densities (Fig. 5.2). In order to reduce this erroneous impression a map has been prepared showing absolute increases of population per area, in other words population growth density (Fig. 5.3). Using this index, practically all of Siberia and the Far East are smoothed out into an extensive region which shows the lowest population increase of the entire country. On the other hand, many smaller regions of higher population densities which showed only moderate percentage growth rates now show up as areas having extremely high growth densities. Such are the highly urbanized and industrialized oblasts of Moscow, Kiev, and Donetsk, as well as such heavily populated, relatively small territories as the Crimea, Moldavia, and Armenia. It can now be seen that in terms of absolute numbers the highest growths by far during 1959–70 were in the southern portions of the country, particularly in a discontinuous belt extending eastward from western Ukraine across Moldavia and southeastern Ukraine, the North Caucasus and the Transcaucasus, into portions of Central Asia.

Present Distribution of Total Population—Summary

Generalizing the current spatial distribution of people over the vast domain of the USSR, probably the most striking feature is the unevenness of its distribution, and this in spite of the fact that plains and lowlands greatly predominate (Fig. 5.4). Mountainous terrain is chiefly confined to eastern Siberia. Notwithstanding the country's recent industrialization and urbanization, the gross pattern of population distribution still pretty much reflects the agricultural potential of the land. The country's East European Plain, which for centuries has been a crossroads of population movement, comprises less than one-sixth of the national territory, but it contains close to two-thirds of the total population. Within the European Plain settlement is concentrated in the western and central parts where the agricultural potential is highest. There rainfall, temperature, and soil conditions are most suitable for sedentary agriculture. Population thins out very rapidly north of about latitude 50° where climatic and soil handicaps become serious, and it thins also to the south and east where the climate becomes too dry.

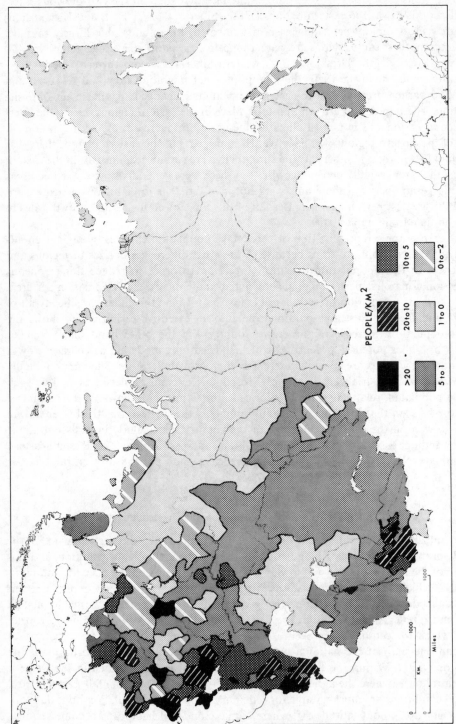

Fig. 5.3. Population growth densities by Oblast, Kray, and ASSR, 1959–70. After Lydolph and Pease.

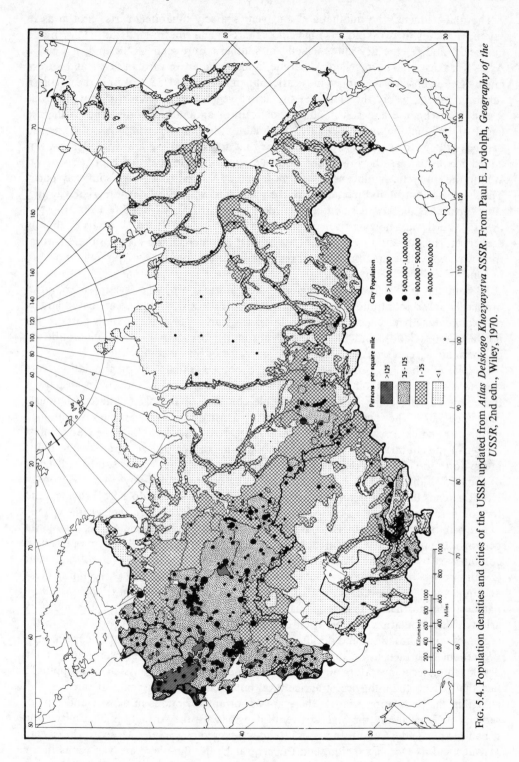

FIG. 5.4. Population densities and cities of the USSR updated from *Atlas Delskogo Khozyaystva SSSR*. From Paul E. Lydolph, *Geography of the USSR*, 2nd edn., Wiley, 1970.

The non-ecumene, the uninhabited and very sparsely inhabited parts, enormous in extent, is mainly of two kinds: (1) the cold subarctic and tundra lands of the north and northeast, and (2) the dry lands, chiefly in southern European USSR and in Central Asia–Kazakhstan. The repellent subarctic lands broaden toward the east and so are much more extensively developed in Asiatic than in European USSR. Within the northern subarctic region, where the characteristic native vegetation cover is mainly coniferous forest, both climatic and soil handicaps discourage agricultural settlement. While the frigid winters may be hard to endure, it is mainly the short growing season, or period between killing frosts, and the cool summers that act to limit the growing of crops. But added handicaps are the low grade podzolic soils and the prevalence of permafrost. Within the subarctic significant settlement is mainly limited to its most southerly parts. This is especially true in Siberia, where the main routeway, the Trans-Siberian rail line, closely parallels the USSR's southern border. Noteworthy also is the fact that most of the large northward-flowing rivers in subarctic USSR are paralleled by bands of slightly denser settlement, reflecting no doubt the modest commercial use made of these natural routeways, as well as the somewhat more favorable conditions for agriculture that prevail in some of the riverine lowlands.

In both the cold and the dry regions where normal cropping is largely excluded, ordinarily only discontinuous and scattered settlements exist, and these are based largely on exploitive activities such as mining, lumbering, and a few river mouth ports in the northern forest lands, and nomadic herding in the dry country. Without doubt the northern lands represent the modern pioneer fringe of Slavic colonization.

In spite of what has been said previously about a gradual shift of population from west to east, the USSR's inhabitants still remain concentrated in the European part of the country where some 70% of the people continue to live. Here the continuously populated part of the country, where population density exceeds 65 per km^2, is contained within a triangular or wedge shaped area whose broad base lies along the westernmost border of the country, and extends from about the latitude of Leningrad on the Baltic in the north to Odessa on the northwest shore of the Black Sea in the south, a distance of some 1500 km (Fig. 5.4). From that western base the population wedge in European USSR extends eastward in an ever narrowing belt across the middle Volga valley and the southern Ural Mountains into western Siberia, with its apex in the general vicinity of Novosibirsk and the Kuznetsk coal field and its industrial concentration. As a narrower belt of settlement, a few hundred miles wide, astride the Trans-Siberian railroad, it continues eastward to the shores of Lake Baikal, beyond which, and even to the Pacific Ocean, it exists in the form of isolated spots of settlement coincident with mining areas and moderately fertile valleys and basins. Everywhere the population triangle is terminated on the north by subarctic climate and its low grade soils, and on the south by aridity. The population triangle itself corresponds rather closely in areal extent to the region of mixed broadleaf and deciduous forest, wooded steppe, and pure steppe natural vegetation, with their associated brown podzolic, black, and chestnut soils, all of them developed under temperature and rainfall conditions that are permissive for cropping, a fact that reflects the influence of agricultural potentialities on original settlement.

Within the population triangle there are important variations in density and type of settlement. Expectantly the highest overall densities are the strongly industrialized and urbanized parts: the Central Industrial Region centered on Greater Moscow, the eastern Ukraine and its Dombas region, and the central Urals. But there are variations in the density of rural settlements as well, with the highest densities lying west of the Volga and extending from the Carpathians across the region of better soils in the wooded steppe into the intensively developed black earth country, which earlier suffered from a pervasive overpopulation, and from which there has been a strong out-migration. Similar high rural densities prevail in the Moscow region and eastward from there to the Volga.

Lying well beyond the southern borders of the great population triangle, where population densities in general exceed 65 per km², and separated from it by extensive dry country, are two important outliers of relatively dense settlement, one in the Caucasus region (27m. inhabitants) and the other in parts of Central Asia (14m.–15m.). Both population clusters owe much of their close settlement to the greater availability of water. In the Caucasus region the high east–west mountain range separates a dominantly Russian population on the north from Transcaucasia to the south where there is a mixture of ethnic groups including Turks, Azers, Georgians, and Armenians. That part north of the Caucasus, with some 15m. inhabitants, has sufficient rainfall over its western black earth steppe to support moderately dense, widely distributed settlement; on the higher piedmont greater availability of irrigation water, together with petroleum resources, has resulted in greater localized densities than in the steppe lands. South of the Caucasus, in Transcaucasia (12m.–13m.), where the climate is milder, and in general more humid, lowland densities are still higher, with the small plain at the eastern end of the Black Sea supporting over 325 persons per km². Dense settlement is also found in the oil fields around Baku.

The region of Soviet Central Asia and southern Kazakhstan, situated east of the Caspian Sea, exhibits striking contrasts in density of settlement between the relatively empty desert steppe lowland and the crowded oases along the highland margins on the east and south. In this dry land nearly everywhere water is the key to settlement. Over the extensive dry lowlands in general, where nomadic Turkish peoples prevail, low population densities of between 8 and 26 per km² are the rule. The main exceptions lie within two corridors of irrigated land which follow the courses of the Amu and Syr Darya from their mountain sources across the dry lowlands to where these streams empty into the Aral Sea. Within these Nilotic riverine strips settlement densities of 195–325 per km² are prevalent. But the population of Soviet Central Asia is concentrated, not on the dry lowlands, but on the rich alluvial and loess soils of the foothill basins and the piedmont belt of the mountain borderlands along the east and south where irrigation water is available from numerous mountain streams. Some non-irrigated farming is practiced, to be sure, and even in such localities population density usually exceeds 195 per km² and in places it may be over 650. But settlement is much denser in the oasis localities. Among the latter the Ferghana Basin is outstanding, for there the inhabitants number 3200–5150 per km². Large nucleated villages and cities are numerous, some of the latter like Tashkent, Samarkand, and Bukhara having great fame as ancient centers of commerce and culture situated on old caravan routes connecting the Orient with the Middle East and Europe. In Soviet Central Asia, with its 14m.–15m. inhabitants, native Asian peoples (Uzbeks, Kazakhs, Tazhiks, Turkmen, Kirgiz) still make up the predominant element. But during recent decades there has been a large in-migration of other nationalities, especially Slavic groups (Russians and Armenians), but also Jews, Germans, Poles, and others, with the result that the present population has a motley composition.

Over the whole USSR population densities in individual political units vary from as low as 0.02 per km² in the Evenki NO in central Siberia to 280.6 per km² in heavily urbanized Moscow Oblast and 261.5 per km² in predominantly rural, irrigated Andizhan Oblast in the Fergana Basin of Central Asia. Some 27.9% of the country has less than one person per km², and 68.6% of the entire country has a population density of less than 5 per km². Less than 2% of the territory of the entire country has a population density of more than 75 per km². The bulk of the population, 63.2%, live in areas with population densities between 10 and 75 per km²; 9.3% of the total population lives on 0.4% of the land which has population densities of more than 150 per km² (Table 5.2).

TABLE 5.2. DISTRIBUTION OF THE SOVIET POPULATION BY
DENSITY CATEGORIES, 1969

People per km²	1000 km²	1000 people	% of total	
			People	Area
< 1.0	6,210.0	2,736	1.1	27.9
1.1– 5.0	9,063.2	20,685	8.7	40.7
5.1– 10.0	1,558.5	10,219	4.3	7.0
10.1– 25.0	2,470.2	39,465	16.5	11.1
25.1– 50.0	1,757.6	65,987	27.6	7.9
50.1– 75.0	778.4	45,667	19.1	3.5
75.1–100.0	174.5	14,271	6.0	0.8
100.1–150.0	163.4	17,642	7.4	0.7
>150	100.5	22,233	9.3	0.4
Total	22,276.3	238,905	100.0	100.0

Source: Valentey and Sorokina (eds.), *Naselenie trudovye resursy SSSR*, p. 141.

In the countryside the rural population generally lives in small clusters, ranging in size all the way from individual households, most numerous in the northwest part of the country, to communities with more than 5000 population, these being most common in the southern part. In 1970 7.1% of the rural population lived in units of less than 100 inhabitants, 49.1% lived in settlements with populations between 100 and 1000, and 43.8% in settlements with populations of more than 1000 inhabitants each. During the 1959–70 period large rural settlements grew at the expense of middle sized and small settlements.

The largest rural settlements are generally found in the southern part of the country, particularly in western Ukraine, Moldavia, the North Caucasus, Armenia, and southeastern Kazakhstan where more than 70% of the rural population live in villages of more than 1000 inhabitants each. The smallest settlements are most numerous in the northwestern part of the country where more than 40% of the rural population lives in villages of fewer than 100 inhabitants each. Throughout the large remaining territory of the country, including central European USSR and most of Siberia and the Far East, the rural population lives primarily in intermediate sized villages.

In 1970 21.2% of the urban population lived in small cities of less than 20,000 population; 23.2% lived in cities with populations between 20,000 and 100,000; 28.2% in communities with populations between 100,000 and 500,000; 19.7% in places with populations between 500,000 and 2m.; and 7.7% lived in Moscow and Leningrad. Except for the two largest cities, a greater percentage of the urban population resided in larger cities in 1970 than in 1959; 47.9% of the total urban population lived in cities with populations between 100,000 and 2m. in 1970, but only 40.1% in 1959.

CHAPTER 6

USSR: CHARACTERISTICS OF THE PRESENT POPULATION

PAUL E. LYDOLPH

University of Wisconsin—Milwaukee, USA

Vital Rates and Age–Sex Structure

At the time of the most recent Soviet census on January 15, 1970, the Soviet Union had a total population of 241,720,000 people, which made it the third most populous nation on earth after China and India. The crude birth rate was 17.4 per 1000 and the death rate was 8.2, so that the natural increase was 9.2 per 1000. The life expectancy for men was 65 years and for women 74 years; 46.1% of the total population were men and 53.9% were women (see Table 5.1). Since the census the population has grown to exceed 250m.

Age–sex structure, which is closely interrelated with vital rates, is still very abnormal in the USSR (Fig. 6.1). There are constrictions of numbers in the age groups centering on 51, which represent the birth deficits during the tumultuous years of the beginnings of the Bolshevik regime; those centering on 36, which probably relate to the havoc and famine that resulted from the collectivization of agriculture in the early 1930s; and those centering on 26, which represent the birth deficits during World War II. In addition, in the age groups above 38, females outnumber males, and the discrepancy between the sexes becomes greater with increasing age.

By age 65 women outnumber men more than 2 to 1. This sex discrepancy is due to the facts that more men than women have lost their lives during times of strife, and that under normal circumstances women on the average live longer than men.

The reduction of numbers below the age of 9 in 1970 is due to two factors: the coming to age of the "thin generation," the surviving babies of World War II, who are now becoming the primary parents of the present generation of newborn; and a significantly declining fertility rate in all ages of women, which reflects growing antinatalist attitudes among Soviet women.

In spite of its generally pronatalist intentions, the Soviet government has been faced with ideological tenets and economic realities which have resulted in governmental policies and individual actions which in most cases have had antinatalist results. Half-hearted governmental attempts to compensate women for having children have been counterbalanced by the ideological premise that parents have the right to decide whether or not a child should be born. This has led to free and legal abortions during much of the Soviet period and wide dissemination of contraceptives and birth control information.

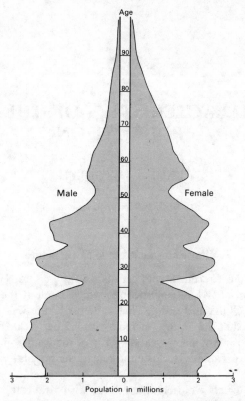

FIG. 6.1. USSR; age–sex structure of the population, 1970.

In addition, the rapidly expanding economy and the shortage of adult men in the popula-tion have acted to urge women to enter the labor force. Low family incomes have also induced the wife to seek outside work. In 1971 women made up 51% of the total labor force of the country; the 1959 census showed that 67% of all women above the age of 16 were economically active. This, of course, has had antinatalist effects, as has also the widespread prevalence of scarce housing. The aggregate results of these multiple influ-ences have been decreasing birth and death rates and, in the last decade or so, reduced natural increase, features common to all societies that are undergoing industrialization and urbanization (Fig. 6.2).

Before the Bolshevik Revolution birth and death rates were both high and the natural increase was moderate. Birth rates declined drastically during the 1930s as the industrial-ization drive got under way, accompanied by a large rural–urban migration. At the same time, with improved living conditions and health standards, the death rate declined moderately, while the natural increase dropped rapidly. During World War II the birth rate plunged—no one knows how much. After the war birth rates and death rates decreased at about the same rate until around 1960, so that natural increase remained essentially constant from 1950 to 1960. However, after 1960 there was a renewed drop in the birth rate, and the death rate leveled off and even began to increase a little as the population became older. Thus, at the present time the USSR has a low birth rate, low death rate, low natural increase, and an aging population.

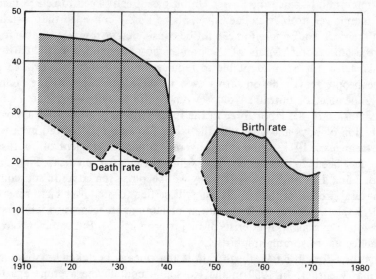

FIG. 6.2. USSR; birth and death rates per 1000 inhabitants, 1913–71.

The death rate reached a low of only 6.9 per 1000 in 1964. Since then it has risen slowly as the population aged. In 1971 it was estimated at 8.2 per 1000. The birth rate reached a low of 17 per 1000 in 1969 after which it has risen slightly. In 1971 it was estimated at 17.8 per 1000. Natural increase also reached a minimum in 1969 with 8.9 per 1000. In 1971 it was estimated at 9.6 per 1000.

The plunging birth rate between 1960 and 1969 can be largely attributed to the coming to age of the "thin generation" of World War II babies. But it cannot all be attributed to that. Generally fertility rates have been decreasing in all age groups of women since pre-World War II days. Overall, the fertility of women between the ages of 15 and 49 reached a low point of 65.7 per 1000 women in 1969–70, and since then it has risen only slightly. Whether this slight upturn is the beginning of a trend or is simply an oscillation about some leveling-off point cannot yet be determined.

Soviet Concern About Fertility

Most Soviet leaders consider an actively growing population to be a good thing and agree that a stimulation of the presently sagging birth rate is desirable. Such attitudes probably reflect the traumatic experiences of the past rather than rational thoughts about the inevitable consequences for the future. The first 30 years of the Soviet period were filled with so many catastrophies that the average annual growth rate of the population was reduced to less than half that of the United States. Only during the 1950s and early part of the 1960s has the USSR experienced rapid population growth. The Soviets have become so conditioned by these past events that they automatically view with alarm any drop in the growth rate. Their fears range all the way from such vague ideas that the future prestige of the Soviet Union depends upon its maintaining its relative standing in world population, to such precise problems as the manning of new industries in an ever expanding economy. The latter concern probably takes precedence in most people's minds, since the Soviet Union has already been forced to face up to a number of manpower problems. The Soviets have finally conceded that certain unused elements of their present population cannot be considered as reserves eligible for recruitment into the labor force. Many of the non-Slavic nationalities, particularly those in Central Asia, have not been adaptable to regular hours of factory work. In addition, most of the people remaining on farms even in the Slavic areas of the country, predominantly uneducated, untrained older women, are unsuited to such employment. Thus the expansion of the labor force in the future will have to depend almost entirely on the induction of boys and girls into the labor force at age 16. And even within the present five-year plan, 1971–5, the actual average annual increment of youths into the labor force has been approximately 2m., while the plan is predicated on an annual increment of 2.5m. This obvious discrepancy will become even larger in subsequent years when the natural growth of the population will be tied to the lower birth rates of recent years. Add to this a general maldistribution of labor with respect to labor needs, and one can see looming a manpower crisis of major proportions. But so far the government has been ineffectual in stimulating births.

One suggestion for lifting the birth rate is that means be taken to stimulate young people to marry earlier. In 1959 in the Russian Republic the average age for newly married couples was 29 + for men and 27 + for women, and the ages were increasing. This was considered by many to be one of the prime deterrents to higher birth rates. On the other hand, in Central Asia the average marriage age was in the low twenties and was stable.

A number of demographers and medical personnel, concerned with the high abortion rate and its effects on the health of potential mothers, have called for more effective contraceptives. They have pointed out that in 1965 there were about 2.5 times as many abortions as there were live births. They argue that an abortion reduces the likelihood of a woman having a child for many months afterward. Therefore if abortions can be reduced by the use of better contraceptives, this might in the long run stimulate births.

Regional Variations in Vital Rates

The Soviet population is far from homogeneous, and different backgrounds and different ways of life result in wide regional differences in birth rates, natural growth rates, and population age–sex structures (Table 6.1). Such structures vary with nationality and region, and between city and country within regions. The greatest differences exist among nationality groups. The Baltic and Slavic groups have much lower birth and natural increase rates than do the Central Asians and Transcaucasians. Currently the two extreme cases at the union republic level are the Latvians (in Baltic USSR) and the Tadzhiks (in Central Asia). In 1971 the Latvian SSR had a birth rate of 14.7 per 1000, a death rate of 11.0, and a natural increase of only 3.7. The Tadzhik SSR had a birth rate of 36.8 per 1000, a death rate of 5.7, and a natural increase of 31.1. Thus the Tadzhik Republic at the present time has a population natural growth rate that is almost nine times greater than that of the Latvian Republic. This, coupled with the fact that the latter has suffered much more from recent wars and civil strife, has produced tremendous differences in the age–sex distributions of the two populations.

The large Russian Republic, which contains more than half of the total population

TABLE 6.1. BIRTHS, DEATHS, AND NATURAL INCREASES BY REPUBLIC AND ECONOMIC REGION, PER 1000 POPULATION

Republic and economic region	1950 Births	1950 Deaths	1950 Natural increase	1960 Births	1960 Deaths	1960 Natural increase	1971 Births	1971 Deaths	1971 Natural increase
USSR	26.7	9.7	17.0	24.9	7.1	17.8	17.8	8.2	9.6
RSFSR	26.9	10.1	16.8	23.2	7.4	15.8	15.1	8.7	6.4
Northwest	25.2	10.1	15.1	20.6	7.5	13.1			
Center	22.1	8.9	13.2	18.5	7.8	10.7			
Volga–Vyatka	27.2	10.8	16.4	24.6	8.0	16.6			
Central Black Earth	21.7	8.3	13.4	21.8	7.7	14.1			
Volga	26.0	9.8	16.2	25.6	7.6	18.0			
North Caucasus	22.1	7.7	14.4	24.0	7.2	16.8			
Urals	31.9	11.8	20.1	25.1	7.3	17.8			
W. Siberia	32.9	12.0	20.9	26.7	6.9	19.8			
E. Siberia	36.0	12.2	23.8	27.7	6.8	20.9			
Far East	42.5	14.0	28.5	24.9	6.2	18.7			
Ukraine	22.8	8.5	14.3	20.5	6.9	13.6	15.4	8.9	6.5
Donets–Dnieper	22.5	7.6	14.9	19.9	6.6	13.3			
Southwest	23.3	9.6	13.7	21.3	7.2	14.1			
South	22.6	7.5	15.1	19.9	6.9	13.0			
Baltic	22.1	12.5	9.6	19.7	8.7	11.0			
Lithuania	23.6	12.0	11.6	22.5	7.8	14.7	17.6	8.5	9.1
Latvia	17.0	12.4	4.6	16.7	10.0	6.7	14.7	11.0	3.7
Estonia	18.4	14.4	4.0	16.6	10.5	6.1	16.0	10.9	5.1
Kaliningrad Oblast	45.5	10.3	35.2	24.2	4.7	19.5			
Transcaucasus	27.9	8.5	19.4	34.6	6.6	28.0			
Georgia	23.5	7.6	15.9	24.7	6.5	18.2	19.0	7.4	11.6
Azerbaydzhan	31.2	9.6	21.6	42.6	6.7	35.9	27.7	6.5	21.2
Armenia	32.1	8.5	23.6	40.3	6.8	33.5	22.6	4.9	17.7
Central Asia	31.9	8.8	23.1	38.8	6.0	32.8			
Uzbek	30.9	8.8	22.1	39.9	6.0	33.9	34.5	5.4	29.1
Kirgiz	32.4	8.5	23.9	36.8	6.1	30.7	31.6	7.0	24.6
Tadzhik	30.4	8.2	22.2	33.5	5.1	28.4	36.8	5.7	31.1
Turkmen	38.2	10.2	28.0	42.4	6.5	35.9	34.7	6.7	28.0
Kazakh	37.6	11.7	25.9	36.7	6.5	30.2	23.8	6.0	17.8
Belorussia	25.5	8.0	17.5	24.5	6.6	17.9	16.4	7.5	8.9
Moldavia	38.9	11.2	27.7	29.2	6.4	22.8	20.2	7.7	12.5

Sources: *Narodnoye khozyaystvo SSSR v 1967 g.*, pp. 40–41, and Leedy, *Demographic Trends in the USSR*, p. 449.
Note: statistics have not been given for economic regions since 1967.

of the Soviet Union, and which within itself contains many non-Russian nationality groups, shows an age–sex distribution somewhere between these two extremes. But within this huge territory there are regional differences even within the Russian nationality group. The eastern parts of the Russian Republic still tend to have somewhat higher birth rates than do the older settled areas in the west, although these differences are steadily waning as time goes on. Unfortunately regional data within republics have not been made available since 1967, but during that year the two extreme cases within the Russian Republic were the Central Industrial Region, which had a birth rate of 12.0 per 100, a death rate of 8.9, and a natural increase of 3.1, and eastern Siberia, which had a birth rate of 17.2 per 1000, a death rate of 7.1, and a growth rate of 10.1.

Some of this contrast could probably be accounted for by differences in the rural–urban ratio of the two regions. In 1967 the Central Industrial Region was 69% urban and 31% rural, whereas the East Siberian region was 61% urban and 39% rural. Since in most areas the rural population still has a somewhat higher birth rate than the urban population has, one would expect the rural areas to have the higher natural growth rates. But perhaps even more significant are different age structures in different regions which have been brought about by migrations. It is the younger adults who are the most mobile, and therefore those areas which are experiencing in-migration have more people in the highly reproductive age categories than do those areas which are experiencing out-migration. For example, Maritime Kray in the Far East, which has been an area of modest in-migration, has 20.1% of its urban population and 16.1% of its rural population in the age group 20–29. Kirov Oblast, on the other hand, in the Volga–Vyatka region, which historically has been an area of heavy out-migration, has only 13.6% of its urban population and 8.3% of its rural population in the age group 20–29. Since across the entire Soviet Union the fertility rates are far higher for the age group 20–29 than for other age categories, it is natural to expect that Maritime Kray would have a higher birth rate than Kirov Oblast.

Since much of the migration in the Soviet Union is from rural areas to urban areas there is a great contrast in age–sex structure between the rural population and the urban population (Fig. 6.3). The pyramid for the rural population dramatically reveals the out-

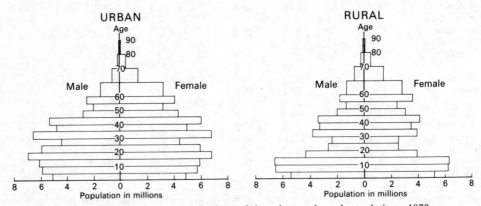

FIG. 6.3. USSR; age–sex distributions of the urban and rural populations, 1970.

migration from rural areas of young people in the 20–29 age group. In regions where migration has been heavy, either in or out, the differences in numbers of the 20–29 age group between cities and villages have become so great that birth rates have actually become slightly higher in the cities than in the countrysides. This is particularly true in some parts of the Baltic republics.

As was mentioned before, the greatest differences in vital rates correspond to differences in nationality. However, these differences are probably conditioned more by stage of socio-economic development than by inherent characteristics such as religious beliefs and mores, which actually are rapidly disappearing under the Soviet system. It is apparent that each nationality group in turn, as it has been drawn into the mainstream of Soviet life, has undergone a rapid decline in births. The Baltic and Slavic peoples lead in this decline, but the process is evident in different stages in all parts of the country, and, except for the Tadzhiks, it has already begun in the two last remaining strongholds of high birth rates—the Caucasus and Central Asia. The Georgians in the Transcaucasus have already evolved most of the way to a low birth rate. It is the remaining peoples of the Caucasus, and the peoples of Central Asia, who are maintaining the average birth rate of the USSR even at the clearly modest rate at which it now stands. The other peoples of the country have quite low birth rates. As the Caucasians and Central Asians are drawn more and more into the socio-economic mainstream, their birth rates undoubtedly will drop rapidly, and this will allow the average birth rate to continue to decline.

The average birth rate in the huge and socially complex Soviet Union at the present time is not too meaningful, since it is not representative of many groups of peoples, but only an average between two extremes, a higher one which is undergoing rapid decline, and a lower one which cannot change significantly. Therefore it is unrealistic at the present time to compare the average birth rate and average growth rate of the USSR with its very heterogeneous population to the average birth rate and average growth rate of a country whose population is quite homogeneous. One can expect much more rapid fluctuations in the former situation than in the latter.

Nationalities

The 1970 census, which allowed individuals to classify themselves into any ethnic or linguistic denominations, resulted in a list consisting of more than 800 ethnic denominations corresponding to 122 major nationalities, and over 300 linguistic and dialectic classes corresponding to 114 languages. Not all of these were recorded in the final census results, but population figures were still given for 104 individual nationality groups, and 151,942 people were lumped together in "other nationalities" (Table 6.2; Fig. 6.4).

Those whose languages belong to the Indo-European family are by far the most numerous, comprising over 84% of the entire population. This family includes the Slavs of which the Russians themselves made up 53.4% of the total population in 1970, the Ukrainians comprised nearly 17%, and the Belorussians 3.7%. While the Slavs came into being in the European part of the USSR, later they have moved into almost every region of the country. Russians and Belorussians have been the most mobile of all the nationality groups and have been the primary migrants who have moved into all cities of the USSR to man new industries. Most cities, no matter in what part of the country they are located, have become populated predominantly by Russians. Another Slavic nationality which numbers more than 1m. people is the Poles, who also are scattered widely in the country.

Other nationalities of the Indo-European family who number more than 1m. people each are the Moldavians in the southwest next to Romania, the Lithuanians and Latvians in the Baltic region, the Armenians in the Transcaucasus, the Tadzhiks in Central Asia, and Jews and Germans who are scattered.

The Altaic language family, which comprises more than 11% of the total population, includes the numerous and widespread Turkic groups. Important concentrations are to be found in the Middle Volga Basin, the Caucasus, Central Asia, and eastern Siberia. The Uralic family includes more than 2% of the total population; these people are scattered in several parts of European USSR. The third large language family, the

E

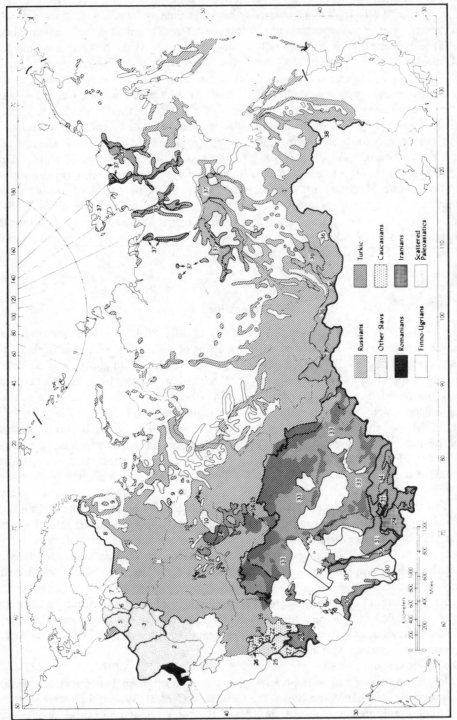

FIG. 6.4. Nationalities in the USSR. After *Atlas Narodov Mira*, Akademiya Nauk SSSR, Moscow, 1964.

TABLE 6.2. MAJOR NATIONALITIES IN THE USSR

Nationality group	1970 population (000s)	% change 1959–70	% speaking national language as native language	% speaking second USSR language fluently	
				Russian	Other
Total USSR	241,720	15.8	93.9	17.3	4.2
Indo-European	198,109	12.5			
Slavs	180,371	12.0			
Russian	129,015	13.1	99.8	0.1	3.0
Ukrainian	40,753	9.4	85.7	36.3	6.0
Belorussian	9,052	14.4	80.6	49.0	7.3
Pole[a]	1,168	−15.4	32.5	37.0	12.7
Romanian	2,817	21.4			
Moldavian	2,698	21.9	95.0	36.1	3.6
Lett–Lithuanian	4,095	9.9			
Lithuanian	2,665	14.6	97.9	35.9	1.9
Latvian	1,430	2.1	95.2	45.2	2.4
Armenian	3,559	27.7	91.4	30.1	6.0
Jew[b]	2,151	−5.2	17.7	16.3	28.8
German	1,846	14.0	66.8	59.6	1.1
Altay	32,788	39.2			
Turk	32,284	39.4			
Uzbek	9,195	52.9	98.6	14.5	3.3
Tatar	5,931	19.4	89.2	62.5	5.3
Kazakh	5,299	46.3	98.0	41.8	1.8
Azerbaydzhanian	4,380	49.0	98.2	16.6	2.5
Ural	4,510	4.8			
Finn	4,281	4.5			
Mordvinian	1,263	−1.7	77.8	65.7	8.1
Estonian	1,007	1.8	95.5	29.0	2.0
Iranian	2,762	45.1			
Tadzhik	2,136	52.9	98.5	15.4	12.0
Caucasian	5,667	29.2			
Georgian	3,245	20.5	98.4	21.3	1.0
Mongol	452	25.9			
Buryat	315	24.5	92.6	66.7	2.7
Paleoasiatic	28	18.3			

Source: *Itogi vsesoyuznoy perepisi naseleniya 1970 goda*, vol. IV, pp. 9–11.
[a]Many Poles considered their native language to be Russian, Ukrainian, or Belorussian.
[b]In 1970 78.2% of the Jews stated Russian as their native language. Most of these did not speak a second language.

Caucasians, is concentrated in the Caucasus region. Extensive Siberia and the Far East originally were very sparsely occupied by groups of Paleoasiatic, Uralic, and Oriental peoples, but these indigenous groups are presently far outnumbered by immigrant Russians.

When the Bolsheviks took over in 1917 they recognized the political advantage of appealing to the many nationality groups by guaranteeing them the right to national self-determination. And although this has not been allowed to proceed to its ultimate consequence, secession from the Union, wherever significant concentrations of nationality groups exist, the Soviet regime has made an effort to award them some political recognition. The larger, more culturally advanced groups that are located along the borders of the country have been accorded the political territorial status of Soviet

Socialist Republic; those which are less populous, or less advanced, or are located within the interior parts of the country have been accorded lower status—either Autonomous Soviet Socialist Republic, Autonomous Oblast, or National Okrug, in descending order. Thus the Soviets have deemed the nationality characteristics of the population to be significant enough to influence profoundly the political administrative map of the country.

Some populous nationalities are so scattered that they have not been accorded political regions. Such are the Germans, Poles, and Jews. Germans are presently numerous in northern Kazakhstan, western Siberia, and Central Asia. Poles are dispersed throughout the western regions, particularly in some of the territory acquired as a result of World War II in what is now western Ukraine and Belorussia. Jews are scattered throughout much of the country, and characteristically live in the cities. They are particularly numerous in some of the larger cities in the west, such as Kiev, Moscow, and Leningrad.

As has already been noted, vital rates vary widely from one nationality group to another, and this, of course, continually alters relative numbers among the groups. Since in general the Central Asians and the Caucasians have much higher rates of natural increase than do the Slavs and Baltic peoples, the former groups are increasing relatively at the expense of the latter. During the 1959–70 intercensal period peoples in the Slavic groups declined from 77.1% of the total population to 74.6%, while the peoples of the Turkic groups increased from 11.1% to 13.4% of the total population. Russians, who had constituted 54.7% of the Soviet population in 1959, constituted only 53.4% in 1970. The Ukrainians decreased from 17.8% to 16.9%.

Among the major nationality groups, the ones that gained the most during the 1959–70 intercensal period were the Uzbeks and Tadzhiks in Central Asia, each of which increased by 52.9% during the 11 year period. During the same time span the Russians gained only 13.1%, the Ukrainians 9.4%, and the Estonians only 1.9%. Actual decreases in numbers have occurred in some nationality groups. Most populous among these are the Jews who diminished by 5.2%, Poles by 15.4%, Mordvinians by 1.7%, Karelians by 12.6%, Finns by 8.2%, Czechs by 16%, and Slovaks by 20%. These decreases were due primarily to assimilations, although in some instances there were emigrations and repatriations to other countries.

There is an inevitable process of Russification that accompanies the industrialization and urbanization of the country. Russian has become the *lingua franca* of the factories and the cities. In order to get ahead young men of all nationalities must learn the Russian language and act as Russians do. The nationality groups that are most susceptible to Russification and assimilation are those who are closest in their nationality characteristics to the Russians, such as the Belorussians and Ukrainians, and those who are widely scattered throughout the country.

The Jews, probably more than any other group, are becoming Russified in a society which has scattered them among the other peoples of the country and repressed their national institutions. Only 17.7% of the Jews who reported themselves as Jews in the 1970 census reported Yiddish as their native language; 78.2% reported their native tongue as Russian.

Language is a good indicator of degree of assimilation. The next step after the switch to the Russian language is often a changeover in the nationality itself. And since people are recorded in censuses simply as they say they are, there are significant numbers of changeovers. Changeovers occur particularly frequently between generations, since a young person of mixed parentage, when his internal passport is issued at the age of 16, has the choice of declaring himself a member of the nationality of either of his parents.

Groups which have the highest percentage of persons who have shifted to another language also show a high percentage who speak some second language fluently (Table 6.2). Both of these indices are lowest among the major nationality groups who constitute the union republics. They are higher among the peoples who constitute the autonomous republics and autonomous oblasts, and highest among the peoples who are dispersed geographically and more liable to assimilation. In 1970, in addition to almost 100% of the Russians who claimed Russian as their native language, 13m. non-Russians named Russian as their mother tongue. An additional 41.9m. indicated Russian as the second language which they spoke fluently. Thus 54.9m., or approximately half of the non-Russian population of the USSR, is in perfect command of Russian: 76% of the total Soviet population speak Russian well.

Some of the smaller non-Russian nationality groups constantly are being assimilated either by Russians or by neighboring groups. The number of nationalities recorded in the censuses has decreased from about 200 in 1926 to 108 in 1959 and 104 in 1970. This is not very surprising since many of the less culturally developed peoples, particularly in the Asian part of the country, felt no nationality ties before the Soviet regime identified their nationalities for them. On the other hand, such peoples as the Ukrainians, Baltic peoples, and Caucasians have fierce nationalistic feelings and are determined to maintain their identities in the face of in-migrating Russians, intermarriage, and the growing use of the Russian language.

Migration among regions is a potent factor in changing nationality mixes within regions. Since it is the Slavic groups, and the Russians particularly, who are most apt to migrate, most of the nationality groups are becoming diluted with Russians. This has caused many anachronisms among the political units of the country which allegedly are established on nationality principles. The Kazakh SSR, for instance, now has only 32.4% of its population made up by the titular group, while Russians make up 42.8%. In the Kirgiz Republic the titular group, with 43.8% of the total population, remains a plurality but not a majority. Hence, neither of these republics any longer satisfies the constitutional requirements for a republic. In fact scarcely any of the Autonomous Soviet Socialist Republics continue to satisfy the constitutional requirements any more. Russians now predominate in almost all of them.

Education

The Soviets have transformed the educational structure of the population during the last half century. Compulsory universal education has been established for the young, and numerous opportunities have been provided for continuing adult education. As late as 1920 only 44% of the population in the age group 9–49 were literate; today the comparable figure is 99.7% (Table 6.3). As late as 1920 there were great educational discrepancies between men and women, between urban and rural populations, and between different regions of the country: 57.6% of the men were literate whereas only 32.3% of the women were; 73.5% of the urban dwellers were literate but only 37.8% of the rural dwellers. The highest literacy was in the Ukraine where 51.9% of the people could read and write, and the lowest was in the Tadzhik Republic (in Central Asia) where only 3.1% were similarly accomplished.

TABLE 6.3. LITERACY, PERCENTAGE OF TOTAL POPULATION AGE 9–49

	1897	1920	1939	1970
USSR	28.4	44.1	87.4	99.7
RSFSR	29.6	47.3	89.7	99.7
Ukrainian SSR	27.9	51.9	88.2	99.8
Belorussian SSR	32.0	47.4	80.8	99.8
Uzbek SSR	3.6	8.0	78.7	99.7
Kazakh SSR	8.1	18.3	83.6	99.7
Georgian SSR	23.6	44.1	89.3	99.9
Azerbaydzhan SSR	9.2	19.7	82.8	99.6
Lithuanian SSR	54.2		76.7	99.7
Moldavian SSR	22.2	41.1	45.9	99.5
Latvian SSR	79.7		92.7	99.8
Kirgiz SSR	3.1	3.5	79.8	99.7
Tadzhik SSR	2.3	3.1	82.8	99.6
Armenian SSR	9.2	15.3	83.9	99.8
Turkmen SSR	7.8	8.7	77.7	99.7
Estonian SSR	96.2		98.6	99.8

Source: *Itogi vsesoyuznoy perepisi naseleniya 1970 goda*, vol. III, p. 570.

Among some of the indigenous populations of Central Asia and northern Siberia illiteracy was almost universal. Some peoples had no written language at all. By 1959 most of these regional differences in literacy had been erased, and by 1970 the differences amounted to only fractions of 1%. Literacy of the total population in age group 9–49 ranges from a low of 99.5% in Moldavia to a high of 99.9% in Georgia. The 1970 census recorded only about 440,000 illiterate people in the whole nation, and they were mainly persons who had been prevented from going to school because of poor health.

In 1970 almost 80m. people were taking some sort of schooling. This amounted to approximately one-third of the entire population. All Soviet children enter primary school (grades 1 to 3) at age 7 and are required to continue through the secondary education program (grades 4 to 8). Compulsory education stops after the eighth grade, but the Soviet government is seeking to extend it to include high school (grades 9 and 10). In 1972 more than 86% of the eight-year graduates continued their education either in secondary schools, specialized secondary schools, or vocational–technical programs. About 20% of the high school graduates were admitted to higher educational institutions.

The level of educational attainment still varies considerably from group to group and from region to region. In 1970 throughout the entire population 483 persons out of every 1000 above the age of 10 had completed at least 8 years of educational training. This ratio ranged from a high of 554 per 1000 in Georgia to a low of 382 per 1000 in Lithuania. The range was even greater among some of the minor political subdivisions. This is especially true in a number of the sparsely populated outlying areas where young, well trained Russian immigrants form significant portions of the total population.

Of the 483 people per 1000 of the total population who had completed at least 8 years of schooling in 1970, 241 had completed only 8 years, 187 had completed a secondary education, 13 had taken some college work, and 42 had graduated from a four- or five-year college course. The greatest portion of the most highly educated people, of course, live in the cities. In 1970 62 out of every 1000 persons in cities had completed a college education, while only 14 per 1000 in the rural areas had done so. Among the total population who have completed college training, men still considerably outnumber women, but it has been reported that among current graduates women slightly outnumber men. In 1969–70 women made up 48 % of all students in higher education and 54 % of students in paraprofessional secondary education institutions.

Among the major nationalities of the Soviet Union, the Georgians have the greatest proportion of their population in higher educational institutions; the Moldavians have the least. For the country as a whole, 19 students per 1000 population are found in higher educational institutions; among the Georgian and Moldavian nationality groups the comparable figures are 27 and 11. The Russians have 21.

Occupation

The universal education of the USSR population, coupled with urbanization and industrialization, has transformed the structure of the labor force of the Soviet Union (Table 6.4). Whereas in 1913 mining, manufacturing, and construction employed only

TABLE 6.4. PERCENTAGE DISTRIBUTION OF CIVILIAN POPULATION ENGAGED IN THE NATIONAL ECONOMY

Occupied in	1913	1940	1950	1960	1971
Mining, manufacturing, and construction	9	23	27	32	37
Farming and forestry (including subsidiary private plots)	75	54	48	39	26
Transport and communications	2	5	5	7	8
Trade, public catering, material and technical supplies, state purchases	9	5	5	6	7
Education, health, social maintenance, science and connected services, arts, culture	1	6	8	11	16
Management, public and cooperative agencies, finance and insurance	4	3	3	2	2
Other national economy sectors (housing and communal services, etc.)		4	4	3	4
Total	100	100	100	100	100

Sources: Pokshishevsky, "Reports," p. 83, and *Narodnoe khozyaystvo SSSR 1922–1972*, p. 343.

9 % of the labor force, in 1971 it occupied 37 %, the largest of any general sector of the economy. Farming and forestry, which had employed 75 % of the labor force in 1913, employed only 26 % in 1971. Although this is still a rather high percentage for a developed country, it does represent a remarkable change. The category "education, health, social maintenance, and so forth" has shown the largest percentage gain, increasing from 1 % of the labor force in 1913 to 16 % in 1971.

Role of Women

The role of women in the labor force has been growing constantly throughout the Soviet period. Initially, this growth was no doubt in response to the large deficits of males in the working age groups. But as time has gone on and the male deficits have risen up the age ladder, the percentage of women in the labor force has continued to increase, so that it now appears that working women have become a way of life in the Soviet Union which has transcended its original stimulation. Women now constitute more than half of the entire labor force of the country (Table 6.5). This is more than double the

TABLE 6.5. WOMEN AS A PERCENTAGE OF ALL WORKERS AND
EMPLOYEES IN THE USSR, 1968

Entire economy	50
Industry	47
Agriculture	43
Transport	24
Communications	67
Construction	28
Trade	74

Source: Lydolph, *Manpower Problems in the USSR*, p. 333.

percentage in 1924 when women comprised only 24% of the labor force. They make up almost half the labor force in the two main production sectors of the economy—industry and agriculture—and they comprise almost three-quarters of the labor force in trade. They are particularly prevalent in certain professions. In 1966 they accounted for 56% of all the administrators in the country and 72% of the medical doctors. They are even more preponderant in some of the so-called "auxillary enterprises" which lie outside of socialized labor and which therefore have no official statistics, such as the intensive working of private plots of land which are allotted to families on collective farms and in some industrial settlements. In those places they account for as much as 90% of the labor performed in raising garden produce and livestock.

Population Mobility and Migration

One great problem as it relates to the labor force is its transitory nature in many regions of the country. It has been reported that in 1970 31% of all the workers in the country changed jobs; 67% of these people changed jobs on their own volition without any government planning involved. In some sectors of the economy, such as construction work, mobility is even greater. Altogether, in 1970 it has been estimated that 100m. man-days were lost because of job changes.

The Soviet population is becoming increasingly mobile; each year about 12m.–15m. people change residence. Much of this movement is over short distances, as between country and city and between one city and another, or even within a given city, as people change jobs voluntarily and look for better situations. Although according to Soviet law all changes of abode must be done under government auspices, the government has become so lax in controlling movement that people have fallen into the habit of leaving jobs and residences in one place and simply showing up looking for jobs and residences in other places. It has been reported that in recent years 90% of all new hirings by industrial enterprises have been done "at the gate."

A significant number of the moves involve longer distance migrations between regions, often from rural areas in one region to urban areas in another. But flows are not primarily unidirectional any more, in general from west to east, as they have been in the past. There is a great deal of cross-movement of people coming and going between regions, and the net migration during the 1959–70 intercensal period has been primarily southward into the southern Ukraine, North Caucasus, and Central Asia. There has also been significant net migration into the northwest and the Far East. The central portions of the country, including the Urals and much of the better populated parts of southern Siberia, have experienced net out-migration. Unfortunately migration data are still largely lacking, and net in-migrations must be computed by subtracting natural increase figures, which themselves are scanty and suspect, from total population growth figures for regions.

The best estimates of net migrations for the entire period 1959–70 are presented in Table 6.6. Among the major regions, it can be seen that out-migration is very high in the

TABLE 6.6. NET MIGRATION INTO MAJOR ECONOMIC REGIONS, 1959–70

Economic region	Thousands net of migrants	Net migrants per 1000 of 1959 census population	Ratio of net migration to total population increase
Northwest	245	22.5	.189
Baltic	365	55.3	.378
Belorussia	−266	−33.0	−.281
Center	90	3.5	.047
Central Chernozem	−500	−64.4	−2.185
Volga–Vyatka	−831	−100.7	−8.749
Volga	46	2.9	.019
North Caucasus	911	78.6	.340
Don–Dnieper	402	22.6	.176
Southwest	−589	−30.9	−.356
South	753	150.3	.548
Moldavia	76	26.5	.112
Urals	−888	−62.3	−.883
West Siberia	−732	−65.1	−.854
East Siberia	−117	−18.1	−.119
Far East	140	28.9	.148
Transcaucasia	13	1.4	.005
Central Asia	737	53.3	.120
Kazakhstan	875	95.6	.237

Source: Peter J. Grandstaff, Economic aspects of interregional migration in the USSR (1959–1970), manuscript of paper presented at annual meeting of AAASS, March 1972, p. 13.

Urals, Volga–Vyatka region, western Siberia, the southwest, and the Central Chernozem region. The Volga–Vyatka and Central Chernozem regions have long been areas of out-migration, but the addition of the Urals and western Siberia, and to a certain extent the southwest, is a new development. Eastern Siberia, too, had a net migration loss, as did Belorussia.

Some of the regions of high out-migration, particularly in the Volga–Vyatka and Central Chernozem regions, were regions of low natural population increase, and therefore the regions which could least afford to sustain out-migrations. The central zone of the country is losing a significant portion of its natural population increase by out-migration, and the southern parts of the country in general are receiving significant

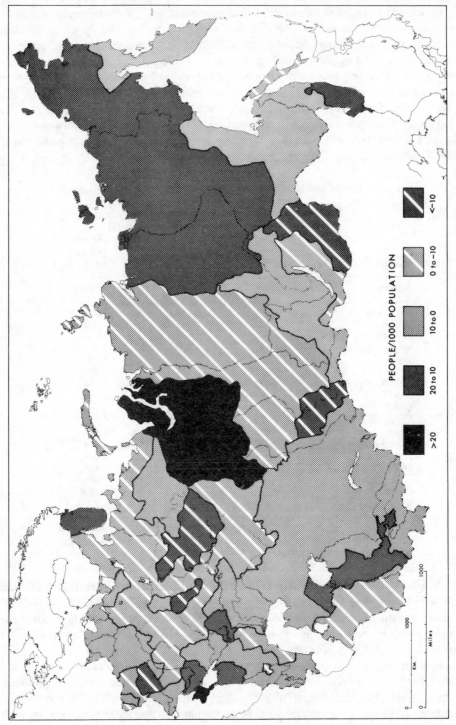

PEOPLE/1000 POPULATION

>20   20 to 10   10 to 0   0 to -10   <-10

Fig. 6.5. USSR; net migration by Oblast, Kray, and ASSR, 1965. After Lydolph and Pease.

in-migration, amounting to as much as 30% of the total increase in Kazakhstan and 10–30% in much of Central Asia as well as in parts of the Transcaucasus, Moldavia, and the Baltic.

One of the characteristic features of migration at the present time is its spotty nature (Fig. 6.5). Great differences exist within major economic regions. Subregions of high in-migration exist in juxtaposition with others of high out-migration. Net migration in 1965 was negative throughout large portions of the European Plain, Urals, and large portions of Siberia, including some of the more populous parts. Sakhalin Island experienced out-migration throughout most of the period 1959–70 which in some years even exceeded the natural increase, so that Sakhalin Oblast actually experienced an absolute population decline. The highest population influx was into the Crimea.

The present pattern of migrations is exacerbating manpower problems rather than solving them and is completely irrational as far as the government is concerned. Apparently there is a general movement southward to more favorable natural living conditions where winters are easier to tolerate and living quarters can be built more simply and cheaply, where people can spend more time out of doors, and where improved opportunities for gardening can provide low cost fruits and vegetables. These reasons are particularly valid for the North Caucasus and the Crimea. The Armenian Republic in the Transcaucasus is experiencing high in-migration of Armenians from other parts of the country as well as from other countries. There seems to be a continuing repatriation of Armenians to the Soviet part of their homeland in the Armenian Plateau country, a region which spreads over parts of the Soviet Union, eastern Turkey, and northwestern Iran. In Central Asia much of the influx has been to provide industrial workers in the burgeoning cities, for the rapidly growing native populations here so far have not solved the industrial labor problems. The influx of industrial workers into this region at present includes primarily Russians and Ukrainians entering from western Siberia and the Urals.

Rural–Urban Composition

One of the outstanding characteristics of the Soviet period has been rapid urbanization. In 1926 only 18% of the population were classified as urban. Beginning with the five-year plans in 1928 and their ensuing industrialization, urbanization took place at a very rapid rate up until World War II. By 1939 the population was 33% urban. World War II interrupted the urbanizing process, but immediately after the war it continued at a rapid pace, although not as rapid as during the pre-war period.

The total urban population is continuing to increase at a rapid absolute rate in spite of the fact that its percentage increase is gradually decreasing as the urban base grows larger. In fact, during the 1959–70 intercensal period, the absolute urban growth rate was faster than in any previous period and this, in spite of government efforts during recent years to slow down the rural–urban migration and retain some of the more able young people on farms. It appears that absolute rural–urban migration continued to increase throughout the last intercensal period. The average annual rural–urban migration for the period 1961–5 was 1.4m. persons, while during the period 1966–70 it was 1.7m. At the time of the 1970 census 56% of the total population of the USSR were classified as urban; by August 1973, 59% were so classified.

The Soviet government is particularly eager to restrict movement into the larger cities, but these efforts seem to be failing also. The plan for Moscow called for a very small population growth in the green belt and suburban zone around the city, but the census figures for 1959 and 1970 show that during that intercensal period population increased by 64.5% in the green belt, 33.2% in the suburban zone, and 24.5% in the outer zone.

During the 1959–70 period the most rapid population growth took place in the 140 cities of the country with populations between 100,000 and 250,000, where the total increase was 44%. Growth rates consistently decreased for successively larger cities. The 48 cities with populations between 250,000 and 500,000 grew by 40%; those 23 cities with populations between 500,000 and 1m. increased by 38%; the 8 cities with populations between 1 and 2m. grew by 35%; and the population in the 2 cities, Moscow and Leningrad, with more than 2m. inhabitants each, grew by 18%. In the 5238 cities and towns each with less than 100,000 inhabitants the growth rate was 36%. Thus, even if the populations of the 664 cities and towns established between 1959 and 1970 are included, these smaller urban places grew at a slower rate than did all classes of larger cities except those above 1m. in size.

Thus it appears that the Soviet policy which seeks to promote the growth of smaller cities and towns is not working out very successfully. One way or another people are moving into the larger cities whether the Soviet leaders like it or not. Some Soviet economists have taken note of this fact and are beginning to rationalize this natural tendency for larger cities to continue to grow by reasoning that it is more economical to increasingly locate industry and people in larger cities than in smaller ones. But this is not the policy of the government.

Sources of Urban Growth

Urban population growth has three contributing elements: rural–urban migration, natural increase within the cities themselves, and conversions of rural villages to urban settlements; of these the first is most important. But although migration still accounts for more of the urban growth than either of the other two factors, the rural–urban flow is slowing down as the total population becomes more urban and there are fewer people left on the farms to migrate. Whereas prior to 1959 the rural–urban migration accounted for 63% of the urban population growth, during the intercensal period 1959–70 it represented only 45.5%. Natural increase within the cities was becoming almost as important, while conversions of rural villages to urban-type settlements were continuing at about the same pace as previously if one discounts war years.

The proportions of urban growth accounted for by natural increase and net migration vary considerably from one part of the country to another. In the Central Asian republics and in Azerbaydzhan, where natural increases are still large, that factor considerably outweighs in-migration. For example, in Azerbaydzhan (Transcaucasia) during the intercensal period 1959–70, urban population grew by 562,000 from natural increase, 118,000 from net migration, and 114,000 from reclassification of rural villages. In the Tadzhik Republic (Central Asia) the comparable figures were 238,000, 131,000, and 62,000. In the western part of the country, on the other hand, Moldavia, which is the least urbanized of all the republics, and which experienced a very rapid rate of urbanization during the 1959–70 period, 123,000 of the total urban growth was attributed to natural increase within the cities, 271,000 to net migration, and 95,000 to reclassification of rural villages. In the Baltic republics, where natural population growth is very slow, the urban increase during 1959–70 was one-third attributable to natural increase within the cities and two-thirds to net migration. Comparable data for regions within the Russian Republic are not yet available.

Regional Distribution of Urban and Rural Growth

Urban and rural population growth, and therefore changes in the spatial distribution of the people, have proceeded very unevenly across the country. Between 1926 and 1959 urbanization went on most rapidly in those regions where the tempo of industrialization had speeded up, which included the Central Industrial Region centered on Moscow, the Donetz–Dnieper region of the Ukraine, the Urals, and southwestern Siberia. Rapid urban growth, but of lesser magnitude, also characterized certain areas in the Far East, the north, and Central Asia and Kazakhstan, most of them sparsely settled, in which mineral exploitation had become active. In the well populated part of European USSR, urbanization was taking place only very spottily, for intervening areas between the most industrialized parts were for the most part bypassed.

The pattern of population growth changed considerably in the 1959–70 period, when the urban population grew most rapidly in many regions where previously cities had not been numerous. A "filling in" process took place in the European part of the country where well populated areas that had previously been predominantly rural were undergoing rapid industrialization.

More conspicuous areawise were some sparsely settled regions in Kazakhstan and western Siberia which were undergoing rapid urbanization in conjunction with mining activities, particularly those associated with oil and gas. But these more extensive eastern areas did not account for as many urban people as did the smaller, more densely populated areas of the west, nor did the eastern regions undergo as much urbanization as did those in the west, since in the east rural populations generally were increasing also.

High rates of natural increase in the predominantly rural areas of Central Asia, Kazakhstan, eastern Caucasia, and portions of Siberia and the Far East caused significant increases in the rural population of these same regions in spite of significant rural–urban migrations. Much of European USSR continued to experience rather rapid rural population decline, as had been the case throughout much of the Soviet period, but the 1959–70 period saw large parts of Siberia and the Urals also experiencing rural population declines as well as Sakhalin Island and Kamchatka Peninsula in the Far East.

During the 1959–70 intercensal period the larger cities of the country (100,000 population and above) experienced particularly rapid growth rates in the southern half of European USSR, portions of the Caucasus, and Central Asia, as well as in some scattered centers throughout the rest of the country. This regional pattern of urban growth during 1959–70 was in sharp contrast to that during earlier periods (Fig. 6.6). Almost all cities in the European part of the country west of the Volga River experienced increases in growth rates during the 1959–70 period as compared to the 1939–59 period. Cities in the middle Volga Valley, Urals, and western Siberia, as well as in parts of northern Kazakhstan, eastern Siberia, and the Far East, experienced decreasing growth rates. The Urals region was the hardest hit. During 1959–70 it had the lowest urban growth rate of any major region in the country, whereas in previous years it had some of the highest growth rates.

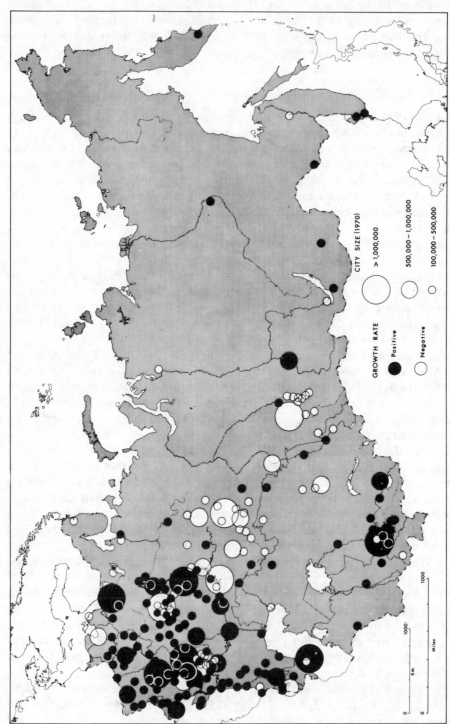

FIG. 6.6. USSR; changes in mean annual growth rates of cities with populations greater than 100,000; (1959–70 rate) minus (1939–59 rate). After Lydolph and Pease, *Changing Distributions of Population and Economic Activities in the USSR*, p. 254.

At the present time the most highly urbanized regions, those areas having the greater portion of their population classified as urban, are the heavily industrialized areas of the Central or Moscow region, the eastern Ukraine, the Urals, the Kuznetsk Basin in western Siberia, and the Leningrad region in the northwest, as well as sparsely settled portions of the country which are dominated by one or more urban developments, more often than not based upon mining activity. Thus high urbanization is experienced in some of the most densely populated parts of the country and also in some of the most sparsely populated parts.

References for Chapters 5 and 6

Allworth, Edward (ed.) (1971), *Soviet Nationality Problems*, Columbia University Press, New York, 296 pp.

Brook, S. I. (1972), Population of the USSR: changes in its demographic, social, and ethnic structure, *Geoforum*, **9**, 7–22.

Eason, Warren W. (1973), Demography, in Ellen Mickiewicz, *Handbook of Soviet Social Science Data*, The Free Press, New York, pp. 49–63.

Goldhaven, Erich (ed.) (1968), *Ethnic Minorities in the Soviet Union*, Praeger, New York, 351 pp.

Harris, Chauncy D. (1971), Urbanization and population growth in the Soviet Union, 1959–1970, *Geographical Review* **61** (1), 102–24.

Kovalev, S. A. (1972), Transformation of rural settlements in the Soviet Union, *Geoforum*, September 1972, pp. 33–45.

Lewis, Robert A. and Leasure, J. William (1966), Regional population changes in Russia and the USSR since 1851, *Slavic Review* XXV (4), 663–8.

Lewis, Robert A. and Rowland, Richard H. (1969), Urbanization in Russia and the USSR: 1897–1966, *Annals of the Association of American Geographers*, **59** (4), 776–96.

Lorimer, Frank (1946), *The Population of the Soviet Union: History and Prospects*, League of Nations, Geneva, 289 pp.

Lydolph, Paul E. and Pease, Steven (1974), Changing distributions of population and economic activities in the USSR, *Tijdschrift voor econ. en soc. geografie* 63 (4), 244–61.

Perevedentsev, V. I. (1969), Contemporary migration in the USSR, *Soviet Geography: Review and Translation* X (4), 192–208.

Pokshishevsky, V. V. (1969), Migration of USSR population described, in *Translations on USSR Resources*, no. 52 JPRS 49279, November 19, 1969, pp. 51–66.

Pokshishevsky, V. V. (1972), Urbanization in the USSR, *Geoforum* 9, 23–32.

(1972) The Soviet peoples: population growth and policy, *Population Bulletin* XXVIII (5), 25 pp.

CHAPTER 7

THE UNITED STATES AND CANADA: SPATIAL ARRANGEMENT OF POPULATION

CLARENCE W. OLMSTEAD

University of Wisconsin—Madison, USA

Introduction

At the highest level of generalization, the areal distribution of population in North America north of the Rio Grande may be described rather simply. There are three very general regions: a southeastern quarter of moderately dense and continuous settlement; a southwestern quarter of much sparser and discontinuous or spotty settlement; and a northern half with few people and vast, virtually empty spaces (Figs. 7.1 and 7.2). As a consequence of the east–west trend of their international border, the United States and Canada, although roughly equal in area, share the total population at a ratio of about 10 to 1. The United States, excepting Alaska and Hawaii, comprises most of the two populated southern quarters; Alaska and most of Canada fall into the relatively empty northern half. Approximately nine-tenths of all Canadians live within 200 miles of the international border. Furthermore, this small populated fraction of Canada is separated into five or six settled areas, each separated from the others by southward extensions of sparsely occupied land or water. Four of these Canadian populated areas are contiguous with settled American regions across the border.

The consequences of this distribution for the two nations, especially Canada, are of great significance. There is the problem for Canada simply of living so close and in economic and cultural interdependence with a giant ten times as populous. There is the cost for Canada of linking its separated concentrations of population together into a unified economy and society. In much of Canada and Alaska, and to a lesser degree in the interior western United States, there is the problem of administering to small numbers of people scattered over a vast territory, and of appraising and using wisely minerals and other land resources also widely scattered. On the other hand, in parts of eastern United States and adjacent Canada, there are problems of congestion which arise from millions of people crowded into limited urban spaces.

Development of the Spatial Arrangement of Population

The locational arrangement of population at any given moment is the cumulative result of countless past locational decisions made by individuals or groups, each within

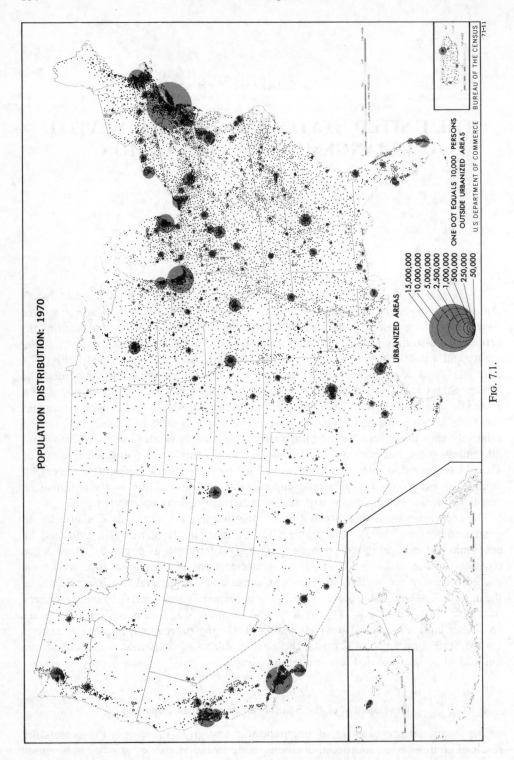

POPULATION DISTRIBUTION: 1970

URBANIZED AREAS

15,000,000
10,000,000
5,000,000
2,500,000
1,000,000
500,000
250,000
50,000

ONE DOT EQUALS 10,000 PERSONS
OUTSIDE URBANIZED AREAS

U.S. DEPARTMENT OF COMMERCE

BUREAU OF THE CENSUS

FIG. 7.1.

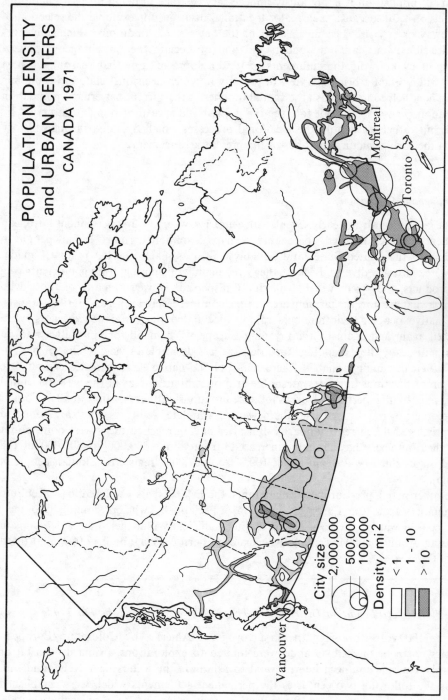

FIG. 7.2. Sources: Census and National Atlas of Canada.

the context of a contemporary set of conditions. In order to understand current areal patterns of population it is obviously unnecessary to trace in detail all past conditions and decisions. But because each major locational decision, for example the selection of a routeway or city site, becomes a part of the new set of conditions which influences later decisions, one can only understand and appreciate the present geography of population by knowing the rudiments of its development. For that reason, the next section will attempt a brief overview of the way in which decisions related to economic development helped to establish the spatial outlines of the current patterns of population distribution. The object is not to trace the growth and spread of population period by period, but rather to identify the locational processes which operated through history to form the early structural outlines of the present arrangement.

The Indigenous Population

In the late sixteenth and early seventeenth centuries, when the first permanent European settlements were established, there were perhaps a million or more Indian people in what is now the United States and possibly a fifth as many in what is now Canada. They were culturally diverse. Because they lived mainly by hunting, fishing, and gathering wild products, they were widely and thinly dispersed. However, many of those who occupied what are now the farming areas of the continent were also crude agriculturalists. These native people, their numbers rapidly decimated by introduced diseases, were displaced again and again by the invading Europeans' demand for land, always to an area appraised by the expanding Europeans as less desirable in view of the set of conditions then pertaining. That is where many of the native American descendants are now—on reservations in the less desirable arid or semi-arid areas of the western United States, and in the peripheral areas of discontinuous settlement in Canada. Caught between their own destroyed, and the newer unassimilated, cultures, most are poor and underprivileged by current standards. But after having reached the lowest point about 1900, their numbers have rapidly increased (from about 240,000 to 800,000 in the United States since 1900; from about 100,000 to 257,000 "registered" Indian people in Canada).

The other major pre-European inhabitants, the Eskimos, also suffered loss of culture and numbers from the European invasion, especially by whalers coming into their Arctic coastal waters: they, too, have adapted sufficiently that their numbers are again increasing. About 28,000 live along the coast of western Alaska, about 17,000 in northern coastal Canada.

Early Outlines of Population Distribution: The Role of Fishing and the Fur Trade

In the 100 years following the first voyage to America by Columbus, European activities north of the Rio Grande were limited to explorations, primarily coastal or within the extreme southern interior, and to fishing in the waters near Newfoundland. During the following two centuries the permanent settlements which were established were almost exclusively devoted to collection, production, or trade of primary goods. Within the first two decades after 1600, agricultural and fur-trading settlements were estab ished by French and English colonists along the Atlantic between the St. Lawrence and James rivers. During the same period Spanish settlement was extended from its outposts in New Spain (Mexico) northward into the Pueblo Indian territory of the Rio Grande Valley. In addition to the motives related to furs and farming, the colonizing nations were concerned with establishing political and military dominance and with converting Indian people to their particular forms of Christianity. The important question to ask for our purpose is: How and to what degrees did the various settlers and their motives and activities exert lasting effects upon the geographical arrangement of settlement and population? One simple but very important observation is that the settlement of Canadian and American territory was dominated by Europeans, especially British and French, expanding westward from the Atlantic coast.

The fishing conducted in Newfoundland waters by several European nations resulted in no permanent settlements during the sixteenth century. Even during the seventeenth and eighteenth centuries, when permanent land bases replaced the temporary summer bases on harbor shores or shipboard, fishing settlements were limited to the coasts. By contrast, the fur trade involved deep penetration of itinerants into the continent, but established only a very skeletal network of routeways and tiny trading posts. Although the volume and value of the furs taken were considerable, of greatest long term importance to future settlement was the knowledge of the continent gained by the traders, largely from the Indian people who were the primary hunters and trappers. Many of the routeways and trading post locations became of lasting importance.

Penetration of the continent by fur traders followed several major avenues, primarily along the waterways. The French were based in the St. Lawrence Valley (Montreal, Quebec). Their trading activities, from the early seventeenth century until the loss of Canada in 1763, extended along two major routeways, the one via the southern Great Lakes into and along the Ohio, Missouri, and upper and lower Mississippi valleys, with major posts at modern Detroit, Pittsburgh, St. Louis, and Minneapolis; the other via the Ottawa Valley and the northern Great Lakes to the Lake Winnipeg area with centers at the Straits of Mackinac, Thunder Bay, and the site of Winnipeg. The British trade penetrated from three directions, surrounding and competing with the French. One penetration overlapping in space and time with the French was inland into the Ohio and Mississippi valleys and Great Lakes area from the agricultural settlements along the New England and middle Atlantic coasts. A second penetration, in the nineteenth century, was inland from Victoria, Vancouver, and the lower Columbia River Valley. The third and major British network was via Hudson Bay into much of central and western Canada. The Hudson's Bay Company, using this network, not only came to dominate the fur trade of Canada but held complete control over much of the area east of the Rocky Mountains and north of the St. Lawrence and Ottawa valleys, known as Rupert's Land, from 1670 until the vast territory was sold to the new Canadian government in 1869.

The final fur-trading penetration into North America was that by Russians. During the late eighteenth and early nineteenth centuries they established bases in coastal Alaska and almost as far south as San Francisco Bay. The lasting effect upon population distribution was minimal but the competition may have stimulated the establishment of a string of Spanish settlements along the coast of California northward as far as San Francisco after 1769 as well as the penetration to the Pacific of American and British explorers and traders from the east.

Early Outlines of Population Distribution: The Role of Agriculture

Fishing and the fur trade, especially the latter, provided incentive for the accumulation of much knowledge about North America and for the establishment of routes and trade centers, some of which have continued and increased in significance. But it is the appraisal, settlement, and use of land for agriculture that established many of the persisting areal arrangements of population and settlement. Agriculture is the base for much of the widespread, continuous settlement in the southeastern quarter of Anglo-America. It is or was the base for many of the scattered clusters of population in the southwestern quarter. Its virtual absence coincides with the absence of continuous settlement in the northern half of the continent (Figs. 7.1 and 7.2).

The fur trade was characterized by mobility along far flung routeways connecting tiny trade centers. Consequently its overlapping, competing systems penetrated rapidly and deeply into the central and northern interior of the continent. By contrast, and assuming an adequate land resource, agriculture required and supported a much higher and more uniform population density, larger trading centers, and a denser network of routes. Consequently, its areal spread was relatively slow. We now consider such spread of agricultural settlement over most of the southeastern quarter of Anglo-America.

When France lost its claim to Canada in 1763, the French-speaking population in the St. Lawrence Valley numbered about 65,000. Although the area functioned as a major center for the far flung fur trade, most of the people were farmers. They were concentrated along the banks of the St. Lawrence from below Quebec to Montreal. During the next century, prior to the confederation of Canada in 1867, agricultural settlement filled the elongated lowland. It pushed against the escarpment of the thin soiled Canadian shield which confines the left-bank section of the lowland to a strip only 10–30 miles deep (Fig. 7.3). Southeast of the river, the settled lowland reached further downstream and extended further from the St. Lawrence into the margins of the Appalachian Highlands. It is estimated that about 10,000 French people emigrated to the St. Lawrence Valley between 1608 and 1763. Their natural increase accounts for most of the 65,000 people in 1763, and for a majority of the more than 1m. in Quebec at the time of confederation, or the more than 6m. today.

Further south, agricultural settlements along the Atlantic also expanded slowly but the dimensions of contiguous spread were far greater than in Canada (Fig. 7.3). During the seventeenth century, settlements established as early as 1607 (Jamestown, Virginia) spread outward in the coastal plain from centers near Boston, New York, the Delaware River, Chesapeake Bay, and Charleston, South Carolina. By 1750 much of the northern Appalachian piedmont was occupied and settlers were pushing into the parallel valleys of the eastern Appalachians. After the American Revolution, settlement began to penetrate through the Appalachians into the Bluegrass and Nashville basins and the upper Tennessee and Ohio river valleys. By 1800 it had advanced through the Hudson–Mohawk and Lake Champlain lowlands and was approaching Lake Ontario and joining with the expanding settlement of the St. Lawrence Lowland where emigrating American loyalists had pushed between the French-speaking St. Lawrence settlements and the Appalachians (Fig. 7.3). In the far southeast, westward expansion was slower, being confined to eastern Georgia before 1800 except for some expansion of the early settlement at New Orleans.

West of the Appalachian Highlands, agricultural settlement again expanded as a

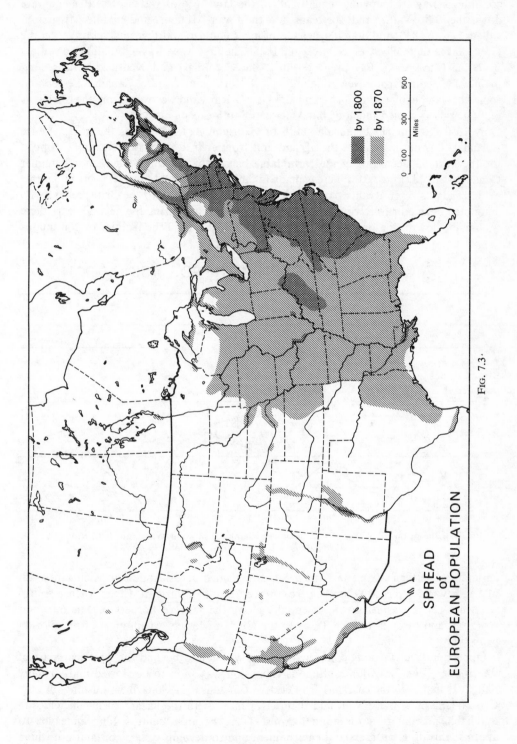

by 1800   by 1870

Miles

0   100   300   500

SPREAD
of
EUROPEAN POPULATION

Fig. 7.3

continuous wave, occupying virtually all of the land. Major waves of settlement were down the Ohio Valley and upstream into the lower Missouri and middle Mississippi valleys before 1830, and along both sides of lakes Ontario and Erie and via travel on the Great Lakes themselves, especially after 1825. The first wave was fed mainly by settlers from the Chesapeake Bay area, Virginia, the Carolinas, and Kentucky; the second mainly by people from New England, New York, and eastern Canada. Lesser and somewhat later expansions upstream from New Orleans and westward from the Carolinas and Georgia occupied much of the American South except Florida.

By 1850 the Ontario Peninsula south of Georgian Bay, as well as the St. Lawrence Lowland, was occupied, and the agricultural frontier in Canada was virtually stopped for the next half century by the formidable barrier of the thin soiled, short summer Canadian Shield (Fig. 7.3). Whereas many inhabitants of Canada in 1850 were emigrants or descendants of emigrants from the United States (loyalists to the British cause who emigrated during or following the American Revolution), during the next 50 years there was major flow in the opposite direction (Fig. 7.4). By 1850 the frontier of continuous

CANADA DEMOGRAPHIC TRENDS, 1861 - 1971

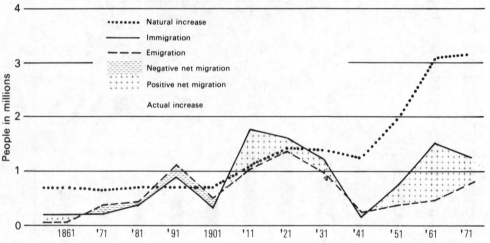

FIG. 7.4. Based on T. R. Weir, "The People", chapter 6 in John Warkentin (ed.), *Canada, A Geographical Interpretation*, Methuen, Toronto, 1968.

agricultural settlement in the United States extended across southern Michigan south of Saginaw Bay, across Wisconsin from Green Bay to Prairie du Chien, thence south-westward across eastern Iowa, essentially along the western borders of Missouri and Arkansas and through eastern Texas to the Gulf of Mexico. Again most of the Florida peninsula was excluded.

Opportunity for farming continued to exist within and beyond the American part of the frontier (Fig. 7.3). But continuous expansion was soon to be slowed and virtually halted, as had been the case earlier in eastern Canada. By 1890 farmers pushing into the Great Plains west of 98°W found themselves faced with the hazard of insufficient and unreliable precipitation for annual crops. There began a century long endeavor to appraise this different grassland environment and to develop systems of land use which will support individual families but not destroy the soil and plant resources. Despite the partial success of that effort, the western margins of the eastern zone of continuous, moderately dense agricultural settlement have changed little in general outline since about 1890.

Ironically, as these frontier limits were reached in the United States, a new agricultural frontier opened in Canada. For half a century, land-seeking Canadians had been one of the streams of immigrant settlers into the Midwestern United States. Now they were able, first via American railroads and then in the 1880s by means of the new Canadian rail line across 800 miles of agriculturally barren Canadian Shield north of the Great Lakes, to reach, penetrate, and settle in the grassland area of the Prairie Provinces. Within 30 years, by 1920, the roughly triangular grassland area marked by the apex sites of Winnipeg, Edmonton, and Lethbridge was occupied by farms, and the major area of continuous, moderately dense settlement in North America was complete (Fig. 7.2). During these first two decades of the twentieth century, when the zone of continuous settlement was expanding only in Canada, the net flow of agricultural settlers between the two countries was reversed. That is, there was migration of farm people from the United States into the Canadian Prairie Provinces (Fig. 7.4). In addition, large numbers of settlers came to the Canadian grasslands from eastern Canada, the British Isles, and eastern and western Europe.

Development of Patterns of Discontinuous Population Distribution in Western North America and the Margins of Settled Canada

The first remote cluster of European population in western North America was the small nucleus established by the Spanish near Santa Fe in the Rio Grande Valley about 1600. During the mid nineteenth century, several groups of settlers penetrated far beyond the frontier of continuous agricultural settlement advancing from the east to establish new nodes of population in the west, and, incidentally, to develop routeways, many of which are of lasting importance. Two of the earliest settlements were agricultural. The Willamette Valley of Oregon was settled in the 1830s and 1840s by people who established and followed the Oregon Trail along the North Platte, Upper Snake, and Lower Columbia rivers, a route later followed by major transcontinental railroads and highways. Taking advantage of information gained from explorers, fur traders, and missionaries, they developed the largest contiguous area west of the Great Plains suitable for non-irrigated, annual crop agriculture (Fig. 7.3). In the late 1840s Mormon people also trekked along the Platte River and through the Wyoming Basin to establish their religious oriented settlement at the western base of the Wasatch Range in what came to be Utah. Unlike the Oregon settlers, they had to develop irrigated farming or other techniques of moisture-conserving agriculture.

Discovery and exploitation of minerals, especially gold and silver, were the incentives for many of the other early clusters of population west, and later north, of the frontier of continuous agricultural settlement. Most notable was the famous rush to central California beginning in 1848. Mining was in the western foothills of the Sierra Nevada but San Francisco became the economic capital. During the following decade mineral discoveries stimulated settlement nodes at Denver; Carson City, Nevada; Virginia City, Montana (south of modern Butte); Boise, Idaho; and in the central Fraser Valley,

British Columbia (Fig. 7.3). Near the turn of the century, gold discoveries stimulated similar rushes but more ephemeral population clusters at Nome and Fairbanks, Alaska, and Dawson, Canada.

Many of the isolated population nodes in the west developed both additional functions and internodal transport connections. Mining usually stimulated supply functions of irrigated agriculture or dry fallow farming (if small areas of suitable land were available), livestock ranching (much more widespread), forestry and, of course, urban and transport functions. But areal spread has remained limited; the population pattern is still markedly spotty (Fig. 7.1).

During the twentieth century, discovery and exploitation of mineral or other earth resources have continued to produce scattered or even remote clusters of population, but under quite different technological conditions and means of dealing with remoteness. Examples include the development of the great clay belt–gold belt area midway between Georgian Bay and James Bay after 1910, the opening of the iron mines in the wilderness along the Quebec–Labrador border in the 1950s, or the development of oilfields in northern Alaska or the James Bay Power Project in northwestern Quebec in the 1970s.

The Growth of Population: Industrialization and Urbanization

The foregoing paragraphs have reviewed, very briefly, the way in which people involved in primary economic activities (fishing, fur trade, agriculture, forestry, and mining) appraised and utilized the land and resources of North America, and, in so doing, established before 1900 the major outlines and patterns of the present distribution of population. What has been omitted, of course, is consideration of the secondary (manufacturing) and tertiary (trade transportation, services), economic activities which now occupy most Americans and Canadians and which are concentrated mainly in cities. However, because the rapid growth of industries and services and the consequent concentration of population in cities has been recent, especially since 1900, these processes will be considered in the following discussion of current areal distribution of population rather than in this brief historical preview.

The Sources of Population Growth

The two large, economically advanced nation states north of the Rio Grande are the product of a set of circumstances unique in the history of the world. Here Europeans discovered a vast territory containing unparalleled agricultural and other resources. The area was only sparsely occupied by people much less advanced in technology and military power than the Europeans. Finally, the new lands became available at the very time in history when the developing Industrial Revolution provided new incentives and a burgeoning set of ideas and tools for their development.

One phase of this unique development in human history and geography was the migration of millions of Europeans to settle in the newly discovered lands, especially in North America. It is estimated that more than a third of a million people came to North America during the eighteenth century. But during the century 1830–1930 the number of immigrants to the United States and Canada exceeded 44m.

During the last half of the nineteenth century more people left than immigrated to

Canada (Fig. 7.4). This was the period during which the westward-moving agricultural frontier was temporarily halted by the Canadian Shield and when many people moved from Canada into the American Midwest or to newly expanding industrial cities of New England. All of Canada's population growth during that period was due to natural increase. During the twentieth century, however, Canada's population has grown through both natural increase and net migration (Fig. 7.4).

The origin of the French-speaking population of Canada has been briefly discussed. That population has developed primarily through natural increase from the estimated 10,000 who had come to the St. Lawrence Valley and parts of maritime Canada before 1663. Most of the 23m. people in the United States classified as black also represent natural increase from the people who were brought from West Africa as slaves during the eighteenth and early nineteenth centuries.

The majority of immigrants to Canada and the United States before about 1840 were from the British Isles. During the middle and late nineteenth century increasing numbers came first from Scandinavia and central Europe and later from southern and eastern Europe. Consequently, the Midwest received many Scandinavian and German settlers. Many eastern Europeans came later; for example, Ukrainians to the Prairie Provinces. During the late nineteenth century, and especially after 1910, the majority of immigrants stayed in the growing cities.

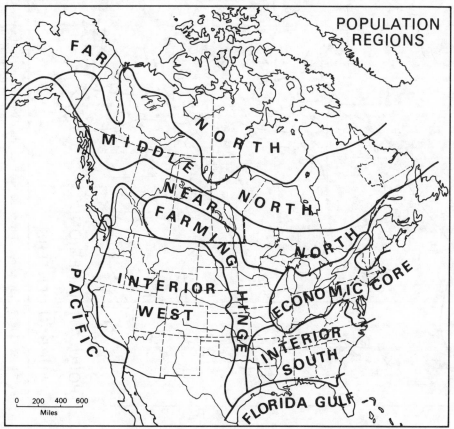

Fig. 7.5.

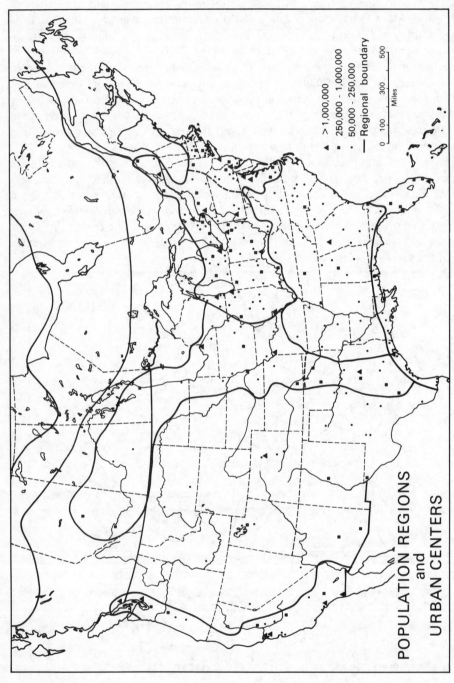

POPULATION REGIONS
and
URBAN CENTERS

Fɪɢ. 7.6. See Fig. 7.5 for names of regions. From census data by urbanized areas in the United States, 1970, and for census metropolitan areas in Canada, 1971.

Current Areal Distribution of Population

To facilitate the discussion of the distribution of population in the United States and Canada, regions have been established as shown in Figs. 7.5 and 7.6. The regions are differentiated on the basis of both the areal density and the spatial pattern or arrangement of population which, in turn, are related to economic activities and use of land. Related data are presented in Tables 7.1, 7.2, and 7.3.

The regions in the southeastern quarter of the continent (Economic Core, Interior South, Florida–Gulf, and Farming-Hinge) include about 70% of all Canadians and 80% of all Americans in much less than a quarter of the combined national areas (Tables 7.1 and 7.2). These regions are characterized by a continuous pattern of dispersed rural population of moderate density and an overlying network of cities (Figs. 7.1 and 7.2).

The three northern regions together with the Interior West comprise more than nine-tenths of Canadian and over half of American territory, but account for less than a quarter of the Canadian population and only 7% of the American. These areas are characterized by discontinuous patterns of clustered population with low average density, or by virtual absence of people. The Pacific Coast region has attributes of each of the above groups of regions; the areal pattern is a clustered one, but areal densities and numbers are relatively high, and growth in recent decades has been rapid.

The Agricultural Population Base

Farm people now comprise only about 5% of the population of the United States and Canada (Table 7.4). But farmers provide an economic base for far larger numbers of people who handle the produce from and supply goods and services for the farms. More important, and as already stated, farming was the dominant segment of the economy in what came to be the areas of contiguous settlement during those earlier times when the locations of towns, cities, and transportation routes were being established.

By 1900 farming people had become distributed somewhat uniformly over most of the Interior South, Farming-Hinge, and Economic Core regions. The principal areas of exception are the Appalachian and Ozark–Ouachita highlands and the Florida–Gulf region (Fig. 7.1). Many farms were established in the highlands during the nineteenth century, but in the twentieth century only those with gentler slopes and better soils, such as in the valleys of the parallel ridge and valley section of the eastern Appalachians, have been able to survive. In much of the Florida–Gulf subregion, soils were either too sandy or poorly drained to attract a contiguous pattern of farm settlement.

Some of the earliest farming settlements in eastern North America were in Maritime Canada. But there, as in neighboring New England and Quebec, steep slopes, thin soils, and a short growing season limited the spread of a uniform pattern of farm population to coastal lowland or valley areas (Fig. 7.2). In interior eastern Canada, as has been stated, contiguous farm settlement was confined to the St. Lawrence Lowland and southern Ontario south of the Canadian Shield. From Lake Huron northwestward to the Rocky Mountains, the northern margins of the Economic Core and Farming-Hinge regions are marked by a transition to relatively infertile soils as well as a short growing season.

The western margins of the Farming-Hinge region are characterized by a more

TABLE 7.1. UNITED STATES, POPULATION BY REGIONS, 1970[a]

Region	% of US land area		Population 1970 (000's)		Urban		Rural		Population per sq. mile	% increase 1960–70	
	Total US	48 states	Region	% of US	% of region	% of US	% of region	% of US		Region	% of US
Economic Core	8.7	10.3	97,421	48.2	79.8	52.3	20.2	36.7	316.8	11.4	42.2
Atlantic	2.1	2.4	45,799	22.7	85.2	26.3	14.8	12.6	630.8	13.5	23.0
Midwest	6.6	7.9	51,621	25.5	75.0	26.1	25.0	24.1	219.7	9.7	19.2
Near North	3.9	4.6	3,223	1.6	38.1	0.8	61.9	3.7	23.5	4.2	0.6
Northeast	1.6	1.9	1,629	0.8	37.4	0.4	62.6	1.9	28.7	4.3	0.3
Great Lakes	2.3	2.7	1,593	0.8	38.9	0.4	61.1	1.8	19.9	4.1	0.3
South	16.9	20.1	44,179	21.8	58.0	17.2	42.0	34.6	73.5	13.2	21.8
Interior	14.2	16.8	31,371	15.5	48.7	10.3	51.3	30.0	62.3	8.3	10.2
Florida–Gulf	2.7	3.3	12,808	6.3	80.7	7.0	19.3	4.6	132.0	27.4	11.6
Farming-Hinge	10.4	12.3	19,513	9.7	68.6	9.0	31.4	11.4	53.1	10.8	8.0
Northern	8.1	9.6	12,911	6.4	62.0	5.4	38.0	9.1	45.3	6.3	3.2
Southern	2.3	2.8	6,602	3.3	81.4	3.6	18.6	2.3	79.8	20.8	4.8
Total East	39.8	47.4	164,335	80.9	71.8	79.1	28.2	86.0	116.3	11.7	72.0
Total Northeast	20.6	24.5	113,554	55.9	76.6	58.3	23.4	49.3	155.7	10.6	45.6
Total Southeast	19.2	22.9	50,781	25.0	61.0	20.8	39.0	36.7	74.3	14.2	26.4
West	44.4	52.7	37,808	18.7	80.8	20.6	19.2	13.5	24.1	20.7	27.4
Interior	39.6	47.0	13,828	6.8	67.2	6.3	32.8	8.5	9.9	11.9	6.2
Pacific	4.8	5.7	23,980	11.9	88.7	14.3	11.3	5.1	142.1	26.4	21.1
48 states	84.2	100.0	202,143	99.5	73.5	99.5	26.5	99.5	67.8	13.3	99.1
Alaska	16.0		300	0.1	48.4	0.1	51.6	0.3	0.5	32.8	0.3
Hawaii	0.2		769	0.4	83.1	0.4	16.9	0.2	119.6	21.5	0.6
Total US	100.0		203,212	100.0	73.5	100.0	26.5	100.0	57.5	13.3	100.0

[a]Regions and subregions are shown on Figs. 7.5 and 7.6. Data are compiled from US Census Reports for economic subregions, state economic areas, states, and counties.

TABLE 7.2. CANADA AND ALASKA, POPULATION BY REGIONS AND CITIES, 1971

	Approx. pop. 1971 (000's)	Estimated % of Canada or Alaska		No. of census metropolitan areas				Number of cities
		Pop.	Area	Over 1m.	500,000– 1,000,000	250,000– 500,000	100,000– 250,000	50,000– 100,000
Economic Core	11,737	54.4	1.7	2	1	5	1	8
Quebec sector	4,999	23.2	0.7	1		1		2
Montreal CMA	2,743	12.7		1				
Ontario sector	6,738	31.2	1.0	1		4	1	6
Toronto CMA	2,628	12.2		1				
Pacific Region	1,526	7.1	0.1	1			1	
Prairie Region	3,355	15.6	5.6		1	2	2	
Interior West	525	2.4	2.9					
Near North	4,223[a]	19.6[a]	19.9[a]				6	1
Atlantic Canada	2,368	11.0	2.5				3	
Quebec South Shore and Gaspe	362	1.7						
New Brunswick	635	2.9					1	
Nova Scotia	789	3.7					1	
Prince Edward Island	112	0.5						
Newfoundland Island	471	2.2					1	
Quebec North Shore and Interior and Labrador	635	2.9	4.6				1	
Central Ontario	955	4.4	4.3				2	1
Western Sector	265	1.2	8.5					
Southern Alaska	208	69.3	16.0					
Middle North	239							
Canada	189	0.9	37.1					
Alaska	50	16.7	18.0					
Far North	56							
Canada	14	0.1	32.7					
Alaska	42	14.0	66.0					
Total North	4,426	20.6[a]	89.7[a]					
Total Canada[b]	21,568	100.0	100.0	3	2	7	10	9
Total Alaska	300	100.0	100.0					

[a]Canada only.
[b]These are national totals, not column totals.

gradual transition and greater irregularity in both the agricultural resource base and the areal distribution and density of population. The boundary line is drawn so as to separate the area dominated by annual crops supported by natural precipitation on the east from areas dominated by dry fallow farming and livestock ranching to the west. The latter kinds of land use, necessary because of the deficient and unreliable precipitation, do not support a pattern of contiguous, moderately dense population (Figs. 7.1 and 7.6).

Excepting the unusual areas listed above, farm people have been widely spread over the Interior South, Economic Core, and Farming-Hinge regions for three-quarters of a century (somewhat less in the Canadian Prairie subregion). Depending upon generally sufficient and reliable rainfall they raised annual crops, as well as livestock, on farms of approximately 40 to a few hundred acres in size. Such a settlement pattern of farm people alone could account for population densities in the range of only 10 to 70 people

TABLE 7.3. UNITED STATES, DISTRIBUTION OF URBANIZED AREAS, BY REGIONS, 1970[a]

| | Category by population | | | | | | | | | | |
| | Over 2m. | | 1–2m. | | 500,000– 1,000,000 | | 250,000– 500,000 | | 100,000– 250,000 | | 50,000– 100,000 | |
	No.	Cum. No.[b]	No.	Cum. No.[b]	No.	Cum. No.[b]	No.	Cum. No.[b]	No.	Cum. No.[b]	No.	Cum. No.[b]
United States	8	8	17	25	21	46	35	81	91	172	76	248
Economic Core	6	6	7	13	9	22	15	37	42	79	27	106
Atlantic	4	4	1	5	3	8	9	17	19	36	9	45
Midwest	2	2	6	8	6	14	6	20	23	43	18	61
Near North									1	1		1
South			3	3	5	8	7	15	29	44	22	66
Interior			1	1	2	3	2	5	23	28	15	43
Florida–Gulf			2	2	3	5	5	10	6	16	7	23
Farming-Hinge			3	3	3	6	6	12	5	17	10	27
Northern			2	2		2	4	6	4	10	8	18
Southern			1	1	3	4	2	6	1	7	2	9
Total East	6	6	13	19	17	36	28	64	77	141	59	200
Total Northeast	6	6	9	15	9	24	19	43	47	90	35	125
Total Southeast			4	4	8	12	9	21	30	51	24	75
West	2	2	4	6	4	10	6	16	14	30	17	47
Interior			1	1	1	2	4	6	8	14	12	26
Pacific	2	2	3	5	3	8	2	10	6	16	5	21
48 states	8	8	17	25	21	46	34	80	91	171	76	247
Alaska												
Hawaii							1	1				1

[a]Regions are shown on Fig. 7.6. Definition and populations of urbanized areas are from US census.
[b]Cumulative numbers.

per square mile. However, the great transformation of agriculture since 1940, with a large input of capital and technology and consequent reduction of labor, has resulted in an increase in size and a decrease in the number of farms. This, along with a decrease in family size, has pushed the rural farm population densities toward the lower end of the range mentioned above. Farm people now comprise only about 5% of the total population of the two countries (Table 7.4).

Superimposed on the base pattern of a somewhat uniformly distributed farm population in the eastern United States and southeastern Canada, now averaging about 8 to 24 persons per square mile, is a correspondingly widespread and somewhat uniform pattern of trade centers. Although the size range of such agglomerated settlements is continuous, they may be thought of for our purpose as being comprised of a three-rank hierarchy. Lowest in the hierarchy are hamlets and villages. They are considered by the national censuses as belonging to the rural category of population if smaller than 2500 people in the United States or 1000 in Canada. In most of the continuously settled farm areas, such hamlets or villages were originally established about 5 to 10 miles apart, providing each farm with accessibility to such a center by horse-drawn vehicle. The next higher order of trade center, those with populations of 2500 to about 10,000, were often about 25 miles apart, each providing higher-order services for the twenty or so villages and hamlets and the one or two thousand farms within its trade area. Such a town often served as the county seat or administrative center. The third order of trade centers would include cities of 10,000 up to 50,000. Such places were relatively few before 1900, but by 1970 numbered more than 1900 in the United States, four-fifths of them in the eastern half of the country. Unfortunately, the spatial arrangement of this hierarchy of agglom-erated settlements cannot be seen in Fig. 7.1; all are represented by black dots, un-differentiated from each other or from farm population. However, the map does reveal the relatively continuous and uniform pattern of this rural and small town population in the eastern humid half of the United States (the pattern in southern Ontario is similar) in stark contrast to the sparse and spotty distribution of population in most of the western half.

The uniform, farm based population pattern is most obvious in the Farming-Hinge Region, which is dominantly agricultural in character (Figs. 7.1, 7.2, and 7.6). A triangle with apexes at Lubbock in Texas, Columbus in Ohio, and Edmonton in Canada contains more than half the productive cropland of North America; the Farming-Hinge Region falls mainly within this continental cropland triangle. In the Farming-Hinge part of the cropland triangle, productive, contiguous farms extend uninterrupted for hundreds of miles so as to dominate both landscape and economy.

In the western more agricultural part of the Economic Core Region, and in parts of the Interior South, especially the Atlantic coastal plain, the base of rural farm population is also widespread and relatively uniform (Figs. 7.1 and 7.6). In some parts of the South, which specialized in labor intensive production of cotton or tobacco and where input of capital and technology lagged as compared with the Midwest, densities of rural farm population are higher than in either the Farming-Hinge or the Midwestern parts of the Economic Core.

Although the foregoing discussion of the areas of widely dispersed, contiguous farm based population has been necessarily brief and general, many readers will have been able to visualize the typical areal arrangement in greater detail. Such an image would reveal a rectangular pattern of governmental areas, roads, farms, and fields with the home of each farm family situated in an assemblage of structures (farmstead) on its own farm. Such an image is representative for most areas settled after 1800, that is the Ontario and Midwest sectors of the Economic Core Region, much of the western Interior South, and all of the Farming-Hinge region. Most exceptional to this arrange-ment was the pattern of settlement in the St. Lawrence Valley and other French settled areas such as near New Orleans. There long, narrow, rectangular farms were arranged in strips, the first one fronting the St. Lawrence or other navigable stream, and later ones along roads oriented parallel to the rivers and original strip of farms. Each farm home was situated at the end of the long lot farm next to the river or road. As long lot farms became subdivided into even narrower and more numerous properties, the settlements came to resemble long one-street villages. Despite this different and interesting pattern of settlement, however, the St. Lawrence Valley, as well as other older settled areas east of the Appalachians in the United States, also came to have widespread, moderately dense farm based population.

The Economic Core Region

Superimposed on the relatively continuous and uniform distribution of farms, villages, small towns, and small cities in the eastern United States (all are represented in Fig. 7.1 by black dots) and in southeastern Canada is a hierarchy of larger urban centers. For convenience, we might divide these also into three size categories: large, medium, and

F

TABLE 7.4. UNITED STATES, DISTRIBUTION OF POPULATION BY CENSUS REGIONS, 1900–70

	United States				Northeast				North Central				South				West			
	1900	1950	1960	1970	1900	1950	1960	1970	1900	1950	1960	1970	1900	1950	1960	1970	1900	1950	1960	1970
Total population (millions)	76.2	151.3	179.3	203.2	21.0	39.5	44.7	49.0	26.3	44.5	51.6	56.6	24.5	47.2	55.0	62.8	4.3	20.2	28.1	34.8
% of US total	100.0	100.0	100.0	100.0	27.6	26.1	24.9	24.1	34.6	29.4	28.8	27.8	33.2	31.2	30.7	30.9	5.7	13.3	15.6	17.1
% change, decade	21.4	14.5	18.5	13.3	20.9	9.7	13.2	9.8	17.5	10.8	16.1	9.6	22.4	13.3	16.5	14.2	31.9	40.4	38.9	24.1
Urban population New definition (millions)		96.8	125.3	149.3		31.4	35.8	39.4		28.5	35.5	40.5		23.0	32.2	40.5		14.0	21.8	28.9
Old definition (millions)	30.2	91.1	113.1		13.9	29.8	32.5		10.2	27.2	33.0		4.4	21.1	29.0		1.7	12.1	18.6	
% of region New	39.6	64.0	69.9	73.5	66.1	79.5	80.2	80.4	38.6	64.1	68.7	71.6	18.0	48.6	58.5	64.6	39.9	69.5	77.7	82.9
Old		59.6	63.0			75.4	72.8			61.1	63.9			44.6	52.7			59.9	66.1	
% of US total New	100.0	100.0	100.0	100.0	46.0	32.3	28.6	26.4	33.8	29.5	28.0	27.1	14.6	23.7	25.7	27.1	5.6	14.5	17.5	19.4
Old		100.0	100.0			33.0	28.7			30.2	29.2			23.4	25.7			13.4	16.5	
% change, decade New	36.7	20.6	29.3	19.2	35.5	8.0	14.2	10.1	37.0	16.0	24.5	14.1	35.6	37.8	40.1	26.1	48.0	43.8	55.3	32.4
Old			25.4				9.3				21.4				37.5				53.5	

Rural population																				
New definition																				
(millions)		54.5	54.1	53.9		8.1	8.8	9.6		16.0	16.1	16.1		24.2	22.8	22.3		6.2	6.3	5.9
Old definition																				
(millions)	46.0	61.2	66.2		7.1	9.7	12.1		16.2	17.3	18.6		20.1	26.1	26.0		2.6	8.1	9.5	
% of region																				
New		36.0	30.1	26.5		20.5	19.8	19.6		35.9	31.3	28.4		51.4	41.5	35.4		30.5	22.3	17.1
Old	60.4	40.4	37.0		33.9	24.6	27.2		61.4	38.9	36.1		82.0	55.4	47.3		60.1	40.1	33.9	
% of US rural																				
New		100.0	100.0	100.0		14.8	16.2	17.8		29.4	29.7	29.9		44.5	42.1	41.3		11.4	11.6	11.0
Old	100.0	100.0	100.0		15.4	15.8	18.3		35.2	28.2	28.1		43.7	42.7	39.3		5.7	13.2	14.3	
% change, decade																				
New			−0.8	−0.3			9.0	8.5			1.1	−0.3			−5.9	−2.4			1.7	−5.1
Old	12.5	6.5	8.3		−0.1	15.3	25.1		7.8	3.4	7.8		19.9	−1.0	−0.5		31.3	35.7	17.3	
Rural non-farm																				
(millions)		31.5	38.5	43.3		6.3	7.7	8.6		8.6	10.3	11.5		12.3	15.6	18.3		4.3	4.8	4.9
% of region		20.7	21.4	21.3		15.9	17.2	17.5		19.3	20.0	20.3		26.0	28.4	29.1		21.3	16.7	14.2
Rural farm[a]																				
Date	1920	1950	1960	1970	1920	1950	1960	1970	1920	1950	1960	1970	1920	1950	1960	1970	1920	1950	1960	1970
Number																				
(millions)	32.0	23.0	15.6	10.6	2.5	1.8	1.1	1.0	10.2	7.4	5.8	4.6	17.1	11.9	7.2	4.0	2.2	1.9	1.5	1.0
% of region	30.1	15.3	8.7	5.2	8.6	4.5	2.5	2.0	29.7	16.7	11.3	8.1	51.3	25.2	13.0	6.4	24.7	9.9	5.4	2.9
% of US farm	100.0	100.0	100.0	100.0	7.8	7.8	7.2	9.3	31.7	32.2	37.1	43.4	53.4	51.9	46.1	37.7	6.9	8.3	9.6	9.5
% change, decade[a]		−24.5	−32.2	−21.3		−25.7	−37.5	−8.6		−20.5	−21.5	−14.7		−27.5	−39.8	−32.6		−19.2	−21.2	−17.4

[a]Rural farm data for 1920, 1950, and 1960 are from the series of Farm Population Estimates published by the US Department of Agriculture. Data for 1970 are from the Census of Population. Percent change from 1960 to 1970 is computed from Census of Population figures.

small metropolitan areas, with urbanized area populations of at least 1,000,000, 250,000, and 50,000, respectively. It is the concentration, size, and functions of cities which distinguish the Economic Core region (Fig. 7.6). In this region containing only about 10% of the area of the American 48 states (less than 9% of the national area) live almost half of the country's people (Tables 7.1, 7.4). The concentration in Canada is even greater: more than half the national population in less than 2% of the area (Table 7.2). Four-fifths of the people in both national sectors of the region live in cities. Fifteen of the total of twenty-eight urbanized areas with more than a million people each are located here, as are 88, or nearly half, of the 194 urbanized areas with at least 100,000 population (Tables 7.2 and 7.3; Fig. 7.6).

The Economic Core Region is comprised of a large American and a smaller Canadian part. The Canadian area, in turn, is made up of the small St. Lawrence Lowland sub-region centering on Montreal and an Ontario subregion with Toronto the principal center (Fig. 7.2). In the United States the Economic Core is separated by the Appalachian Highlands into the small original Atlantic sector (Megalopolis) and a larger Midwestern sector.

The term economic core represents more than mere concentration of population and cities. It implies that this area is the core or heartland in the economy of both nations. Not only is there concentrated within this relatively small area a major part of both national populations and production but, more significantly, also a majority of the decision-making power and activities by which the economies of both countries, and indeed a significant part of the world, are directed.

The economic core first began to evolve along the Atlantic seaboard, in the area that has since become Megalopolis, when during the early nineteenth century the seaport cities of the area began to collect, process, and trade the products of the agricultural South and developing Midwest, and to perform business and financial services and economic direction for those areas. For a variety of reasons, including its superior harbor and its lowland Hudson Valley/Mohawk Valley gateway through the Appalachian Highlands to the Great Lakes and Midwest, New York City forged ahead of its rivals to become the major overseas gateway and primary node of the developing economic core, even though it shared the core functions with Philadelphia, Boston, and Baltimore and with Montreal and later Toronto in Canada.

In the beginning, emphasis was mainly on the trading and handling of goods, especially agricultural, and on rudimentary manufacturing. During the later nineteenth and early twentieth centuries, manufacturing multiplied both in kind and amount, first in the large and smaller port cities and inland cities of the seaboard area, then along the routeways into the Midwest. Factory cities sprang up and multiplied in size. Millions of immigrants, mainly from Europe, flooded into the gateway cities, especially New York. Millions stayed there to man the factories, move the goods, and build the cities; others moved along the railroads and Great Lakes into the Midwest where they joined westward-moving Americans on new farms or in new cities. Some of these cities, along the Ohio River, such as Pittsburgh or Cincinnati, and particularly along the southern Great Lakes, such as Buffalo, Cleveland, Chicago, and Toronto, began to rival the older seaboard cities in size, factory output, and commercial functions.

The economic core functions, and consequently the Economic Core Region, had leaped across the Appalachians to form a Midwestern segment, including the Ontario sector. Both the Atlantic and Midwestern segments were aided by discovery and exploitation of remarkable earth resources. During the late nineteenth century the anthracite coal of northeastern Pennsylvania became the base not only for local concentrations of mines and their workers (Fig. 7.1) but also for the heat and energy supplying the factories, offices, and homes of the growing seaboard cities. Somewhat later the great bituminous coal resources of the dissected Allegheny tableland, from southwestern Pennsylvania and southeastern Ohio to the Kentucky–West Virginia–Virginia border area, attracted thousands of miner settlers to that area (Fig. 7.1) and fueled the iron and steel mills and factories in both the older seaboard sector and newer Midwest sector of the Economic Core. After the opening of a major ship lock at Sault Ste. Marie in 1855, iron ore from the great resources in the western Lake Superior area likewise not only gave rise to local mining populations but, more importantly, supplied the burgeoning needs of new iron and steel mills along the southern Great Lakes at or near Chicago, Detroit, Cleveland, Buffalo, and Hamilton and inland to Pittsburgh. The Great Lakes, supplying low cost means of transport, at first for passenger vessels, but continuously for freight, especially for bulk goods such as coal, ores, limestone (used as flux in the iron-making blast furnaces), and grain, and also unlimited supplies of fresh water for lakeside factories and cities, became a magnet for city growth. Of the nine giant cities in the Midwest–Ontario section of the Economic Core, six are located on the Great Lakes, the other three being along the Ohio or Mississippi rivers (Fig. 7.6).

Finally, these cities, like those of the Atlantic sector and Montreal, perform manufacturing and commercial functions not only for the millions of people within the cities themselves and for the region, but for the two nations and beyond. For example, much of the enormous surplus production from the agricultural Midwest, the Farming-Hinge Region, the near North, and the West is funnelled into these Midwest and Ontario Core cities for processing, trading, and shipping eastward to or through the seaboard gateway cities of Megalopolis and Montreal.

Because of the need to understand how the Economic Core Region came to be, we have emphasized the historical development of its cities as centers of commerce and manufacturing. Much of the two nations' commerce and manufacturing is still carried on in the cities of the Economic Core. Within many of them, from one-fourth to two-fifths of all workers are employed in factories, another fifth are involved in retail and wholesale trade, and still others provide transportation services. During recent decades, however, an increasing proportion of all workers has been engaged in the provision of other services such as banking, insurance, advertising, business management, health, education, entertainment, and government. Many of these service jobs are concerned directly or indirectly with the management of the two nations' and the world's economies. It is for such high level decision making that the Economic Core is most distinctive. For example, it has been estimated that Megalopolis (the Atlantic section of the Core) alone handles as much as 90% of the volume of American money transactions and 80% of all stock transactions, or that it possesses two-thirds of the large advertising agencies and the headquarters of 40% of the 500 largest corporations in the United States. For Canada, such management functions are even more concentrated in Toronto and Montreal, or in New York and American core cities.

The relationship between the areal concentration of population, on the one hand, and of the Economic Core functions, especially decision making, on the other, is a complex one whose analysis challenges geographers, economists, and demographers. The concentration of employment opportunities in manufacturing and services obviously encourages concentration of population. In turn, the large and growing population creates an expanding market for goods and services. But the relationship may be changing as technology, resources, and even human values change. The manufacturing of the two countries not only continues to spread outside the Economic Core, especially into the far West and American South, but also employs a decreasing proportion of all workers. Furthermore, with improved devices for communicating, recording, and processing information, it becomes increasingly possible for high level decision makers to be separated, not only from their production line workers but also from the bulk of lower level administrators and clerical workers. For example, a corporation may have its top decision makers and management in New York, its accounting and other administrative and clerical offices in Detroit or even Los Angeles, and its factories and production workers in various parts of the United States and Canada. Problems of congestion and pollution in crowded cities of the Economic Core Region may serve as further incentives for people to seek or to establish employment opportunities elsewhere. These trends, although merely touched upon here, may help to explain the slow but significant and probable continuing decline in the proportion of people who reside in the Economic Core Region, especially in the case of the United States.

Examination of Figs. 7.1, 7.2, and 7.6 reveals the arrangement of cities and population within the Economic Core Region. The Atlantic Megalopolis and St. Lawrence subregions are dominated by the great port cities which serve as gateways between Anglo-America and the rest of the world, especially Europe. New York is dominant in size as it is in business management. Because of the increasing role of government in the direction of the American economy and society, Washington shares with New York the central role in decision making and has been the fastest growing of the five great Megalopolis nodes during recent decades. In Canada, Montreal shares the gateway function and number one rank with Toronto; fast-growing Ottawa plays the important government role. Figure 7.6 recognizes the recent southward expansion of the Economic Core to include the port centered urbanized areas of Norfolk–Portsmouth and Newport News–Hampton.

In Canada the St. Lawrence lowland and the plain north of lakes Ontario and Erie form the axis of the long, narrow Core Region. In the United States, two major trans-Appalachian corridors connect the Midwest sector of the Core to Megalopolis. The only trans-mountain lowland route, along the Hudson and Mohawk valleys and Lake Ontario Plain to Lake Erie, utilized first by the Erie Canal and then by the New York Central Railroad and finally the New York Thruway, became densely populated and occupied by industrial cities such as Rochester, Syracuse, Utica, Rome, and Albany–Schenectedy–Troy (Figs. 7.1 and 7.6). The largest urban area, Buffalo–Niagara Falls, is both an industrial center and the transfer point for national and international water and land shipment. The second and less open trans-Appalachian corridor, reaching westward from Megalopolis toward Pittsburgh at the head of the Ohio River Valley, represents a more difficult crossing of the Appalachian Highland. Although it has been served by a number of separate railroad and highway routes, it is less densely populated and urbanized than its northern counterpart.

In the Midwest and Ontario sectors, the greatest node is centered on Chicago and Milwaukee, where the Great Lakes waterway reaches furthest into the productive agricultural heartland of the country. Chicago serves not only as the greatest industrial and commercial center for a large and highly productive region, but also as the principal gateway between the Economic Core and the western half of the United States. These roles are shared, on a much smaller scale, by the old, industrial river port and rail center of St. Louis.

There are two concentrations of Midwestern cities which may be considered as lying along axes between the two trans-Appalachian corridors just previously noted and the western anchors of Chicago and St. Louis. The greater of these is centered around the southern and western shores of Lake Erie. The location of Cleveland in the heart of the Economic Core is strategic, commanding the water and land routes from the Midwest toward the Buffalo–New York corridor as well as the overland routes toward the Pittsburgh–Megalopolis corridor. Its functions are diversified among commerce, manufacturing, and services. The Detroit–Windsor urban node commands the water route from the upper Great Lakes into the Economic Core and is a major crossroads between the American and Canadian parts of the Economic Core Region. Its growth, and that of many smaller cities of southern Michigan and adjacent Ontario, Ohio, and Indiana, have been particularly associated with the motor vehicle industry.

The southern concentration of urban centers (Columbus, Dayton, Indianapolis, Cincinnati, Louisville) in the Midwest Core commands both the Ohio River and the overland routeways between St. Louis and the Pittsburgh–Megalopolis corridor. This was the most important area of early development in the Midwest; Cincinnati was not surpassed in population by Chicago until the 1870s nor Louisville by Detroit until a decade later (Fig. 7.3). Growth and sharing in Economic Core functions by the two Ohio River cities, and especially by Columbus, Dayton, Indianapolis, and smaller nearby cities, has again increased in the mid twentieth century.

The Interior South

As previously indicated, the Interior South has a widespread distribution of rural and small town population but with relatively high densities occurring in restricted areas. Until the mid twentieth century there had been marked correlation of spatial distribution between intensive production of tobacco or cotton, on the one hand, and both density of rural population and ratio of black to white people, on the other. The agricultural system for both crops was labor intensive and especially dependent upon black people who were bound to the system, and hence to particular areas, first as slaves and then, until the mid twentieth century, by lack of alternative opportunities. Although agriculture in the South has recently been undergoing rapid change, with many white and especially black people migrating to cities, the effects of the persistent labor intensive system are still present in the patterns of current population distribution. A major tobacco-growing area with relatively dense rural population is centered in the inner coastal plain of North Carolina and extends southward into South Carolina and northwestward into the Piedmont along the Virginia–North Carolina border (Fig. 7.1). Other areas with somewhat lesser population densities related in part to tobacco production include the southwest Georgia–Florida border area, the northern part of the Great Valley in eastern Tennessee, and central Kentucky from the Bluegrass Basin southwestward into the Pennyroyal area along the border with central Tennessee. Relatively dense populations of white and especially of black people engaged in cotton production were much more widespread in the Interior South than those related to tobacco. Areas of more than average density and of concentrations of rural black people included the inner coastal plain of South Carolina and Georgia, northern Alabama centering on the Tennessee River Valley, and the Mississippi River floodplain from southeastern Missouri through eastern Arkansas and western Mississippi into northeastern Louisiana (Fig. 7.1).

There are two other areas of relatively dense rural population in the Interior South. The major one is based on the coal-mining industry in the Cumberland Mountains of southern West Virginia, eastern Kentucky, southwestern Virginia, and neighboring Tennessee (Fig. 7.1). Close observation shows settlement to be concentrated in the dendritic patterned narrow stream valleys deeply incised in the rugged hill and mountain country. During earlier times, many of the mining people were part time farmers. A smaller area of relatively dense rural and small town settlement is the bayou country to the west and south of New Orleans. It has long been an area of cane sugar plantations which used large amounts of hand labor. It is also the area of "Cajun" people and culture. The "Cajuns" are the descendants of French-speaking people who were exiled from Acadia (Nova Scotia) in the eighteenth century and settled along the then remote bayous to become farmer fishermen. Finally, since the mid twentieth century, on-shore and off-shore oil drilling and production along the Louisiana coast have brought many new people as well as aspects of modernization to this area of relatively dense rural and small town population.

As compared to the Economic Core Region, the Interior South is an area of later and lesser urbanization. The region has about 17% of the 48-state area and 15.5% of the population. But whereas four-fifths of the Economic Core people are urban, more than half of the population in the Interior South is still rural (Tables 7.1 and 7.4). Atlanta is the only urbanized area in the Interior South with a population of at least 1m.; there are thirteen such cities in the American Economic Core (Table 7.3). There are only five urbanized areas with populations of 250,000 or more in the Interior South as compared with 37 in the much smaller Economic Core.

In both the Interior South and the Economic Core regions there had developed by the mid nineteenth century a widespread population base of rural farm and small town people. But the development upon this base of many rapidly growing cities in which there became concentrated not only much of America's manufacturing but also much of the management and decision making for its economy and society occurred only in the Economic Core. Only since the mid twentieth century has urbanization and economic change in the Interior South begun to reduce the marked imbalance between the two regions (Table 7.4).

As previously suggested, the early agricultural economic base in the two regions was different. In the Economic Core, especially the Midwest sector, farms were family operated and commercial from the beginning. Each farm family made its own decisions, performed most of its own labor, and sought to produce as much as possible for the marketplace. The land resource was exceptional both in quality and quantity. The combined conditions meant that labor was scarce and expensive relative to land; that incentive was great to increase capital input, in the form of technology and non-human energy, in order to increase yields per man hour. The relatively large numbers of increasingly productive and informed farm people wielded strong influence in encouraging local, regional, and national governments and business to develop agricultural education, technology, and institutions for the improvement of production and marketing. The growing cities which manufactured the agricultural machinery and supplies and processed, traded, and transported the farm products became an ever-growing regional market as well as forwarding system for those products. As numbers of farm people have declined since the 1940s (but not their productivity nor their buying power) most Economic Core cities continue to develop from the earlier base and momentum.

The Interior South was different. To be sure it had an early advantage in agricultural production. With its long growing season and mild winters it could produce products which were in demand in Europe and the northern United States but which could not be grown in those cooler areas. The products whose choices came to dominate the agriculture and even the economy and society of the Interior South were most importantly cotton, secondarily tobacco, and to a much lesser extent sugarcane and rice. From the appraisal of the set of conditions which existed during the seventeenth, eighteenth, and early nineteenth centuries came the dominant system of plantation agriculture and slave labor. The soils which had developed under the humid subtropical conditions of the Interior South were generally much less fertile and durable than those of the Midwest. Richer alluvial soils were limited in extent and expensive to drain and reclaim. The combined conditions were thus opposite to those in the Midwest. After the importation and multiplication of a black slave population, labor was comparatively plentiful and low in cost relative to productive land—there was little incentive to substitute the input of capital and technology for labor. Manufacture of machinery, implements, and farm supplies was limited. First step processing of farm products such as ginning of cotton, pressing of cottonseed, or refining of sugar was not sufficient to support manufacturing cities. Black people, whether first as slaves or later as share croppers, were extremely limited in the opportunities to acquire education, income, or buying power. Until the mid twentieth century most of them were rural farm people but, unlike farm people in the Economic Core, they provided little base for the functions or growth of cities. The small scale white farmers, although greatly outnumbering the plantation operators, were nevertheless locked into the same labor intensive, rather static, and impoverished economic system. Attempts to improve agricultural technology and education for the mass of rural people were limited; poor farmers and laborers, especially black slaves (share croppers after emancipation) lacked the power, while large landholders and associated urban tradesmen and investors lacked incentive to change the system.

Resting upon a labor intensive, relatively poor agricultural base, cities of the South continued to be primarily service and commercial centers for their surrounding regions. Urbanization was comparatively retarded (Table 7.4). Atlanta and Memphis were the two largest cities, Memphis serving as a great cotton and lumber market and Atlanta as the trade and transport center for the southern parts of the Piedmont, coastal plain, and Appalachians. Coastal cities of the Gulf South region served as seaports. What most southern cities lacked until well into the twentieth century were the functions of manufacturing for regional and especially for national markets and significant non-local business management and decision making. Small scale, lower level management was carried out on plantations or in local banks, offices, and governmental centers. Much of the higher level, larger scale functions, such as ownership and financing of railroads, or managing the export and processing of cotton, was performed in cities of the Economic Core.

Recent Urbanization in the Interior South

Since the mid twentieth century cities in the South have been growing faster than those in the Economic Core (Table 7.4). Growth is related to expansion of the two earlier lacking or lagging functions, manufacturing and the services, the latter including increased participation in business management. Four groups of growing cities may be identified.

First are the cities which have long served as regional centers, of which Atlanta and Memphis have already been mentioned. Atlanta is located centrally in the whole southeastern area and commands major rail and highway routes along either side of the southern Appalachians, northeastward toward Megalopolis and northward toward the Midwest Economic Core. Rapid expansion of both business and industry made it the second fastest growing large urbanized area (over 1m. inhabitants) in the United States during the 1960s. Memphis is the major commercial center along the Mississippi River land and water routeways and for the agriculturally productive Mississippi Valley from Missouri to Louisiana. Smaller regional commercial centers whose functions and growth are somewhat similar include Nashville, Little Rock, Shreveport, Jackson, and Montgomery.

The second notable group of cities in the Interior South is much more localized in the Piedmont region of the Carolinas and Georgia, the most urbanized and industrialized area in the Interior South (Figs. 7.1 and 7.6). Manufacture of cotton textiles—the oldest and most significant industry—was developed in the Piedmont after the Civil War, especially after 1880. The industry, like traditional agriculture in the South, is labor intensive and began to draw surplus rural white laborers to factories located at or near water power sites in small towns along the numerous Piedmont streams. Using the available factory sites, power, and southern cotton, but especially the low cost labor, the area was able to surpass the older New England cotton textile region in importance by 1920, and to go on to dominate that industry and to achieve preeminence in manufacture of hosiery, underclothing, blankets, carpets, and other goods made of cotton and synthetic fibres. Charlotte and Greensboro (North Carolina) and Greenville (South Carolina) are the largest of many medium sized and a great number of smaller textile-making cities. Two other industries in which the Piedmont has come to lead the nation are the manufacture of cigarettes and furniture. Supplies of tobacco grown in the Piedmont and coastal plain, and hardwood from the Piedmont and southern Appalachians, are convenient. But the furniture industry, like cotton textiles, is labor intensive and has used low cost surplus labor from Piedmont farms and the southern Appalachians to achieve leadership. Both the furniture and tobacco industries are centered in North Carolina and Virginia, tobacco in larger cities such as Raleigh, Winston Salem, and Durham, furniture in High Point and many small cities.

A third much less concentrated group of cities is strung along the fall line junction between the resistant rocks of the Piedmont and the geologically younger, less resistant materials of the coastal plain. Early settlements and water powered mills were established at river falls and rapids along the Fall Line. Roads and railroads were developed to serve the line of settlements. Fall line settlements which have become medium sized cities include Raleigh, Columbia, Augusta, Macon, Columbus, and Montgomery (Figs. 7.1 and 7.6). They serve the agriculturally developed inner coastal plain and share in textile and other manufacturing developed in the Piedmont.

The cities of the final group are located in the Great Appalachian Valley, the most prominent and continuous lowland of the parallel ridge and valley segment of the Appalachians which extends along the eastern side of the Highlands from eastern Pennsylvania southwestward into Alabama. The largest urbanized area, third largest in the Interior South, is Birmingham. Together with Gadsden in the valley to the northeastward, it comprises the major center of integrated iron and steel manufacturing in the whole South. The industry was originally based on local raw materials but now uses imported ore. Some of the steel is further processed in highly industrialized Chattanooga, Tennessee. Still further northeastward are Knoxville, with more diversified functions, including the University of Tennessee and administrative offices for the Tennessee Valley Authority, and a concentration of small cities and dense rural population near the Tennessee–Virginia border. Many people in the latter area including the cities of Bristol, Kingsport, and Johnson City, are employed in the manufacture of synthetic fibres, textiles, photographic film, chemicals and paper. The last of the string of Great Valley cities within the Interior South is Roanoke, a railroad, manufacturing, and commercial center.

Florida and the Gulf Coast

In the character and causes of population distribution, Florida and the Gulf Coast differ greatly from the Interior South. First, as indicated earlier, most of this outer coastal plain region did not develop a widespread base of contiguous farm settlement, although it has more recently developed highly productive specialized agriculture in restricted areas. Secondly, the region has become highly urbanized. With only 3.3% of the 48-state area, the region has 6.3% of the population, four-fifths of it urban (Table 7.4).

Growth of both population and urbanization has been recent. The population of Florida has multiplied seven times since 1920. Before 1920 only one of the region's cities had as many as 100,000 people, New Orleans having reached that size by 1840 on the basis of its functions as a port near the mouth of the Mississippi River. By 1970, sixteen urbanized areas within the Florida–Gulf Coast Region had reached that threshold, two of them having over a million people and three more over a half million each (Table 7.3 and Fig. 7.6).

Most of the cities continue to serve as ports not only for the increased population within the region but, especially in the case of Houston, New Orleans, and smaller cities in the center and west, for expanded production in hinterlands reaching well into the interior. In the central and western parts of the region also, great resources and production of petroleum and natural gas as well as sulfur have stimulated development of petrochemical, aluminum refining, and related industries. The space exploration program has stimulated growth especially at and near Houston, New Orleans, and Orlando, Florida. Finally, the recreation industry and the development of retirement and second homes have brought large scale net in-migration, permanent as well as seasonal, especially to Florida. The Florida–Gulf Coast Region might be thought of as having been annexed by the Economic Core Region to serve as winter fruit and vegetable garden, recreation and retirement area, and space exploration laboratory.

The Farming-Hinge Region

As shown in Figs. 7.5, 7.6 and Table 7.1, this region is divided into three subdivisions, a Prairie subdivision in Canada, and northern and southern subregions within the United States. The whole region is identified on the basis of two components of population and their respective functions. The first is the widespread, remarkably uniform distribution of rural farm and small town population (Figs. 7.1 and 7.2). The rural farm people operate a major portion of North America's cropland. Included are all of the Canadian Prairie region, much of the highly productive American corn belt, the western part of the Midwest dairy region, most of the annually cropped portions of the American spring and winter wheat regions, and the black soiled prairies of east central Texas. Each farm family typically lives on its own farm comprised of one or more rectangular blocks, the farms increasing in size from a typical 240 acres in the moister east to near 1000 in the drier west. The system of land survey has imposed rectangularity not only upon farms and fields but upon road networks, on small and large political divisions, and upon the spatial arrangements of farm population and the hierarchy of small towns and cities, as well as upon the internal form of the latter.

The second component of the population is made up of cities which, considering the dominance of agriculture in the economy, are notable in number, size, and locational arrangement. Two-thirds of the population in this outstanding agricultural region is urban (Table 7.1). Three of its urbanized areas have populations over a million, four others have more than half a million, and another eight more than 250,000 (Tables 7.2 and 7.3; Fig. 7.6). Each of these, and of the 17 additional centers with at least 50,000 population, serves as a commercial, transport, and service center for the highly capitalized, productive agriculture in its region. But the functions of the largest cities reach far beyond their immediate hinterlands within the Hinge Region. These large cities serve as connecting links or gateways between the relatively densely populated eastern and the more sparsely settled western or northwestern sections of the two countries.

The three largest American centers—Minneapolis–St. Paul, Kansas City, and Dallas–Fort Worth—dominate this gateway function for the northern, central, and southern latitudes, respectively, of the United States. The major railroads and even highways which span the western half of the country along near parallel latitudinal lines converge upon these cities, particularly the Twin Cities and Kansas City, from which they focus on the Chicago and St. Louis gateways, respectively, to and from the Economic Core. During recent decades these three major collecting and distributing centers have begun increasingly to perform manufacturing as well as business management functions so that each might be thought of as a developing outlier of the Economic Core Region. Omaha, although smaller than the big three, performs a similar hinge or connecting link function.

The medium size cities such as Saskatoon, Regina, Fargo, Des Moines, Lincoln, or San Antonio perform more as regional commercial centers than as interregional connecting links. Oklahoma City, Tulsa, Wichita, and the centers in Texas and Alberta serve the oil and natural gas industries as well as agriculture. Much of their rapid population growth has been stimulated by the former function.

In the American section the large and medium size Hinge cities are located in a pronounced north–south alignment (Figs. 7.1 and 7.6). This arrangement arises from their being regional centers for the western side of the great cropland triangle, and collection and distribution centers for the sparsely settled Great Plains to the westward, as well as east–west gateways. The northernmost cities are located in the fertile Red River and Missouri River valleys and serve as river crossings. It is not strange, though it is highly significant to the economy, politics, and society of each of the American Great Plains states, especially the four northern ones, that the dominant city of each lies along or near its eastern margin. Small towns and service centers in the American section are arranged in east–west linear orientation in keeping with the dominant pattern and interregional linkage function of major railroads and highways, some of which follow major river valleys.

In Canada the eastward gateway function is remarkably concentrated in Winnipeg, located at the southeastern apex of the Prairie subregion where it is squeezed between the Canadian Shield and the international border. All rail and highway traffic between eastern and western Canada pass through it. At the western margin of the Prairie sub-region the linkage function to Vancouver is shared by Edmonton, Calgary, and Leth-bridge. In addition, Edmonton is a gateway and service center for vast areas to the north and west including central British Columbia, the Peace River Valley, the Athabasca–Mackenzie Lowland, and the Alaska Highway. Development of the petroleum industry since 1947 has greatly stimulated the diversification of the economy and growth of population in Alberta. Small towns and rural service centers in the Prairie subregion tend to be aligned along the railroads and highways which radiate westward and north-westward from Winnipeg.

The Pacific Coast Region

The area comprising the sparsely populated western half of the coterminous United States and adjacent parts of Canada is here divided into two unequal sized regions, the larger Interior West and the less extensive Pacific Coast Region (Fig. 7.6). Both are strongly characterized by nodes or islands of population, both rural and urban, separated by sparsely settled territory (Figs. 7.1 and 7.2). But the settlement clusters in the smaller Pacific Coast Region are much more extensive and populous than those of the Interior West. As a consequence, the relatively small Pacific Coast Region is exceptional to the generalization of overall sparse population in the western part of the continent. It has nearly 12% (24m.) of the people of the 48 contiguous American states in less than 6% of the area, and 7% of Canadians in a tiny fraction of the national area (Tables 7.1 and 7.2). Approximately nine-tenths of the people live in cities, a higher proportion than even in the Atlantic section of the Economic Core. The region has six urbanized areas, each with more than a million people, and three more with over half a million each (Tables 7.2 and 7.3; Fig. 7.6). It resembles the Economic Core Region both in that so much of its population is concentrated in giant cities, and also that these cities perform a larger than normal proportion of the business and business management and the manufacturing of the two countries. This development is recent, since mid century, but the Pacific Coast Region may now be considered as a developing secondary economic core.

More than four-fifths of the regions' people live in California, which has advanced from statehood to being the most populous state in the country in little more than a century. Over half of the 20 + million Californians are concentrated in two main clusters, both overwhelmingly urban: a northern one in the Bay region, with San Francisco and

Oakland as the principal cities (some 3m. people in urbanized area), and a southern one with Los Angeles as the primate city (more than 8m. people). Lesser urban and rural settlement nodes are to be observed in the San Diego area to the far south, in the Great Valley lying inland, and in numerous smaller intermontane valleys and coastal lowlands (Fig. 7.1).

There have been three major boom periods in the story of continuous growth in the population and economy of California. The gold rush to central California in the mid eighteenth century established San Francisco–Oakland as the first significant population node, a superior port, gateway, and commercial center, first for the mining activity in the Sierra Nevada and then for the productive agriculture developed in the great Central Valley and smaller coast range valleys opening toward San Francisco Bay (Fig. 7.3). This node became the terminus of the first transcontinental railroad in 1869. The second boom developed during the 1880s. It was stimulated by the new railroads connecting both San Francisco and southern California to the east, by the development of irrigated agriculture, food processing, and refrigeration which permitted conversion of the alluvial lowlands of California into fruit and vegetable gardens supplying the rapidly developing Economic Core Region 2000 miles distant, and by the developing image of mild, sunny, mountain girt California as a healthful, ideal place to live. This second boom in California's development focused particularly upon the south and led to the rapid growth of Los Angeles, although that city did not surpass San Francisco in size until 1920. The third spurt in the continuous population and economic growth came during and following World War II when the tremendous expansion of shipbuilding, aircraft, electronics, and associated industries changed the Pacific Coast cities from moderate regional to major national industrial centers. Los Angeles–Long Beach has become the second, and San Francisco–Oakland the sixth, largest urbanized area in the United States. Both San Diego and San Jose, each to some degree a satellite of the respective larger nodes, have surpassed a million population.

The second boom phase of California's growth was based in significant part on the development of a highly capitalized, technical, large scale, irrigated agriculture supplying especially fruits and all season vegetables for the populated eastern United States. Such agriculture resulted in relatively dense population in the 400-mile long Central Valley, the smaller linear valleys in the central coast ranges, the Los Angeles basin, and the Imperial Valley (Fig. 7.1). The third boom phase of urbanization and industrialization, while centered in the two major urban nodes, has pushed outward to dominate and even displace farming over extensive areas. Even the once dominantly agricultural Central Valley now claims one urban center of over half a million population, Sacramento; one with a quarter million, Fresno; and three more with more than 100,000 (Fig. 7.6). The spectacular increase of population and urbanization have further affected the intensive, productive agriculture which was originally focused toward distant eastern markets, by providing within the Pacific Coast Region itself a market of approximately 25m. people.

Not only national, but also international rearrangements of population, production, consumption, and trade have affected California and the Pacific Coast Region, especially since 1940. The major seaport nodes of Vancouver, Seattle, Portland, San Francisco–Oakland, Los Angeles–Long Beach, and San Diego serve as gateways to and from the Pacific. World War II necessitated a tremendous effort which was centered at and funneled through those gateways. During the quarter century since, possibly the greatest economic growth of any nation has been that of Japan, whose leading trade partners are in North America. The long-continuing military activity in southeast Asia, the recent development of all the western Pacific countries including China, and now the improvement of relations between China and the United States, have brought and will continue to bring increased importance to the Pacific Coast Region and its development. One might observe that the United States and Canada, having faced primarily toward the Atlantic since the beginnings of European settlement have, especially since 1940, become oriented toward both oceans.

Population in the northern part of the Pacific Coast Region is equally or even more areally concentrated than that in California. Most people live in the narrow structural lowland between the Cascade and British Columbia Coast Mountains to the east and the lower coast ranges of Oregon, Washington, and Vancouver Island to the west. There are three concentrations of population, one in the Willamette Valley focused on Portland, a Washington segment in the Puget Sound Lowland centered on Seattle (Figs. 7.1, 7.2, and 7.6) and a third concentration in Canada. The Seattle and Vancouver urbanized areas each have more than a million people, Portland somewhat fewer.

The Willamette Valley is the oldest node in the West; it was established by settlers moving overland from the distant agricultural frontier in the humid East, in this case beginning before 1840 (Fig. 7.3). The Valley was recognized as being unusual within the arid West, having mild winters and long growing season but a shorter summer dry period than California to the south, and more ample and reliable precipitation than in the Interior West. There were better soils, more lowland area, and much less dense forest of big trees to be cleared than in the small lowlands between the mountains and arms of the sea in Washington or British Columbia.

The California Gold Rush provided market opportunities after 1850 for the small community of grain and livestock farmers in the Willamette Valley. The Willamette node of population and those in Washington and British Columbia also shared, somewhat differently and to less degree, in the two later boom phases of growth that affected California. Agriculture benefited from railroad connections to eastern markets in the 1880s, but it was primarily unirrigated in character and much more related to markets closer at hand than was true in California. Nor was the image of the ideal place to live so romanticized, popularized, and effective as in the case of California. The northern areas have been affected, again to a somewhat lesser degree than California, by the urbanization–industrialization phase, Seattle sharing, for example, in the shipbuilding and aircraft industries.

Whereas the hinterland of California beyond the Sierra Nevada and San Bernardino Mountains is a vast desert or semi-desert area, very sparsely settled until the relatively recent population growth in Arizona and Las Vegas, the hinterlands of Vancouver, Seattle, and Portland beyond the British Columbia Coast Mountains and Cascades have been considerably more productive. The irrigated agriculture of the Yakima, Wenatchee, and Okanagan valleys, the Columbia River basin and the Snake River Plain, and the mineral and forest industries of the Cascades and northern Rocky Mountains, while oriented mainly toward eastern or overseas markets, have had a considerable part of their commerce centered in and through Portland, Seattle, and Vancouver. Portland, at the confluence of the Willamette and navigable lower Columbia River, became a seaport node for rail and highway routes and local river commerce southward toward California, northward toward Seattle, and eastward through the Columbia Gorge in the Cascades to the Columbia–Snake and northern Rocky Mountain region. The Seattle–Tacoma node, without a similar low level route across the Cascades, nevertheless became the focus of three transcontinental railroads. It became the major center of management and commerce for the fishing, mining, forest, and defense economy of Alaska and for a great lumber industry. The Seattle and other ample harbors of Puget Sound compete strongly for the growing Pacific Ocean commerce as well as national defense functions. Lacking local resources of coal or petroleum, the Seattle and Portland nodes have utilized the vast hydroelectric power generated along the Columbia River system and now receive petroleum, natural gas, and hydroelectric power from western Canada. In Canada, Victoria was the leading Pacific port until after a Canadian transcontinental railroad was completed to New Westminster and then Vancouver in the 1880s. Victoria has remained the provincial capital and the commercial center for southern Vancouver Island. But Vancouver has assumed the increasingly important role as major Canadian gateway to the Pacific as well as to Pacific Coastal United States.

Because the twentieth century growth of population, industrialization, and urbanization have been so rapid in the Pacific Coast Region, especially California, and because that growth was both caused and encouraged in significant part by a widely diffused image of these areas as ideal places to live, the conflict of the perceived ideal with resulting present congested conditions is now stark and dramatic. We have come to expect and have long accepted overcrowding, congestion, pollution, and ugliness in parts of New York, Chicago, or Detroit. But suddenly we realize that it has happened in the utopian valleys of Los Angeles and Yosemite and near San Francisco Bay. California, long the second and still the third largest petroleum-producing state in what was an oil rich country, must now import vast amounts of petroleum and other forms of energy. Third largest of the states, most populous, and first in agricultural production, California is now faced with problems of insufficient land and water for homes and farms as well as factories. Now that California's once glorified living spaces appear to many to have become overcrowded and despoiled, North Americans seem to be turning to alternative utopias, first Arizona for example, and now Colorado, Oregon, and British Columbia.

The Interior West

The interior West comprises almost half the area of the coterminous United States but has less than 7% of the population and an average density of less than 10 persons per square mile (Table 7.1; Figs. 7.1 and 7.6). Sparse population is likewise characteristic of the British Columbia segment. Ironically, two-thirds of the people in these wide open spaces live in cities, and many of the remainder in small, widely separated rural concentrations. For this nucleated majority there is a sense of community within the insular congregations of people, but a feeling of remoteness from other nodes and especially from the primary and secondary cores of population in the distant East and along the Pacific Coast. For the minority of Western people who live outside the scattered population concentrations, there is remoteness at all scales, local, regional, and national. Distance becomes a major fact of everyday living.

To repeat, the dominant characteristic of population in the dry Interior West is its overall sparsity. But almost equally striking is the fact that the scant population is strongly coagulated into clusters or nodes, a goodly number of which are linear in shape. Such features of spatial arrangement are related both to the nature of the land and resources and to the culture of the people who have appraised and occupied the land. The Interior West, especially in American history, has always been an area remote—a kind of land reserve, a region either passed over or not yet entered (Fig. 7.3). Until the mid nineteenth century it was beyond the westward-spreading frontier of agricultural occupance. Then, with the settlement of Oregon's Willamette Valley and the gold rush and development in California, the Interior West became a 1200-mile wide lacuna to be surmounted in the functioning and development of a nation comprised of a major eastern and a lesser distant western part (Fig. 7.3). The significance and cost to the functioning of the American nation of this great partial lacuna, separating the primary eastern and secondary western parts of its ecumene, has been alleviated by advances in the technology of communication and transportation, but has not been overcome, even today. In Canada the Interior West subregion is a partial lacuna between the Pacific Coast and Prairies; it represents part of a far greater distance to be overcome between Vancouver and the Economic Core Region.

Because of the number of population clusters, each with considerable individuality in terms of size, origins, and sustaining economies, it is impossible here to discuss them singly. Broad generalizations must suffice. One of the prime causes for variations in the density and spatial arrangement of population is the differences in the forms of land use, including not only agriculture but also mining, forestry, and recreation. Three common forms of agricultural land use in these dry lands, arranged in ascending order of potential for supporting population, are livestock ranching, dry fallow farming, and irrigated farming.

The land use which is most widespread is livestock grazing. Because of varying degrees of aridity and sparseness of pasture, the limited availability of water, and in parts the rough and mountainous terrain, individual family operated ranches must contain from 2000 to upwards of 20,000 acres, including lands rented or leased often from the federal or provincial governments. Consequently ranching, while very widespread, directly supports an extremely sparse population. The better the physical conditions the more animals that can be supported and thus the smaller the ranches and the denser the population. Areas too dry even to support grass and ranches include much of the Mohave–Colorado Desert in western Arizona, southeastern California, and southern Nevada; the Great Salt Lake Desert and many of the larger alluvial basins within the Great Basin in Nevada, western Utah, and southeastern Oregon; parts of the higher, rougher Rocky Mountains especially in central Idaho and neighboring Montana and parts of British Columbia; high rough parts of the Arizona Highlands in east central Arizona and west central New Mexico; and sections of the deeply dissected dry canyon lands of the Colorado Plateaus in southeastern Utah. These are the least populous regions (Fig. 7.1).

The best ranching areas, where pasture and water are most dependable, lie in the less arid parts of the Great Plains nearest the Farming-Hinge Region, or in mountain piedmonts and valleys. In much of the Great Plains, ranching is interspersed with dry-fallow farming and restricted areas of irrigated farming. Great Plains areas which are more exclusively used for ranching, because of rough terrain as well as aridity, include the Dakotas and southeastern Montana south and west of the Missouri River, and the Edwards and Stockton plateaus of southwestern Texas. The Nebraska Sand Hills of central northern Nebraska are too sandy and hilly for cropping but have dependable pasture and water for beef cattle ranching. Note the sparsity of population in each of these areas (Fig. 7.1). Livestock ranches west of the Great Plains are usually situated in the mountain valleys or along mountain piedmonts at the margins of basins and plains. Commonly livestock are herded upward to the high mountain pastures in summer; they descend again in the fall to graze and be fed at lower elevations.

A second type of agricultural land use, with a somewhat higher potential for supporting population, is designated as dry-fallow farming. Such a system of agriculture adapts to the rainfall deficiency by alternating a summer of moisture-conserving cultivated fallow with a summer of cropping, usually of wheat. With modern technology and machinery, a single farmer may operate more than a thousand acres of such crop and fallow land. These areas obviously support a very low population density. Nevertheless, it is in extensive areas of dry-fallow farming, in the western Great Plains and the Columbia Plateau, that the population pattern is most uniformly widespread, although not without some linearity. In all other parts of the Interior West, the settlement pattern is markedly nucleated, but also with linearity (Fig. 7.1).

A third kind of agricultural land use in the dry Interior West is irrigated farming. As compared with livestock ranching or dry-fallow farming, it uses much smaller areas of land and develops them much more intensively. Irrigated farming needs relatively flat land situated at relatively low elevations and with sufficiently long growing season, fertile alluvial soils, and water. Consequently, irrigated areas are situated along mountain piedmonts and in valleys leading out of the mountains. Because irrigated farming is intensive and productive, it supports a relatively dense farm population as well as market and service towns. Consequently, to a much greater degree than ranching or dry farming, irrigated farming provides the base for nucleated, linear concentrations of population.

Irrigated crops are of great variety, including those for feeding livestock (alfalfa, corn, grain sorghum) as well as cash crops (sugar beets, vegetables, grains, cotton, and various fruits). Some of the more important nodes of population, based at least in part on irrigated agriculture, are the Colorado Piedmont near Denver, the Wasatch Mountain valleys and piedmont near Salt Lake City, the Salt and Gila valleys in southern Arizona near Phoenix, the Snake River Plain in Idaho, and the Yakima, Wenatchee, and Okanagan valleys in Washington and British Columbia (Fig. 7.1).

Much of the vast area between the Great Plains and the Pacific Coast Region is publicly owned. Because of its inability to support farms, it was never homesteaded or purchased by individuals. Some large areas are Indian reserves, some especially scenic areas have been set apart as national or provincial parks, other very barren areas are used for military purposes. The two largest categories of public land in the United States are national forests and federal grazing lands. Clearly, public lands have few permanent settlers.

Mining provides the basic or supplementary economic support for many population nuclei. Examples include the Kimberley–Trail area in British Columbia, Coeur d'Alene in northern Idaho, Butte–Anaconda in western Montana, or Bisbee–Douglas in southern Arizona (Fig. 7.1). Mining and processing of minerals contribute significantly to the economy of larger population centers such as Spokane, Salt Lake City, Provo, Phoenix, Tucson, Pueblo, and El Paso. Lumbering is also of importance to Spokane and some smaller northern or mountain centers.

The most recent and rapidly developing base for population concentration and growth in the Interior West is the recreation industry. In southern Arizona, as in California, warm, sunny winters and desert and mountain scenery were widely advertised to attract seasonal and permanent residents seeking health and recreation. Throughout the Interior West, spectacular scenery—some preserved in national or provincial parks—attracts many summer visitors and seasonal and permanent residents to serve them. Prehistoric cliff dwellings, mining ghost towns, and other artifacts of the romanticized early west are similar lures. Increased popularity of skiing, together with new or improved facilities, have made year around resorts of such places as Sun Valley, Idaho, Aspen and Vail, Colorado, or Lake Tahoe on the California–Nevada border. Finally, man created structures such as Hoover or Grand Coulee Dams, or whole recreation oriented cities such as Las Vegas and Reno, Nevada, attract many visitors and residents. As urbanization increases in the Interior West, the remarkable scenic and recreational resources are required to serve not only increasing numbers of visitors from the distant densely populated parts of the two countries but also the demands from increasing numbers of local residents. It seems urgent that steps be taken to control the use and exploitation of these unusual but fragile resources lest their recreational powers be denied to future generations.

Interior Western Population Nuclei and Interregional Connections

Finally, there is still another coarse pattern of population arrangement within the Interior West that is worthy of brief mention. It was suggested earlier that the American Interior West was for long, and to a considerable extent continues to be, a lacuna to be surmounted in the functioning of nations comprised of primary eastern and secondary far western cores. The lacuna is overcome to a degree by means of lines of communication and transportation, the latter comprised in modern times of railroads, highways, and airways, as well as circuitous ocean routes. These railroads and highways have had a major role in determining the spatial arrangement of the region's population and in the functioning of its economy. Because they connect East and West, they impart something of an east–west alignment to the pattern of population distribution.

It has also been pointed out that for the mining, irrigated farming, and recreation industries, resources tend to be highly localized, as they are to a lesser degree for lumbering, dry-fallow farming and even livestock ranching. In nationally integrated economies these widely dispersed small concentrations of economic activity, together with their sparse and frugal regional and local rail and highway networks, to be viable must be connected to the main national east–west transport lines. The result in the Interior West of this set of interrelated national, regional, and local conditions is a spatial arrangement of population which not only is highly nucleated but also has the nuclei arranged roughly in east–west alignments.

Served by the central east–west routeways are several of the region's largest population clusters. Easternmost of these is the Colorado Piedmont, lying along the eastern base of the central Rocky Mountains, and containing Denver, the largest urban center in the entire Interior West (Fig. 7.1). Here the extensive piedmont settlements have utilized the rich alluvial soils and the waters of the South Platte river system to create a major center of irrigated agriculture. In the adjacent mountains earlier mining and more recent recreational developments provided supplemental sources of wealth. Across the Central Rockies, at the western foot of the Wasatch Mountains, is another populous piedmont region with Salt Lake City as its metropolis. Here Mormon settlers created a nucleus of irrigated farming together with some dry-fallow farming and livestock ranching. Rich mineral and scenic resources in its surrounding area have made Salt Lake City a center of mineral production and refining as well as of outdoor recreation. Further west the same central routeways serve the great arc of irrigated farms and trade centers coincident with the Snake River plains and the lesser settlements along the Humboldt Valley leading toward Reno.

The southern routes, including the Santa Fe and Southern Pacific rail lines, and later established highways, link a number of important population clusters, most important of which is the Phoenix–Tucson concentration in southern Arizona. Irrigated agriculture, mineral wealth, and the attraction provided by the dry, sunny, and mild winter climate have all contributed to the growth of this population node. Smaller population nuclei are those associated with the Imperial Valley, Yuma, El Paso, and Albuquerque, all of them centers of irrigated agriculture, and the last two supported by mining as well. A relatively new area of population concentration has developed in the High Plains of western Texas, with a major area of irrigated agriculture centered around Lubbock, and oil development in the vicinity of Odessa and Midland, while Amarillo serves as a trade center for the petroleum industry, dry-fallow farming, and ranching.

The northern routeways across the Interior West serve fewer and smaller population clusters than do those of the center and south (Fig. 7.1). Largest is that where the three major northern American rail lines converge at Spokane, which is the regional center for important mining and forest industries in the nearby mountains, for surrounding ranching and dry-fallow wheat farming in the Palouse, and for irrigated farming in the Columbia Basin further to the west. Smaller population nodes center on Butte and Anaconda, famed for copper production, and at Great Falls, Missoula, and Billings in irrigated valleys and ranching areas. In British Columbia the lines of settlements along the railroads which wind through the mountains west of Lethbridge and Calgary, respectively, are very thin and interrupted, especially along the more northerly route (Fig. 7.2).

The North

In the preceding discussion of population distribution we have accounted for about four-fifths of the people but only a tenth of the land area of Canada (Table 7.2). For the United States, by contrast, considerable areas, but relatively few people, have been omitted (Table 7.1). The fact of overriding importance for Canada is that over three-fourths of its population is concentrated in two major regions (Economic Core and Prairie subregion of the Farming-Hinge Region) and one tiny one (Pacific), each of which is a contiguous extension of a similar region in the United States but which is widely separated from the others in Canada by sparsely populated territory (Table 7.2; Fig. 7.6).

The remaining parts of the two countries, characterized by sparse population arranged discontinuously over area, are designated as the North. This vast area is divided into three regions—the Far North, Middle North, and Near North (Figs. 7.5 and 7.6). The two sections of the Near North which extend into the United States are designated as the Northeast and Great Lakes subregions (Fig. 7.6; Table 7.1).

The simple names selected for these northern regions correctly suggest the locational relationships which explain their character as population regions. They occupy a position which is peripheral, frontier, and subsidiary to the Pacific, Farming-Hinge, and especially the Economic Core regions to the southward. During the more than four centuries of appraisal, settlement and economic development of North America by people mainly of European origin, these northern regions, together with parts of the Interior West, are the areas which have been found least attractive. Furthermore, they have been generally regarded, especially during the twentieth century, as less attractive for permanent settlement than for economic development. That is, their resources are sought and exploited especially by and for people of the Economic Core Region, but the exploitation is carried out with a minimum of permanent settlement within the northern regions. This important generalization is increasingly true as one progresses away from the Economic Core through the Near, Middle, and Far North regions, respectively. This basic locational–functional relationship also explains the characteristics of population distribution in the North—it is sparse and largely confined either to a few projections of settlement into the area from the southward or to scattered small clusters. The number and size of population clusters decrease from the Near through the Middle to the Far North regions.

The strategy of exploitation with minimum settlement seems obviously related to the severe climate of the area, including the difficulties of life in winter and the limitations for agriculture in summer. But the strategy is a human one and is also related to the perceived need by most people for the many social amenities and conveniences that can only be provided by agglomerations of population. In other words, the North fails to attract permanent settlement not only because of severity of climate or even limited resources, but also because of sparse population itself (and consequently few amenities).

The Near North

Although the Near North is the smallest of the three northern regions, it contains all but a tiny fraction of their total population (Table 7.2). In terms of both the areal distribution of population and of the underlying economic development, the Near North is transitional between the Economic Core and other regions to the southward and the Middle and Far North to the northward. Although the Near North shares frontier character with the further north regions, parts of it have a long history of settlement and economic development. The delayed establishment of permanent fishing settlements on the coast of Newfoundland, and the thin network of routes and trading posts established by the fur trade in the interior, have been mentioned. The different, denser, continuous areal distributions of population associated with agriculture have also been discussed (Fig. 7.3). Settlements based on forestry vary in character. Before 1900 they tended to be small and often impermanent, like many mining settlements. In the twentieth century they remain relatively small but are often associated with large, fixed, processing plants and associated service establishments.

Settlements based on these primary economic activities—fishing, fur trade, agriculture, and forestry, including some processing, trading, and shipping of their products—were established in Atlantic Canada and the American Northeast section of the Near North in the seventeenth and eighteenth centuries. But the extent of the resources and therefore of the size and distribution of settlements was limited. With the development of the interior of the continent during and since the mid nineteenth century, the American

Northeast and Atlantic Canada subregions of the Near North have found their locations to be increasingly peripheral and their economies marginally competitive nationally. Increasingly since 1950, the recreation industry has added to the support base, especially in the American Nórtheast where the attractive Adirondack and New England mountains are close to Megalopolis. In Atlantic Canada the tourist industry is favored by a kind of remote, historic charm, but is handicapped by distance from the Economic Core.

Although the Atlantic Canada subdivision of the Near North is less urbanized than the Canadian parts of the Economic Core and Pacific Coast regions, or even much of the Prairie subdivision of the Farming-Hinge Region, still more than half the population is urban (Tables 7.2 and 7.5). Urban population is dominated by the three provincial

TABLE 7.5. CANADIAN PROVINCIAL AND PRINCIPAL METROPOLITAN AREA POPULATIONS, 1971

			Provincial			
Prov. name	Metro. area	Metro. pop.	Total pop.	% increase 1961–71	% urban	% urban change since 1961
Ontario			7,703,106	23.5	82.4	+ 5.1
	Toronto	2,628,043				
	Ottawa	602,510				
	Hamilton	498,523				
	St. Catharines	303,429				
	London	286,011				
	Windsor	258,643				
	Kitchener	226,846				
Quebec			6,027,764	12.3	80.6	+ 6.3
	Montreal	2,743,208				
	Quebec	480,502				
British Columbia			2,184,000	34.1	75.7	+ 3.1
	Vancouver	1,082,352				
Alberta			1,627,874	22.2	73.5	+10.2
	Edmonton	495,702				
	Calgary	403,319				
Manitoba			988,247	7.2	69.5	+ 5.6
	Winnipeg	540,262				
Saskatchewan			926,242	0.1	53.0	+10.0
Nova Scotia			788,960	7.6	56.7	+ 2.4
	Halifax	222,637				
New Brunswick			634,557	6.1	56.9	+10.4
Newfoundland			522,104	14.0	57.2	+ 6.5
Prince Edward Island			111,641	6.7	38.3	+ 5.9
Northwest Territories			34,807	51.3	48.3	+ 4.4
Yukon Territory			18,338	25.7	61.0	+26.6
			21,568,311	18.3	76.1	+ 6.5

capitals and major ports (Halifax, St. John's, and Saint John), Sydney, an old steel-making center, and Moncton, a regional trade and transport center in one of the better agricultural areas. All are on or near the coast (Fig. 7.2). The population engaged in fishing and much of that associated with agriculture and forestry are also coastal. Agriculture is confined to coastal lowlands (Prince Edward Island, southeastern New Brunswick) or to narrow valleys (Saint John–Aroostook along the New Brunswick–Maine border, Annapolis–Cornwallis in western Nova Scotia). Each of these small concentrations of population tends to be isolated from the others by sparsely populated land or water, as all in turn are isolated from the major concentrations in the Economic Core.

The outstanding geographic fact about the Great Lakes–St. Lawrence subdivision of the Near North (Quebec north of the St. Lawrence, Ontario, Michigan, Wisconsin, and Minnesota) is its location adjacent to the Economic Core and, for Canada, its location between the Core and the populated Prairie and Pacific regions (Figs. 7.2 and 7.6). The clusters of population in this subregion are related either to the transport links between the Core and the West or to northward penetrations from the Economic Core to exploit resources for agriculture, minerals, forestry, hydroelectric power, or recreation. Some population clusters benefit from a combination of these economic supports.

Some agriculture, often economically marginal, has survived on glacial drift soils in the northern parts of the three American states and even on the edges of the Canadian Shield, although east of the Ottawa Valley the edge of the Shield is remarkably coincident with the northern boundary of the farming area. Three clusters of population within the Shield are partly based on agriculture—the Lake St. John Lowland and the Great and Little Clay Belts (Fig. 7.2). Each represents a pocket of soils developed from materials deposited in lakes that existed during the glacial period. In the Lake St. John Lowland and Saguenay River Valley, the small dairy-farming population is subsidiary to the much larger urban population which is related to aluminum refining based on hydroelectric power and to forest industries. Chicoutimi–Jonquière have a population of 134,000 in the census metropolitan area (Figs. 7.2 and 7.6). In the Clay Belts also agriculture has become secondary to mining and forest industries. The Great Clay Belt extends in a narrow 300 mile long east–west band across the Quebec–Ontario border near Lake Abitibi; the Little Clay Belt is also astride the provincial border further south near Lake Timiskaming. They were opened to agricultural colonization after 1900 by the building of the Canadian National Railroad from the St. Lawrence Valley westward through the Great Clay Belt toward the Prairies, and a connecting line from Toronto northward through the Little Clay Belt. As had happened during the building of the first transcontinental Canadian railroad through the Sudbury area in the 1880s, minerals were discovered and their exploitation became the major base of the local economy. The Great Clay Belt and environs to the southward are now a major mining area for gold, silver, copper, zinc, and associated metals. Small towns strung along the rail line and its spurs service the mines and some large pulp and paper manufacturing plants. Sudbury to the southwest of the Little Clay Belt, and a center for mining and refining of nickel, copper, and precious metals, is the largest agglomeration of people in the three northern regions, with more than 150,000 in the census metropolitan area (Fig. 7.2). North Bay, to the east, is a crossroads of the east–west Ottawa Valley–Sault Ste. Marie routeway with the north–south route from Toronto to the Clay Belts.

The three remaining urban areas in the Near North with populations near 100,000 all function as transport centers. Thunder Bay (formerly Port Arthur–Fort William), on the northwestern shore of Lake Superior, is a vital link in the railway, waterway, pipeline, and highway connections between the Economic Core and Canadian West and Northwest. For example, much of the grain from the Prairie region and iron ore from western Ontario is transferred from rail to lake shipment here. Duluth–Superior serves similar functions, shipping iron ore from the Mesabi Range and grain from the American spring wheat region and even serving pipelines transporting petroleum and natural gas from Alberta to the Canadian Economic Core area. The international twin city of

Sault Ste. Marie (five-sixths of the population is on the Canadian side) serves the ship locks along the Great Lakes waterway. Duluth and Sault Ste. Marie, Canada, have iron and steelmaking plants, the one in Canada accounting for a fifth to a quarter of Canadian production. All three cities serve mining, forest, and recreation industries in their areas.

The recreation industry as a support for permanent settlement is relatively important along the few highway and rail routes through the Great Lakes–St. Lawrence subregion and, by means of access by airplane, even away from routeways. But such industry supports few permanent residents. Recreation based population is much more numerous both seasonally and permanently along the shores of the great and small lakes and in scenic areas nearest the Economic Core such as in the margins of the Canadian Shield north of Toronto, Montreal, and Quebec, and in the northern Great Lakes states.

Except for the Indian economy and fur trade, settlement and economic development of the western Canadian section of the Near North (west of Ontario) has been later and smaller. The western section accounts for only about 6% of total population of the Near North (Table 7.2). The most widespread cluster of population represents agricultural settlement, mainly after 1920, in the Peace River Valley, an outlier northwest of the Prairie subdivision of the Farming-Hinge Region (Fig. 7.2). Recent population growth in the British Columbia portion has been stimulated by development of petroleum and natural gas. Flin Flon, Manitoba, with about 10,000 people, is representative of a mining settlement established in the wilderness and then connected to the ecumene by railroad and highway. Prince Rupert was established as a second transcontinental railway terminal and port on the Pacific after 1914, but has been unable to compete effectively with Vancouver.

Southern and southeastern Alaska are placed in the Near North, not because the areas are near to populous parts of the United States but because they share the characteristics of the Near North as a population region, that is, sizable prongs or clusters of population as compared to the Middle and Far North. The largest is the Anchorage urban area, by far the fastest-growing of the eight urban areas with populations of 100,000 or more in the Near North. It is the dominant center for administration of government, military, business, transport, and service activities in Alaska. The former capital, Juneau, and the several other small fishing–forestry towns and villages in the southeastern panhandle region are growing slowly or not at all. More than two-thirds of the 300,000 people in Alaska in 1970 lived in the coastal Near North region (Table 7.2).

The Middle and Far North Regions

These two subdivisions of the greater North share the characteristics of extremely sparse population widely dispersed in very small isolated settlements. They comprise approximately 70% of the area of Canada and over four-fifths of Alaska but have a total population of less than 200,000, smaller than that of metropolitan Kitchener, Ontario, or Madison, Wisconsin (Table 7.2). Yet the two regions are different. The Middle North has been penetrated by the construction of transport routes and the establishment of sizable resource-exploiting settlements; the Far North has not.

The Alaska Highway was constructed to provide a land route from the American and Canadian ecumene to Alaska during World War II. It leads from the Peace River population cluster through Yukon Territory to Fairbanks. Settlements along it are few and small except at Fairbanks. A second important routeway is that through the Athabaska and Mackenzie valleys from Edmonton to the Arctic. It has combined rail and highway (now as far as the south and north shores of Great Slave Lake, respectively) with water transport (by barge on the Mackenzie–Slave River system including the three great northern lakes). This system has been developing steadily since World War II to serve mining settlements (Yellowknife, Pine Point), increasing oil exploration in the Mackenzie Valley and Arctic, and Indian and Eskimo settlements.

A grain-exporting railroad was completed from the Prairie region to Churchill on Hudson Bay in 1929, but Churchill remains a small center with limited shipping season and facilities. Branches of the railroad now lead to the major nickel-mining centers of Thompson and Lynn Lake in the Middle North as well as to older Flin Flon in the Near North.

Three significant developments since 1950 have led, or may lead, to new population clusters in the eastern part of the Middle North. The oldest is the mining of iron ore along the border between Quebec and the western bulge of Labrador. One 350 mile long railroad and several shorter ones now carry millions of tons of iron ore annually from sizable mining towns situated in a wilderness virtually uninhabited before 1950. The other two developments with potential for new population clusters are huge hydro-electric power installations, one partially completed and producing on the Churchill River in Labrador, the other under construction on rivers entering James Bay from Quebec.

In the Far North settlements are still tiny and access is by sea or air. Some of the settlements are those of coastal Eskimos still living partly from the sea. Others are administrative posts often with installations for military or scientific purposes. Some are for mineral exploration. It is the latter which may well result in new clusters of population or new routeways, and thus necessitate revision of the regional boundaries as outlined here. A case in point is the building of the Alaska pipeline from the new oil fields on the Arctic Coast to Valdez. It is stimulating boom growth in Fairbanks, currently the largest center of population in the Middle North, and will result in penetration of road and pipeline beyond the Middle North as represented in Fig. 7.5. But although the regional outlines change, the strategy which underlies the population geography of the greater North continues—maximum exploitation of its resources mainly by and for the Economic Core but with minimum migration and settlement from the Core.

Changing Regional Distribution of Population

This chapter is concerned with the areal distribution of population at the present time. But since the areal distribution is continuously changing, it is appropriate to consider the most significant changes which are currently in progress. Two processes related to population which have occurred throughout the history of the United States and Canada, and which still continue, are increase in numbers and westward spread.

Comparing the two countries, the percentage rate of increase was higher in the United States during the last half of the nineteenth century (when westward expansion of agricultural settlement in Canada was temporarily blocked by the Canadian Shield) but has been higher in Canada since 1900. During the 1950s population increased 30% in

Canada and 18.5% in the United States, the highest rate in each country since the first decade of the century. During the 1960s the rates were 10 and 13%, respectively (Tables 7.4 and 7.5). In Canada the rate of natural increase has varied but declines in rate have exceeded gains, bringing the rate to 10.1 per 1000 in 1970, the lowest in history. A general decline in rate of natural increase has also occurred in the United States where in 1972 the average number of children produced per family was reported to have dropped for the first time below 2.1, the number considered necessary to achieve zero population growth. Total population will continue to increase because of the large number of persons already born but not yet of child-bearing age. However, if the replacement level of 2.1 children per family were to continue, the total national population would level off at approximately 320m. in about the year 2040.

The spread of population westward, a process also as old as either nation, continued during the last decade. In 1970 the northeast and north central census regions in the United States accounted for 24.1 and 27.8%, respectively, of the country's residents, down from 26.1 and 29.4% in 1950 (Table 7.4). The precentages of population gain for the two areas during the last decade were 9.8 and 9.6, respectively, considerably less than the national increase of 13.3%. The South gained 14.2% during the decade, a little above the national average, its share of the United States population rising slightly from 30.7% in 1960 to 30.9% in 1970. Since the South was essentially maintaining its relative position during 1960–70, the relative loss in the Northeast and North Central regions had to be offset by gains in the West. An increase of 24.1% during the decade, almost twice the national average, helped the West to raise its share of the national population from 15.6 to 17.1% (Table 7.4). Among Canadian provinces, British Columbia has recorded the largest percentage population increase in every decade since 1920 (Table 7.5); during 1900–20 when the Prairie Provinces were being settled, they led in rate of growth.

Areas of Population Loss

The populations of the United States and Canada had a combined gain of more than 27m. people during the 1960s. Only three states (North and South Dakota and West Virginia, plus the District of Columbia), and no Canadian provinces, experienced losses. In view of these facts it is remarkable that during the 1960s more than two-fifths of the approximately 3100 American counties and one-third of the census areas of Canada lost population (Fig. 7.7). The main area of loss is in the Great Plains extending from Saskatchewan to Texas. Identified earlier was a great cropland triangle whose apexes are located at approximately Columbus (Ohio), Lubbock (Texas), and Edmonton (Canada), which contains a majority share of the cropland of North America. This cropland triangle corresponds closely with the large area of population loss. There are two discrepancies. First, in the United States the area of population loss extends beyond the western border of the cropland triangle to the base of the Rocky Mountains, thus including also the dry-fallow farming and ranching areas of the western Great Plains (Fig. 7.7). Second, the large area of population loss does not include the apex of the cropland triangle east of the Mississippi River, except for the less urbanized, more agricultural parts of southern Illinois and the Wabash Valley of Indiana. That is, the more urbanized Economic Core Region segment of the cropland triangle is excluded from the vast area of population

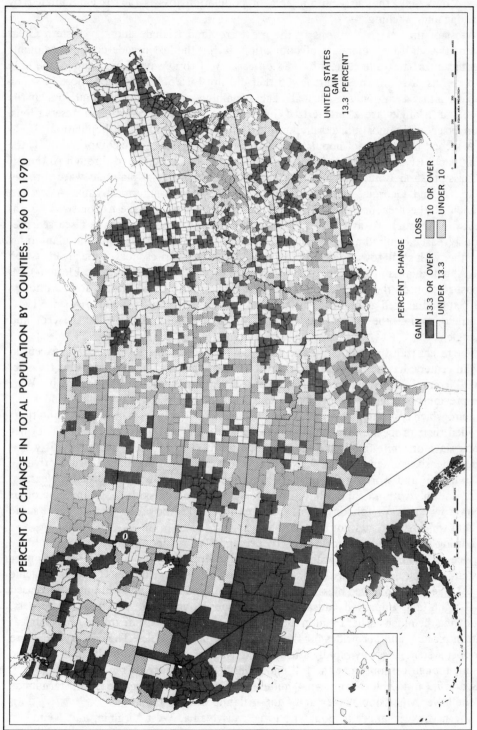

PERCENT OF CHANGE IN TOTAL POPULATION BY COUNTIES: 1960 TO 1970

UNITED STATES
GAIN
13.3 PERCENT

PERCENT CHANGE

GAIN
13.3 OR OVER
UNDER 13.3

LOSS
10 OR OVER
UNDER 10

FIG. 7.7. Source: US Bureau of the Census.

loss. Conversely, the vast interior area of population loss is the area dominated by farming and ranching.

Most of the census divisions in the great cropland triangle and the western Great Plains that did not suffer loss of population during the last decade contain regionally significant urban trade centers located on east–west routeways. For example, the only two census divisions in Saskatchewan that did not lose population are those in which Regina and Saskatoon are located. The remaining census units without loss in the cropland triangle are characterized by recreation industry or Indian reservations. Conversely and almost universally, non-urban agricultural units lost population.

A second major area of population loss (Fig. 7.7) is the great arc comprised of (1) the Mississippi River flood plain from southeastern Missouri southward through Arkansas, Mississippi, and Louisiana, and (2) the Gulf–Atlantic coastal plain eastward through Alabama and Georgia, and thence northeastward into southern Virginia. A western branch of the area occupies the inner coastal plain from northern Louisiana south-westward through Texas. This is the part of the Interior South that, as discussed previously, early acquired a nearly continuous pattern of contiguous farms and plantations together with small town trade and service centers. It comprises most of the area between the Appalachian and Ozark–Ouachita uplands, on the one hand, and the Florida–Gulf Coast Region on the other. It has been overwhelmingly an agricultural area. Although farmed land as well as numbers of farms has decreased in much of the area since 1940, it still comprises the largest area of cropland in the continent outside the cropland triangle.

The recent transformation of agriculture and consequent loss of population, except in urban centers, has been as dramatic in this area as that in the great cropland triangle, but different. In an earlier reorganization of southern agriculture following the Civil War, the previously dominant plantation system was replaced by share cropping. Under this system, which continued down to about 1960, owners or managers of former plantations divided their properties into small 10- to 40-acre plots and assigned each to a former black slave or white family for the growing of cotton or tobacco. Essentially, it was a labor intensive system in which the share croppers exchanged their labor for the privilege of living on and working the land. Because most share croppers, especially Negroes, were not only without capital but also lacked education and skills to do anything other than grow cotton or tobacco, and were often in debt to the landowner, it was a static system which they could not leave or change.

During and following World War II, demands for manpower, both in the military services and in factories and warehouses, began to draw people out of the share cropper system. Young adventurous black and white migrants to Economic Core and Pacific Coast cities were followed by kinfolk and friends. Demands for and winning of increased civil rights and improved education opened more opportunities. Many landowners, following the much earlier trend in the Midwest, began to substitute tractors, mechanical cotton pickers, and herbicides for the work of people and mules. The century old share cropper system gave way rapidly after 1940 and almost disappeared by 1970. A dramatic result, though certainly not the full and painful human story, is revealed in Figs. 7.7, 7.8, and 7.9 and Tables 7.4 and 7.6—millions of black and white people left the farmlands of the lower Mississippi Valley and Gulf–Atlantic Coastal Plain.

The negative changes in population in Pennsylvania, West Virginia, and Kentucky and immediately adjacent areas were related to loss of employment in coal mining.

INTER - REGIONAL MIGRATION

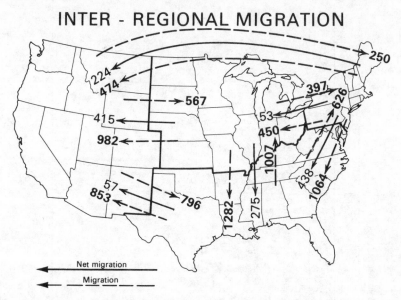

FIG. 7.8. Migration based on change of residence (1965–70) of population 5 years old and over, 1970. Source: US Bureau of the Census, US Census of Population: 1970, *General Social and Economic Characteristics*, Final Report (PC1)-Cl, United States Summary, US Government Printing Office, Washington DC, 1971, Table 137.

NET MIGRATION, 1960 - 1970

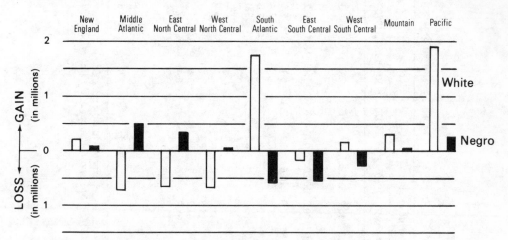

FIG. 7.9. Source: *Statistical Abstract of the US, 1972*, p. 26.

Examination of Fig. 7.7 can further test the relationship. The major area of bituminous mining extends from southwestern Pennsylvania and southeastern Ohio through West Virginia and eastern Kentucky into adjacent Virginia and Tennessee. The greatest concentration of mining and production is centered near the junction of the Kentucky–Virginia–West Virginia borders. The second most important area of bituminous mining

TABLE 7.6. UNITED STATES, NEGRO POPULATION AND MIGRATION

	United States				Northeast				North Central				South				West			
	1920	1950	1960	1970	1920	1950	1960	1970	1920	1950	1960	1970	1920	1950	1960	1970	1920	1950	1960	1970
Total Negro population (millions)	10.5	15.0	18.9	22.6	0.7	2.0	3.0	4.3	0.8	2.2	3.4	4.6	8.9	10.2	11.3	12.0	0.1	0.6	1.1	1.7
% of total US Negro population	100.0	100.0	100.0	100.0	6.5	13.4	16.0	19.2	7.6	14.8	18.3	20.2	85.2	68.0	59.9	53.2	0.8	3.8	5.8	7.5
% of region population	9.9	10.0	10.6	11.1	2.3	5.1	6.8	8.9	2.3	5.0	6.7	8.1	26.9	21.7	20.6	19.2	0.9	2.9	3.9	4.9
% change, decade			25.4	19.7			50.1	43.4			54.7	32.7			10.6	5.8			89.3	55.2
% urban	34.0			81.3	77.3			97.0	83.4			97.0	25.3			67.5	73.9			96.9
% rural	66.0			18.7	22.7			3.0	16.6			3.0	74.7			32.5	26.1			3.1
% farm				3.0				0.2				0.3				5.4				0.2
Total non-white population (millions)		15.8	20.5			2.1	3.2			2.3	3.6			10.3	11.5			1.0	2.2	
% urban		61.7	72.4			93.6	95.2			91.3	93.9			47.6	58.2			71.6	78.8	
% rural		38.3	27.6			6.4	4.8			8.7	6.1			52.4	41.8			28.4	21.2	
% farm		21.2	7.8			0.7	0.2			2.5	0.9			30.5	12.9			11.1	3.3	
Net migration, 1960–70																				
White				2.3				-0.5				-1.3				1.8				2.3
Negro				-0.1				0.6				0.4				-1.4				0.3

Sources: Population data from reports of United States Census.
Migration data from *Statistical Abstract of the United States, 1972*, p. 26.

in the country extends from western Kentucky into adjacent southern Illinois and Indiana. Finally, in the Parallel Ridge and Valley section of central eastern Pennsylvania is the old and major area of anthracite mining, where decreasing production and employment have been a problem for nearly half a century. The correspondence of all of these coal-mining areas to the loss categories in Fig. 7.7 could hardly be closer. The map suggests the fact and reasons, but again not the human problems, of population loss.

A final extensive area of population loss includes much of the eastern half of the Near North, especially Atlantic Canada and Quebec with adjacent parts of northern New England, as well as the northern part of the American Great Lakes subregion (Fig. 7.7). As indicated earlier, the eastern areas were settled early but by the mid nineteenth century people were migrating from them to better endowed farming areas in Ontario and the Midwest and to growing cities in the developing Economic Core Region. Some revival of economy and populations during the mid twentieth century is related to development of second homes and the recreation industry. The latter trend is directly related to accessibility from the urbanized areas to the southward. The fact that it is the northern, most remote parts of both American subdivisions of the Near North, the Northeast, and Great Lakes subregions that have lost population, whereas the southern more accessible areas have gained, suggests that the development of second homes and recreation facilities is significant (Fig. 7.7).

Areas of Population Gain

The above discussion of population loss has implied that most of the gain has been in and near urban centers or in areas considered attractive for recreation and pleasant living conditions. The Economic Core Region demonstrates the first relationship (Figs. 7.6 and 7.7). Gains are widespread throughout this highly urbanized region except in districts previously noted: the coal-mining areas in Appalachia and in western Kentucky–southern Illinois, and some of the more agricultural counties of Illinois and Indiana. In the three counties with losses in northernmost highland Pennsylvania, conditions are more akin to those in the Near North than to domination by either coal-mining or agriculture. Figure 7.7 suggests two subregions of more rapid growth within the Economic Core Region, the one centering on Megalopolis, and a more diffuse western one near the southern Great Lakes. The latter extends into Canada in an uninterrupted area of gain, during the 1960s, from Detroit–Windsor through Toronto to Montreal.

A contiguous area of gain extends southwestward from Megalopolis, along the Great Appalachian Valley to include most of the Appalachian Piedmont. These areas have been discussed as the most urbanized and industrialized in the Interior South. The extension of an area of gain southward from the Midwest Economic Core through central Kentucky and Tennessee is more difficult to explain. The three included districts of greatest gain are among the most urbanized in the general area: the Bluegrass and Nashville basins and the Tennessee Valley of northern Alabama. The areas surrounding these three cores, while largely agricultural, were not dominated by the share cropper system of cotton or tobacco production whose demise was associated with marked population loss in the coastal plain and lower Mississippi Valley.

The Florida–Gulf Coast Region was characterized, in the discussion of Fig. 7.6, as an area of recent dramatic urbanization. Only a few of the most rural counties failed to register above average gains in population during the last decade (Fig. 7.7). The Pacific Coast Region and southwestern part of the Interior West, characterized by rapid population gain, have likewise been noted for their rapid urbanization, generally related either or both to industrialization and the search for ideal living conditions.

The quest for recreation, including second homes, would seem important in understanding population growth in the Ozark–Ouachita Highlands, parts of the southern and eastern Appalachians, and in Rocky Mountain districts from northern New Mexico to western Montana. The Ozark–Ouachita area, like other once deforested, marginal agricultural areas, for example parts of northern Wisconsin and Michigan, lost population during much of this century until the revival during the last decade. These southern highlands are now attracting vacationers and retirees from newly prosperous southern as well as northern cities. One important element in the attraction consists of the several large new artificial lakes along streams of the White and Arkansas River systems.

Recent study suggests that population growth in such areas as the Ozark and northern Great Lakes regions during the 1960s was the beginning of a major reversal in the long term rural–urban migration in the United States. During 1970–3 the average gain of population in nonmetropolitan counties was 4.2% compared to only 2.9% in counties containing a city of 50,000 or more. See Calvin L. Beale, *The Revival of Population Growth in Nonmetropolitan America*, Economic Research Service, US Dept. of Agriculture, 1975.

Finally, compare Figs. 7.6 and 7.7 to note the significant islands of marked population gain in the Farming-Hinge Region. In the cropland triangle scattered districts that are exceptions to the widespread distribution of population loss were identified as small trade and routeway nodes. In the Farming-Hinge Region each of the important east–west gateway cities is the nucleus of an area of rapid population growth. Note Minneapolis–St. Paul, Omaha, Kansas City, Tulsa, Oklahoma City, Dallas–Fort Worth, and San Antonio. The case of Canadian Prairie cities such as Winnipeg, Regina, Saskatoon, Calgary, and Edmonton has been mentioned.

Interregional Migration

Change in population numbers is made up of two components—natural increase (excess of births over deaths) and net migration. During the decade 1960–70, natural increase for the whole United States averaged about 2m. annually. However, as indicated earlier, the rate of increase of national population has been declining, due mainly to declining birth rate. Natural increase declined from about 2.6m. in 1960 to less than 1.7m. during 1971. Net civilian immigration into the country during the late 1970s averaged about 400,000 annually.

Since all parts of the United States experienced some natural increase during the decade 1960–70, those areas with population losses must be ones from which significant numbers of people have migrated. Migration of people from farming and coal-mining regions has been discussed in accounting for areas with net population loss. But many areas which did not experience a net loss nevertheless lost people through net out-migration. In fact, states or counties which had population gains significantly below the national average gain of 13.3% must have lost people by migration. We may now examine Table 7.6 and Figs. 7.8 and 7.9, which show gains and losses by census regions and divisions, in relation to the familiar Figs. 7.6 and 7.7.

New England shows a net in-migration during the decade, comprised of both black and white people (Fig. 7.9). This may include several components: (1) black and white people moving from southern farms to New England cities; (2) movement from the core of the New York metropolitan area into suburban Connecticut; and (3) movement into the accessible parts of the Near North subdivision of New England for pursuit of recreation. Figure 7.9 suggests that large numbers of black people moved into the Middle Atlantic metropolitan areas, whereas over half a million white people left. Figure 7.8 indicates, for the northeast census region as a whole, a net loss to each of the other three census regions. Apparently the loss, mainly of white people to the South and West, more than offset the large influx of black people from the South (Table 7.6).

The north central census region had a net migration loss during the decade of nearly 900,000. Every state was in the loss column except Michigan, where inflow and outflow were equal. Both the east and west census divisions lost over 600,000 white people (Fig. 7.9), the western section from a smaller population base. We have argued that this represents the great flow of people off farms of the cropland triangle, although many of the farm surplus people must have gone to cities within as well as outside the census region. The net loss of rural white people was partly compensated in the eastern division by a net inflow of 356,000 black people to cities (Fig. 7.9). Figure 7.8 indicates a very large exchange with the South and West, resulting in net outflow from the north central region. Presumably the exchange with the South was comprised mainly of white out-migrants and black in-migrants.

The South, aside from a considerable but almost balanced exchange with the West, presents almost a mirror image of what happened in the New England Middle Atlantic and east north central census divisions. In sum, there was a great out-migration of black people that was more than offset by in-migration of whites. But whereas all three southern census divisions lost large numbers of black people presumably to northern and western cities, almost all of the net gain of white people was to the South Atlantic division (Fig. 7.9). Furthermore, Fig. 7.7 indicates that in-migration was far from uniform within that division; more than 70% of the net in-migration of white people went to Florida. Most of the remainder went to Maryland and Virginia (Washington and other urban areas) and to Georgia (Atlanta urban area?). As was indicated in the earlier discussion of Fig. 7.7, there has been very significant rearrangement of population in the South, with marked loss (both black and white people) from farming areas and (mainly white) from coal-mining districts, and great gains in the cities, especially in the Florida–Gulf Coast Region but also in the Piedmont and more scattered urban areas.

The West gained during 1965–70 in the exchange of migrants with each of the other three census regions (Fig. 7.8). Most of the gain, of both white and Negro people, went to the Pacific census division (Fig. 7.9). As with the other census regions, Figs. 7.8 and 7.9 merely corroborate the differential population growth analyzed earlier (Fig. 7.7). They do indicate that Americans are indeed a mobile people, especially when it is recognized that the majority of changes of residence are less than interregional and are not shown. Figure 7.8 shows also that the exchanges are not simple one-way movements. For example, in order to register its marked migration gain during 1965–70, the West had to offset more than 1.6m. out-migrants.

Movements of black population account for a very significant part of the regional

G

rearrangements of total population in the United States during recent decades. Outstanding has been the movement of blacks from the rural South to the urban North and West (Table 7.6; Fig. 7.9). During the decade 1960–70, 1.4m. black people left the South. Every southern state except the border ones of Delaware and Maryland had a net loss of black population, each of those from North Carolina southward and westward through Louisiana losing at least 150,000. All three of the other census regions had substantial in-migrations of black people, although three-fourths of the southern exodus went to the urbanized states of New York, California, New Jersey, Illinois, and Michigan. Northern New England, the western Midwest, the Great Plains, and the interior West gained only small numbers of Negroes. Three major streams of black migration may be recognized. From the South Atlantic area, Virginia to Georgia, the movement has been mainly to Megalopolis. Most black migrants from Alabama, Mississippi, and Arkansas have moved directly northward into the Midwest segment of the Economic Core. From the western South the exodus has been mainly to urban centers of Texas, Colorado, Arizona, and the Pacific coast.

The migration of black people has markedly altered their present areal distribution. As late as 1910, nine out of ten blacks lived in the South, mainly in the belt of rural farms and communities on the coastal plain from Virginia through the Mississippi River bottomlands to the Texas Black Prairies. In 1950 the South's portion of black population was down to two-thirds and by 1970 to 53.2% (Table 7.6). About two-fifths now live in the cities of the Economic Core Region.

In Canada, the century old net out-migration from the Atlantic region westward still continues. The net out-migration from the Prairie region, most notably from Saskatchewan with its agriculture oriented economy, is of lesser duration but has been consistent since 1930. The only large areas, aside from cities, to gain consistently from net migration are the Economic Core Region, especially the Ontario sector, and the small Pacific region.

Summary

This chapter has attempted to describe the current and changing areal distribution and arrangement of people in the United States and Canada and to suggest some of the explanations. The distribution varies greatly, the greatest contrast being that between (1) the southeastern quarter of the combined area with its widespread, continuous distribution of rural population and its relatively dense pattern of small and large cities, and (2) the vast interior western and northern areas with sparse population arranged in scattered clusters. Population in the Pacific region is highly clustered but also relatively dense, highly urbanized and growing rapidly. The great significance of this general arrangement to Canada, with its widely separated major concentrations, has been emphasized.

Most notable features of change have been the continuing but declining rate of increase (compounded out of natural increase and net immigration); the differential growth rates resulting in regional shifts, especially from Atlantic Canada toward the Economic Core Region and from the American Economic Core toward the Pacific Coast, southwest, Florida, and Gulf Coast; the flow from rural farm and coal-mining areas to the cities, a flow whose source is diminishing in numbers; and the rapid shift of black population, especially from southern farms to northern and western as well as southern cities (a movement whose reservoir is also decreasing in volume). Two additional important trends, observable at a larger map scale, are (1) the relative or even absolute decline of numbers in urban cores and concomitant rapid growth of surrounding suburbs, and (2) the increase and rearrangement of rural non-farm population. These are treated in Chapter 8.

References

Borchert, John R. (1967) American metropolitan evolution, *Geog. Rev.* **57**, 301–32.

Fremlin, Gerald (ed.) (1974) *The National Atlas of Canada*, 4th edn., Ottawa.

Gerlach, Arch C. (ed.) (1970) *The National Atlas of the United States of America*, US Dept. of the Interior, Geological Survey, Washington DC.

Gottman, Jean (1961) *Megalopolis: The Urbanized Northeastern Seaboard of the United States*, Twentieth Century Fund, New York.

Hart, John Fraser (1960) The changing distribution of the American Negro, *Annals Assoc. Am. Geog.* **50**, 242–66.

Olmstead, Clarence W. (1960) The application of a concept to the understanding of a region: people, time, space and ideas in the Economic Core Region of Anglo-America, *J. Geog.* **59**, 53–61.

Sale, Randall D. and Karn, Edwin D. (1961) *American Expansion, A Book of Maps*, The Dorsey Press, Homewood, Ill.

Trottier, Louis (ed.) (1972) *Studies in Canadian Geography*, six regional volumes published for the 22nd International Geographical Congress, Toronto, University of Toronto Press.

Vance, James E., Jr. (1972) California and the search for the Ideal, *Annals Assoc. Am. Geog.* **62**, 185–210.

Warkentin, John (ed.) (1968) *Canada, A Geographical Interpretation*, Methuen, Toronto. See especially chapter 6, "The People" by T. R. Weir.

Zelinsky, Wilbur (1962) Changes in the geographic pattern of rural population in the United States, 1790–1960, *Geog. Rev.* **52**, 492–524.

CHAPTER 8

CHARACTERISTICS OF POPULATION IN THE UNITED STATES AND CANADA

PAUL D. SIMKINS

Pennsylvania State University, USA

Introduction

For over 250 years the United States grew westward and behind that advance the land filled rapidly with farms and cities. With increasing development the early pattern of high fertility and mortality finally broke and rates began a long downward trend, first in the northeast with the declines later diffusing irregularly to the west and south. These changing differentials in vital rates altered regional patterns of growth and progressively modified the spatial arrangements of population characteristics. Moreover, as the opportunity surface of the country rose, warped streams of migration developed, enlarged, or withered. These streams did not simply carry a cross-section of the originating population; rather, they selected persons with certain qualities and, by so doing, further altered the population composition of the various parts of the country. Across this span new immigrants, responding to the economic pulse of the nation, joined the streams of the native-born in search of something better, adding their contribution to the changing population trends of the United States. These elements of fertility, mortality, and migration continue to change in proportion and intensity and to reshape the distribution of population characteristics of the United States.

Fertility Patterns

Although there is lacking the necessary data for determining with any precision the fertility levels during the early history of the United States, there can be little doubt that these levels were high and considerably above those prevailing in Northwest Europe at the time. Estimates of crude birth rates for the late Colonial and early Republic periods suggest levels in excess of 50 per 1000. But well before the Civil War, perhaps as early as 1820, at a time when the nation was still over 90% rural, the crude birth rate of the white population began to inch downward irregularly but persistently in a gradual reduction which was to continue for a century. Already by 1820 distinct regional contrasts in fertility existed within the United States, with relatively low rates characteristic of the northeastern states, particularly southern New England, and higher fertility levels typical of regions to the south and westward to the frontier. This basic regional pattern of fertility persisted through the period of the development of the United States and into the twentieth century.

In contrast with the earlier persistent decline in fertility levels and the relative stability of regions of high and low fertility, the period since 1930 in the United States has been marked by large fluctuations in national fertility levels and rather sharp changes in the regional distribution of fertility patterns, particularly in areas of low birth rates. The long term decline in fertility abruptly steepened during the 1920 decade and the onset of the economic depression to reach a low in 1933 when the crude birth rate for the total population stood at 18.4 per 1000. However, with the progressive recovery of the national economy and a rebirth of optimism, the decline in fertility was reversed and toward the end of the 1930 decade birth rates in all of the states began to rise, an increase that accelerated sharply after the end of World War II. By 1947 the crude birth rate for the nation (26.6 per 1000) had regained the level which prevailed some 25 years earlier. This rapid and sharp increase in fertility was not unexpected—similar increases had taken place following other major conflicts as families were reunited or created. What was unexpected was the persistence of the higher fertility rates. In European countries elevated fertility levels were short-lived, most countries returning to pre-war fertility patterns within a few years. In the United States, however, the higher fertility plateau was maintained, and for 10 years after the war crude birth rates remained at or near 25 per 1000. Indeed, the use of the crude birth rate softens the impression of increased fertility during the immediate post-war years, for the large number of infants born are added to the denominator upon which the calculation is based and tends thereby to restrain increases in the rate.

A better appreciation of the elevated fertility of the United States after World War II is provided by the general fertility rate, i.e. the number of births per thousand women, aged 15–44 years. Since the base is not total population but women in their reproductive years, the measure is unaffected by the addition of births to the population and is, therefore, a more sensitive indicator of fertility change. In contrast to the relative constancy of the crude birth rate in the immediate post-war period, the general fertility rate continued to climb after 1950 to peak at 122.9 in 1957 (Fig. 8.1). It is indicative of the high fertility levels of the 1950 decade that the general fertility rate crested in the same year that the most fertile female age group (20–24 years), to whom are born somewhat more than one-third of all births, declined to its smallest post-war size (Fig. 8.2). Thus, females born between 1933 and 1937, at the lowest ebb of depression fertility, themselves contributed greatly to the record number of births in 1957.

From 1957 onward birth rates in the United States declined, slowly at first but gathering momentum toward the middle of the 1960s. By 1967 the crude birth rate had fallen to 17.9, a level below that reached in any of the depression years. Throughout the 1960 decade, however, the number of women entering their reproductive years progressively enlarged. The number of women aged 20–24 years, about 5.3m. in 1947, increased to over 7.5m. by 1967 and continued to increase thereafter as the larger birth cohorts of the immediate post-war years matured. It was expected that these growing numbers would shortly reverse the trend of declining fertility and diminishing number of births. When both birth rates and numbers did register slight increases in 1969 and again in 1970, it appeared that the delayed "echo effect" might be emerging. However, the upward trend was not maintained and in 1971 the crude birth rate fell to 17.2 and continued downward to 14.9 in 1974, in which year it was slightly below the European average.

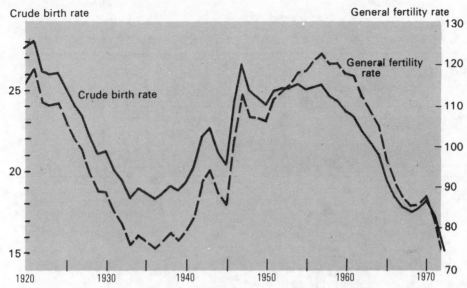

FIG. 8.1. The United States: crude birth rates and general fertility rates, 1920–72.

The general fertility rate of the total United States population likewise underwent a progressive decline after 1957. By 1965 that rate had declined below 100 for the first time since 1945. Although the rate continued downward, it remained above the record low of 75.8 established in 1936 until the sharp fertility reduction during 1972 brought the rate to 73.4. Thus, in 1972, both the crude birth rate and the general fertility rate had reached historic lows in the United States, with fertility in that year falling below the replacement level.

Regional Contrasts in Fertility Levels, 1940

During this period of rising and falling birth rates the states and regions of the United States exhibited rather large differential adjustments. In 1940, before the great upward surge in birth rates, the fertility levels within the United States were in rough accordance with regional developmental status. The urban–industrial states from southern New England to Illinois, together with Kansas and Nebraska, maintained the below average levels that had long characterized the region. Among the states, New Jersey had the lowest fertility with only 57 births per 1000 women in the reproductive ages compared with a national average of about 80. General fertility levels were also relatively low in the three Pacific coast states. The more rural states, especially those with relatively low incomes and high proportions of nonwhites, had higher fertility levels. Every state south of the Ohio River, except Florida, and every state between the Great Plains and the Pacific coast states had fertility above the national average. The highest general fertility rates among the states in 1940 were in New Mexico (136.2) and South Carolina (122.9).

The regional fertility pattern of the nonwhite population in 1940 generally duplicated the broader features of that of the total population, although with higher levels in each

Females Ages 20 - 24
(in millions)

Number of Births
(in millions)

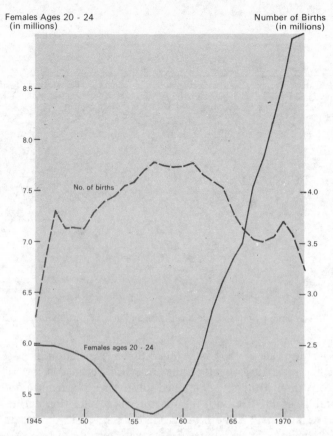

Fig. 8.2. The United States: estimated number of females ages 20–24 and number of births, 1945–72.

state. Relatively low fertility characterized the nonwhite population of the manufacturing states and California with higher levels elsewhere. The major difference between the two patterns was the exceptionally high levels in nonwhite fertility in the North-central and Mountain states relative to the South—a result of the extraordinarily high fertility of the Indian population that contributed the bulk of nonwhite births in the western states. The general fertility rate of the nonwhite population of Arizona was in 1940 208.1, over two and one-half times the national rate for all races combined.

Regional Changes in Fertility Levels, 1940–60

Between 1940 and 1960 the general fertility rate of the total United States population increased sharply from 79.9 to 118.0 and increases were registered in every state except West Virginia and South Carolina. However, during this period of rising fertility rates, the greatest relative increases occurred in states which had had exceptionally low fertility rates in 1940. New York State, for example, which had a general fertility rate of 57.5 in 1940, began the 1960 decade with a rate of 104.9. Alabama, on the other hand, had an increase in its fertility rate only from 106.1 to 120.9 during the same period. Thus, one result of the changing fertility levels in the post-war period down to 1960 was to narrow considerably the range of fertility levels among the states.

Along with the decrease in the magnitude of state fertility differentials, there was also a significant shift in the regional distribution of low fertility. Although the basic regional fertility patterns that existed in 1940 were preserved in 1960, with low rates across the more urbanized Northeast and along the Pacific coast, and with generally higher rates elsewhere, the rather sharply delineated area of low fertility concentrated in the manufacturing states had become blurred and much less distinct by 1960. Only those states from southern New England to Ohio still maintained below average fertility; increases in rates in the urban states west of Ohio had raised fertility rates of these states to a level above the national average.

Whereas sharp rises in birth rates in the area of traditionally low fertility had brought intermediate levels to much of this area, smaller increases in the South between 1940 and 1960 brought that region closer to the national average. Indeed, general fertility rates in the peripheral southern states of Virginia, North Carolina, Tennessee, and Oklahoma by 1960 had fallen below the national norm.

Changing Patterns of White Fertility, 1940–60

The shift to moderate fertility, relative to the national average, among several of the southern states was largely the result of changing fertility patterns of the white population. In 1940 every state south of the Ohio River, with the single exception of Florida, had a white general fertility rate well above the national average. At this date (1940), when the general fertility rate for the national white population was 77.1, most of the states of the South had rates over 90 and in three (Arkansas, Kentucky, and West Virginia) the corresponding rates exceeded 100.

Between 1940 and 1950, during which time national fertility rates rose substantially, white fertility rates in the South rose but slightly and around the margins of the region fertility levels began to approximate more closely the national average. The smaller gains in white fertility in the South relative to the nation continued in the 1950 decade. Indeed, during this decade of fertility increases, five states of the South (West Virginia, Kentucky, Tennessee, South Carolina, and Arkansas) experienced a decline in white general fertility rates. Thus, by 1960, the traditional high fertility of Southern whites had virtually disappeared. At this date, every state in the South in an arc from Mississippi to Virginia (except Florida) had a general fertility rate for whites lower than that of Illinois, Indiana, or Ohio.

Regional Contrasts in Fertility Levels, 1960

While the fertility levels in the South were moving into closer approximation to the national norm between 1940 and 1960, high fertility continued throughout the northern Great Plains and Mountain states. In 1960, when the general fertility rate for the nation was 118.0, the corresponding rate in most of the western states inland from the Pacific coast states was over 130. The highest level (156.2) was reached in New Mexico. Only to a small degree can this high level of fertility in the Mountain and northern Great Plains states be attributed to the nonwhite, chiefly Indian, population. Although the crude birth rate of the Indian population in 1960 (42.2 per 1000) was well above that of the nation (23.7 per 1000), in no state did the Indian component comprise a large part of the total population. The largest proportional representation was in New Mexico where Indians made up about 6% of the state's population. Thus, high fertility in the Mountain and northern Plains states was very largely the result of high white fertility.

Regional Fertility Changes since 1960

Records of fertility published by the National Center for Health Statistics do not yet allow the determination of general fertility rates by state or country for 1970. Thus, it is difficult to determine the degree to which the changing regional fertility patterns that had emerged after World War II have continued or have become arrested. However, the 1970 United States Census of Population reports two fertility measures by county that can be used to confirm in greater areal detail the generalizations already made. These two measures are child–woman ratios, i.e., the number of children under 5 years per 1000 women aged 15–49 years; and the number of children ever born per 1000 ever married women of different age groups in 1970. The former measures, child–woman ratios, therefore would reflect survivors of births between 1965 and 1970; the latter, number of children ever born, would indicate cumulative fertility of women of different ages.

The most conspicuous cluster of counties with low child–woman ratios in 1970 was in Oklahoma and eastern Kansas. Around that core to the east and south, below average child–woman ratios occurred in an arc of counties from southern Iowa to eastern Texas. Of the states included in this mid continent core of apparent low fertility, only Oklahoma had a general fertility rate below the national average in 1960. There is considerable uncertainty, however, of the degree to which this concentration of low child–woman ratios identifies a region of emerging and expanding low fertility. Much of this area has experienced long continued migration losses concentrated chiefly among young adults. The removal of young females by out-migration could greatly increase the proportion of older and less fertile women in the reproductive ages, thus reducing the child–woman ratio and leading to an understatement of the fertility performance of the resident female population.

The other large area of low child–woman ratios in 1970 was in central and northern California with isolated outliers northward into Oregon and Washington, states which did have relatively low general fertility rates in 1960. The majority of the counties with low rates experienced net in-migration between 1960 and 1970, so the indicated low fertility would not seem a result of age selective migration.

The urban, manufacturing states from southern New England to Illinois, long an area of distinctly low fertility, is indistinguishable as a region in 1970 when child–woman ratios are used as an index of fertility levels. The expected association between predominately urban counties and areas of low fertility shows clearly only in the eastern portion, and even here much of the low fertility area is in Pennsylvania counties which have experienced losses of young people by out-migration. The lowest child–woman ratios in the east are displaced south of the more urban states in a fragmented belt that runs down the ridge and valley region, crosses Tennessee and Kentucky, and merges into the mid continent core of low child–woman ratios in southern Missouri.

This belt of low fertility through Appalachia appears even more distinct and continuous when completed fertility of ever married women who were 35–44 years in 1970 is used as a measure of fertility levels (Fig. 8.3). The virtue of this measure is that it exercises control both over the age composition of the population considered and over marital status as well. The measure does not record so well recent changes in fertility since one assumes that women 35–44 years in 1970 had most of the births occurring to them some 15–20 years earlier, i.e., near the peak of the post-war "baby boom."

In 1970 there were 3132 children ever born per 1000 ever married women 35–44 years of age. Fertility levels below this figure were largely concentrated in a belt which followed Megalopolis from Connecticut to Washington DC, but then continued southward through western Virginia, the western Carolinas, northern Georgia, and Alabama. This zone of low completed fertility then curved northward to include most of the counties of Tennessee and western Kentucky. This arc of low fertility through the Appalachian region and into the south most likely reflects a continuation and deepening of the declining white fertility beginning to emerge there in the late 1950s.

The mid continent area of low fertility indicated by child–woman ratios in 1970 appears as well on the map of completed fertility but as a region sprinkled with isolated counties and small clusters of counties having low fertility, dispersed in an area of intermediate fertility. It may be that a region of genuine low fertility is beginning to emerge in the mid continent, but its definition and delimitation must await better and more recent fertility data.

The distribution of counties having high fertility in the period since 1960, measured either by child–woman ratios or completed fertility, is not greatly changed from earlier periods. The Deep South, especially coastal North Carolina, central and southern Georgia, most of Mississippi, and much of Louisiana, where the concentrations of nonwhites are especially high, continues to be characterized by high fertility (Fig. 8.3). Completed fertility in 1970 was especially high along the Mississippi floodplain. In Issaquena county, Mississippi, for example, 5972 children had been born for every 1000 ever married women ages 35–44 in 1970. Westward, the belt of high fertility largely disappears in eastern Texas to reappear again in the south along the Rio Grande. High completed fertility also characterizes most of the counties of New Mexico, eastern Arizona, and the state of Utah. The nearly uniform high completed fertility exhibited in these states breaks apart northward in Idaho and western Montana in a confusion of counties of alternating high and low fertility. This jumbled pattern in Idaho and western Montana also marks the western end of a belt of moderate to high completed fertility along the northern border of the United States from Montana across the Dakotas, Minnesota, Wisconsin, and Michigan. Given the levels of education and general well being in these latter states, the maintenance of uniformly high completed fertility is puzzling. There was not a single county in North Dakota, Minnesota, or Wisconsin, and only one county each in Michigan and South Dakota that, in 1970, had a completed fertility level below that of the national average.

Although the details as yet remain unclear, it would appear that the dominant theme in the changing regional differences in fertility levels in the United States over the last three or four decades was one of convergence—a narrowing of the range between the regions of highest and lowest fertility. As the national fertility levels rose sharply or dropped as precipitously, those regions whose birth rates departed most from the national average tended to make the largest adjustment in their fertility. Although

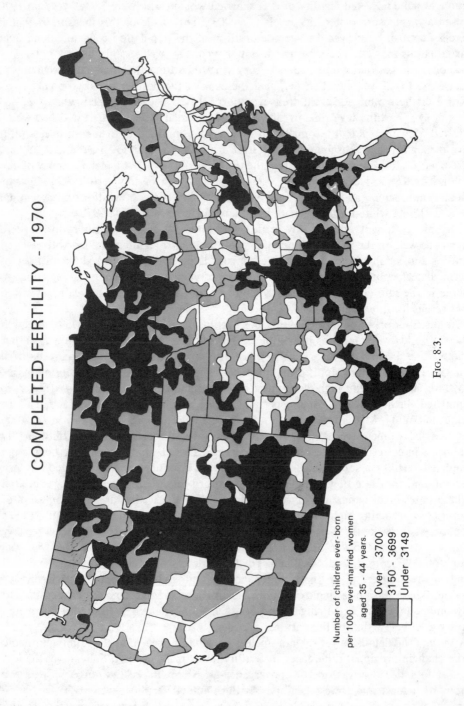

COMPLETED FERTILITY - 1970

Number of children ever-born
per 1000 ever-married women
aged 35 - 44 years.

Over   3700
3150 - 3699
Under 3149

FIG. 8.3.

downward adjustments have occurred, the highest fertility levels tend to persist in those areas which contain large proportions of minority groups in their populations—the Deep South, the lower Mississippi Valley, the Mexican–American areas of the Rio Grande and Southwest, and the Indian areas of the West. The major exceptions to this generalization would be Utah and the northern tier of states from Montana to Michigan. The most significant regional change in fertility levels since World War II would appear to involve areas of low fertility, i.e., the southward displacement of the areas of lowest fertility from the urban and industrial Midwest to Appalachia and the border states from Tennessee to Virginia.

Mortality Patterns

The data at our disposal are too fragmentary and incomplete to allow an exact reconstruction of the course of mortality across the history of the United States. Even so, early mortality was relatively high even in good years, with this level punctuated at intervals as epidemics and local food shortages took an abnormal toll. One can assume, however, that during much of the nineteenth century, especially during the latter part, there was a slow and irregular downward drift in the risk of death so that by 1900 the crude death rate of the United States had dropped to 17.2 per 1000. This downward drift in death rates was sharply interrupted in 1918 when the massive influenza epidemic is estimated to have added nearly half a million deaths to the expected total. Re-established in 1919, the progressive decline in crude death rates continued but at a slower pace. Throughout the 1930 decade the death rate hovered around 11 per 1000, declining by another point during the early 1940s. Around 1950 the downward drift of the crude death rate ceased, and for the last 20 years has generally fluctuated between 9.4 and 9.6 per 1000.

Changes in Differential Mortality Since 1900

Not all of the elements of the population of the United States have benefited equally from the reduction in mortality risk since 1900. Among age groups, the greatest improvement has taken place among children ages 1–4 years. With each advance in age group thereafter the relative reduction in mortality rate since 1900 progressively lessens. Thus, the percentage decline in the death rate for the total population between 1900 and 1960 was about 45%; among children 1–4 years, 94%; and among the older population, 75–84 years, only 29%.

The trend in infant mortality since 1900 has followed an outline similar to that of the total population, a progressive decline until the early 1950s at which time the rate of decline greatly slowed. Although the reduction in infant mortality was considerable, from about 100 deaths to infants less than 1 year of age per 1000 live births in 1915 to 26 in 1960, there was, nevertheless, great concern felt over the 1960 level because a number of European countries had achieved substantially lower infant loss. A major contributory cause of the higher infant mortality in the United States was the continuing high loss among nonwhite infants. Since 1960, infant mortality in the United States has again declined but the discrepancy between races still remains. In 1971, infant mortality

among whites was 16.3 deaths per 1000 live births; among nonwhites the comparable
rate was 29.3.

The decline in mortality since 1900 has also favored females over males. From 1900
to the present the female death rate has been consistently below that of males, but after
about 1930 the gap between the two rates has progressively widened. The difference in
rates is particularly significant in those ages just before retirement. In 1971, the death
rate for males 55–64 years was 22.4 per 1000; the rate for females in that same age
group was 10.5. The explanation for this widening sex differential is as yet uncertain.
It is possible that women may have a greater constitutional resistance to degenerative
diseases. Thus, as deaths from maternal mortality, tuberculosis, and the like have been
greatly reduced or largely eliminated and deaths from heart disease and cancer have
progressively increased, the sex differential in mortality has grown. The heavier male
mortality, especially at the older ages, has been partly responsible for the marked
decline in sex ratios of the United States population since 1910.

The decline in crude death rates among the nonwhites population since 1900 has
followed a trend similar to that of the total population, i.e., sharply declining rates early
in the century, with the rate of descent decelerating as the rates reached lower levels.
Crude death rates among nonwhites have become more or less stable over the last
decade at about 9.6 or 9.7 per 1000, only slightly above that of the white population.
Indeed, the estimated crude death rate of the nonwhite population in 1971 was slightly
below that of whites, 9.1–9.3 per 1000 respectively. The use of the crude death rate as
an indicator of mortality risk, however, distorts the comparative mortality experience of
the two groups. The nonwhite population, because of a higher fertility, has a median
age below that of whites and, therefore, smaller proportions in the older ages among
whom risks of death are high. A comparison of death rates by age group in 1971, when
the crude death rate favored nonwhites, makes the point effectively (Table 8.1). Only at
the extreme older ages are the age specific death rates for nonwhites below those of

TABLE 8.1. RATIO OF MALE DEATH
RATES TO FEMALE DEATH RATES
UNITED STATES TOTAL POPULATION

Ages	Sex differential		
	1900	1954	1971
Under 1 year	1.23	1.31	1.26
1– 4	1.07	1.18	1.29
5–14	0.97	1.50	1.67
15–24	1.02	2.29	2.71
25–34	1.00	1.82	2.10
35–44	1.09	1.58	1.70
45–54	1.10	1.74	1.84
55–64	1.11	1.18	2.13
65–74	1.11	1.57	1.91
75–84	1.08	1.28	1.52

Sources: 1900 and 1954 data from Bogue,
D., *Principles of Demography*, p. 595; 1971
data from US Dept. HEW, *Monthly Vital
Statistics Report, Annual Summary for the
United States 1971*, p. 15.

whites. At all other ages, and particularly between the ages of 25–44 in which nonwhite rates are more than double those of whites, the risk of death falls most heavily on the nonwhite population.

The degree to which the rural–urban differential in death rates has altered over time in the United States is uncertain. The evidence available for Massachusetts and New York states and for Boston and New York City around 1900 suggests that at that date mortality was higher in urban than in rural places. It appears to have been particularly high in the large cities, and in these cities, especially among infants. With the development of medical technology and the spread of health facilities, both concentrated in larger cities, the excess mortality of these large cities has disappeared. However, the relative change in mortality rates among residential classes since 1900 remains obscure; the growth of suburbs and the blurring of distinctions between rural and urban classes makes such a determination an almost insurmountable task. Nevertheless, differentials do remain among urban and rural places, especially in infant mortality. The differences, however, are reversed between white and nonwhite groups. Among whites, infant mortality tends to be highest in large cities (greater than 500,000 population), intermediate in other urban areas, and lowest in rural areas. Among nonwhites, the differences in infant mortality among these residential classes are stronger and rates are highest in rural areas and lowest in the large cities.

Regional Differences in Mortality

As mortality has declined differentially among groups within the United States, and as levels of economic well being have altered among the regions, the distributional patterns of mortality have likewise shifted. Unfortunately, published data are insufficient to trace adequately the details of these shifts in mortality patterns. Although crude death rates by state are published annually by the National Center for Health Statistics, these rates are of limited value in assessing differential risks of mortality among states or regions of the country, for they are strongly influenced by the age structure of the various populations. For example, the average crude death rate for Missouri for the period 1959–61 was 11.0 per 1000, the third highest crude death rate among the states. However, the age–sex standardized death rate for Missouri for the same period was below the national average. The reason for the discrepancy, of course, is the large proportion of older people in the state's population, people who are exposed to heavy mortality risks.

One method by which the effect of age structure differences can be minimized is to examine the regional differences in death rates by specific age groups. Rather than investigating all age groups, the following discussion compares mortality rates among persons 1–4 years, who are especially subject to the economic and environment influences on mortality, and persons 55–64 years, among whom degenerative diseases are more common.

Regional Contrasts in Childhood Mortality, 1939–41

The average death rate during the three years 1939–41 for persons 1–4 years of age in the United States was 3.0 per 1000. The regional distribution of death rates among this age group was relatively simple; south of the Ohio River and continuing westward to Arizona, every state had mortality rates for this age group above the national average. Every state north of this group of states, except Colorado and Montana, had mortality rates for children 1–4 years below the national average. The highest childhood death rates were in New Mexico and Arizona, both states having rates more than double the national average. No small part of this mortality distribution can be credited to the high proportions of nonwhites in the high death rate states among whom the incidence of poverty was especially severe and whose children would be susceptible to dietary deficiencies and infectious diseases. But the distributional pattern of deaths among young children, 1939–41, was not entirely the result of excess mortality among nonwhites, the arrangements of states having higher than average mortality remain almost identical if the white population alone is considered.

Regional Contrasts in Mortality in Preretirement Ages, 1939–41

The risks of mortality among older people in the years 1939–41 were distributed quite differently than the risks of death among children. During the 1939–41 period, the average death rate for the population aged 55–64 years was 21.9 per 1000. Death rates above that average were strongly concentrated in east coast states. Every state which borders the Atlantic Ocean from Massachusetts to Louisiana had a death rate for those in the preretirement ages in excess of the national norm. Outside that belt of states only Illinois, Arizona, and Nevada had comparable death rates for that age group. This particular distribution fits well with no commonly recognized factor related to mortality. Certainly the Atlantic–Gulf coastal belt was not uniform with respect to the degree of urbanization, *per capita* income, sex ratio, ethnicity, or race. Possibly the distribution pattern of high mortality in this older age group reflected the combined operation of two sets of factors: high morality among nonwhites of all ages in the South, and excess mortality from the more degenerative diseases associated with the large cities of the Northeast. Whatever the causes, the pattern of high mortality states shifts considerably when death rates among persons 55–64 in 1939–41 are examined separately by race and sex.

The distribution of high mortality in 1939–41 among nonwhite males 55–64 years of age was much less regionally concentrated than was high mortality among the total population of this age group. Generally, high mortality was prevalent among the eastern states with highest rates found in Illinois (48.0 per 1000) and in Pennsylvania (45.0 per 1000). Although most southern states had higher than average mortality among their older nonwhite males, the excess mortality would not seem so severe as in the manufacturing states. It is possible, of course, that underregistration of nonwhite deaths in the South might have been more frequent during the 1939–41 period than in the Northeast.

The regional contrast in death rates for persons aged 55–64 in 1939–41 was especially strong between white males and white females. Among white males of these ages, the distribution of death rates by state did not depart greatly from that of the total population, except that the areas of highest mortality were restricted more closely to the New England and Middle Atlantic states. The southern states were divided about equally between those having higher than average white male mortality in preretirement ages and those having below average rates. High mortality among females in this age group in 1939–41, however, was even more restricted to the northeastern states than was high male mortality. Outside of this area, only Arkansas and Arizona had death rates for white females ages 55–64 years which exceeded the national average.

Regional Contrasts in Mortality, 1959–61

Over the next 20 years after 1940 the death rate in the United States for both children and the older population declined, though in neither case was the decline great. Nor was there any considerable shift in the distributional pattern of high and low mortality in either age category. Generally those states which had experienced exceptionally heavy mortality in the earlier period achieved the greatest relative reduction in death rates resulting in a convergence of rates among the states and the emergence of several additional states in the below average mortality category. For example, the Border States from Virginia to Missouri, which had had relatively high mortality rates among children in 1939–41, had death rates for this age group below the national average 20 years later.

It is difficult to generalize in any meaningful way the patterns of death rates by age groups for sex and race into one comprehensive map of differential risks of death by regions of the United States in 1960. Nevertheless, a few general statements are possible. The northern interior states from Kansas to the Dakotas and eastward through Iowa, Wisconsin, to Michigan had below average mortality risks for both children and the older, preretirement population. This low risk of death was true for both sexes. Northern New England, i.e., Maine, New Hampshire, and Vermont, had somewhat higher than average risks for both sexes and both age groups; the manufacturing states from southern New England south to and including Maryland and Delaware, and westward to Illinois generally, had death rates among children well below the national average but death rates among adults aged 55–64 years well above the average for the country. The Southern and Mountain states were generally characterized by rather high mortality. The pattern of death by age in these latter states, however, was the reverse of that of the urban–industrial states of the Northeast. In the South and Mountain West, death rates among children 1–4 years were generally above average, whereas risks of mortality among older people 55–64 years were considerably below those in the northeastern states.

A recent publication by Kitagawa and Hauser gives data on age adjusted death rates for 1959–61 for total nonwhites and separately by sex for whites by 121 economic sub-regions of the United States. These data largely confirm the observations made above relative to states. The areas of lowest mortality risk for whites are largely concentrated in the Great Plains states from the Dakotas to Central Texas. Areas of high mortality risk largely front the Atlantic Ocean from New York to northern Florida or are located in the intermontaine West (Fig. 8.4).

The regional pattern of the mortality experience of the United States since 1960 cannot be determined easily from published data. Data that do exist for crude death rates and life expectancies suggest that the trend toward convergence of rates among the states continues, but that the general distribution of high and low mortality remains similar to that of 1960.

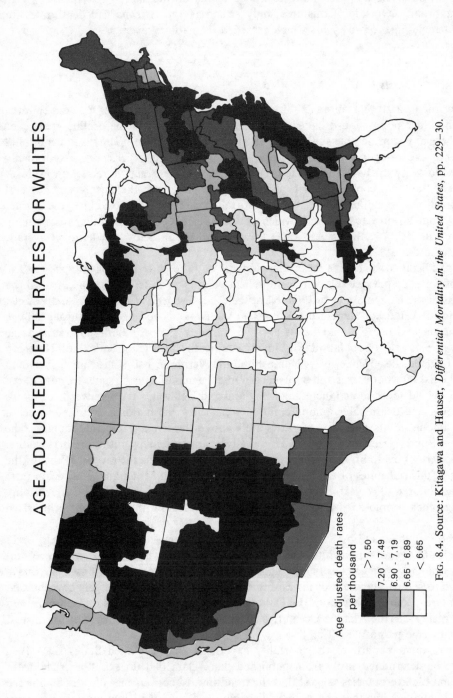

AGE ADJUSTED DEATH RATES FOR WHITES

Age adjusted death rates
per thousand

> 7.50
7.20 - 7.49
6.90 - 7.19
6.65 - 6.89
< 6.65

FIG. 8.4. Source: Kitagawa and Hauser, *Differential Mortality in the United States*, pp. 229–30.

Regional Differences in Death by Cause

One aspect of mortality to which geographers have paid scant heed and which deserves considerably more attention is the distribution of death by specific cause. As medical science has developed and has overcome many of the infectious and parasitic diseases which formerly took such heavy tolls, the list of major killing diseases has shortened. As late as 1930, tuberculosis (all forms) was responsible for 6.3% of all deaths in the United States; by 1971 only slightly more than 0.2% of all deaths resulted from this cause. Diphtheria and typhoid fever, which still appeared on lists of major causes of death in 1930, have been largely eliminated. Diseases of the heart, however, which claimed 19% of all deaths in 1930, contributed double that proportion in 1971. Two diseases alone, malignant tumors and diseases of the heart, are now responsible for over half of all deaths occurring annually in the United States (Table 8.2).

TABLE 8.2. DEATH RATES FOR THE TEN LEADING CAUSES OF DEATH:
UNITED STATES, 1971

Rank	Cause	Death rate	Percent of total deaths
1	Diseases of heart	358.4	38.6
2	Malignant neoplasms	160.9	17.3
3	Cerebrovascular diseases	100.6	10.8
4	Accidents	53.8	5.8
5	Influenza and pneumonia	27.2	2.9
6	Certain causes of mortality in early infancy	19.2	2.1
7	Diabetes mellitus	18.2	2.0
8	Cirrhosis of liver	15.5	1.7
9	Arteriosclerosis	15.5	1.7
10	Bronchitis, emphysema, and asthma	14.5	1.6
	All other causes	145.3	15.6

Source: Public Health Service, *Monthly Vital Statistics Report, Annual Summary for the United States, 1971*, **20**, (13), Aug. 30, 1972.

Although each disease has its own particular pattern of distribution, the precise reasons for these patterns remain obscure. Some causes of death, such as suicide and homicide, have distributions which appear to be linked to regional differences in culture and behavior, whereas other causes of death—tuberculosis, gastritis, hypertensive heart disease, and certain malignant tumors—show greater associations with regional economic levels and environmental differences.

Suicide

Suicide accounts for only a small fraction of all deaths in the United States; in 1960 the age adjusted death rate from this cause was only 10.4 per 100,000. Rates above this level were concentrated in western states. In 1960, every state in the Mountain and Pacific regions had death rates from suicide above the national average.

Homicide

Death from homicide is considerably less common in the United States than is death from suicide; in 1960 the age adjusted death rate for the latter cause of death was 4.9 per 100,000. Whereas high rates of suicide are largely found in the West, above average levels of death from homicide are largely restricted to the South and Southwest. In 1960, North and South Carolina, Georgia, and Alabama had rates more than double the national average.

Arteriosclerotic Heart Disease and Malignant Tumors

The two leading causes of death in the United States, arteriosclerotic heart disease and malignant neoplasms, exhibited a wide range of rates among the states in 1960. For example, the age adjusted death rate from arteriosclerotic heart disease varied from a maximum of 285.8 per 100,000 in Rhode Island to a minimum of 143.2 in New Mexico. Above average rates of death from either cause were strongly concentrated in the northeastern states from New England to Illinois. Outside of these states, the only other state to have above average rates for both causes of death in 1960 was Louisiana.

Other causes of death likewise often exhibit strong regional concentrations. Distributional patterns, however, tend to alter sharply across the age spectrum, among the races, and between the sexes. Were the explanations of these patterns simple, most likely the causal linkages would already be known.

Migration Patterns

Although it does not appear as such in any of the state seals or flags, the wheel in many ways may be considered a symbol of America; the wagon or train wheel which early carried the nation westward, or the automobile wheel that moves it now increasingly to and from metropolitan centers. The United States has long been a mobile nation. From the beginning of record in 1850, every census count has found about one-fourth of the population living outside their state of birth. The same, consistent high rate of movement is suggested as well by other evidence. Beginning in 1947, the Bureau of the Census each year has sampled the mobility status of the population. These samples have all shown that in every year almost one-fifth of the population changes residences. For 6% of the population the move carries them across a county boundary; for 3% across a state line.

Yet it would be easy to exaggerate the mobility of Americans. By far a majority of the population still lives in the state of birth. Indeed, a residential history survey conducted in 1958 suggests that about one-fourth of the adult population of the United States have spent their entire lives in their current place of residence. The proportion of movers varies with age, being highest among young people and declining with increasing age. Nevertheless, of those 65–74 years of age reached by the sample, about 19% had always lived in the same city or unincorporated portion of the county of their 1958 residence. Thus, a relatively small part of the population is involved in long distance moves in any one year, and a significant share over their lifetimes never move or move only short distances from their birthplaces. No small part of the high mobility rates of the United States population is imparted by the repeated moves of the same persons.

Nevertheless, the expansion and development of the country has demanded relatively high mobility. Regional differentials in natural increase and in the demand for labor have required adjustment by migration. Over time several major streams have emerged to dominate migration flows within the country. The first of these streams was east–west following the advance of the frontier and the westward expansion of settlement. These streams generally followed latitude belts, with people from New England and the

Northeast moving westward to the Lake States and the Northwest, and people from the Old South tending to move toward Texas and the Southwest. With progressive industrial development, however, the principal destinations of migrants increasingly became cities. Thus, the major currents of movement altered to an implosion of moves from hinterland to urban centers, with these local systems crossed by a movement from the interior of the country eastward, an increasing exchange between the South and the Northeast, and a continued flow westward, particularly to California and the Southwest. Although the movement away from the South has always been chiefly of whites who form the majority population, nonwhites have increasingly participated in the out-migration, especially in the period following World War I.

The stimulus which sets these currents into motion across the country is largely regional disparities in economic opportunity. The push to the frontier, the flight from farms, the move to the metropolis—all reflect this basic drive. Economic differentials among places, however, is not the only force generating migration. Associated with this basic drive is a multitude of other motives as varied as the people who comprise migration streams. Increasingly, the search for more pleasant living conditions has become an important generator of movement in the United States.

Migration, however, does not always satisfy the desires which originally lead to relocation. The local topography of the national economic and social opportunity surface is never known to any degree of completeness by potential migrants. All respond to their own image of what that surface is, an image created from such disparate sources as popular literature, letters from friends, propaganda from promoters, and job advertisements. Not uncommonly migrants have found their images of a destination unmatched by reality and so return to their original homes or move again in search of their original intent. The major currents of migration as they are customarily defined in the United States are only the more visible of a complex swirl of streams, eddies, and counter flows, each carrying its own burden of migrants distinct in their characteristics from other flows and from the population left behind.

One characteristic which varies among migration streams is the age of migrants. Within the United States the highest rates of mobility are reached during the years of early adulthood as persons leave home for marriage, college, or the job market. With advancing age migration rates tend to decline. During the twelvemonth period ending in March 1971, nearly 44% of the persons aged 22–24 years changed residence; 18% of that age group moved from one county to another. Among the older population, those 65 years and over, only 2.7% had migrated across county boundaries during the survey year. The destinational choices of various age groups, moreover, differ markedly.

Age Differential in Net Migration, 1950–60

During the 1950 decade net migration flows were largely to metropolitan areas and away from nonmetropolitan counties. Nearly all ages were attracted to the metropolitan areas, with peak rates in the 20–29 year age group. On the contrary, nonmetropolitan areas lost population in almost all ages, particularly young adults. Only in the retirement ages, 65–74, did nonmetropolitan areas gain a greater number than they lost.

The directions taken by present migration streams within the United States continues in broad outline the major historical relocations—the move away from farms, the exodus of nonwhites from the South, the gain of population by the western states, and the growth of cities, especially their suburbs, throughout the country.

The Movement Away from Farms and Rural Areas

The drain from farms since World War II, especially among young adults, has been particularly heavy. During the 1940 and 1950 decades this migration runoff reached flood proportions and is estimated to have removed more than 20m. persons, a volume of off-farm migration unequalled in any previous score of years. By 1960 the farm population of the United States had declined to about 15.6m. Further reduction occurred during subsequent years so that by 1971 only an estimated 9.4m. persons lived on farms—4.6% of the total population. This recent out-migration from farms has been disproportionately heavy for nonwhites. During the 1960 decade the average annual decrease in the total farm population was 4.6%; among nonwhites the comparable figure was 9.7%.

The movement away from farms, together with the more general rural–urban migration, shows conspicuously on maps of net migration by county for both the 1950 and 1960 decades. During both periods only a small handful of rural counties across the South, the Middle West, northern Great Plains, and northern Mountain states managed to attract net migrants. During the earlier decade, 1950–60, the heaviest losses to the rural population occurred in the states of the central South. Out-migration from Arkansas and Mississippi was sufficient in magnitude to result in absolute losses in population. Throughout the Great Plains net migration losses occurred in nearly all age groups. In the South, losses were most severe among the labor force ages. In Arkansas, for example, the male group aged 25–29 years in 1960, living in nonmetropolitan counties, was only half as large as it would have been had there been no migration during the decade. Throughout many counties of the South the heavy out-migration in other age groups was partially offset by net in-migration of persons of retirement age.

In the 1960–70 period, the area of heaviest rural loss by out-migration shifted northward. Rural population losses which had occurred in most counties of the northern Great Plains during the previous decade widened to other counties and generally intensified. Of the 308 nonmetropolitan counties in the four states from Kansas northward, 241 ended the 1960 decade with a population smaller than they had at the beginning of the decade. Indeed, out-migration from both Dakotas was sufficient in volume to produce an absolute loss in the total populations of the two states. Although rural losses were general throughout the Great Plains and the Mountain states, the axis of heaviest out-migration tended to shift westward. Montana and Idaho, which had gained in rural population during the 1950s, experienced rural population losses during the 1960s. For Idaho, this was the first decade since enumerations began in 1870 in which the rural population declined in number. Heavy out-migration between 1960 and 1970 was also characteristic of most counties in the panhandle of Texas and in New Mexico.

The Movement of Nonwhites Away from the South

The general loss of population by migration in the southern states during the 1960 decade was due almost entirely to the continued heavy outward movement of nonwhites, mainly blacks, for every state in the South except West Virginia, Kentucky, Oklahoma, and Alabama gained white migrants. Although net out-migration of nonwhites from the South has occurred in every census decade since 1910, the movement has been greatly intensified after World War II. During the 1950–60 interval the net migration loss of nonwhites from the three census divisions which comprise the South involved an estimated 1.46m. persons. In the most recent census period the volume of the nonwhite exodus from the South may have slackened somewhat, but the net migration loss still appears to have exceeded 1.2m. persons. Among the southern states, a net loss of nonwhites occurred in all but the peripheral border states of Delaware, Maryland, Kentucky, Oklahoma, and Texas. The greatest loss, both relatively and absolutely, occurred in Mississippi which had a net out-migration of nearly 277,000 nonwhites, a number which represents 30% of its 1960 nonwhite population. In addition to Mississippi, net out-migration of non-whites from Alabama, Arkansas, and South Carolina was sufficient to produce an absolute decline in their nonwhite populations. The pattern of heaviest nonwhite migration losses in the South between 1960 and 1970 corresponds closely to the areas of relatively strong nonwhite population concentrations. Loss by net migration equal to one-fourth or more of the 1960 population occurred through the lower Mississippi River floodplain and in a broad arc of counties from Mississippi to southern Virginia. In contrast, the states of the South added more than 1.8m. whites by net migration between 1960 and 1970. Over 1.3m. of these, however, were added by Florida alone.

Metropolitan Gains by Migration

Over each of the last two decades the population growth of the United States has been absorbed largely by the metropolitan areas. During the 1960 decade the combined population of Standard Metropolitan Statistical Areas increased by almost 20m., representing about 83% of the national population gain during the decade. This gain in metropolitan population was general throughout the country; of the 50 largest SMSAs only Pittsburgh, Pennsylvania, experienced a net loss in population. The contribution of migration to this metropolitan gain, however, can be easily overstated for, despite the large movement from rural and nonmetropolitan areas to the large cities, about three-fourths of the population increase in these metropolitan areas was due to natural increase.

In 1970 there were 457 metropolitan counties in the United States of which three-fifths (277) gained by net migration. The regional pattern of metropolitan gain or loss reflects in considerable measure the economic health of the areas in which the city was located. Most of the metropolitan areas in the urban belt from Boston to Washington DC gained by migration during the 1960s, as did those in Florida and in the Pacific coast states. Other areas of substantial gain by net migration include the cities of North Carolina; Atlanta, Georgia; the larger metropolitan areas of eastern Texas; and many of those in the central and western part of the manufacturing belt. On the other hand, metropolitan areas whose economies were supported mainly by older, basic industries, or that were located in areas of general population decline, more often lost by net migration. The metropolitan areas of the eastern part of the manufacturing belt had a mixed pattern of net migration during the 1960 decade. Whereas migration gains occurred in most metropolitan counties of Massachusetts, Connecticut, and New Jersey, losses were more common in the metropolitan areas of New York, Pennsylvania, and Ohio. Of the 26 metropolitan counties of New York, half experienced net migration losses; in Ohio and Pennsylvania a majority of metropolitan counties lost population by migration. In each of the three states there was a net out-migration from all metropolitan counties combined.

This record reflects in part the relatively slow growth in total population of the states of the Northeast. All three states, New York, Pennsylvania, and Ohio, increased in total population less than the national average over the 1960 decade. But the net migration loss in the metropolitan counties of these states also is mute testimony to the inadequacy of the SMSA definition to include all of the population functionally related to and dependent upon the metropolitan complex. The suburban and exurban growth so dominant in the 1960s has removed large numbers of people from the definitional confines of the SMSA to towns and rural areas in adjacent counties.

The trend in metropolitan movement throughout the United States during the 1960 decade was clearly away from the central city to the suburbs. By 1970 more people were living in suburbs than in either the central cities or in the nonmetropolitan areas. However, the simple distinction between central city and suburb is no longer adequate to illustrate differential growth within metropolitan areas; suburbs must be separated between those near to and those removed from the central city. In general, the 1960 decade was a period in which the central cities lost population by migration, the inner and older suburbs either gained or lost slightly, and it was the outer suburbs which experienced the heaviest net in-migration. The distinction between the inner and outer suburbs is difficult to make using data by county, for rarely are county sizes and shapes such that suburbs of varying ages can be isolated. One such area where differential migration growth within a metropolitan area can be determined is in the St. Louis, Missouri SMSA. The political unit which contains the city of St. Louis is rather small and corresponds closely to the older central city. During the 1960 decade out-migration from the city was equal to about one-fourth of the 1960 population. The adjoining counties in Illinois experienced a slight net loss by migration. St. Louis county, which borders the city to the west, gained moderately from net migration. However, St. Charles county, further to the west, had a net migration gain equivalent to 50% of its 1960 population. The metropolitan area of Washington DC experienced a similar pattern of growth. The District of Columbia lost sufficient population through migration to more than offset the gain from natural increase, leading to a decline of about 1% in the total population. However, the adjoining counties in Maryland (Montgomery and Prince Georges) and Virginia (Fairfax) gained more than 482,000 net migrants during the same period. Outward from these counties numerical gains declined but relative gains by net migration increased. Prince William county, Virginia, immediately to the south of Fairfax county, gained only 41,000 net migrants, but this was equivalent to 82% of its 1960 population.

The Washington DC metropolitan area illustrates another change common to the metropolitan areas of the northeastern and north-central parts of the country. Although the District had a net migration loss of about 100,000 people during the 1950s, there was a net migration gain among nonwhites of some 37,000 persons. Partly as a consequence of this differential migration, the proportion of nonwhites in the district increased from 54 to 71% between 1960 and 1970. Substantial redistributions of white and nonwhites occurred in most other large northern metropolitan centers. In 1940, the total Negro population included in all central cities was 4.4m.; by 1970 that population had increased to 13.1m. and accounted for a little more than one-fifth of the total population of central cities.

Areas of Migration Reversal, 1960–70

Although most persons moving in the 1960 decade traveled routes followed by earlier migrants, there were some striking changes in the directions taken by migrants or in the numbers moving in given directions. It is too early to tell whether these changes are temporary or signal the emergence of new migration trends. However, certain of the changes prompt speculation about changing motives of migrants. In several areas of the United States there has been a reversal of previous migration trends; areas which had long lost population by out-migration gained migrants during the 1960 decade. The location of these areas suggests that Americans may be reordering the priorities assigned to given amenities, increasing the importance attached to winter sports, water recreation, and less congested areas.

One of these areas of migration reversal is in northern New England. New Hampshire and Vermont have had intercensal rates of population growth below that of the nation since the 1810–20 decade until the 1960s when the growth rate of each state was greater than the national average. Between 1950 and 1960 only 4 of the 40 counties of the three northern New England states gained net migrants; in the 1960 decade, however, 22 counties increased by migration. Similar reversals of past trends occurred in many counties in the northern part of the Lake states, particularly in the northern counties of the lower peninsula of Michigan, in parts of the northern Rockies, and especially in several of the nonmetropolitan counties of Colorado. Colorado gained more than 215,000 net migrants during the 1960s with the greater part of this growth received by the metropolitan cities along the front of the Rockies, chiefly Denver. However, gains by migration spread westward into the Mountain counties well beyond the commuting shed of Denver.

Migration Reversal in the Ozarks

The largest area in the United States in which there was a reversal of past out-migration trends comprised a belt of counties running diagonally from southern Missouri, across northeastern Arkansas and eastern Oklahoma, and into northeastern Texas. What makes this Ozark–Ouachita area of particular interest is its nonmetropolitan, for the most part rural, character. While there have been some gains in manufacturing and other forms of urban employment in the towns embedded in the Ozarks, such growth hardly seems sufficient to explain the reversal in growth trends, associated with expanding in-migration, over so wide an area. Perhaps equally involved has been the growth of tourism based partly on the creation of several large artificial lakes. The system of artificial lakes in Oklahoma, Arkansas, and Missouri now rivals that of the TVA region. The suggestion that much of the in-migration is a search for amenities receives support from the fact that young adults, ages 20–24, are still leaving in sizeable numbers and that net in-migration has largely involved the middle and older aged persons. The moderate climate, rather rugged scenery, relatively low cost of living, and the lack of congestion may combine to make this area attractive to many. One interesting possibility is that a substantial part of the in-migration may be the return of persons who moved out of the area earlier. This is suggested in part by the reversal of the migration exchange with the Los Angeles SMSA. Between 1955 and 1960 almost every State Economic Area in the Ozarks sent more migrants to the Los Angeles area than it received in return, a loss by exchange which had its beginnings much earlier. However, in the 1965–70 interval, nearly the whole of the Ozarks area received more migrants from the Los Angeles area than they sent.

Migration of Older Persons, 1965–70

The Ozarks, in fact, may be emerging as a major retirement center of the United States. Between 1965 and 1970 the areas of the United States having a net migration gain of persons 65 years or over included most of the State Economic Areas of the Pacific coast, the Southwest, the Lake States, northern New England, the Border States of North Carolina and Tennessee, the Ozarks, and Florida (Fig. 8.5). Of these receiving areas, Florida was by far the most significant. Between 1965 and 1970 over 150,000 net migrants who were at least 65 years at the time of the 1970 census were added to Florida's population. The volume of this net movement was a little over one-third the size of Florida's 1960 population aged 55 years or over. The only other state to receive a relatively large absolute influx of persons of retirement age was Arizona, but this movement involved a net flow of little more than one-tenth the volume of the Florida movement. Other states with above average gains of older migrants were, in order: California, Oregon, Arkansas, Texas, and Oklahoma. While the number of people of retirement age migrating to the Ozarks between 1965 and 1970 was rather small, the volume of that move apparently increased considerably over earlier decades.

Although the Ozarks did not receive during the 1960 decade a flow of older people comparable to the numbers moving to Florida or Arizona, it does share one characteristic of these states—the in-migration of the aged was selective for males. For the whole of the United States, the sex ratio of the population 65 years and over in 1970 was about 72 males for every 100 females. Sex ratios of the older migrants into the major retirement areas of Florida and Arizona between 1965 and 1970 were generally above 90 and commonly over 100. Contrary to what popular opinion may hold, there were more older males moving to Florida between 1965 and 1970 than there were older females.

A fairly large proportion of the cities and suburbs of the northeastern part of the United States experienced a net migration of the aged in the last half of the 1960 decade. In nearly every instance this migration was selective for females. For example, the sex ratio of older in-migrants to Fairfield county, Connecticut, which abuts the New York city metropolitan area, was 49. Although data on the origins of these persons are not available, a reasonable assumption would be that the bulk of the movement was local. The distribution of sex ratios of older migrants reinforces an observation commonly made for adult migrants of all ages, i.e., as the distance moved increases, so also does the sex ratio of the migrants involved.

Areas with Reduced Net Migration, 1965–70

The emergence of new areas of migration gain accompanied, and in fact may be related to, another change in migration patterns in the United States. Several areas which

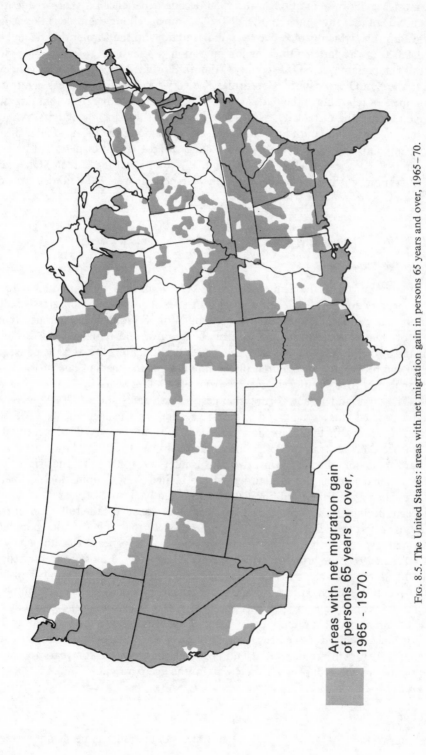

Areas with net migration gain of persons 65 years or over, 1965 - 1970.

FIG. 8.5. The United States: areas with net migration gain in persons 65 years and over, 1965–70.

gained most heavily by migration in the 1950 decade experienced a sharp reduction in the magnitude of that movement in the 1960s. The most striking example is Los Angeles county, California, which gained over a million migrants in the former decade and only about 250,000 in the latter. Other major migration destinations to receive a reduced number of net migrants were Dade county (Miami), Florida; Maricopa county (Phoenix), Arizona; and San Diego county, California. The very success of these areas in attracting large numbers of migrants in the past, and the congestions resulting from that migration, may have reduced the attractiveness of these areas for subsequent migrants. Although these urban areas in the South and Southwest remain among the most popular destinations for migrants, there is some evidence suggesting a wider dispersal of migrants during the 1960 decade. In the 1950–60 period, 677 counties of the United States gained by net migration. During the subsequent ten-year period over 940 counties gained by net migration.

Components and Consequences of Population Change

Changing Age Structure

The modernization of the United States was accompanied by a gradual reduction in both mortality and fertility levels and with these reductions came progressive alterations in the age and sex composition of the population. So long as comparatively large numbers of children were born, the base of the age pyramid remained broad and the median age of the population was kept low. With declining fertility and the consequent decline in the proportion of children in the population, the median age of the United States population rose steadily, increasing from about 17.2 years in 1830 to 26.5 years in 1930. The large and rather abrupt changes in birth rates since 1930, however, has greatly interrupted this regular and progressive climb in the median age. The sharp reduction in fertility in the depression years led to an abrupt rise in the median age which reached 30.2 years in 1950. The post-war recovery in fertility, however, reversed the upward trend, and during the last two census intervals, for the first time since census records became available, the median age of the United States population declined. In 1970 the median age of the total population had fallen back to 28.1 years.

The recent decline in the median age, however, does not reveal the full effect of recent undulations in fertility levels on the age composition of the United States population. The elevated level of birth rates between 1946 and 1955 has meant that the age group 15–24 years in 1970, the group in which life cycle changes are most concentrated, was almost 50% larger than the corresponding age group in 1960. As the number of births has subsequently declined, successive age groups have become smaller. The number of children 5–14 years of age in 1970 was about 15% larger than that age group in 1960, whereas the number of children under 5 years of age was smaller in 1970 than in 1960. The distortions produced in the age structure of the United States by the fluctuations in fertility since 1930 will require social and economic adjustments for years to come as the inequalities in age groups work their way up the age pyramid.

Changes in Sex Ratios

The trend of the sex ratio of the United States population has been more irregular than that of the median age. During most of the nineteenth century, mortality differences between the sexes exercised only a modest influence on the national sex ratio. Far more important was the effect of the male-dominant immigration from Europe. Following the restriction of immigration and with the growing disparity between male and female mortality, the sex ratio of the United States population has dropped sharply. By 1970 there were about 95 males in the country for every 100 females, with females outnumbering males in the population by more than 5,387,000. The highest sex ratio is found among children less than 5 years of age (104.0), with the ratio dropping progressively by age to reach 56.0 among persons 85 years and over.

Changing Racial Proportions

The proportional representation of races and ethnic groups in the population of the United States is a result of differential natural increase and immigration. So long as immigration from Europe remained substantial, numerical increases in the nonwhite population were offset by even greater gains among whites. Thus, throughout the nineteenth century and continuing until 1930, the proportion of nonwhites in the total population of the United States progressively declined. At the time of the foundation of the Republic perhaps as much as one-fifth of the population was nonwhite; by 1930 this proportion had dropped to about 10%. More recently, restrictions on the volume of immigration and the higher natural increase among nonwhites have allowed them to reverse this decline in their proportional representation in the population. By 1970, nonwhites comprised 12.7% of the total population, about the same proportion as a century earlier. Although the share of nonwhites in the United States population has remained relatively constant over the past century, their distribution within the country has not. In 1860 about 90% of the Negro population lived in the South and in the Border States, nearly all in rural areas. This concentration did not begin to break until the early twentieth century. Even by 1910, only 17 cities in the United States contained more than 5000 Negroes, which combined included less than 5% of the total Negro population. The massive moves of Negroes from the rural South to southern and, especially, to northeastern cities has profoundly changed their distribution within the country. In 1970, only slightly more than half (53%) of the Negro population lived in the South. In all regions of the country, Negroes were more urban than were whites. Even in the South, which holds 93% of all Negroes living in rural areas, two-thirds of the Negro population was resident in urban places.

Population Change and Composition

Within the United States, given the regional convergence of birth and death rates, it is increasingly net migration which governs regional differences in rates of growth and changes in local population composition. Between 1960 and 1970 about 44% of the counties of coterminous United States declined in population numbers, net migration removing a larger number than was added by natural increase. For the most part, these counties of loss were the rural reservoirs of the Great Plains, the Mountain states, the South, and Appalachia which have long supplied young migrants to the cities. Fully one-half of the counties of Missouri and two-fifths of the counties of Iowa reached their maximum populations in 1900 or earlier. The long-sustained loss of young people from these and adjacent states has produced a high median age of the resident population throughout much of the mid-continent. The State Economic Area which comprises the north central tier of counties in Kansas has a median age of 40.5 years, higher than that of the Tampa–St. Petersburg, Florida SMSA (37.7 years).

In some counties the continued loss of youth has so sharply altered the age composition, increasing the proportions of the aged, that more deaths than births were recorded during the 1960 decade. In the entire United States there were 125 counties with natural decrease during the 1960s. The largest share of these counties were arranged in a broken ring around Kansas City. Missouri alone had 34 counties of natural decrease in the 1960–70 period. The only other concentration of counties of natural decrease outside of the mid-continent area was Florida. In this instance, the cause was the large in-migration of older people.

Between 1960 and 1970, 1718 counties in coterminous United States gained in population. The largest share of these counties (1260), however, gained only because the volume of net out-migration was insufficient to offset the natural increase which had accrued in these counties during the 1960 decade. All but 46 of the counties of population gain, but negative migration, were nonmetropolitan. The spatial arrangement of these counties forms no clearly defined pattern. However, the majority are located intermediate between areas of population gain and loss, most often some distance away from major metropolitan centers. Thus, many of these counties are scattered widely throughout the Mountain and Pacific states juxtaposed between agricultural areas of population loss in the Great Plains and the regions of population gain along the Pacific coast and the Southwest. Others are located in a discontinuous belt from Maine across northern and western New York into northern Ohio and Indiana. The remaining area of concentration of counties with population gain but net migration loss circles the Appalachian region of limited economic opportunity and population loss. Because relatively smaller numbers of young adults were removed from these counties by migration than was true in the counties of absolute population loss discussed earlier, median age tends to be lower and to approximate more closely the national average.

The remaining 897 counties, about 30% of all counties of coterminous United States, gained in population between 1960 and 1970 from both natural increase and net migration. Although a larger number of these counties are nonmetropolitan (622) than are metropolitan (275), a much greater proportion of the metropolitan counties (60.3%) gained from both sources of growth than did nonmetropolitan (23.8%). Because a considerable, but variable, share of the population growth of these counties of combined gain has been contributed by natural increase, the impact of migration on population composition has been less severe than in counties of net migration loss. Indeed, given the numbers involved in the migration from rural to urban areas, it is surprising that the age composition of the two populations are so similar. Partly because of a somewhat higher fertility, rural areas have a slightly larger share of their population composed of children than do urban areas. In 1970, about 30% of the rural population of the United States was less than 15 years of age compared with 28% of the urban population. Many of these children in rural areas are subsequently removed by migration, and the rural age pyramid breaks inward at about age 20. The result of this migration away from rural areas is that persons 20–29 years are relatively more numerous in the urban population. The proportions of people in the middle years of life are almost identical for rural and urban areas, but progressively with advancing age differential, migration and mortality alter the relative composition of the two populations—but only slightly. Persons 65 years and over in 1970 made up 9.8% of the urban population and 10.1% of the rural. A greater contrast between the older populations of rural and urban areas is in the distribution by sex. The greater tendency for older males to remain in or move to rural areas gives these areas a higher sex ratio among the aged (88.8) than is found among the aged in urban places (66.8). It seems reasonable to assume that as fertility and mortality levels within the United States continue to converge, and as the nation continues to urbanize and suburbanize, regional contrasts in population composition will continue to diminish.

Summary

The 1960–70 decade was a period of rapid and sustained decline in birth rates, a decline which toward the end of the decade had brought fertility down to near replacement levels. By 1972, both the crude birth rate and the general fertility rate were at record lows. During the same period, death rates remained nearly constant. As a result of these changes in vital rates, fewer births and a greater number of deaths occurred than during the 1950 decade, slowing considerably the national rate of population growth and forcing a downward readjustment in the projections of future population size.

The decline in fertility has occurred among nearly all socio-economic groups within the country. Generally the adjustment was greatest in those groups which earlier departed most from the national average. This adjustment in fertility has produced a narrowing of the range in fertility among the different regions of the United States. The decline was particularly striking among southern whites who, by 1970, would appear to have a fertility level near or below the national average. Nevertheless, regional differences in fertility still persist in the United States; relatively high fertility levels remain in areas in which nonwhites predominate, in much of the Mountain West, and in the Northern Great Plains.

Redistribution of the population continued during the 1960–70 census interval with large numbers moving away from the rural interior of the country to the cities, and from central cities outward to new suburbs. Most migration, however, originated and ended in urban centers. Gains, as in the past, were most pronounced in areas possessing economic opportunities and desired amenities. Where these two attractions occurred in combination growth was particularly rapid. The West continued to grow more rapidly than other regions of the United States. Much of that growth occurred in urban areas. By 1970, the West had become the most urbanized region of the country with California the most populous and the most urban state in the nation.

In contrast, older areas of the Northeast generally grew at rates below the national average. Pennsylvania, whose population increased only 4.2% in the decade, lost in absolute numbers more from out-migration than did any other state. This migration loss not only occurred in rural areas but extended as well to many of the older cities whose economies were based on extractive or basic industries. For the first time in its history, Pennsylvania fell slightly below the national average in the percentage of its population classed as urban.

Rapid population gains occurred also in the South with the largest part of these gains in Florida, the Washington DC area, Atlanta, Georgia, and in the cities of east Texas.

The in-migration of whites into many of the southern states was countered by continuing heavy out-migration of the nonwhite population, which approached in numbers the massive exodus of the 1950 decade.

These processes altered, and will continue to shape, the maps of population composition of the United States. Although regional convergence in population traits has narrowed the range of internal differences, the United States remains a rich mosaic of variable population groups.

Canada, Population Characteristics

Vital Rates

Canada's average national crude birth rate in 1970 was 17.4 per 1000, but this figure was derived from relatively large regional differentials (Table 8.3). Highest were those

TABLE 8.3. PRINCIPAL VITAL STATISTICS, BY PROVINCE, 1970 (per 1000)

Province or territory	Live birth rate	Death rate	Natural increase rate	Crude fertility rate (1969)[a]	Infant mortality rate
Newfoundland	24.2	6.4	17.8	126.0	21.8
Prince Edward Island	17.8	9.2	8.6	95.7	22.0
Nova Scotia	18.5	8.8	9.7	88.9	17.3
New Brunswick	18.5	7.9	10.6	92.2	19.7
Quebec	15.3	6.7	8.6	70.8	20.6
Ontario	17.6	7.4	10.2	82.1	16.9
Manitoba	18.6	8.0	10.6	90.3	18.9
Saskatchewan	17.5	7.9	9.6	95.1	22.4
Alberta	20.0	6.3	13.7	94.3	19.1
British Columbia	17.2	8.0	9.3	83.2	16.9
Yukon Territory	28.2	6.8	21.4	154.0	30.5
Northwest Territories	40.5	7.7	32.8	206.1	68.1
Canada	17.4	7.3	10.1	82.4	18.8

[a] Rates per 1000 total women 15–44 years of age.
Source: *Canadian Yearbook, 1972.*

of the Northwest (40 per 1000.5) and Yukon (28.2) Territories, both frontier regions where the proportions of native peoples are high. Among the provinces, birth rates range from a high of 24.2 in Newfoundland to a low of 15.3 in Quebec. The latter figure, for a province that is so strongly French Canadian and Roman Catholic in composition, may seem unusual. But actually the demographic factors operating for the rest of Canada have functioned in Quebec as well, so that from the mid nineteenth century to the 1930s there was a downward trend in birth and death rates among French Canadians, paralleling those of the rest of the population, except that both were higher among those of French origin. But over recent decades this differential has gradually waned, with the result that in 1970 Quebec's birth rate was the lowest among the provinces and its death rate was one of the lowest. Urbanization, improved education, the spread of family planning, and the tendency of French Canadian youth to marry at a later age than their counterparts elsewhere in Canada probably represent the answer to Quebec's low fertility. Why Newfoundland's birth rate (24.2) is so much higher than those of the other provinces is not clear. Crude fertility rates (births per 1000 married women 15–44 years of age) in 1969 reveal much the same intra-Canada distribution as do the crude birth rates; among the provinces, Newfoundland's is much the highest and Quebec's distinctly the lowest, with those of the two Northern Territories well above the rates of the provinces.

Provincia! differentials in death rates are small, ranging only from a low of 6.3 in Alberta to a high of 8.8 in Nova Scotia. Rates are below the national average in four provinces (Newfoundland, Quebec, Alberta, Yukon Territory), but the reason for this situation is not evident. The Canadian rate of infant mortality is low (18.8) and the differentials among the ten provinces are small. By contrast, they are markedly higher in the two territories where native peoples are relatively numerous—68.1 per 1000 in Northwest Territories and 35.5 in Yukon.

In 1970 the average rate of natural increase in Canada was 10.1 per 1000, or somewhat higher than that of the United States where the average death rate is also higher. Among the 12 provinces and territories the range in natural increase is noteworthy—from highs of 32.8 in Northwest Territories and 21.4 in Yukon Territory to a low of 8.6 in both Quebec and Prince Edward Island. Among the 10 provinces the rate is especially high (17.8) in Newfoundland and moderately so in Alberta (13.7), where birth rates are also above average.

Sex Ratios

In Canada in 1971 there was essentially a perfect equality between the numbers of males and females within the total population. But this balanced sex ratio (males to females) of 100 has been reached only within the past few years. As late as 1931 the ratio of males to females was 107, but the discrepancies have been slowly dwindling since that time. An imbalance between the sexes still prevails within certain population groupings, however. Thus among the urban dwellers there are only 98 males to 100 females. But within the rural nonfarm group the male predominance rises to 107, and within the rural farm population it reaches 116. Slight sex ratio differences prevail even among cities within different size categories; large cities (over 100,000 population) have an average sex ratio of only 97; in small cities and towns (under 10,000) it is close to 100. Among the provinces, only the two most populous and urbanized ones, Ontario and Quebec, have a predominance of females, and merely a slight one at that. In the others, males are more numerous, but not significantly so. Only in the Northwest and Yukon Territories, where frontier conditions still prevail, is there a strong predominance of males (sex ratios of 111 and 117 respectively).

Ethnic Composition and Languages

Since 1867 the ethnic composition of Canada's population has changed appreciably. Those of British ancestry have declined from 60 to 44%; the French proportion has changed little, remaining slightly under one-third; but those whose lineage goes back to other parts of the world have increased their proportion from 6 to slightly over 20%. It is in the Atlantic provinces that the oldest elements—English, Scots, Irish, French

—of Canada's ethnic mosaic overwhelmingly predominate, this conservative group comprising over 95% of the total population in Newfoundland, New Brunswick, and Prince Edward Island. Only the French Canadians, who by reason of their history, language, and religion tend to stick together, represent to some degree a separatist group; the others are first and foremost Canadians. Although all of the provinces contain a certain proportion of French Canadians, Quebec is the only one with a French majority, amounting there to 80% of the total population. Still, almost a quarter of the French Canadians live outside Quebec province, mainly in those parts of Ontario and New Brunswick bordering on southern Quebec. This continuous block of territory forms the core region of French Canada. The remainder of the French Canadians exist in the form of small scattered groups, separated from the main nuclear group, and forming a significant minority only in Manitoba, Nova Scotia, and Prince Edward Island. Nearly 27% of the Canadian population give French as their mother tongue, and in Quebec Province this figure rises to slightly less than 81%. The only other province where the percentage rises above 7% is New Brunswick, where it is 34%. It is estimated that roughly only one-quarter of the French Canadians are bilingual. The strong desire to maintain and develop the French Canadian heritage is greatly influenced by the Roman Catholic clergy, the French Canadian universities, and the French press, radio, and television stations.

In addition, there are the original native peoples of Canada, about 261,000 in number, which comprise only a little more than 1% of the population. These may be divided into two groups—Indians (244,000) and Eskimos (17,000). The latter form small clusters of settlement along the inhabited parts of the Arctic and Atlantic coasts. They are gradually becoming more localized, and also more Canadian in their ways of living. By contrast, the more numerous Indians are concentrated along the northern margins of the Canadian ecumene where characteristically they live on reserves and are thereby eligible to receive tax, welfare, and health benefits.

Age Structure

As of 1971, 29.6% of the Canadian population was under 15 years of age and 8.1% was over 65 years. If the dependent young (0–14) and the dependent aged (65 and over) taken together are considered to be an economically unproductive group, then 62–63% fall within the productive ages, and are potentially a part of the nation's labor force. In 1971 Canada's age–sex pyramid showed a pronounced constriction in that bracket representing the age group 30–39 years; it reflects the shrunken birth rate during the depression decade of the 1930s. The relatively broad base of the pyramid signifies the increased birth rate of the two subsequent decades. But since the late 1950s, and continuing through the 1960s and into the 1970s, there has been a decline in the birth rate, with the result that the age–sex pyramid for 1971 reveals a significant drawing in at the very lowest tiers of the base. Regional variations in the proportions of the dependent young (0–14 years) are chiefly noteworthy in Newfoundland and the two territories, where they are distinctly above the country average, which is also true of the crude birth rates.

Rural–Urban Components

Currently, Canada is one of the world's most urbanized countries, for in 1971 the census reported that 76.1% of the inhabitants lived in places of 1000 or more population; the figure was 71.1 a decade earlier, and a very low 19.6% a century before, in 1871. Thus within a century Canada has undergone transformation from a rural oriented society engaged predominantly in primary production to one that now resides mainly in metropolitan areas and earns its livelihood in the secondary and tertiary economies. Cities of 100,000 or more inhabitants numbered only one in 1871; a century later there were 22 such metropolitan centers. In 1871 cities of over 100,000 inhabitants represented 3.3% of the total population; in 1971 the comparable figure was 55%.

Rural population is made up of two components, farm and nonfarm, the latter including, according to the census, persons living in small communities of under 500 inhabitants, as well as in scattered isolated residences, none of whom till the land. Over the decades as the urban proportion of the total population had steadily increased, so the rural share has waned, but the two rural components have fared differently. Between 1931 and 1971 the proportion of the total population living on farms shrank from 31.2% to 6.6%, a decline which represented a mass exodus from the land mainly to urban places. By contrast, over the same period, the rural nonfarm population increased its

TABLE 8.4. CANADIAN PROVINCIAL AND PRINCIPAL METROPOLITAN AREA POPULATIONS, 1971

Provincial name	Metropolitan area	Metropolitan population	Provincial Total pop.	% urban	% urban change since 1961
Ontario			7,703,106	82.4	+ 5.1
	Toronto	2,628,043			
	Ottawa	602,510			
	Hamilton	498,523			
	St. Catherines	303,429			
	London	286,011			
	Windsor	258,643			
	Kitchener	226,846			
Quebec			6,027,764	80.6	+ 6.3
	Montreal	2,743,208			
	Quebec	480,502			
British Columbia			2,184,000	75.7	+ 3.1
	Vancouver	1,082,352			
Alberta			1,627,874	73.5	+10.2
	Edmonton	495,702			
	Calgary	403,319			
Manitoba			988,247	69.5	+ 5.6
	Winnipeg	540,262			
Saskatchewan			926,242	53.0	+10.0
Nova Scotia			788,960	56.7	+ 2.4
	Halifax	222,637			
New Brunswick			634,557	56.9	+10.4
Newfoundland			522,104	57.2	+ 6.5
Prince Edward Island			111,641	38.3	+ 5.9
Northwest Territories			34,807	48.3	+ 4.4
Yukon Territory			18,338	61.0	+26.6
			21,568,311	76.1	+ 6.5

proportion from 16.1 to 17.3%, a slight percentage increase to be sure, but one that represented a healthy gain in actual numbers. The proportion of the population that is rural is especially large in the Atlantic provinces, where in 1971 it amounted to 44.1% compared with only 23.9% for all Canada. Still, in Newfoundland less than 0.9% of the population dwells on farms. In 1961 only 12–13% of Canada's labor force was employed in primary industry (agriculture alone about 10%), but nearly 21% in the secondary and 67% in the tertiary industries.

The proportion of the population classed as urban by the 1971 census (places with 1000 or more inhabitants) varies widely among the 10 provinces—from a high of 82.4% in Ontario and 80.6% in Quebec to a low of 38.3% in Prince Edward Island. Only Ontario and Quebec have urban proportions above the national average (76.1), although British Columbia (75.7) and Alberta (73.5) are not far below. If metropolitan population (in places of 100,000 or more) instead of all urban is considered, the provincial ratings are considerably changed; Ontario still rates first with 65.7 living in metropolitan areas, but British Columbia, Alberta, and Manitoba rank next in order, all of them with 50–60%. Quebec has a low 22.3%, while Prince Edward Island has no metropolitan population. Canada has three metropolitan centers with over a million inhabitants— Montreal and Toronto each with over 2.5m., and Vancouver with slightly over a million. Urban congestion is greatest in the Great Lakes Lowland, followed by the St. Lawrence Lowland. Fully half of Canada's population is contained in the 14 metropolitan areas each having over 200,000 inhabitants; nine of these are in the Great Lakes–St. Lawrence Lowland; only one is in the Atlantic provinces; three are widely scattered within the Prairie Provinces, and one is situated on the Pacific coast (Table 8.4).

References

Beale, Calvin L. (1969) Natural decrease of population: the current and prospective status of an emergent American phenomenon, *Demography* **6** (2) 91–99.

Bogue, Donald J. (1959) *The Population of the United States*, The Free Press, Glencoe, Illinois.

Bowles, Gladys K. and Tarver, James D. (1965) *Net Migration of the Population 1950–60*, Vol. 2, *Analytical Grouping of Counties*, US Department of Agriculture, Economic Research Service, Washington DC.

Hauser, Philip M. (1971) The census of 1970, *Scientific American* **225** (1) 17–25.

Kiser, Clyde V., Grabill, Wilson H., and Campbell, Arthur A. (1968) *Trends and Variations in Fertility in the United States*, Harvard University Press, Cambridge, Mass.

Kitagawa, E. and Hauser, P. M. (1973) *Differential Mortality in the United States: A Study in Socio-economic Epidemiology*, Harvard University Press, Cambridge, Mass.

Lewis, G. M. (1969) The distribution of the negro in the coterminous United States, *Geography* **54** (4) 410–18.

Murray, Malcolm A. (1967) Geography of death in the United States and the United Kingdom, *Annals of the Association of American Geographers* **57** (2) 301–14.

Schwind, Paul J. (1971) *Migration and Regional Development in the United States 1950–1960*, The University of Chicago, Department of Geography, Research Paper No. 133, Chicago, Ill.

Taeuber, Irene B. and Taeuber, Conrad (1971) *People of the United States in the 20th Century*, US Department of Commerce, Bureau of the Census, Washington DC.

Weir, T. R. (1968) The people, in J. Warkentin, *Canada: A Geographical Interpretation*, Toronto, pp. 137–76.

Zelinsky, Wilbur (1962) Changes in the geographical patterns of rural population in the United States, 1790–1960, *The Geographical Review* **52** (4) 492–524.

CHAPTER 9

JAPAN

GLENN T. TREWARTHA

University of Wisconsin—Madison (Emeritus), USA

Populationwise Japan is not without distinction. Not only is it the world's sixth most populous country (110m. in 1974), but it is also situated in the midst of population giantism, for four of the earth's six giants lie along the rimlands of eastern and southern Asia, a region where dwell 54% of the world's people. But Japan is the only one of these Asian giants qualifying for inclusion in the economically more developed realm. It is also the sole representative of that realm whose people are non-Caucasoids.

Occupied by civilized peoples for upwards of two millenniums, the land of Japan bears an indelible imprint of a long and intensive tenure, not only in its exclusively manmade features but in modified natural ones as well. The crowding of many men on little land is a dominant feature. Yet, in spite of a threefold multiplication of population numbers over the past century, with a commensurate increase in density, a greatly increased economic prosperity causes the modern Japanese to enjoy much improved living standards, far greater longevity, and to be healthier, taller, more robust, and better educated than were their forebears.

Racial and Cultural Origins

While the precise origins of the present Japanese and their culture remain in dispute, it is agreed that they represent a blend of several strains, very likely both indigenous and imported, the latter derived from Asiatic source regions. Spurred, perhaps, by the activities of the expansionist Hans in eastern mainland Asia, there began as early as 400 BC an infiltration into Japan of Mongoloid peoples from the mainland. Archeological evidence indicates that at about this time Japan underwent a transformation that led to a new life style, and one which contrasted with that prevailing during the long previous period of the Jomon hunting–fishing–gathering culture. The new culture complex, known as Yayoi, involving as it did such features as the tillage of crops (including cultivation of wet rice), iron tools, and weaving, undoubtedly can be linked to an intrusion of cultural patterns from outside. In fact, the formation of the historic Japanese people begins with Yayoi, which also probably produced the main genetic component of Japan's modern population. Appearing first in northern Kyushu, the nearest point of contact with mainland Asia, Yayoi culture spread east and north until by AD 300

221

it had modified the earlier Jomon culture over the entire country as far north as Hokkaido.

The establishment of paddy rice as the stable food crop of Japan was of special importance, for not only did it foster social stability and permit high densities of rural population, but in addition it tended to strongly focus settlement on the restricted areas of level and fertile new alluvium where water was available for inundating the rice fields.

Population in Pre-modern Japan (Prior to 1868)

Little is known with any degree of certainty concerning the size of the Japanese population during the formative centuries of the State. However, there is some evidence that in the late twelfth century it may have numbered between 6m. and 9m.; by the sixth or seventh decades of the nineteenth century it probably had expanded to over 30m., but the intervening growth rates remain obscure.

Of particular importance, as it relates not only to population but to many cultural features of modern Japan as well, are the two and one-half centuries of Tokugawa rule (1615–1867) that immediately preceded the restoration of the emperor in 1868 and the advent of modern Japan. During this period of relative peace and stability, society and government were organized along feudal lines, with actual power in the hands of a Tokugawa military overlord, called a *shogun*, who ruled from Edo, now Tokyo. The emperor, largely without real power but ceremonially supreme, continued to reside in Kyoto. Thus, only slightly more than a century ago Japan was a feudally structured society.

The two and one-half centuries of Tokugawa rule saw important population changes. During the first half, as a strong central government damped the devastating internal wars and instituted land reclamation programs, population grew moderately, estimated from about 18m. at the end of the sixteenth century to about 26m.–27m. in the first quarter of the eighteenth. These added numbers of people were able to occupy mainly newly reclaimed agricultural lands. But during the latter half of Tokugawa rule, as readily reclaimable good lands dwindled, growth of population slowed markedly. The relative stagnation in numbers at around 26m.–27m. for about a century (1728ᴘ1822) is usually ascribed to a variety of factors, among them a prevalence of infanticide and induced abortion, delayed marriage, and natural disasters such as famines and pestilence, all of these perhaps stimulated by the fact that population had increased to a near maximum which the agricultural land could support at the technical levels of the closed feudalistic economy then prevailing. Unemployment, most of it of the hidden variety, was rife in feudal Japan. But although the country as a whole showed a nearly static population during this century or more, still there were sharp temporal as well as regional changes, with the regional ones sufficiently compensatory to provide a stability in population numbers for the country as a whole.

Distribution of the 25m.–30m. inhabitants in Tokugawa Japan exhibited many of the present-day patterns. Density of population was already high, about 67 commoners per km² (173 per square mile) of total land area in 1750, and these figures rise to 91 (235) if largely unoccupied Hokkaido is excluded. The above numbers must be multiplied 7–10 times if nutritional density, or inhabitants per unit area of cultivated land, is sought. Even at present only about 14% of the total land area is under cultivation, and in mid-Tokugawa the tilled land amounted to not more than 3m. hectares, or one-half to three-fifths what it is today. Moreover, the agricultural techniques employed were simple, and alternative employment opportunities outside of agriculture were few. The predominantly agricultural population was strongly concentrated on the small alluvial lowlands (mostly coastal), so that a discontinuous and clustered pattern was conspicuous. Already in the Tokugawa Era settlement was densest in a belt that included the Pacific borderlands extending from Edo (now Tokyo) and the Kanto Plain on the northeast to Kinki at the eastern end of the Inland Sea, and thence along the seaward margins of that waterway to northern Kyushu. Within this population belt the greatest concentrations were those of Kinki (Osaka–Kyoto region), the lowlands around Ise (Nagoya) Bay, and southern Kanto (Tokyo region). Most striking contrast between population distribution in feudal Japan of 1860 and that of 1970, little more than a century later, is that the former lacked the great increment of population, mainly urban, which has been added, chiefly during the last century as the nation's economy has modernized and industrialized. As at present, most of the highland country, excepting the intermontane basins, was meagerly settled, and frontier Hokkaido had only about 65,000 inhabitants. The addition of some 70m. people since 1872 has not been primarily associated with an expansion into new frontier lands, except in Hokkaido, but rather with a further piling up of population on the alluvial lands which formed the earlier ecumene. So while the population density differentials intensified, the overall pattern of distribution was not greatly altered.

By the middle of the nineteenth century the limits of development in feudal Japan (excluding Hokkaido) under the social, political, and economic system then prevailing seem to have been reached. A change was called for.

Population Growth and Redistribution in Modern Japan (after 1868)

On the threshold of its modernization period overall conditions in Japan were scarcely favorable for economic take-off—resources were scanty, population was large and dense, capital accumulation was small, a traditional social organization prevailed, and science and technology were undeveloped. The two principal favorable conditions were a low rate of population growth and an increased level of education permeating the general public, both features inherited from the preceding Tokugawa feudal period.

In the following critical preparatory period for economic take-off under the Restoration Government, lasting from about 1870 into the 1890s, the average rate of population increase was only about 0.5% per year. At the same time the rate of economic growth was close to 4% per year, which is high for an agricultural economy, and 8 times the rate of population growth. This then was considerably above the minimum ratio (economic growth to population growth) of 4–5, thought to be necessary in order to complete the preparation for an economic take-off within 15–20 years. It should be noted, also, that in the preparatory period for economic take-off the Meiji Restoration Government very wisely placed emphasis on continued improvement of public education as part of the modernization program.

Japan between 1880 and 1940 provides the almost perfect example of the classic assumption concerning the interaction of economic and demographic factors. As

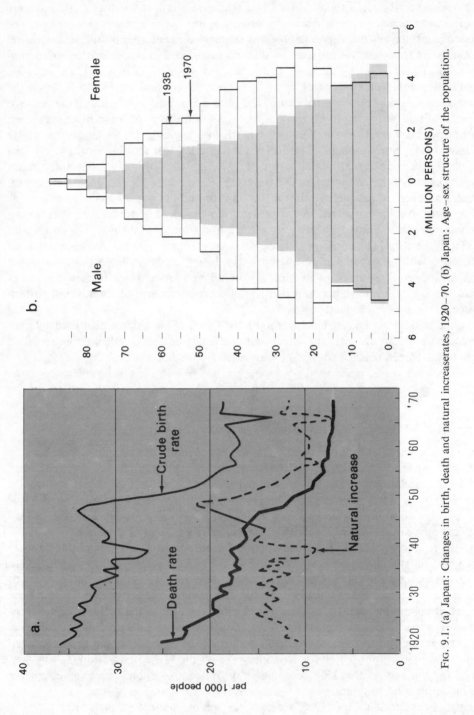

Fig. 9.1. (a) Japan: Changes in birth, death and natural increaserates, 1920–70. (b) Japan: Age–sex structure of the population.

modernization, industrialization, and urbanization proceeded, birth and death rates both declined, especially after about 1920 (Fig. 9.1). During this six-decade period after 1880 economic expansion was paralleled by population growth, and while the latter was not unusually rapid, never exceeding 1.7% per year between 1880 and 1940, still over this period of six decades a massive total of about 35m. persons was added, compelling a significant regional redistribution of population (Table 9.1). Especially after about 1900 it was the half dozen largest cities, in addition to frontier Hokkaido, that gained population most rapidly, with two-fifths of the total national increment between 1900 and 1920 being absorbed in five metropolitan prefectures. In 1888 the six largest cities contained only 6% of the nation's population; by 1918 this figure had risen to 11%. In 1888 only 12.9% of the nation's people lived in communes of over 10,000 population, but this had risen to 20.6% in 1906, 27.6% in 1913, and 31.9% in 1920. The rapid growth in urban population was beginning. Thus, for centuries the growth of Japan's population was a reflection of the country's economic evolution and was in step with it. Only during the last decade or two has the biological increase begun to lag well behind the soaring economic expansion, a momentous fact having remarkable consequences. Not the least of these are the rise in the standard of living and the greater mobility of the population.

It is generally considered that the demographic transition in Japan had its beginnings as of about 1920 (Table 9.2). At that time both birth and death rates began to fall nearly simultaneously; the usual lag in fertility decline was absent. Over the first four pentads of the transition, or down to about 1940, the synchronized declines in both vital rates were moderate (Table 9.2). Average pentad *death rates* in that period fell from 23.0 to 17.4, or a total of 5.6 points. But then came an abrupt change in the downward mortality trend, for, disregarding the abnormalities of the war years, the average death rate for the first post-war quadrennium 1947–50 dropped to a new low of 12.1. This represented

TABLE 9.1. TOTAL POPULATION GROWTH RATES, 1880–1970

Year	Population (000's omitted)	Annual average increase rate (%)	Population density per km²
1880	36,649		101
1890	39,902	0.6	106
1900	43,847	0.8	115
1910	49,184	1.1	129
1920	55,391	1.2	146
1925	59,179	1.3	156
1930	63,872	1.5	168
1935	68,662	1.4	181
1940	71,400	0.8	188
1945	72,200	0.2	196
1950	83,200	2.9	226
1955	89,276	1.4	242
1960	93,419	0.9	253
1965	98,275	1.04	266
1970	103,720	1.10	280

Data for 1880 through 1910 are estimates made by the Cabinet Bureau of Statistics. Beginning in 1920 the population figures are from the Population Census of Japan.

TABLE 9.2. VITAL RATES (PER 1000 POPULATION)

Year	Crude birth rate	Crude death rate	Natural increase rate
1900–5	32.1	20.4	11.7
1905–10	32.2	21.0	11.2
1910–15	33.7	20.3	13.4
1915–20	32.5	22.6	9.9
1920–5	35.0	23.0	12.0
1925–30	34.0	19.8	14.3
1930–5	31.8	18.1	13.6
1935–40	29.3	17.4	11.9
1940–3	30.7	16.3	14.4
1947	34.5	14.7	19.9
1950	28.3	10.9	17.3
1955	19.5	7.8	11.7
1960	17.3	7.6	9.7
1961	17.0	7.4	9.5
1962	17.1	7.5	9.6
1963	17.4	7.0	10.3
1964	17.8	7.0	10.8
1965	18.7	7.2	11.5
1966	13.8	6.8	7.0
1967	19.4	6.8	12.7
1968	18.6	6.8	11.8
1969	18.5	6.8	11.7
1970	18.7	6.9	11.8

Source: *Selected Statistics Indicating the Demographic Situation of Japan*, Institute of Population Problems, October, 1971.

a decline of 5.3 points from the 17.4 average of the last pre-war pentad, or nearly as great a slump as occurred over the four pentads from 1920 to 1940. There was a further rapid drop to 8.8 per 1000 (Fig. 9.1a) in the 1950–5 pentad, but after that the rate steadied, with the three succeeding pentads showing death rates of 7.8, 7.2, and 6.8. These qualify as being among the earth's lowest national mortality rates. Doubtless the fall in death rates since 1920 is related to an increase both in the general well being and cultural attainments of Japan's population and, more specifically, to a betterment of the public health services and to the success attained in greatly reducing the effects of some of the more killing diseases, especially tuberculosis, nephritis, pneumonia-bronchitis, and dysentery.

Birth rates also gradually declined (35.0, 34.0, 31.8, 29.3) over the first four pentads after 1920 (Table 9.2; Fig. 9.1a). But this downward trend was reversed sharply just after the war, and in the three-year period 1947–9 the national birth rate surged upward to 33.8, representing a return to the level of the 1920s. From the high water mark of 34.5 in 1947 a rapid decline set in, so that the 1947 crude birth rate was halved by only 10 years later. There were 2.7m. births in 1947; this was reduced to 1.6m. in 1957. The general fertility rate (births per 1000 females, ages 10–49) was 109.1 in 1947 but only 54.2 in 1957. So while the downward trend in Japan's fertility began as of about 1920, the rapid and complete transition from high to low fertility occurred in the decade after the war. The pre-war gradual decline in births was preparatory for the post-war precipitous one.

All years since 1964, and down to 1974, have had birth rates in excess of 18 per 1000, which represents a very slight upward trend. Japan's present birth rate of about 20 per 1000 is higher than those of Europe and Anglo-America.

Synchronized declines in birth and death rates after about 1920 resulted in moderate annual rates of natural increase (12–14 per 1000), the trend of which, in spite of irregularities over short periods and for individual years, did not change drastically over the past half-century (Table 9.2; Fig. 9.1a). Still, the problem of absorbing each year 700,000 to over a million additional inhabitants, in a country of limited resources, became more serious with each passing year. Then came the deluge, for in a brief period of three or four years just after the war, when Japan was materially and spiritually in the slough of despond, birth rates soared, mortality slumped, and as a consequence the *natural* increase moved upward to its highest levels, reaching 21–22 per 1000 in 1948 and 1949. Concurrently there was a large net repatriation of 5m. persons, so that in the pentad 1945–50 the annual rate of *total* population increase climbed to 29 per 1000, and the number of inhabitants grew by 11m., thereby producing a dilemma that jolted the then discouraged and economically destitute country into taking firm and prompt action aimed at slowing population growth.

Sanctioned by the national government, the Japanese people responded to the nation's population plight by a prompt and determined application of most of the then known demographic checks on fertility, including abortion, contraception, sterilization, and postponed marriage. The concerted action was spurred in part no doubt by the country's poverty following the war. But even more it derived from the fact that, given the situation of a rapid and sustained drop in mortality, the Japanese people felt constrained to alter their fertility behavior so as to better take advantage of the opportunities offered by a reviving economy stimulated by the Korean War. The prime urge was the individual's desire for self-improvement. A rapidly declining birth rate after 1949 was a major national accomplishment, the result of which was to make Japan demographically unlike other Asian countries.

Expectably, the recent vital revolution in Japan has subsequently manifested itself in alterations of important population characteristics such as age structure (Fig. 9.1b), proportions of dependants, and size of the labor force, and also in the geographical and occupational distributions of the country's people. Some segments of the Japanese economy are now confronted with an actual shortage of labor, especially of young males, and if this situation becomes aggravated it might even lead to propaganda favoring a return to higher fertility.

Population Characteristics and Their Regional Distribution

Vital Rates

In 1970 the average national *crude birth rate* of Japan was 18.8 per 1000 inhabitants. Among the 46 prefectures the rates ranged from a high of 23.7 in Saitama to a low of 13.6 in Shimane, or a spread of 10.1 points. (See Fig. 9.2 for names and locations of regions and prefectures of Japan.) Nine prefectures, together representing 46–47% of the nation's total population, yet less than 11% of its area, had birth rates *above* the country average, but since two of these, Nara and Shizuoka, were so slightly above they may be disregarded (Fig. 9.3a). Significantly, the remaining seven, all with crude birth

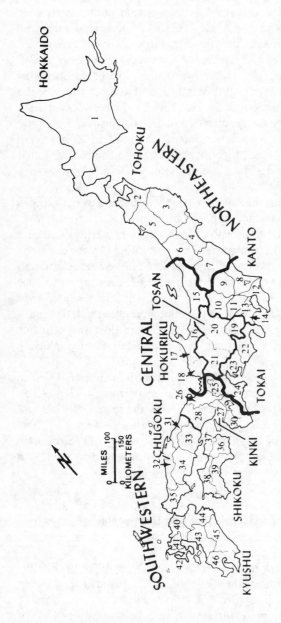

Index map of prefectures and main regional subdivisions of Japan.

1	Hokkaido	11	Saitama	20	Nagano	29	Nara	38	Ehime
2	Aomori	12	Chiba	21	Gifu	30	Wayakama	39	Kochi
3	Iwate	13	Tokyo	22	Shizuoka	31	Tottori	40	Fukuoka
4	Miyagi	14	Kanagawa	23	Aichi	32	Shimane	41	Saga
5	Akita	15	Niigata	24	Mie	33	Okayama	42	Nagasaki
6	Yamagata	16	Toyama	25	Shiga	34	Hiroshima	43	Kumamoto
7	Fukushima	17	Ishikawa	26	Kyoto	35	Yamaguchi	44	Oita
8	Ibaraki	18	Fukui	27	Osaka	36	Tokushima	45	Miyazaki
9	Tochigi	19	Yamanashi	28	Hyogo	37	Kagawa	46	Kagoshima
10	Gumma								

FIG. 9.2. Index map of prefectures and main regional subdivisions of Japan.

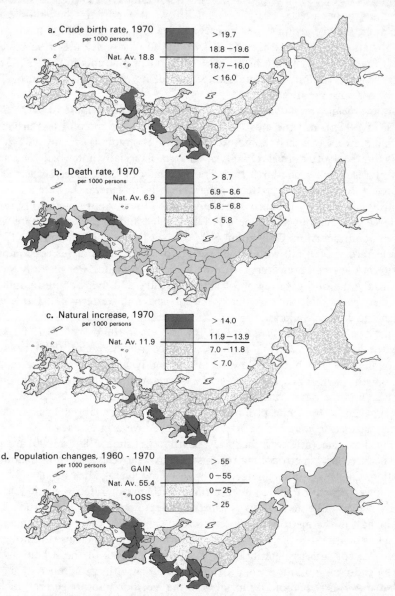

FIG. 9.3. (a) Crude birth rate (per 1000), 1970. (b) Crude death rate (per 1000), 1970. (c) Natural increase (per 1000), 1970. (d) Population change (per 1000), 1960–70.

rates well above the national average, are strongly urbanized and contain all or parts of five great metropolises (Tokyo, Kanagawa, Chiba and Saitama prefectures include the Tokyo–Yokohama conurbation; Aichi contains Nagoya city; Osaka Prefecture includes Osaka city; and Hyogo Prefecture has the metropolis of Kobe). In present-day Japan high birth rates appear to correlate with metropolitization, a situation that derives from the large scale net in-migration in the 1960s of young adults attracted by the employment opportunities in the giant industrial–commercial centers. Thus the age structure of the metropolitan prefectures is heavily weighted toward cohorts in the child-bearing ages. For example, the age group 15–34 years inclusive represents 43–44 and 40–41% of the total population in highly urbanized Tokyo and Osaka prefectures respectively, where a large young adult in-migration has prevailed, but it amounts to only 31–32% of the total in the six predominately rural prefectures of northeastern Honshu, or Tohoku, a region of net out-migration.

Birth rates *below* the national average of 18.8 are characteristic of 37 of the 46 prefectures (Fig. 9.3a). For the most part these are the less populous, less urban, and less industrial prefectures; their combined populations amount to only 53–54% of the nation's total in 1970, but nearly 90% of its area. Especially noteworthy is the group of 13 prefectures where crude birth rates are unusually low, or under 16 per 1000. While these prefectures are widely scattered geographically, in general they are a mountainous, backward and meagerly urbanized group in which the current low fertility relates both to the large scale net out-migration of young adults, and to the recent more widespread practice of contraception. Only about 30% of the total population in these 13 low birth rate prefectures (1970) fall within the age group 15–34 years inclusive, compared with over 40% in the seven prefectures with the highest birth rates. Peripherally located with respect to the nation's core region of major industry and metropolitan population, the 13 low birth rate prefectures are mainly in northern and western Honshu, Kyushu, and southern and eastern Shikoku.

The national average *death rate* in 1970 was 6.9 per 1000, one of the earth's lowest. Among the 46 prefectures the mortality rates range from a high of 10.8 in isolated, rural, and mountainous Kochi, to a low of 4.8 in highly urbanized Kanagawa prefecture containing the metropolis of Yokohama, or a spread of 6.0 points. In only eleven prefectures was the death rate *below* the national average of 6.9 per 1000, and significantly in seven of these the proportions of the total population that are urban were *above* the national average of 53.5%; in three they were in excess of 70% urban (Fig. 9.3b). The five prefectures with the lowest death rates (under 5.8 per 1000) are all located within the three great metropolitan regions; all have above average proportions of urban population. Of the six other prefectures with below average death rates (5.8–6.8), but not the lowest, three of these also are highly urbanized. Life expectancy at birth, or longevity, which in some respects is a better index of mortality than crude death rate, is also highest in the metropolitan prefectures. Apparently there is a strong correlation between low death rates and a high degree of urbanization, and this situation prevails in spite of a recent serious deterioration of several elements of the urban environment, more especially air pollution, that are injurious to health. A number of factors have contributed to this reduction of mortality in the metropolitan prefectures, including the favorable cultural and economic environment, the sharp decline in fertility (net reproduction rate), and the large influx of young adults, ages 15–34, among whom the death rate is expectably low. Also as the net reproduction rate declined and family size shrank, more care could be given to the fewer children, resulting in a reduced overall mortality. Among Japan's urban population it is the mortality rates of infants, small children, and adolescents that are especially low.

In 1970, 35 of the 46 prefectures had death rates that *exceeded* the national average of 6.9 per 1000, so that nearly 65% of the country experienced above average mortality (Fig. 9.3b). But in only 8 of the 35 high mortality prefectures were death rates as high as 8.7 and over, or notably above the mean, and all of these were relatively poor, backward, rural prefectures in southwesternmost Japan, from which there has been a large post-war net out-migration of young adults, resulting in residual populations having a high proportion of the elderly. Only 29–30% of the population in these eight prefectures of highest mortality fall within the ages of 15–34 inclusive. The comparable figure for the five urban prefectures with the lowest death rates is nearly 41%. But while prefectural differentials in both birth and death rates continue to be significant, noteworthily they have been gradually shrinking, so that Japan is becoming geographically more homogeneous in its vital rates.

Natural increase rates, representing the balance between births and deaths, show much stronger regional contrasts than do either births or deaths. The highly urbanized metropolitan prefectures, where birth rates are well above the national average and death rates below, usually have natural growth rates that are three to four times those of some of the most rural and backward prefectures (Fig. 9.3c). For the whole country the natural increase rate in 1970 was 11.9 per 1000 persons, or 1.19%. Only 8 of the 46 prefectures had annual natural increase rates equaling or exceeding the national average, and all but one of these lie within the three great metropolitan regions of Japan. Thirty-eight prefectures had natural increase rates below the national average of 11.9; in nine of these the rates were below 7. A majority of the 38 are distinctly rural in character, a feature that is especially marked in the nine with rates under 7. The latter are peripherally situated, in both the southwestern and northeastern extremities of the country. In them birth rates have recently declined, for reasons noted earlier, while at the same time death rates have continued to remain distinctly higher than in the metropolitan prefectures.

It is noteworthy that in Japan the geography of demographic reproductivity, or natural increase, has shown important changes since about 1960. In 1930, for example, high natural increase was characteristic of Hokkaido, northeastern Honshu, northern Kanto, southern Kyushu, northern and eastern Shikoku, and a few other scattered regions. For the most part these were regions with a low degree of urbanization. Low natural increase at that time was characteristic mainly, but not entirely, of regions where urbanization was well advanced. But since 1960, and therefore reflected in the 1965 and 1970 population censuses, the situation has reversed to a considerable extent, as described in the preceding paragraph. It is believed that this reversal is partly a consequence of geographical changes in sex–age composition caused by the age selective large scale rural–urban population migration of the late 1950s and the 1960s. But it also reflects the increasingly widespread practice of contraception in the more rural and backward prefectures.

Up to 1970, no prefectures had experienced a negative value of *natural* increase, although in several of them the rate presently is very low. But as of about 1965 some 200 of the minor civil divisions (mura and machi), or 6% of the total, experienced more deaths than births. Some 30% of all minor civil divisions in 1965 showed such a very low level of natural increase that they could very well change to a negative value in the near future.

Differential regional rates of population *change*, or *absolute* increase/decrease in number of inhabitants, involves not only natural increase but also net migration. Over the last census decade (1960–70), nearly half of Japan's prefectures experienced absolute *decreases* in population (Fig. 9.3d). Mainly these were peripherally located, mountainous units, where the degree of urbanization was below the country average. The 24 prefectures experiencing an absolute increase in number of inhabitants, while widely distributed, are generally the more urbanized subdivisions. More revealing, however, is the map of population change over the pentad 1965–70 by minor political subdivisions, since these smaller units permit a finer regional screening of the data than do the larger prefectures. Such a map of change reveals that only about 16–17% of the country's total area experienced a gain in population during that late pentad, while over 83% lost in number of inhabitants. This increased concentration of people on about 17% of the area, mainly the densely inhabited districts of the great metropolitan regions, reflects the operation of two factors—natural increase and net in-migration acting in conjunction, and at a maximum, in the highly urbanized regions. In this connection it is noteworthy that the government's population projections made in 1971 by prefectures, and also by larger regions, for 1975, 1980, and 1985, indicate that positive *proportional* growth is anticipated for only three of the country's large regional subdivisions. Stated another way, only three of Japan's nine main regions are expected to increase their proportions of the nation's total population by 1975, 1980, and 1985; these are (1) Tokyo Metropolitan Area, (2) Kinki Metropolitan Area, and (3) Tokai, the latter comprising the Pacific coastal strip between Tokyo and Kinki and including the metropolis of Nagoya (Table 9.3). The other six regions are expected to decline in their proportions of the total population; three of these are also forecast to decline in absolute numbers. The three metropolitan regions where relative population growth is anticipated together comprise what is called the Tokaido Megalopolis, a contiguous region representing only about 15% of the nation's land area, but containing some 57m. people, or 55% of the total.

TABLE 9.3. PERCENTAGE DISTRIBUTION OF THE PAST AND FUTURE POPULATIONS OF JAPAN BY NINE REGIONS: 1950–85

	Census population			Projections as of 1971, medium estimates		
	1950	1960	1970	1975	1980	1985
All Japan	100.00	100.00	100.00	100.00	100.00	100.00
1. Hokkaido	5.16	5.39	5.00	4.79	4.61	4.46
2. Tohoku	10.84	9.98	8.71	8.27	7.84	7.35
3. Tokyo Metropolitan Area	22.90	25.46	29.17	30.37	31.38	32.34
(a) South Kanto	15.69	19.12	23.25	24.48	25.55	26.61
(b) North Kanto	7.21	6.34	5.92	5.89	5.83	5.73
4. Hokuriku–Tosan	8.70	7.69	6.84	6.58	6.38	6.21
5. Tokai	10.66	10.80	11.36	11.76	12.22	12.65
6. Kinki Metropolitan Area	13.95	15.02	16.78	17.26	17.69	18.17
(a) Kyoto–Osaka–Hyogo	10.82	12.21	14.02	14.42	14.74	15.07
(b) Surrounding Area	3.13	2.81	2.76	2.84	2.95	3.10
7. Chugoku	8.17	7.43	6.74	6.55	6.34	6.10
(a) Sanyo	6.35	5.84	5.45	5.35	5.22	5.07
(b) Sanin	1.82	1.59	1.29	1.20	1.11	1.03
8. Shikoku	5.07	4.41	3.76	3.52	3.30	3.11
9. Kyushu	14.54	13.81	11.64	10.90	10.24	9.61
10. Tokaido Megalopolis (3, 4, and 5)	47.51	51.28	57.31	59.39	61.29	63.16

Sources: Population Censuses of Japan, 1950, 1960, 1970. H. Hama, Second revised population estimates by prefectures, Japan: 1975, 1980, 1985 (Provisional), *Journal of Population Problems, Tokyo*, No. 119, July 1971, pp. 43–48.

During the pentad 1965–70 Japan's population increased by 5.4m., and almost the identical increase was experienced by the Tokaido Megalopolis, indicating that the total national gain in inhabitants over that period was absorbed by this restricted urban region. However, it may be significant that the 1971 population projections for 1975, 1980, and 1985 do not infer quite as large gains for the Tokaido Megalopolis and each of its three subdivisions as did an earlier government estimate made in 1964. This may reflect a change that has occurred only very recently in the country's migration patterns—a feature to be described later.

Age Structure

Japan's rapid demographic change during the short span of 10–15 years following the war has resulted in striking modifications in the age structure of her population as expressed in Fig. 9.1b. Over the seven or eight decades separating the Meiji Restoration and the Pacific war of the early 1940s, the relative proportions of the young (0–14 years), the mature (15–64), and the aged (65 and over) in the total population probably changed little, and did not depart significantly from what they were in 1940, viz., 36, 59, and 5. But after 1947, as birth and deaths decreased sharply, the proportion of the population under 15 years of age shrank, and this in spite of improvements in infant and child mortality. By 1955 the percentage that was young fell to 33.4, was reduced to 25.6 in 1965 and 23.9 in 1970, and the shrinkage is likely to continue over the next several decades (Table 9.4). The age profile was drawing in and narrowing at the base (Fig. 9.1b).

In contrast, the proportions of Japan's population, both in the mature (15–64) as well as in the aged (65 and over) groups, expanded noticeably after about 1950. The mature group rose from 59.7% in 1950 to 64.2 in 1960, and further to 69.0 in 1970; the aged increased more sharply—from 4.9% in 1950 and 5.7% in 1960 to 7.1% in 1970.

TABLE 9.4. PERCENTAGE OF POPULATION BY AGE GROUPS

Year	Percentage by age			Ratio of dependent to productive population		
	0–14	15–64	65+	Total	0–14	65+
1920	36.5	58.2	5.3	71.6	62.6	9.0
1930	36.6	58.7	4.7	70.4	62.3	8.1
1940	36.0	59.2	4.7	68.8	60.8	7.9
1947	35.3	59.9	4.8	67.1	59.1	8.0
1950	35.4	59.7	4.9	67.5	59.3	8.3
1955	33.4	61.3	5.3	62.7	54.1	8.6
1960	30.0	64.2	5.7	55.7	46.7	9.0
1965	25.6	68.1	6.3	46.9	37.6	9.3
1970	23.9	69.0	7.1	44.9	34.6	10.3
1980	22.2	68.8	9.1	45.5	32.2	13.3
1990	19.2	69.8	11.0	43.3	27.5	15.8
2000	17.6	67.9	14.5	47.3	25.9	21.4

Sources: Population Censuses of Japan, 1920–70; projections, 1980–2000, Institute of Population Problems, Tokyo.

Between 1955 and 1970 the number of children (0–14 years) declined by 3.05m., while the numbers in the mature or productive ages expanded by 16.5m. and the aged by 2.6m. Earlier high fertility and declining post-war mortality accounted for the large increase in numbers within the mature productive age group.

If the dependent young (0–14) and the dependent aged (65 and over) taken together are considered to be an economically unproductive group, then the *dependency ratio* may be expressed as follows:

$$\frac{\text{young} + \text{aged}}{\text{mature}} \times 100.$$

In Japan the dependency ratio has been declining over the present century; only slowly down to about 1950, but rapidly since then (1920, 71.6; 1950, 67.5; 1960, 55.7; 1970, 44.9). But the dependency ratio is expected to rise again by late in this century as the proportions that are children and mature decline modestly, and the percentage that is aged rises more rapidly (Table 9.4).

Admittedly the current prefectural variations in the proportions of the young (0–14 years) are scarcely striking. In 1970, for example, there was an equal number of pre-fectures in which the proportions of the young were above and below the country average of 23.9%, and both the high and the low groups were widely distributed and also well represented in rural as well as urban parts. It is a fair generalization, though, that the proportion classed as young are somewhat above the national average in a distinct majority of the prefectures situated within the more rural northeastern (Hokkaido and Tohoku) and southwestern (Kyushu) extremities of the country (Fig. 9.4a). But, contradictorily, this is also the situation in a number of the Tokaido metropolitan prefectures. Proportions classed as young population are usually *below* the country average in much of industrially more advanced and more urbanized parts of central and southwestern Honshu. But this is also true in more than half a dozen of the rural and backward prefectures. A rational explanation for this complex distribution is difficult to come by. The problem may be clarified somewhat by observing that in 1960, and even as late as 1965, the distribution patterns of the young age group were both simpler and easier to rationalize than is that of 1970. At the earlier dates, too, the prefectural ranges in the proportions of the young were much greater (6.8 percentage points in 1970, but 11.8 in 1965). Also in 1960 and 1965 the lowest proportions of the young were more closely restricted to the metropolitan prefectures, while the highest proportions were more narrowly identified with the rural prefectures of the northeastern and southwestern extremities of the country. Obviously the pentad 1965–70 witnessed a considerable homogenization among the prefectures in terms of the proportions of the young.

Any explanation for this relative concentration of the young age group in the two extremities of the country, a feature that is presently on the wane, probably involves more than one factor, and likely relates both to regional birth rate differentials and to population migrations. While in recent years crude birth rates in the remote northeast and southwest parts have been somewhat below the national average, in earlier decades, and even as late as the 1950s, they were still significantly above the national average. This situation has operated to maintain even yet a relatively high proportion of children in those more distant parts. Another factor involved is the large scale, internal migration that has taken place in Japan since about 1955, as adults of labor force age, especially young males, have been drained away from the more remote and largely rural regions as

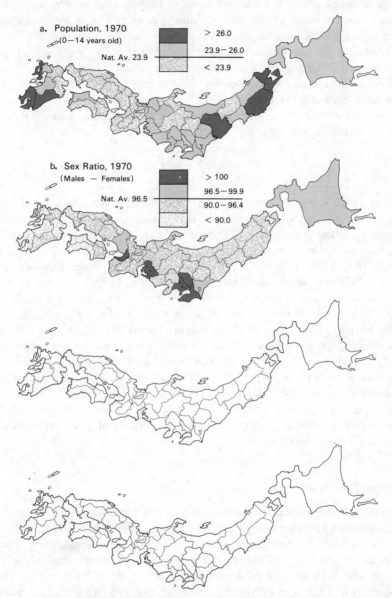

FIG. 9.4. (a) Percentage of young (0–14 years) in total population, 1970, by prefectures. (b) Sex ratio, 1970, by prefectures.

they sought employment in the burgeoning metropolises of central and southwestern Honshu. Both the northern and the southwestern extremities have recently been regions of strong net out-migration, age and sex selective in character, a feature that has resulted in those regions being left with a residual population relatively high in the proportion of children, and, in some prefectures, of oldsters as well.

In 1970 the mature age group (15–64), representing actual and potential labor force, was proportionally above the country average (69%), and so relatively large, in 11 prefectures. Nine of these are situated within the country's main urban–industrial belt and have experienced a large net in-migration, especially of young adults.

As it relates to the distribution of the elderly (65 years and over) as a proportion of the total population, two generalizations appear valid. Their proportions are consistently below the country average of 7.1% in the metropolitan prefectures where their numbers have been diluted by the large in-migration of young adults. Also they are proportionally fewer in the country's climatically harsher north and northeast than in the milder subtropical southwest.

Sex Ratios

Unlike most other Asiatic countries, Japan's population has an excess of females, the ratio being 96.5 males to 100 females. In this population feature Japan resembles the economically advanced countries of Europe. In only 6 of the 46 prefectures do males predominate in numbers, and significantly all six have metropolises of over a million inhabitants (Fig. 9.4b). This male dominance relates to the large male-selective net in-migration which has taken place in the metropolitan prefectures since about 1955 as employment opportunities soared. Three other prefectures, although their sex ratios are below 100, still have proportions of males that are above the national average of 96.5. One of these, Hokkaido, is of much more recent settlement than most of Japan, parts of which still show evidence of semi-frontier conditions. Such a region is likely to selectively attract more males than females. Another of the three, Hyogo, contains the metropolis of Kobe. Of the 37 prefectures with sex ratios *below* the national average of 96.5, there are 6, all in Shikoku and Kyushu in southwesternmost Japan, that have unusually small sex ratios of under 90. These are peripherally located with respect to the urbanized core of the country, are strongly rural, and have experienced a large male-selective net out-migration.

Occupational Structure

As late as 1920 the economic composition of Japan's population, in which nearly 54% of the inhabitants 15 years of age and over were engaged in primary industry, overwhelmingly agriculture, resembled more the present situation in the economically retarded nations than that in the technologically advanced countries of the West. But in the successive decades after 1920, except for a short period following the Pacific war, the proportions of the nation's total population engaged in agriculture waned, while those in the secondary and tertiary economic sectors increased. But it is especially since 1950 that the transformation of the occupational structure of Japan's population has been phenomenally rapid, for by 1970 the proportion of the labor force engaged in primary industry had shrunk to 19%, while those in the secondary and tertiary sectors had expanded to 34 and 47% (Table 9.5). These respective proportions signify that Japan had become an advanced technological society. But although the *proportion* of the total labor force employed in primary industry has generally declined over the past half century, the *numbers* so employed did not decrease sharply until after 1960—14.2m. in 1960, 11.7m. in 1965, and 10.1m. in 1970. This decline in agricultural employment did

TABLE 9.5. JAPAN'S EMPLOYED PERSONS BY
INDUSTRIAL SECTORS

Year	Percentage distribution		
	Primary	Secondary	Tertiary
1920	53.6	20.7	23.8
1930	49.4	20.4	30.0
1940	43.6	26.2	29.6
1947	53.4	22.3	22.9
1950	48.3	21.9	29.7
1955	41.0	23.5	35.5
1960	32.6	29.2	38.2
1965	24.6	32.3	43.0
1970	19.3	33.9	46.7

Source: *Selected Statistics Indicating the Demographic Situation in Japan*, Institute of Population Problems, Tokyo, Japan, October 1971, No. 8, Table 10.

not signify a falling off in agricultural output; rather it denoted a more efficient use of labor. Very recently, however, there has been an actual decline in the gross farm product.

Prefectural variations in occupational structure are significant. Agriculture in 1970 employed 17.8% of the national labor force population, but the proportions ranged from a high of 39.4% in Kagoshima, the southernmost prefecture, to a low of 0.9% in Tokyo prefecture. In 34 prefectures the proportions in agriculture were *above* the national average (Fig. 9.5a). Although these civil divisions are widely distributed, they clearly represent the more peripheral and less urban and industrial parts of the country. The 12 prefectures with employment percentages in agriculture *below* the national average are the more urbanized and industrial ones. They are concentrated within the core region of the country, including the Pacific side of subtropical Japan, the borderlands of the Inland Sea, and northwestern Kyushu. The five prefectures with the lowest proportions (under 10%) of agriculturists are Tokyo, Kanagawa, Aichi, Osaka, and Kyoto, each of them containing a metropolis of over a million inhabitants. It may seem unusual that Hokkaido, the northernmost island, should have a relatively low percentage of its laboring population in agriculture, much lower in fact than the prefectures of northern Honshu. No doubt this reflects, at least in part, the less labor-intensive nature of Hokkaido's agriculture compared with that in the longer settled and milder parts of Japan further south, where paddy rice is a much more prevalent crop.

Japan in 1970 was one of the world's greatest manufacturing nations, with about one-third of its labor force population engaged in secondary industry (manufacturing and construction). This is only slightly less than the proportion characteristic of much of western Europe. Moreover, the ratio has been moving upward rapidly over the past two decades as manufacturing has flourished. Among the country's 46 prefectures the proportion of the labor-force population engaged in the secondary industries in 1970 varied between a high of 45.8% in Aichi prefecture containing the Nagoya metropolis, and a low of 16.6% in Kagoshima, in southernmost Kyushu. Ratios are low, and *below* the country average in 28 prefectures, all predominantly rural, and typically concentrated

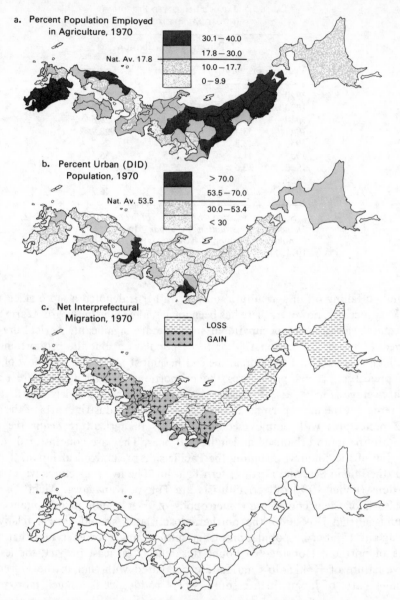

a. Percent Population Employed
   in Agriculture, 1970

Nat. Av. 17.8

30.1 – 40.0
17.8 – 30.0
10.0 – 17.7
0 – 9.9

b. Percent Urban (DID)
   Population, 1970

Nat. Av. 53.5

> 70.0
53.5 – 70.0
30.0 – 53.4
< 30

c. Net Interprefectural
   Migration, 1970

LOSS
GAIN

FIG. 9.5. (a) Percent of total population employed in agriculture, 1970, by prefectures. (b) Percent of total population that is urban, 1970, by prefectures. (c) Net interprefectural migration, 1970, by prefectures.

in the northern and southwestern extremities of the country. *High* proportions characterize the nation's core region that stretches from Tokyo to northern Kyushu, and whose northeastern half is the Pacific Belt Region, with its three great metropolitan areas where in 1970 three-quarters of the country's industrial production was concentrated on only 30% of the total area.

Tertiary industry, as a class, represents a highly composite group of economic activities (wholesale and retail trade; finance and insurance; real estate; transport and communications; electricity, gas and water; educational, government, and other service) that emphasize services and decision making rather than the production of material goods. In general where a large proportion of a population is engaged in tertiary activities, it is indicative of a high degree of national sophistication and an advanced form of civilization. Japan, with 46.7% of its employed population engaged in the tertiary sector, ranks high among the world's nations in this population characteristic.

In only 11 of Japan's 46 prefectures do the proportions of the employed population engaged in tertiary activities *exceed* the national average of 46.7%. A majority of these are well urbanized prefectures situated in the country's Pacific core region. Prefectures having the *lowest* percentages (under 40) engaged in tertiary activities are among the least urbanized; they are especially concentrated in the northern and the mountainous central parts of the country and much less so in the southwest.

Urban Population

Population censuses commonly classify inhabitants into rural and urban categories, inasmuch as urban society presents sharp contrasts to its rural counterpart.

Currently in Japan there are two different ways of counting and representing the country's urban population—by *shi* and by densely inhabited districts. Of long standing is the procedure by which the country, for administrative purposes, has been subdivided into rural units called *gun* (composed of both *machi* or towns, and *mura* or villages) and urban units called *shi*. But a count of the shi inhabitants unquestionably exaggerates the proportion of the total population that is authentically urban, since the shi boundaries usually enclose, in addition to a genuine urban cluster, other small group and dispersed settlements that are more or less rural in character. The second procedure, more precise but only very recent, for determining Japan's urban population relates to the newly created densely inhabited district (DID). A DID is officially defined as an area within a small administrative subdivision (shi, machi, or mura) that is composed of a group of contiguous enumeration districts, each of which has a population density of 4000 or more inhabitants per square kilometer, and a minimum total population of 5000. That Japan's DID and shi populations are far from being numerically identical is shown by the census counts of 1970 which gave the former as 55,535,000 and the latter as 74,353,000. Thus the urban percentage was only 53.5 by DID standards, but 72.2 if the shi unit is employed.

But since the more precise DID concept for urban had its inception with the 1960 census, there is no completely satisfactory way to trace changes in the proportions of rural and urban inhabitants in Japan's population over the past half century or so. However, if one uses the less exact shi statistics from the earlier censuses, down to and including that for 1955, and DID data for 1960, 1965, and 1970, the evidence is clear, even though conformity is lacking, that the urban proportion of the population was expanding rapidly while the rural proportion was shrinking. Thus the effects of steady population growth and mounting overall population density were accentuated by still another feature of population behavior, namely that of rapid general urbanization, and more specifically of metropolization, the latter confined to a few limited areas.

In Japan recent soaring prosperity has become increasingly identified with the city.

But if the proportion of the total population that is presently urban (DID) can be accepted as around 54 %, then it may be noted that this figure is below the comparable urban proportions characteristic of the industrial countries bordering the North Atlantic Basin, in Northwest Europe, and in Anglo-America. On the other hand, it is well above those for the other countries of eastern and southern Asia. In this population characteristic, as in so many others, Japan stands out as the exception in Monsoon Asia.

Distribution of Japan's urban (DID) population is most uneven. It is highly concentrated within the country's manufactural–commercial Pacific zone which extends from the Kanto or Tokyo region, at the belt's northeastern extremity, along the Pacific side of Honshu, and the Inland Sea borderlands to northern Kyushu (Fig. 9.5b). As of 1970 about 61 % of the total urban (DID) population was concentrated in the Tokaido Megalopolis, which forms the northeastern half of this manufactural belt, where six of the great metropolises, each with more than a million inhabitants, are located. This figure rises to nearly 65 % if industrial Fukuoka Prefecture in northern Kyushu, with its two large cities of Kitakyushu and Fukuoka, is added.

The Japanese census recognizes three main metropolitan clusters within the Tokaido Megalopolis, whose eight prefectures in 1970 contained a total urban (DID) population of 33m.–34m. people, or, as noted above, some 61 % of the nation's total urban (DID) inhabitants. Or this trilogy of prime urban nodes may be evidenced in another way. If a circle with a 50 km radius is drawn around each of the three largest cities—Tokyo, Osaka, and Nagoya—the DID population included within these three discrete circles, representing a mere 1 % of Japan's land area, is about 33m. or nearly 32 % of the nation's total number of inhabitants. By far the most populous of the metropolitan clusters is that of Kanto, located furthest to the northest, which in 1970 contained 18m.ᴘ19m. urban residents, or 34 % of the nation's total DID population, and sprawls over parts of at least four prefectures. There Tokyo, the world's second largest city, with over 11m. residents in 1972, and Yokohama are the main urban units, but there are upwards of 15 others with populations exceeding 100,000. Next in size is the Kinki Metropolitan Region, located at the eastern end of the Inland Sea, with 11–12m. people (1970), and including the great metropolises of Osaka, Kobe, and Kyoto. It occupies parts of three prefectures. Third in rank, but much smaller, is the Nagoya metropolitan cluster with 3m.–4m. inhabitants (1970), mainly included within one prefecture (Aichi), and containing one metropolis (Nagoya) only. Some would recognize still a fourth metropolitan region, that of northernmost Kyushu, but including as well the city of Shimonoseki situated across a narrow strait in Honshu. With a total urban population of nearly 2.5m., its two major cities are Kitakyushu (over 1m. inhabitants) and Fukuoka (650,000).

For the 1960–70 decade the DID population in the four Kanto prefectures which, contain most of the Tokyo–Yokohama metropolitan area, increased by 47–48 %. This is to be compared with a 36 % increase for the nation's total DID count, and about 11 % for the country's total population. For the three prefectures that include nearly all of the Kinki Metropolitan Area the 1960–70 DID population increase was nearly 43 %, but for the single prefecture which embraces a great share of the Nagoya Metropolitan Area it was only about 31 %. Clearly, then, Japan over the last decade was rapidly urbanizing; but what is more, the two most populous metropolitan areas were absorbing a disproportionate share of the national DID increase. Japan's inhabitants, as well as becoming increasingly urban, were also accumulating most rapidly in two great metropolitan clusters, those of Kanto and Kinki.

Urbanization is being paralleled by suburbanization. Thus, Tokyo Prefecture, which is overwhelmingly urban and suburban, increased its total population between 1960 and 1970 by over 22%, but Tokyo City (the *ku* or ward area) increased by only 6.4%. Moreover, eleven of the city's individual wards which comprise the central city actually experienced absolute decreases in the number of their inhabitants. Osaka Prefecture underwent a 43.6% increase over the same decade, but Osaka City showed a slight absolute decline, and 16 of its 19 wards also showed declines. Significantly, the central wards of all the cities with over 1m. inhabitants experienced decreases in population. This outward movement from the old city centers to the suburban districts represents a kind of micro-level migration.

But while the growth rate of urban DID population was at a maximum in the two greatest metropolitan areas of Kanto and Kinki, it is scarcely true that accelerated growth is greatest in the group of giant cities with over a million inhabitants. Thus, in the six largest cities, which together contained 38.8% of the nation's DID population in 1960, that proportion dropped to 36.9% in 1965 and 32.4% in 1970. Only Yokohama among the six metropolises surged upward in population at a high rate. By comparison with the six urban giants, Japan's large cities of 100,000 to 1,000,000 inhabitants showed a higher rate of growth. But small cities of 50,000 or less suffered an absolute decline.

Population Mobility and Redistribution

Japan's is a mobile population and the degree of mobility, especially of the labor force, has been increasing in recent years in step with the country's expanding economy. Such migration is as vital as the flow of capital, for continuous economic growth without labor mobility is impossible. Japan's astounding economic expansion over the past decade or two required a large-scale shift of population from rural to urban areas in order to meet the labor demand in the industrializing cities. At least from the time of the first modern census in 1920, the continuity of a drift of population from rural to urban areas has been known to prevail. Such is the classical one-way movement of people typical of a modernizing country, and it is the type that has prevailed in Japan, until very recently at any rate.

For half a century at least, and doubtless for some time even before 1920, two of the nation's principal regions, the Kanto and Kinki metropolitan areas, except for a war-period interruption, continued to experience a net in-migration of population (see Table 9.3). Eight of the country's main regions, rural and more peripherally located, continued to lose population by net out-migration. The remaining three regions—Hokkaido, Tokai, and Kitakyushu—experienced periods of both positive and negative net migration. The basic pattern of population movement, then, has been one that is essentially centripetal in character, with a concentration of migrants from rural areas in the two large metropolitan regions where Tokyo and Osaka are the primate cities. Of the two, the Tokyo region has usually possessed the greater attraction for migrants, but its pull has become relatively much stronger in the post-war period, and it now draws from a distinctly wider area than does its rival.

The annual volume of internal migration in Japan in the early 1920s amounted to a little over 2m. By 1955 the figure had risen to 5.1m., to 5.7m. by 1960, and to 8.3m. in 1970. Migrants represented only 5.7% of the total population in 1955, but 8.0% in both

1960 and 1970. This total migrant flow is almost equally divided between that which involves only short distance, or intra-prefectural, movements and a second usually representing longer distance movements across prefectural boundaries. It needs to be stressed that figures for gross migration are composed of two opposite streams, namely in and out, and therefore do not indicate anything about the changing proportions of each of the two components.

Post-war internal migration in Japan may be separated into two stages. During a period of a few years just after the Pacific war, repatriation and demobilization resulted in a sharp shift in population to the rural areas. The desolation prevailing in the bombed and burned cities made them temporarily unattractive for resettlement. But this early post-war migration to the rural parts was only a temporary circumstance, for shortly the overburdened countryside began to shed its surplus of people as economic reconstruction progressed in the cities. In the period 1947–55, when the average population growth rate for the whole country was only 14–15%, the corresponding rate for the six largest cities was as high as 53–54%. Still, this exaggerated urban growth rate was only sufficient to restore the metropolises to their pre-war size. The economically active population engaged in primary industry numbered about 18m. in 1947; but it dropped to 16m. by 1955 as some 2m. abandoned primary industry and shifted to other occupations in the cities.

The second post-war decade, 1955–65, witnessed a remarkable economic expansion, and correspondingly a larger exodus of people from the farms, attracted by the employment opportunities in the prospering cities. An estimated 16m. employed in primary industries in 1955 shrank to 14m. by 1960, and further declined to 11m. by 1965 and to 10.3m. in 1970. Reflecting this voluminous rural–urban transfer of inhabitants, the urban (DID) population increased from 40.8m. in 1960, to 47.3m. in 1965 and 55.3m. in 1970. Still more striking was the super growth rate of population in the eight metropolitan prefectures that included the six largest cities—from 23.6m. (DID) in 1960 to 28m. in 1965 and 32.7m. in 1970—an addition of over 9m. in one decade.

Regional differentials in population growth rates, and hence population redistribution through time, is affected by both internal migration and by regional differentials in natural increase. But in post-war Japan the dominant role in the redistributing process has been played by migration. This is partly because the traditionally large regional and prefectural differentials in fertility and mortality continuously shrank in the post-war period. But more fundamental was the remarkable shift of population from the rural to the metropolitan prefectures.

Largely because of the recent massive rural–urban transfer of population, the areas of Japan have become strikingly polarized into those that currently are gaining and those that are losing in total population. This dichotomy was described in an earlier section on population change. Areas of decreasing population are very largely the rural administrative units of *machi* (towns) and *mura* (villages). Between 1960 and 1965 as many as 83% of the mura became areas of population decrease.

During 1970 about 4.1m. persons, or nearly 4% of the total population, were involved in the short range intra-prefecture type of migration. Expectably the numbers so involved are greatest in the most populous prefectures, but the *ratio* of migrants to total prefectural population is variable as between prefectures. Intra-prefectural mobility was greatest, and above the country average, in nine prefectures (1970), and in all but one of these the flow was strongly motivated by the pull of a local city (DID) of over 800,000 inhabitants, six of them with over a million. Expectably, such metropolises attract intra-prefectural migrants as well as those from beyond the prefecture.

The total magnitude of the more lengthy interprefecture migration involved about 4.2m. individuals in 1970, or a just slightly greater volume than that which took place within prefectural boundaries. Some 63% of the total *in-migration* occurred within 9 of the 46 prefectures, all of them metropolitan in character and therefore offering attractive employment opportunities. Each of the nine had an annual in-migration exceeding 100,000 persons. Ten other prefectures in 1970 experienced an in-migration in excess of 50,000. While only one of the latter, Kyoto, contains a metropolis, a majority of them do lie within Japan's industrial belt and so are at least moderately urbanized.

Significantly, an important *out-migration* (> 100,000) in 1970 was characteristic of 8 of the same 9 urban prefectures that showed the largest in-migration. Hokkaido is also included, making 9 in all. That large scale in-migration *and* out-migration characterize most of the metropolitan prefectures reflects in part their large total populations. It also signifies the complex nature of the streams of migration existing among the metropolitan prefectures, as well as the outward movement of inhabitants from the core areas of the large cities to suburban locations, not infrequently across prefectural boundaries.

A positive interprefecture *net* migration (immigration) was characteristic of 15 of the 46 prefectures in 1970. While these are widely scattered, they do avoid both the northern and southern extremities of the country, and at the same time tend to concentrate within the country's heartland, or that part reaching from the Tokyo region, southwestward along the Pacific Coast, through Tokai, to Kinki at the eastern end of the Inland Sea, and thence along the Honshu coast of the Inland Sea (Fig. 9.5c). The regions of negative interprefecture net migration (emigration), which cover much the larger part of the country, include Hokkaido and Tohoku in the north, the Japan Sea side of Honshu, all of Shikoku and most of Kyushu. This is peripheral Japan; the outland.

There are certain very recent features of migratory behavior in Japan that warrant brief comment. Obviously a rural-to-urban movement of people cannot continue in-definitely. Already complaints have been voiced about shortages of labor in some rural areas, while urban authorities are having serious difficulties in accommodating their greatly swollen populations. Very recently, there is some evidence indicating that a transformation is occurring in migratory behavior and in the resulting redistribution of population. The urban parts, and especially the metropolitan areas, which for more than half a century evidenced remarkable and consistent increases in net in-migration, have in the recent inter-censal period 1965P70 begun to show a significant slowing in the upward trend. At the same time the rural regions, where a net out-migration has long been the rule, started to manifest a shrinkage in their losses. Hokkaido was the single exception. Using annual rather than pentad data, it appears that the above-mentioned changes in net migration trends began as late as the early 1960s. Seemingly a fundamental alteration in the migration streams has very recently emerged. Particularly noteworthy is the increasing return migration from the metropolitan regions which currently is at a higher rate than the rural exodus. The result is a shrinkage of net out-migration in the rural regions and of net in-migration in the metropolitan areas. This swelling return migration from the great metropolitan regions is one of the most recent redistributive movements of population in Japan. But there are others. Inter- and intra-metropolitan migrations, and also intra-prefectural transfers, are mounting, with the result that the whole migration pattern is becoming increasingly complex. The earlier largely one way rural–urban type of transfer is giving way to a more multi-way movement characteristic of a new period of economic and social change.

In this connection it is also noteworthy that the latest inter-censal period, 1965–70, reveals that the fastest growth rates were experienced by the medium sized cities of 100,000–299,000 inhabitants. Such cities gained population even in regions that were losing as a whole. At the same time, population in the largest cities of over 1m. inhabitants, while still increasing during the period 1965–70, actually increased at the slowest rate compared with any other post-war pentad. Also there has been a remarkable waning in the contribution made by net in-migration to the total metropolitan population increase, while the role of natural increase has expanded. Among the cities of over 1m. inhabitants, only Yokohama still maintains its high rate of increase. Apparently what is happening is that the population concentration in Japan, which for so long represented a national-level clustering within the great Tokaido Megalopolis region, has very recently begun to shift to a regional or local-level clustering. This is designated as "dispersed concentration."

Other Population Characteristics

Japan's is a highly literate and educated population. *Illiteracy* is almost nil, for nearly 100% of the adult population possesses ordinary reading and writing skills. The educational system provides for 9 years of compulsory education (6 years of primary school and 3 years of lower secondary school). Some 85% of those graduated from lower secondary schools in 1971 advanced to the upper secondary schools, with females slightly more numerous than males. Of all upper secondary school graduates, 26.8% went on to junior colleges and universities, in which institutions males outnumber females only very slightly. In Japan one out of every four persons of college age is enrolled in higher academic institutions.

Religion is all-pervasive among Japan's population; dependence on sacred ritual and belief prevails at both the national and the household levels. Religion in Japan is essentially Shintoism and Buddhism, and in the lives of many Japanese a clear-cut distinction between the two does not exist. Shintoism, interpreted to mean all native sacred beliefs, and hence a kind of national mythology or ancestor worship, is the indigenous religion and is therefore to be distinguished from Buddhism, which was introduced from the mainland. It is estimated that Shintoism represents about 45% of the population and Buddhism nearly 51%; Christians make up only about 0.5%.

The *per capita gross national product* in 1973 was estimated to be $1920, by far the highest figure for any country in eastern and southern Asia. On the other hand, it was only two-fifths that of the United States, slightly more than half that of Canada, and was well below the *per capita* average productivity of Northwest Europe as a whole. To be sure, the figure for Japan has been moving upward rapidly in recent years, so that the *per capita* productivity gap between Japan and Western countries has been closing fast. At the same time the gap between Japan and the less developed world has widened.

The range in *per capita* average incomes among the 46 prefectures is large, those in the most affluent prefectures being two to three times what they are in the poorer ones. Highest *per capita* incomes in the fiscal years 1969–70 were in the prefectures comprising the great metropolitan areas; the lowest were in the rural prefectures of the northeastern and southwestern extremities of the country.

Population Density and Distribution Patterns

The census count of Japan's population as of October 1, 1970, was 103,720,000 (estimated 111m. in 1975). Contained within an area of 370,073 km², this count represents a simple man/land ratio of 280 inhabitants per km² (725 per square mile), which is one of the world's very highest national population densities.

But even Japan's exceedingly high arithmetic density figure is scarcely a true indicator of the degree of crowding there, owing to the great prevalence of highlands with slopes so steep as to discourage important settlement. Scarcely 16% of Japan's area is classified as agricultural land (including residential lots, meadows, pastures, reservoirs, etc.), while barely 14% is currently in crops. Thus the population density per unit area of cultivated land reaches the astounding figure of about 1872 per km² (or almost 4850 per square mile). Probably in no other country are human beings crowded together so thickly on the cultivated lowlands, most of them coastal in location. To be sure, slightly over half of Japan's population is classed as urban, but a great proportion of the towns and cities as well are situated on lowlands. Much of mountainous and hilly interior Japan is characterized by population densities that are far below the country average; over considerable areas population is sparse indeed.

A hasty observation of the population map gives the impression that the complex density variations in Japan are mainly a function of terrain character and of the degree of urbanization; doubtless this is the case (Fig. 9.6). But superimposed on this very conspicuous complex pattern is another, more obscure and of coarser dimensions, that has its roots in climatic differences (with associated variations in land productivity), historical antecedents, and recency of settlement. Accordingly, and disregarding local variations, there can be observed an overall decline in general population density (rural density as well) northward from about latitude 37° or 38°. So while the national density average was about 280 per km² in 1970, that for Hokkaido, the northern island, and the region most recently settled, was only 66 persons, or less than one-fourth as great. No other prefecture approaches this modest density. Tohoku, comprising the six northeastern prefectures of Honshu, has an overall density of only about half the national average, but, on the other hand, more than twice that of Hokkaido. To be sure, there are three or four mountainous prefectures in mild southwestern Japan that have densities as low, or lower, than colder Tohoku's average, but these are isolated and exceptional instances. Usually they are highly deficient in lowland areas, and are only modestly urbanized and industrialized. While in Japan northward from about 37° there is an overall decline in population density with increasing latitude, there is no similar progressive change in density throughout subtropical Japan. If, in order to eliminate the effects on population density of the variable proportions of highland and lowland within individual prefectures, cultivated land is substituted for total area, a similar decrease in nutritional density, as in arithmetic density, northward of about 37° or 38° is to be observed. Thus, prefectures in northern Tohoku have nutritional densities only 50–70% as great as those of nonmetropolitan prefectures in subtropical southwestern Japan, while Hokkaido's is only one-fourth to one-third as great.

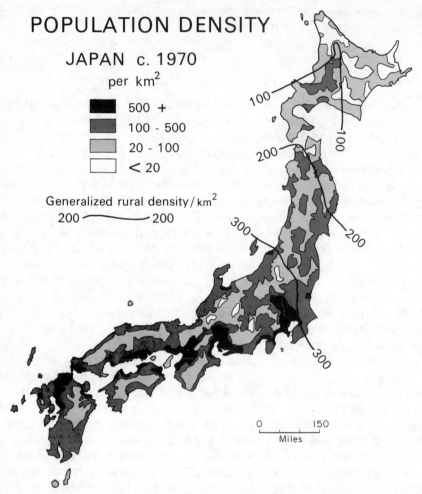

POPULATION DENSITY

JAPAN c. 1970

per km²

■ 500 +

▨ 100 - 500

▩ 20 - 100

□ < 20

Generalized rural density / km²

200 ———— 200

FIG. 9.6. Modified after map in *Atlas of Japan: Physical, Economic, Political,* International Society for Educational Information, Tokyo, 1970.

This progressive decline in population density northward from about latitude 37° or 38° reflects also increasing remoteness from the cultural and economic heart of the country. Because Japanese culture had its origins in the subtropical southwest, the northland has always been looked upon as the provinces and the backcountry, a region where the environment is harsher and the ways of living cruder. As late as 1800 the number of Japanese settlers in Hokkaido may not have exceeded 40,000. Even more important in operating to reduce population density in Japan's northland is the severity of the climate there which makes living conditions harsher and agricultural land less productive, especially for a people strongly bound to subtropical types of agriculture and housing. In these northern regions with cooler summers and shorter growing season, rice-cultivation has been especially disadvantaged, so that until recently rice yields were relatively low and varied greatly from year to year, depending on the weather. Multiple and winter cropping become much more precarious in Japan's microthermal climates, and such practices are entirely absent over large parts of the northland. Similarly, a number of the country's important crops, such as sweet potatoes, tea, citrus, and mulberry, are either absent or of small importance north of 37–38°. As a consequence largely of physical handicaps, agricultural production per unit area in Hokkaido is only one-fourth to one-third what it is in subtropical Japan, while in Tohoku the ratio is about one-half. It is significant in this respect that farms increase in average size northward from about 37° or 38° in order to compensate for this decreased productivity.

Within subtropical central and southwestern Japan population is markedly concentrated in a long, irregular belt, with conspicuous nodes, reaching from the Kanto, or Tokyo, Plain southwestward to northern Kyushu (Fig. 9.6). Its northeastern part is the Tokaido Megalopolis. In Kanto and Tokai the population belt fronts upon the Pacific Ocean, but from about Nagoya westward, and including Kinki, it chiefly coincides with the coastal lands of the Inland Sea. Much of this population belt was included in the region of very early settlement, and has in the last half century come to be the most urban–industrial part of modern Japan. The whole region is easily accessible from the sea, for its indented coastline offers numerous havens for ships. It contains both the ancient and the modern national capitals of Japan as well as its modern centers of industry, business, and finance. As its western end is the nation's most productive coal region, while its eastern parts are served by the country's greatest concentration of hydroelectric development, located in central Honshu. Included within this populous belt are all six of the country's great metropolises, all of its major ports, and over 60% of its cities of over 100,000 population. In a few parts of the population belt where relatively large alluvial lowlands front on spacious bays, greatly expanded nodes of population have arisen. Most noteworthy of these are the Kanto, Kinki, and Nagoya metropolitan regions described previously.

As noted earlier, it is the variations in relief and in proportions of steep slopeland which play a dominant role in affecting the most conspicuous local variations in population density and the most striking patterns of population distribution. In a region of such prevailingly rugged terrain, where lowlands are usually separate and isolated, it is not unusual that a strongly clotted or cellular pattern of population distribution should develop, with the clusters of dense settlement almost coincident in both area and shape with sizable alluvial lowlands. Indeed, it is nearly possible to reconstruct the crude relief pattern of Japan from a detailed population map. In the hill lands themselves there prevail very complex dendritic patterns of population arrangement, with the filaments of settlement becoming finer as the valleys narrow at the higher elevations. In some places smooth upland surfaces, either volcanic ash or older alluvium, and low level areas of weak Tertiary rocks where dissection is well advanced are likewise moderately well settled.

In a paper entitled "Population density by landform division of Japan," prepared by the Geographical Survey Institute to accompany the map "Population density by landform division, 1955" (3 sheets, scale 1:800,000), seven different types of terrain are recognized, and the population density for each type, and for each subdivision of each type, is computed. The population of all urban places with an area exceeding 0.25 km², or close to one-third of the total, was excluded.

It may be observed that mountains and volcanoes, which comprise over three-fifths of the total area of the country, had only 21% of the total rural–small city population. Within these two terrain categories population densities were lowest. Hill lands, with lower relief and wider valleys, had densities that were markedly higher than those of mountains and volcanoes. But it was the lowlands of new alluvium, and to a much lesser extent the low uplands of older alluvium and volcanic ash, that supported the highest densities. These two terrain types, while occupying only 24% of the area, contained 65% of the population; the alluvial lowlands alone, with only 13% of the area, accounted for 45% of the population. It bears emphasizing that the latter figure would be greatly increased if all urban population was included. To be sure, similar landform types within the country's several regional subdivisions support different densities of population. For example, lowlands of new alluvium in Hokkaido have about half the density of those in Tohoku, which is the lowest for any subdivision of Old Japan, and only about one-fifth the density of those of Kinki in southwestern Japan, which is the highest in the nation.

The strong coincidence between plains and areas of dense settlement makes for a decided peripheral or seaboard concentration of people, since most of Japan's lowlands are delta-fans (Fig. 9.6). Hence it is not surprising that many elements of Japanese culture are closely bound to the sea. It is chiefly in Tohoku and Tosan (central highlands region) that the detrital lowlands are interior basins, with the consequence that there more of the population clusters are also removed from tidewater. Coincidence of population with alluvial lowlands is perhaps more pronounced in Japan than in most parts of the world because of the Japanese farmer's strong urge to grow irrigated rice, which requires flattish inundated fields.

Like the Chinese, the Japanese tend to overcrowd the best agricultural lands and neglect the possibilities of the less fertile, or even marginal, and more isolated upland areas. This tendency to depreciate the less productive upland sites is of multiple origin. In part it reflects the dominance of irrigated rice and the difficulties associated with growing that inundated crop on uplands and slopes where irrigation is difficult. In part, also, it is a consequence of Japanese farming techniques being poorly adapted to the exploitation of hilly uplands, since they largely exclude an intensive and rational pastoral activity and fail to emphasize the development of fruit and nut crops. Even more, perhaps, it is a consequence of the Japanese farmer's difficulty in making a living from any but the best land, using the method of spade agriculture, which until recently has been so prevalent. It is interesting to speculate concerning the effects which the greatly expanding use of hand tractors may have on the utilization of infertile upland sites, for even these simple machines considerably increase the area that can be efficiently worked by a farm family. Still, both mechanical and animal power have limited usefulness on steep slopes.

References

Boffey, P. M. (1970) Japan: a crowded nation wants to boost its birthrate, *Science* **167**, 960–2. (Reply by A. R. Sweezy, **169** (1970) 97).
Chard, Chester S. (1974) *Northeast Asia in Prehistory*, the University of Wisconsin Press, Madison.
Kakiuchi, George H. (1969) Impact of modernization on population trends in an Asian nation: Japan, in *Geography of Population: A Teacher's Guide* (Paul F. Griffin, ed.), Feardon Publishers, Palo Alto, California, pp. 135–61.
Kawai, Reiko (1961) Population density of Japan by land form division, *Erdkunde* **15** (3) 226–32.
Okazaki, Yoichi (1965) Migration in relation to future growth of population and its distribution; internal migration and population distribution—Japan, in UN, *World Population Conference, Belgrade*, vol. II.

(1960) Population density by landform division in Japan, *Bulletin of the Geographical Survey Institute (Tokyo)* **6**, (2–3) 155–66.

Taeuber, Irene B. (1958) *The Population of Japan*, Princeton University Press, Princeton.

Taeuber, Irene B. (1962) Japan's population: miracle, model, or case study, *Foreign Affairs* **40**, 595–604.

Trewartha, Glenn T. (1965) *Japan: A Geography*, University of Wisconsin Press, Madison, chapter 5, Population, pp. 101–41.

Tsubouchi, Yoshihiro (1970) Changes in fertility by region, 1920–1965, *Demography* **7**, 121–34.

Wilkinson, Thomas O. (1964) A functional classification of Japanese cities, 1920–1955, *Demography* **1**, 177–85.

I

CHAPTER 10

AUSTRALIA AND NEW ZEALAND

M. G. A. WILSON

Wollongong University College, Australia

Despite their many physical differences, Australia and New Zealand have much in common socially, economically, and historically. In each case European settlement is comparatively recent; in both the early settlers were predominantly of British stock; in each the progress of settlement involved the dispossession of an indigenous population, the exploitation of rich mineral and forest resources, and the gradual establishment of prosperous, export based agricultural and pastoral economies; in each, during the twentieth century, have evolved competing yet increasingly interdependent, affluent, industrialized, highly urbanized, predominantly European societies whose major traumas during the past 75 years have been two world wars and periodic economic recessions.

Tied by blood, by trade, and by tradition to the European hearthland of the demographic revolution of the nineteenth century and subjected to essentially the same external modifiers of demographic behavior, it is not surprising, therefore, that substantially the same path of demographic evolution has been traversed by both Australia and New Zealand as by the countries of Northwest Europe and Anglo-American. In neither case, however, has the process of change been a carbon copy of the motherland's model. Initial or final levels, rates of change, and the spatial manifestations of change, for example, have all been influenced by local conditions. In this chapter, therefore, attention will be directed both to demonstrating the strong similarities between events and patterns in this and other parts of the more developed realm and to the consideration of the manifold differences which are particular to this region as a whole or to one or other of its component parts.

Population Numbers and Growth

Early Settlement

At the time of first European settlement both Australia and New Zealand were already lightly populated by "native" races. In Australia an estimated 300,000 Aborigines occupied a variety of environments from the well watered, forested coastal areas to the desert and semi-deserts of the interior. In New Zealand only slightly fewer Maoris were concentrated mainly in the warmer northern island's forested hills and coastal lowlands.

Early white settlement took several forms. In New South Wales, Tasmania, and Western Australia penal colonies were established during the last decades of the eighteenth and the early decades of the nineteenth century. In New Zealand whalers, sealers, and later missionaries established shore bases for converting blubber to oil and heathens to Christianity. Initially, however, their impact was small. By 1800 Australia's white population had reached 5000, mostly males, almost all either convicts, militia, or administrators. In New Zealand a mere 50 whites were estimated to be in residence. The transportation of convicts to Van Diemen's Land and New South Wales continued well into the nineteenth century, but after 1820 the migration of free settlers was officially encouraged, and during the 1830s and 1840s Wakefield's land settlement schemes were responsible for the foundation of communities in South Australia and later in several areas of New Zealand.

Population Growth

From such small and rather disreputable origins, populations have evolved numbering in 1971 almost 13m. and 3m. in Australia and New Zealand respectively. Australia's population grew rapidly from 1798 to the late 1850s, reaching its first million exactly 70 years after initial settlement. Since the 1860s the growth rate of the Australian population has been rather more sedate and much less variable. Between the 1860s and 1880s annual growth rates ranged between 3 and 4% as high natural increase rates were supplemented by a net in-migration attracted by a plethora of mineral strikes in all colonies, by the opening up of larger pastoral leases to the small farmer, and by the generally expansive mood of the economy. With the depression of the 1890s, however, both birth and migration rates plummeted, departures exceeding arrivals in the period 1896–1905, and the annual growth rate dropped below 2% for perhaps the first time since the early convict period. During the present century rates of growth have hovered around 2%, peaking slightly during good times as migration rates improve, bottoming somewhat during periods of war and economic recession.

In New Zealand, migration to the goldfields resulted in a doubling of the population between 1860 and 1870. A vigorously pursued policy of assisted immigration and public works during the second half of the 1870s continued the high rate of growth, but depression, unemployment, and net emigration during the eighties depressed it to around 2%. Since then the New Zealand rate, like that of Australia, has fluctuated about this level in response to world wars and economic depressions, but rarely with the same degree of variability as has characterized Australia.

In general the occasional quite pronounced growth rate differences between the several Australian states are indicative of the spatio-temporal irregular nature of resource exploitation and development on the Australian continent prior to the last major gold rushes in Western Australia during the 1890s. Since 1900 growth rate differentials have been far less pronounced. In New Zealand the divergent patterns of growth in the two main islands may be similarly explained. Prior to 1860, North Island contained a majority of the white population. The discovery of gold, the easier availability of land in the South Island and the outbreak of the Maori wars in North Island in the sixties reversed this trend, but refrigeration, the opening up of land suitable for intensive grassland farming and the development of the communication network during the 1880s and 1890s restored North Island to its earlier preeminence by the turn of the century. Since then the imbalance has continued to increase.

Growth of the Indigenous Population

For long periods of time since "contact", both Maori in New Zealand and Aboriginal populations in Australia actually declined under the combined onslaught of the white man's firearms, liquor, diseases, and widespread social disintegration stemming from the loss of tribal lands. In New Zealand this decline ceased about the turn of the century, by which time Maori numbers had been reduced from an originally estimated quarter million to something in the vicinity of 40,000 but not until about 1916 was there any significant and continuous reversal of the trend. Since then their numbers have increased steadily, such that by 1971 the statistical Maori population (i.e. greater than one-half Maori blood) had returned to levels only slightly below those at contact. The Aboriginal population in Australia, less well equipped than the Maori to coexist or compete with the invading European pastoralist or agriculturalist, experienced a much more prolonged period of decline. By 1921 only an estimated 70,000 full and half-bloods remained. By 1954 they had been reduced by a further 10,000. In succeeding censuses some improvement, though nothing like the resurgence of the Maori, has been noted.

Population Distribution and Density

With overall population densities of only 2 and 11 per km² respectively, both Australia and New Zealand are, by world standards, only lightly populated. In neither case, however, does this average value have any intrinsic significance, for high proportions of the total populations are concentrated into comparatively restricted areas, leaving large expanses either sporadically and sparsely populated or completely uninhabited. In 1971 two-thirds of all Australians lived in cities of more than 100,000 inhabitants; five-sixths of these were in fact resident in the six state capitals and Canberra, the national capital. Of the remainder, 20% lived in the smaller (1000–100,000 inhabitants) urban areas scattered for the most part through the south and east of the country, and only 14% were classified for census purposes as "rural," only about half of whom were actually resident on rural holdings. In New Zealand a similar situation obtains; 44% are concentrated in the four largest urbanized areas (Auckland, Wellington–Hutt, Christchurch, Dunedin), a further 36% live in smaller urban areas, and less than 20% are rural, of whom about three-quarters appear to be "on farm" residents; and, as in Australia, even these comparatively and absolutely small numbers of farm dwellers are highly concentrated in the few areas which for reasons of environmental suitability or accessibility can most profitably be utilized.

Australia

In 1971 approximately 90% of the Australian population was contained in that third or less of the continent east and south of a line linking Cooktown in coastal northeast Queensland with Moree (northeastern New South Wales), Mildura (northwestern Victoria), and Ceduna (South Australia), and Esperance with Geraldton in Western Australia (Fig. 10.1). The remaining two-thirds to three-fourths of the land mass, despite recent developments in the tropical north, consist mainly of the thinly populated open spaces of "outback" pastoral Australia and the virtually uninhabited arid interior where

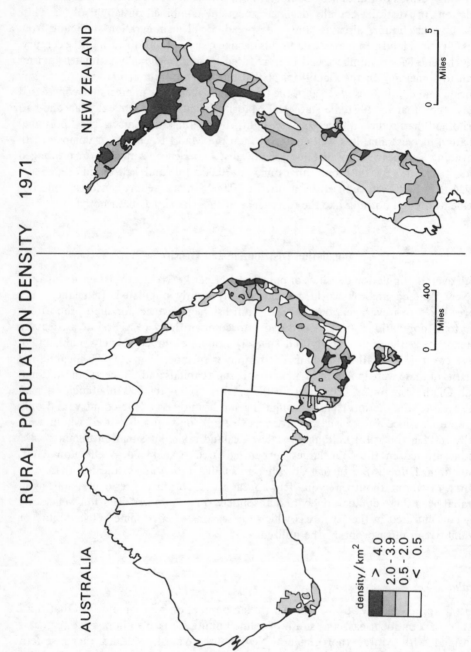

FIG. 10.1. Rural is defined as population living on dispersed home farms and in small settlements not designated as urban (generally under 1000 population).

Aboriginal mission stations and reserves, mining settlements, and isolated "homesteads" comprise the bulk of the permanent settlement.

In the southeast and southwest this peripheral humid to subhumid "populated crescent" extends at its widest point no more than 500 km from the coast and is rapidly pinched out between the ocean and, in the southwest, the drylands or, in the north, heavily forested roughlands. Within it, densities show a general and well marked tendency to decline with increasing distance from the coast and decreasing effective precipitation, though the regularity of this broadly zonal pattern is considerably disturbed by major variations stemming from local or regional differences in the intensity of agriculture and in the size, spacing, and function of urban centers, reflecting the often complex interrelationships between environmental, economic, historical, and political factors.

Within the populated crescent, areas of high population density outside of the major metropolitan areas and their intensively developed rural fringes are at once limited in extent and widely distributed. For the most part densest rural settlement is found in association with intensive agricultural systems such as dairying, sugar cane production (restricted to coastal areas in Queensland and northern New South Wales), fat stock raising or specialist horticulture, orcharding and viticulture (a) on the larger flood plains of the major coastal river systems, (b) inland where water resources, soil, and slope conditions have permitted intensive irrigation (most notably in the Murray–Goulburn–Murrumbidgee system), or (c) in a few other especially favored localities such as the elevated, cooler, Atherton Tableland of north Queensland and the highly productive red and black soil Darling Downs in southeast Queensland. Throughout these areas rural population densities in excess of 10 per km² are general, though locally highly variable, rising in areas of most intensive settlement, for example in the irrigated specialist orcharding, vine growing, and vegetable producing districts along the Murray River, as at Mildura, to two or even three times this level.

Inland the largely uninhabited forested roughlands of the eastern face of the continental divide and the Darling Ranges in the west cause a sharp discontinuity in population distribution. However, where topographic barriers are less pronounced, as in central Queensland, and on the undulating granitic tablelands behind the main escarpments or the basalt and sand plains of southwest Victoria, extensive pastoralism prevails; rural population densities thus rarely exceed 1 per km², and significant urban centers are infrequent. On the lower slopes and plains still further inland, however, over a zone some 150–250km wide extending from the New South Wales and Queensland border through to the shores of the Great Ausrralian Bight and again, in Western Australia from the Bight northwest to the Indian Ocean, densities thicken and distribution patterns become more regular as extensive pastoralism is replaced by the closer settlement of the mixed cropᴘlivestock region where cereal growing, in association with wool sheep and fat lamb production predominates. Throughout this zone rural densities of up to 2 per km² are usual, higher on the humid and southern margins, lower inland and to the north, where holding size and the role of livestock increases. A well developed central-place system, including urban areas with populations of up to 25,000, is also characteristic.

On its arid margins mixed farming gives way to extensive pastoralism, mainly the raising of sheep for wool (except in Queensland, where cattle predominate initially), or to the uninhabited expanses of the arid interior. Where permanent settlement obtains pastoral holdings upwards of 150 per km² are usual. Under such conditions rural densities of from 1 persons to 25 km² to 1 per 250 km² or more are common, while the incidence of urban settlement is extremely low and more often than not associated with mining rather than with agriculture or pastoralism.

An Economic Interpretation

Because each of the Australian states evolved more or less as a quasi-independent, metropolitan dominated space economy it can be posited that the arrangement of land-use systems in each state should reflect not merely environmental factors but also the effect of distance from the metropolitan growth pole. Using data from the 1966 census it has been demonstrated first, that the arrangement of land-use systems is in general accord with the expectations of the von Thunen model, and, second, that this decline in land-use intensity with distance from the metropolis is accompanied by a decline in population density (Table 10.1).

TABLE 10.1. DENSITY OF POPULATION BY LAND-USE ZONE, AUSTRALIA, 1966

Land-use zone	Area (1000 sq. miles)	Density (per sq. mile)	Rural population change, 1961–6 (%)	Median distance from metropolis (km)
Metropolitan	2	3368		
Intensive cropping	15	37	−11.9	197
Dairying	48	21	− 6.4	119
Intensive sheep	86	8	− 5.3	129
Intensive beef	17	8	+ 1.9	145
Wheat–sheep	162	4	− 2.3	180
Extensive sheep	797	0.4	− 0.6	448
Extensive cattle	883	0.3	− 1.7	679

Source: P. Scott (1966), Population and land use in Australia, *Tijdschrift voor Econ. en Soc. Geogr.* **59**, 237–44.

Although accessibility to the dominant metropolis is clearly relevant to the explanation of the spatial arrangement of agricultural activities and of population density variability, it is, of course, not the only factor. Several of the most intensively settled areas owe their origin and continuing existence less to accessibility than to politics. The important irrigation districts of the Murray and Murrumbidgee valleys in southern New South Wales, or the Ord River in the far north of Western Australia, for example, are the products of governmental decision making and support; similarly, the sugar lands of coastal Queensland and increasingly the dairying areas of coastal New South Wales and Queensland, with their high population densities, depend heavily upon government support and protection for their existence. The fact remains, however, that under conditions which in several important respects approach those assumed in the basic model, a clear sequence of land uses has evolved outward from the metropolis, with which is associated a well marked population density decline.

New Zealand

Similar patterns and levels of density are also discernible in New Zealand (Fig. 10.1). Most rural dwellers and significant urban places are concentrated on the fringing coastal plains and lowlands. Hill country pastoral districts support lower populations densitie while the upland and/or roughland cores of each island are largely unpopulated.

Intensive grassland farming, dairying, and fat-lamb raising, singly or in combination, as is characteristic of the well watered and now highly fertile coastal lowlands or rolling hill country of several districts (Waikato, Taranaki, Bay of Plenty, and the Manawatu–Horowhenua), or the more restricted pockets of intensive horticulture, orcharding, and special cropping on the drier coastal alluviums (Hawkes Bay, Nelson, and Poverty Bay), all in North Island, support highest rural densities and correspondingly high urban populations. Within South Island, the drier, more extensively cropped and grazed Canterbury Plains and downlands east of the Southern Alps, comprising the single largest area of regularly dispersed rural settlement in the country, and the colder, wetter, mixed farming area of the Southland Plains support rather lower densities (3–5 per km²), while the extensively grazed tussock grasslands of the alpine foothills and inland basins of the South Island high country (except where irrigated) and the improved pastures of the hill lands in the central and eastern North Island carry lowest overall densities. The intermixing of more intensive forms of agriculture on valley and basin floors with the pastoral activities of the hill and high country does, however, give rise to irregular, frequently linear patterns of population distribution throughout the more sparsely settled districts, an irregularity which is accentuated by the similar distribution of the rural servicing centers.

Density Trends

Recently, under the impact of farm mechanization and accompanying economies of scale and in the absence of expansionary agricultural programs at other than the local level, the drift from the land has become general throughout rural Australia and New Zealand. Rural densities have therefore tended to move downwards, though at different rates depending upon the type of farming. Thus, it has been shown for Australia that between 1961 and 1966 those areas under intensive cropping lost population at an average rate of 12% and that, in general, the rate of population loss, and therefore of density decline, diminished with declining land-use intensity. In short, the resulting redistributionary movements of population resulted in a lowering and flattening of the rural population density surface. In New Zealand no similar spatial regularity is apparent, but there, too, rural densities are generally declining. Since 1966 the lowering of the rural density surface has continued in Australia and in much of New Zealand, but greatest reductions have occurred in the least rather than the most densely populated areas.

Components of Population Change

Vital Rates

In the early 1970s crude birth rates in Australia and New Zealand were slightly in excess of 20 per 1000 and well above the level required for replacement, as gross reproduction rates of 1.46 and 1.39 respectively indicate.

With only periodic reversals, birth rates have declined greatly since registration began during the 1860s. From 1870 to the early 1930s the downward trend was reversed significantly only in the years immediately preceding World War I and again immediately after it. After the depression of the 1930s birth rates rebounded and maintained their upward movement through the war years, peaking in the post-war "baby boom" (24 per 1000 in Australia, 28 per 1000 in New Zealand) and remaining near this level until the early 1960s, when decline again set in.

The early downward trend in fertility set in almost simultaneously in each of the Australian States and in New Zealand, though from somewhat different levels, and the decline can be attributed to changes (a) in the proportion of the reproductive age populations that are married, and (b) in the level of marital fertility.

Spatial Variations in Fertility

During the fertility decline significant differentials between birth rates in urban and rural areas, between higher and lower socio-economic status groups, and between foreign and locally born women were observed. Also apparent, however, was the shrinkage of these differentials with the passage of time. Given this convergence, it is to be expected that present day areal variations in fertility will also have diminished greatly, though in New Zealand the effect of Maori birth rates ought to be observable wherever Maoris form significant concentrations, for example the northern and east coast areas of North Island.

Marital fertility (children 0–4 years per 1000 ever-married women aged 15–49 years) calculated for each major area, and for the residual population in statistical divisions districts in Australia and New Zealand, from data collected at the censuses of 1966 reveals that the long established tendency for fertility to be highest in Queensland, the Northern Territory, and Western Australia and lower in New South Wales and Victoria seems to be maintained, as is the differential between Australian and New Zealand rates. Within individual states, metropolitan fertility is usually lower than that of the largely rural areas, and there is a marked tendency for rural fertility to increase with distance from the metropolitan centers, though there are some significant departures from this pattern; more intensively settled regions, for example the dairying areas of coastal New South Wales and Victoria and Queensland's sugar coast, all appear to have rather lower levels than might be anticipated.

Rural Fertility

Explanations for the detailed pattern of variability in rural fertility in Australia are for the most part nonexistent. In a study made of the spatial variations in rural fertility within the state of Victoria, only the incidence of Roman Catholicism and distance from Melbourne appeared to have any "explanatory" power.

In New Zealand, rural marital fertility is significantly higher in most North Island districts than in all but the southernmost South Island district. Those districts possessing high concentrations of Maoris tend also to have highest fertility. In the northern and eastern districts of the North Island, for example, Maoris comprise between 20 and 50% of the total population and marital fertility rates range from 850 to in excess of 1000.

The importance of variations in the age composition of the female population in the reproductive ages must also be considered. Except where Maoris are heavily represented, fertility varies directly with the proportion of young (20–29 years) ever-married women. When the remaining districts are considered, however, the relationship breaks down owing to the already noted tendency for Maori women to prolong childbearing. In New Zealand, as in Australia, therefore, spatial variability in rural marital fertility seems mainly to depend on age, marital status, and ethnic composition.

Urban Fertility

In both countries urban fertility levels tend to be lower than those of their encompassing or contiguous rural districts, but not unrelated to them. In general, urban areas in high (or low) fertility rural areas will themselves rank high (or low) on the array of urban fertility rates. It is frequently asserted that urban size and fertility levels are inversely related. A detailed examination of this relationship for Australian submetropolitan urban places (over 1000 population) reveals, however, that size, *per se*, "explains" only a very small proportion of the variation in urban marital fertility. Far more important is the age distribution of reproductively aged females. Where high proportions occur in the ages of peak fertility, then the rate will tend to be high.

Apart from the North Island–South Island differential, fertility levels in the New Zealand urban system do not display any clear regional patterning. But, as in Australia, there is a clear positive association between age distribution and fertility. Similarly, there is a strong association between fertility and the importance of the Maori population, as, for example, in Rotorua, Tauranga, Gisborne, and Whangarei.

Death Rates

Current mortality rates are low by standards of the developed realm and have been so for several decades. In 1920 crude death rates were approximately 9 per 1000 and have fluctuated about that level, regardless of changes in age structure, standards of living, public health, and medical care ever since. In this period, however, life expectancy has increased significantly.

In both nations age–sex specific death rates are virtually identical. Under 1 year a death rate of approximately 17 per 1000 is characteristic. This drops precipitously to 0.4 at age 10–14 years and remains low until affluence, aging, and over-nutrition begin to take their toll in the forties. The gains of the last half century have not been evenly distributed across the age structure, however. Infant (under 1 year) and childhood (1–5 years) mortality rates in Australia are now respectively only one-third and one-sixth of their 1920–2 levels, but with increasing age the degree of reduction diminishes fairly rapidly. In general, female rates have declined far more substantially than those for males, particularly for teenagers and women in the post-reproductive age.

While low mortality is the national norm, both societies contain significant minority groups for whom the benefits of the welfare state and the affluent society have been less marked. Maori life expectancy at birth is almost a decade less than that of the white population (though the gap is closing rapidly), and at all ages under 64 years Maori specific death rates are at least one and a half times higher than white rates. The mortality experience of Australia's Aboriginal population is less well documented, but sample surveys demonstrate even more marked differentials. Such pronounced differentials reflect major dissimilarities in ways of life, residential environment, and living standards. In New Zealand this becomes apparent in the distinctive pattern of Maori disease mortality. A high incidence of deaths from tuberculosis, gastro-intestinal diseases, rheumatic heart disease, and accidents indicates their generally lower living standards. Excessive deaths from diabetes and heart disease with hypertension, however, reflect a cultural predisposition to over-nutrition.

Spatial Variations in Mortality

In a detailed analysis of New Zealand's rural and urban mortality during the period

1964–8 it was demonstrated that while there was considerable place-to-place variability in mortality, (a) rural standardized mortality ratios were generally lower and less variable than those for urban areas, (b) highest ratios for both urban and rural areas were particularly concentrated in North Island's heavily Maori East Coast, Northland, and, to a lesser extent, Taranaki districts and in South Island's coal mining West Coast area, and (c) urban SMRs were inversely related to urban size.

In the absence of studies of Australian mortality at a similar level of detail, precisely comparable findings are unavailable. Somewhat more crudely standardized rates have been computed for the larger and more heterogeneous statistical divisions, however, from which it appears that, as in New Zealand, highest SMRs are most prominent in the more remote, sparsely populated localities, perhaps reflecting the predominance of higher risk occupations, a higher degree of environmental stress, and in some areas a more "pioneering" life style. Significantly high SMRs also occur in the Hunter Valley and South Coast Divisions of New South Wales, both of which contain concentrations of high risk coal mining and heavy industry. Metropolitan divisions in all states appear also to experience moderate to high SMRs, but a detailed examination of SMRs among Victorian urban places failed to reveal any inverse relationship between urban size and mortality.

Lowest SMRs are particularly prominent in coastal Queensland and northern New South Wales, inland Victoria, southwestern Western Australia, and the Northern Territory. To some extent this would appear to be a statistical artifact reflecting the discrepancy between the mid winter, visitor inflated census population of 1966 and the population normally resident in these areas.

Infant Mortality

Infant and maternal health early became a matter of public concern in both societies. Since the 1930s infant death rates have halved and in 1971 stood at 17.9 (Australia) and 16.7 (New Zealand). In each country there is, however, a sizable gap between white and nonwhite rates. In New Zealand the Maori stands at 27, in contrast to the non-Maori rate of only 15. At ages over 7 days the Maori death rate is more than twice the non-Maori rate and in the post neo-natal period is more than two and a half times as high. Comparable data are not available for Australian Aborigines. Their situation is substantially worse, however, and is only now being paid the attention it deserves.

This ethnic difference would appear to be largely responsible for the major regional variations in infant mortality in New Zealand for, as with total mortality, the heavily Maori east coast region and its urban areas have highest rates while the largest cities consistently register lowest mortality, possibly reflecting the higher quality of hospital resources available.

In Australia, too, metropolitan rates are generally somewhat lower than those elsewhere, but recent inclusion of aboriginal deaths has tended to modify this situation in some states.

Within the metropolitan areas prior to 1967 statistically significant, temporally consistent, and well marked areal variations in the incidence of infant mortality have been noted that appear to be closely related to the socio-economic structure of the metropolis. In general a center periphery gradient is apparent, with highest rates, both for neo-natal and total mortality, occurring in the central city and lowest rates in the outer suburban municipalities. Superimposed upon this concentric pattern is a clear tendency for higher rates to occur in lower status, industrialized sectors, which suggests a clear relationship between infant death and the incidence of social deprivation, on the one hand, and social disorganization on the other, even in the major cities of affluent, egalitarian, welfare statist Australia.

Internal Migration

Analysis of internal migration in the region has been impeded by the absence hitherto of official enumeration or registration data relating to residential mobility at anything other than the state level. Most studies of population redistribution have therefore been forced to rely upon net migration measures.

In both Australia and New Zealand the pattern of gain or loss by migration is made up of distinct but not independent components. At the broadest level there is, in New Zealand, an apparent South to North Island movement such that between 1966 and 1971 the former experienced a net outflow of some 16,250 persons (equivalent to almost 2% of the total 1966 population), while the latter gained some 14,000 persons by in-migration. In Australia during the period 1961–6 the warmer and more rapidly developing states of Queensland and Western Australia experienced small but significant net inflows, while the southeastern states of Victoria and New South Wales, but particularly Tasmania, were net losers. While climatic/amenity factors have played some part in these broad scale relocations, real differentials in the rate of growth of employment opportunities are mainly responsible—in New Zealand associated with the continuing concentration of manufacturing and commerce in the major urban areas of the North Island, in Australia with the rise of new mineral based development.

Rural Depopulation

At the local level net migration is dominated by continuing depopulation of rural areas and their smaller service centers and by the corresponding growth of larger urban places, most notably the metropolitan areas.

No particular region is completely immune from this tendency though some have suffered less extensively than others. In Australia heaviest out-migration seems recently to have been associated with the depressed and drought-stricken pastoral and mixed crop–livestock farming districts of central and far western New South Wales and western and northwestern Victoria. Dairying districts have continued to lose by out-migration but at rates generally below those experienced in the more extensive systems. In New Zealand similar tendencies seem to be emerging, for although the highest rates of out-migration for the period 1956–61 were not confined to any particular type of farming, settlement pattern, or terrain, in later quinquennia the hill country areas of North Island seem to have experienced generally higher losses than other districts, though high levels are also to be found elsewhere.

Especially involved in these off-farm and out-of-town movements are the school leavers and younger adults for whom the declining rural job market, the centralization of higher education and off-farm employment opportunities, and the bright city lights are all potent motivating forces. In Victoria's Wimmera district, for example, one-quarter of the population aged 10–14 years in 1961 had departed from the region by 1966, while more than a third of the rural females and some 15% of the males in the same age group were lost by migration. And while these proportions are among the highest for any statistical division in that state for that period, a similar age selectivity is generally characteristic and has been noted in New Zealand as well.

Most Australian metropolitan areas experienced significant gains from in-migration. Most (from 65 to 88%) migrants to these areas have their immediate origins in other urban areas or overseas rather than in rural districts, however, but the routes by which migrants reach the largest cities are not yet well defined. In New Zealand the step-migration hypothesis is known to have some relevance, but this up-hierarchy movement from rural to metropolitan areas is clearly only one component of a more complex process of rural migration.

The factors underlying the continuing exodus from farm and country town require little elaboration. The reduction of farm labor requirements in the face of continuing mechanization and amalgamation, marketing difficulties, and declining profitability that has characterized the sixties are, of course, root causes. Losses in the primary sector of the economy in association with changing travel and shopping habits among those remaining have led to consequential reductions in the level of business activity and population in the smaller country towns, particularly those lacking any significant industrial activity.

Departures from this pattern of general rural out-migration are, almost without exception, areas undergoing "development." Rural areas peripheral to expanding urban areas are characteristically net gainers. Occasional areas of agricultural intensification, as for example in irrigated districts in New South Wales and Victoria, also stand out as areas of net in-migration. Far more spectacular, however, are the gains accruing to areas of rapidly expanding mineral exploitation in Northern Australia, or their New Zealand equivalents, the hydro-electric power and forest product projects.

Urban Migration Patterns

Urban centers display more diverse levels of net migration. Larger regional and sub-regional centers in New Zealand, and to a lesser extent in Australia, have continued to gain by migration, but the degree to which this is so depends on such factors as the growth rate of "basic" employment opportunities and the amenity level. In Australia, high net in-migration is characteristic of the mining settlements of the tropical north, centers in which mineral handling and processing industries have been expanding, and mushrooming tourist–recreation–retirement centers of the "sunshine coasts" of New South Wales and Queensland. In New Zealand high net in-migration rates occurred in Auckland, the national metropolis, and in Hamilton the rapidly expanding service, distribution, and educational center for the prosperous and densely populated South Auckland area. In northern South Island, Nelson, noted for its high sunshine hours, also gained significantly. Less functionally specialized urban areas have experienced much lower net migration rates, and in Australia, at least, there has been a widespread reduction of attractive power by all but the most favored few during the last decade. At the other end of the spectrum is a group of urban centers, often of considerable size, which have experienced significant net out-migration. In New Zealand, Dunedin (111,059) and Wanganui (37,982) had negative net migration rates of between 2 and 4%, while in Australia a variety of towns including several mining centers and those of the pastoral districts have been particularly hard hit and seem unlikely to recover.

Population Change in the 1960s

Despite declining birth rates during the 1960s, Australia's growth rate remained virtually constant (*c.* 10%) between 1961 and 1971. In New Zealand, however, a more substantial deceleration was recorded, from just on 11% down to 7%, for the fertility decline there was accompanied by a marked slackening in in-migration such that in the years 1967–9 net out-migration was experienced.

In both nations the drift from the land continued unabated. In the period 1966–71 the rural component in all Australian states except Queensland declined by from 5 to 10%, while in New Zealand the reduction was only marginally less (4.5%). As a result, the proportion of the population resident in urban areas continued to swell. In New Zealand and in all Australian states but Tasmania the population residing in major urban areas increased by more than 10%; those resident in smaller urban areas increased at a somewhat slower rate but still more rapidly than in the preceding period. Locally, population change shows greater diversity. For the most part growth rates reflect net migration differentials rather than variations in birth or death rates.

Rural Population Change

Although the overall rate of rural population decline in both Australia and New Zealand is of the order of 5% for the five-year period 1966–71, losses of from 10 to 20% of the 1966 population are common over large areas, and few localities have experienced population gain (Fig. 10.2).

In general those areas most heavily depopulated are regions of moderately extensive wheat–sheep farming and the more extensive pastoral regions of southwestern Western Australia, western and central New South Wales, and southwestern Queensland. In New Zealand the sparsely settled hill lands of the North Island have been similarly affected. More intensively utilized and settled areas have lost less heavily (0–10%), but only in certain developmental areas, for example in portions of the Murray Valley irrigated areas, or in central Queensland, has decline been averted. The gains characterizing much of the Australian "outback" are also associated with development, but to a large extent they reflect changes in the non-agricultural or pastoral elements.

Urban Population Change

The pattern of urban population change has been remarkable for the continuing rapid growth of the major centers, the high incidence of absolute decline among smaller urban areas, the compensating rapid growth experienced by certain categories of towns, often of quite small size, and by the well marked regionalization of growth which has arisen from these.

Metropolitan Growth

The high rate of metropolitan growth reflects, at least in part, a continuation of the historic tendency towards the centralization of educational, social, and employment opportunities, decentralization policies notwithstanding, and in Australia the continuation of significant international in-migration. Growth rate differentials between the various state capitals and between New Zealand's four major urban areas reflect variations in the growth of these opportunities and in their perceived attractiveness. Thus,

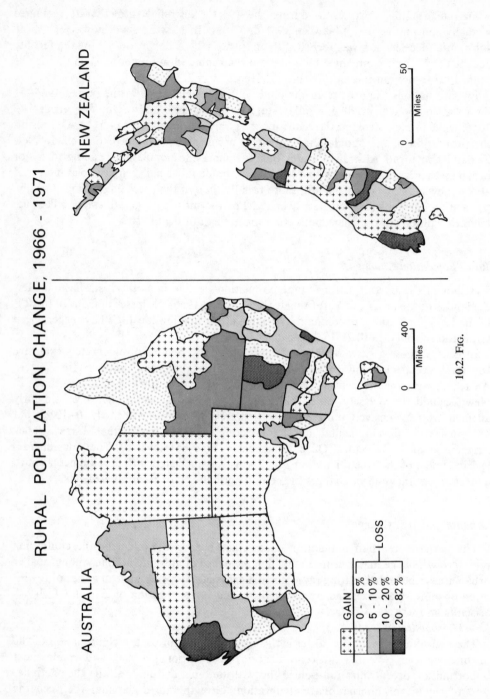

RURAL POPULATION CHANGE, 1966 - 1971

NEW ZEALAND

AUSTRALIA

GAIN
0 - 5 %
5 - 10 %
10 - 20 %
20 - 82 %
LOSS

Miles
0　　50

Miles
0　　400

10.2. Fig.

Canberra, Australia's national capital, has increased in population by more than 50%, largely through inter-metropolitan migration, as its administrative, educational, and cultural roles have burgeoned and with them its local and regional commercial significance. In Western Australia the continuing spectacular growth of Perth is associated with the state's rapid, mineral based economic development, and again interstate and international migration have been important components. In New Zealand the continuing spatial polarization of the economy involving significant shifts of employment from the South to the North Island, and in particular to the Auckland area, has resulted in a continuing high level of growth in Auckland and Wellington–Hutt. Hobart (Tasmania), however, has grown only slowly, reflecting the slower growth of the state economy and its peripheral location to the nation's markets.

Declining Towns

The pattern of "other" urban population change is more complex, for a variety of factors operating at several scales are involved, as is revealed by a consideration of declining towns. Between 20 and 45% of the urban areas in each Australian state (except Tasmania) and in New Zealand lost population during the period 1966–71. The majority were small (less than 3000 inhabitants)—their incidence diminished with increasing size—and located within 30 minutes' driving time of a major regional or subregional center. This phenomenon can be seen as the outcome of rural population decline and the increasing tendency for those remaining on farms to travel longer distances to larger centers for their various needs. In short, towns established in the railway age have become locationally obsolescent in the age of the family car.

Growth Points

Although nearly one-third of all Australian and one-quarter of all New Zealand towns declined in population between 1966 and 1971, rapid growth (more than 10% in 5 years) was generally more characteristic; only in Victoria and Queensland, both hard hit by adverse rural conditions, did declining outnumber high-gaining centers. Larger regional centers figure prominently in this category, but rapid growth seems to have been particularly prevalent among (a) urban places in close proximity to metropolitan centers, (b) resort and retirement towns, and (c) places serving regions of rapid economic development associated with specific institutions or activities undergoing significant expansion.

Population Composition

Ethnic Composition

Three main components occur in the populations of both Australia and New Zealand: (a) the indigenous non-Europeans, i.e. Aborigines and Maoris, (b) the locally born, essentially European (white) population, and (c) the overseas born, also for the most part European. In each the locally born European element constitutes approximately 80% of the total, but there are significant differences in the composition of the remainder; Maoris, for example, comprise some 8% of New Zealand's population, Aborigines less than 1% of Australia's, and there are major variations in the make-up of the foreign born element. Of outstanding importance is the marked difference in the importance of the "British" and other European groups. In both societies the British element is the single largest (61% in New Zealand; 43% in Australia); in Australia, however, they are outweighed by the non-British, particularly southern and central Europeans, whereas in

New Zealand they are absolutely preponderant. Furthermore, Pacific Islanders form a sizable and growing component of the New Zealand population (9% in 1966), but are numerically and proportionately negligible in Australia.

In large part these differences reflect divergent migration policies, particularly since 1945, for while New Zealand has concentrated heavily upon encouraging Britons to emigrate and has, at the same time, special responsibilities for and special relations with several Pacific Island territories, Australia early discarded imperial preference, and over the years has cast her net ever wider to achieve an annual intake of in excess of 100,000 immigrants.

In both societies significant ethnic segregation and concentration is evident. Ninety-five per cent of the Maori population is concentrated in the North Island of New Zealand; 41% were, in 1966, resident in the 18 defined urban areas (as against 62% of the total population); 95% of New Zealand's Pacific Island community is concentrated in urban areas, more than half of them in Auckland: Australia's Aboriginal population is almost exclusively rural; the foreign born component is much more heavily urban and metropolitan concentrated than the Australian born, and there is a clear tendency for ethnic groups of increasing visibility and cultural distinctiveness to cluster more strongly in and within the metropolitan centers.

The Indigenes

Despite the recently increasing degree of urbanization highest concentrations of both Maori and Aborigine are still to be found in rural areas. In New Zealand, Maoris constitute from 20 to 50% of the rural and small town population in the northern and eastern half of the North Island, and form significant concentrations (10% or more) in many of the larger urban areas in that region, particularly those providing unskilled or semi-skilled employment opportunities in meat freezing, milk, fruit, and vegetable processing and forest product industries.

Some 17% of all Maoris now live in the Auckland urban area, and although over the years the degree of residential and occupational segregation there has been reduced, the Maori still tends to occupy a low rung on the socio-economic status ladder. Occupational choice is circumscribed by lower educational attainment; residential choice, though greatly improved by the actions of the welfare state, is still constrained by low incomes. They therefore reside in low-cost housing areas easily accessible to the major employment nodes, though the incidence of longer distance commuting would appear to be slowly rising.

The Australian Aborigine is heavily concentrated in areas most remote from white settlement. Until recently those in gainful employment have been most prominent in the pastoral industry, or, in more intensively utilized areas, as seasonal fruit pickers, vegetable harvesters, or other essentially unskilled occupations. The rise of the mineral industry in their traditional lands has, however, opened up alternative avenues of employment for some.

Pacific Islanders

New Zealand's growing population of Pacific Islanders is heavily concentrated in the Auckland metropolitan area. The remainder are widely scattered, but in general are located in areas providing high wage, low status, unskilled occupations in a narrow range of industries, principally those related to the processing of primary products but also in the public transport and clothing industries and as domestic help. Within Auckland, Polynesians are strongly segregated residentially, in part because of their low incomes but also because of their desire to live in communities with friends, relatives, or fellow Polynesians, preferably from the same island group. Some 40% of all Polynesians therefore reside in the inner city area where they comprise up to 25% of the total population in any locality.

Other Foreign Born

The remaining foreign born components are most heavily represented in the metropolitan areas of the mainland states of Australia and in New Zealand's North Island and in other areas which have undergone rapid economic expansion in the post-war years. The key to this distribution pattern is, understandably, growth of employment opportunities. In both countries rapid growth has been associated with metal processing, motor vehicle and appliance manufacturing and allied industries, mainly concentrated in or around the metropolitan areas, but the post-war boom in construction, e.g. power generation projects, and the mineral industry has also channelled migrants to other areas (Fig. 10.3). High migrant concentrations are especially notable in Wellington–Hutt and Auckland in New Zealand (approximately 20% of their total populations), and in Wollongong and Geelong, in Australia.

The proportions of foreign born are generally lower in rural areas, reflecting the less buoyant conditions of the agricultural sector and more difficult entry conditions. There are, nevertheless, several areas of significant foreign born concentration in rural Australia and tendencies towards this situation in New Zealand, particularly in localities where specialized intensive agriculture is practised, e.g. tobacco growing, viticulture, orcharding, and horticulture, and in Queensland the growing of sugar cane.

As Fig. 10.3 indicates, however, highest concentrations of foreign born in nonurban areas are located in sparsely settled areas of central, northern, and western Australia and in the Snowy Mountains area of southern New South Wales. Such high levels can be accounted for by the rapid growth of the mineral industry, the expansion of international defense and scientific research facilities, and by major construction activities such as the Snowy Mountains hydro-electric project.

Age Structure

In 1966 nearly one in three Australians and New Zealanders was under 15 years of age, about 8% were 65 years or older, and the remainder, close to 60% of the total, were in the "economically active" age groups. Though similar in overall structure, detailed differences between the two countries stem from variations in national fertility and migration rates. Higher proportions of the New Zealand population are found in all age groups up to 20, reflecting New Zealand's higher birth rate. Australia's more active post-war migration program has inflated the proportion in all but the very oldest age groups for both males and females. As a result, Australia has somewhat more favorable youth and total dependency (young plus aged) ratios, 47 and 16 per 100 as against New Zealand's 55 and 69 per 100.

Because both societies have experienced similar patterns of social and economic development in the last 50 years or so, changes in their age structure have followed parallel tracks. Declining birth rates and low or negative net migration through into the 1930s resulted in a steady increase in mean and median ages for both sexes, reaching the low 30s by the mid 1940s. The post-war resurgence of fertility, along with substantial

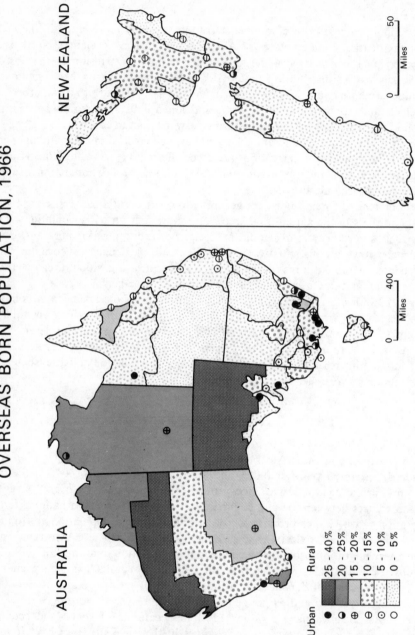
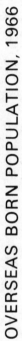

OVERSEAS BORN POPULATION, 1966

AUSTRALIA

NEW ZEALAND

Urban
● ◐ ⊕ ⊖ ⊙ ○

Rural
25 - 40%
20 - 25%
15 - 20%
10 - 15%
5 - 10%
0 - 5%

0   400
Miles

0   50
Miles

Fig. 10.3. Percent of total population born outside of Australia and New Zealand, 1966.

in-migration, however, reversed this trend in the 1950s and 1960s, and by 1966 mean ages had dropped to 1930 levels.

Given the generally low level of variability in mortality, the urban–rural gradient in birth rates and the well defined, age specific migratory movements outlined above, it is to be expected that the highest proportions of the economically active will occur in the major urban areas, while youngsters will be most heavily and oldsters least represented in rural areas. "Other" urban areas, where separately classified, will tend to lie between these extremes. At the macro-scale such expectations have some validity in both Australia and New Zealand, and with only minor modification are also applicable to each of the Australian states. In most states the proportion of youngsters (under 15 years) in the rural population tends to increase with distance from the metropolitan center while the proportions of aged (65 years and over) tends to decrease.

Superimposed upon this system-wide regularity, however, are positive and negative subregional and local effects stemming from such causes as ethnic concentrations, variations in types of farming, levels of prosperity, and so on. The low proportions of youngsters (20%) in northwestern Australia, for example, clearly reflect the preponderance there of young able-bodied males, largely without dependants, associated with mining and construction projects; the extraordinary youthfulness (45% under 15 years) in New Zealand's East Cape district and the lower, but still high, levels (40%) in that country's Northland and South Auckland–Bay of Plenty regions are clearly influenced by high Maori fertility and adult out-migration from those regions.

Urban age composition reflects the impact of both internal and overseas migration and may be explained by interrelated factors ranging from urban size and function to rates of growth and ethnic composition. In both nations a clear inverse association between urban size and the proportion of the population under 15 years of age is apparent, probably reflecting the increasing attractiveness of larger centers to migrating adults. The presence of significant institutional populations, e.g. universities and other higher education establishments, retirement homes, and "labor camp" situations, as in towns associated with mining or construction activities, however, will depress the proportions in this young age group.

Sex Composition

Migration has always been a significant component of population growth in Australia and New Zealand. Since the migration streams have most commonly been male dominant, often heavily so, the sex composition of the national populations has usually also been male dominant, though decreasingly so with time. Not until the last census did the New Zealand sex ratio drop to parity under peace-time conditions. In Australia there are still 101.2 males for every 100 females.

Major sectoral and spatial deviations from the national averages occur in both societies. Generally these reflect differences in the employment, educational, and social opportunity sets available in particular localities or contexts. Almost without exception rural areas have high masculinity: urban areas are generally female dominant, though town size, function, or location may cause major departures from this regularity.

A fairly well marked tendency exists in Australia for the masculinity of rural populations to increase as the intensity of agricultural settlement diminishes toward the interior. This may be interpreted as reflecting the increasing importance of male labor employing enterprises among the pastoral and mixed farming areas of the drier regions in contrast to the family operated units characteristic of more intensively farmed districts. It should be noted, however, that prospecting, mining, construction, and other male dominated activities are also important in the "outback" and will therefore contribute to this situation. Similar tendencies are apparent in New Zealand, even at the level of the statistical district, for highest masculinity levels are experienced in the East Coast, Canterbury, and Southland Districts, all of which contain major pastoral areas and/or developmental projects.

References

Burnley, I. H. (1972) European immigration settlement patterns in Metropolitan Sydney, 1947–66, *Aust. Geogr. Studs.* **10** (1) 61–78.

Curson, P. H. (1966) The changing demographic structure of Auckland, in *Auckland in Ferment* (ed. J. S. Whitelaw), Auckland, 1967, 22–39.

Curson, P. H. (1970) Polynesians and residence in Auckland, *NZ Geogr.* **26** (2) 162–73.

Heenan, L. D. B. (1967) Rural–urban distribution of fertility in New Zealand, *Annals Assoc. Am. Geogr.* **57** (4) 713–35.

Heenan, L. D. B. and McCracken, K. W. J. (1972) On the spatial distribution of mortality in New Zealand, *N Z Med. J.* **75** (47a) 194–200.

Jones, E. F. (1971) Fertility decline in Australia and New Zealand, 1861–1936, *Population Index* **37** (4) 301–37.

Rose, R. J. (1972) *Maori–European Comparisons in Mortality*, Special Report No. 37, Department of Health, Government Printer, Wellington, New Zealand.

Scott, P. (1966) The population structure of Australian cities, *Geogr. J.* **131** (4) 463–81.

Scott, P. (1968) Population and land use in Australia, *Tijdschrift voor Econ. en Soc. Geogr.* **59**, 237–44.

Spencer, G. M. (1971) Fertility trends in Australia, *Demography* **8** (2) 247–60.

INDEX